IN FREEDOM'S SHADE

W0232605

In Freedom's Shade

Anis Kidwai

Translated by Ayesha Kidwai

THE New INDIA FOUNDATION

PENGUIN BOOKS

An imprint of Penguin Random House

PENGUIN BOOKS

USA | Canada | UK | Ireland | Australia
New Zealand | India | South Africa | China | Singapore

Penguin Books is part of the Penguin Random House group of companies
whose addresses can be found at global.penguinrandomhouse.com

Published by Penguin Random House India Pvt. Ltd
4th Floor, Capital Tower 1, MG Road,
Gurugram 122 002, Haryana, India

Penguin
Random House
India

First published in Urdu as *Azadi Ki Chhaon Mein* by Qaumi Ekta Trust 1974
First published in English by Penguin Books India 2011

MIX
Paper from
responsible sources
FSC® C047271

This is a legitimate digitally printed version of the book and therefore might not
have certain extra finishing on the cover.

Contents

Translator's Introduction

I first truly read Anis Kidwai's *Azadi Ki Chhaon Mein* (from now, *Azadi*) in April 2002, in the wake of the Gujarat violence. In the subsequent expressions of anguish and outrage, I heard often that these were no 'riots' but pogroms orchestrated by the Gujarat government, and that the unprecedented scale of sexual violence perpetrated on Muslim women signified a genocidal design. The question that haunted me was how different this massacre was from the slaughter of Sikhs in 1984 marked by similar unilateral, state-sponsored aggression.

My initial stimulus to read *Azadi* was the need to understand the anatomy of a 'true' riot, to contrast this with the many pogroms witnessed in independent India. Partition riots have been enshrined in popular imagination as violent eruptions in a civil war where Muslims, Sikhs and Hindus were evenly matched in religious fervour and bloodlust. I hoped that Anis Kidwai would help me to find the point of departure between 'then' and 'now'.

To my surprise, *Azadi* told quite a different tale. It did not speak of Partition communal riots in the sense I had expected, but of an array of conflicts—from battles to localized pogroms. Then too, religious identity was the pretext for murder, rape, extortion, eviction and abduction, with the benediction of state institutions and functionaries. Its communal violence was different only in that the aggressions were simultaneous across a large geography, each a refraction of the other, victims here turning perpetrators there. Then, as now, the price for returning to a state of calm was amnesia about the complicity of the powerful in abetting the pogrom, along with recasting of the memory of 'riots' as a clash of religious identities.

Azadi is a key that frees us from the imprisonment of our popular imagining of Partition. In its frank delineation of the violence in Delhi between September 1947 and June 1948, this invaluable record of an activist attributes the same temporal depth to the forces of secularism that we ascribe to division and hatred. Partition's victims were not only Hindus and Muslims but also children, lovers, rustics and city-dwellers, refugees and the internally displaced, 'Harijans' and Jats. And those that rescued India were not only Gandhi and Nehru but also widows and unmarried women, students and teachers, pandits and Harijans, swamis and ulemas.

Azadi is a gift of memory that both inspires and liberates. To every story of atrocities committed in the name of religion, one of organized resistance by citizens is added—when Harijans are evicted from a Delhi village, Subhadra Joshi and Anis Kidwai restore them to their homes; when the city is rife with tension between refugees and the remaining few Muslims, students and teachers of Jamia Millia open a school for Hindu and Muslim children to study and play together; when rumours of a fresh wave of rioting on 15 June 1948 course through the province of Delhi, the frenetic efforts by Shanti Dal activists ensure that the date passes by without incident.

By offering us this different perspective on Partition, *Azadi* also points to many important lessons that we should have learnt. Perhaps the most pressing is this one—while we have thus far focused on the forced migration across borders, Anis Kidwai's account foregrounds the issue of internal displacement. As she tells us, a sizeable number of people that took refuge in Purana Qila and Humayun's Tomb camps between September 1947 and March 1948 did not ever leave for Pakistan. Sadly for many of them, their homes no longer awaited their return, having been destroyed or appropriated by strangers or the government. Where did they go? The answer is perhaps lost for all time to come but the lesson that independent India should have learnt, at the very least, was to recognize the reality of internal displacement caused by communal, sectarian and ethnic violence. That the lesson is as yet unlearnt is evident—as people languishing in camps in Gujarat, Kandhamal, Chhattisgarh, Jammu and the north-east will confirm—in the lack of legislation guaranteeing the state's commitment to the rights of the internally displaced to protection, relief, rehabilitation and reparation.

Anis Kidwai begins *Azadi* with a moving account of her husband Shafi Ahmad Kidwai's murder in Mussoorie in October 1947, and ends it with the fervent appeal that her book reaches the young hands of succeeding generations before they lift the burden of new India. In this journey is enshrined the quest for an ideal of restorative justice, akin to that at the heart of South Africa's Truth and Reconciliation Commission—a justice that seeks to repair damage, not by retribution but by directing attention to the victims' needs and participation. As Joe Slovo, one of the Commission's chief architects, said, the best revenge he could have had from the men who murdered his wife was that they be made to live in peace in a system that they had fought so brutally against. While all Indian, Pakistani and Bangladeshi victims of Partition will agree that this goal is yet to be achieved, the readers of *Azadi* will turn the last page with, I hope, a renewed conviction that such justice is indeed possible and necessary.

A Note on the Translation

⸎

Although Anis Kidwai wrote *Azadi* in 1949, the book did not find a publisher until twenty-five years later, when Qaumi Ekta Trust (QET) published it in Urdu in 1974. This was followed by a National Book Trust (NBT) edition in 1978, and a Hindi translation in 1981, also by NBT. These three editions, which differ in minor details, have formed the main texts for my translation. I have also referred extensively to Anis Kidwai's handwritten manuscript of *Azadi* and the draft writings that she recorded in two notebooks. These last two sources were only privately available to me at the time of translation and have since been donated to the University of Jamia Millia.

When compared to the three published editions, the handwritten manuscript differs most radically in terms of chapterization. For reasons that cannot be fully understood now, QET published the eighteen chapters in twenty-one, and NBT in twenty-three—this expansion obscured the text's basically chronological architecture. This translation seeks to restore *Azadi* to its original chapterization, supplemented by subtitles to indicate the months each chapter refers to. Some chapters of the handwritten manuscript have been reorganized to fit in with this design but, as Anis Kidwai's own use of a bi-monthly reference frame was at best indicative, I have refrained from adding supplementary information about actual dates and times of events (wherever they are available).

In addition, some passages that are not to be found in any published editions have been incorporated into this translation. These include short passages deleted in pencil in the handwritten manuscript, in the service of discretion perhaps. As many of these passages find their way back into the NBT edition as footnotes, I have incorporated them all into the main text. The longest addition is an extract from Anis Kidwai's draft notebooks (in Chapter 3). I take this latitude with some confidence, as it appears that she handed over her notebooks with the handwritten manuscript to the QET publishers in 1974 as well. Although not part of the handwritten manuscript, selections from the notebooks—in particular the visit to Alwar in 1949—were already included in this first edition.

In fact, there are reasons to believe that the handwritten manuscript is itself an amended version of the one written in 1949. One indication is the occasional lapse of memory that Anis Kidwai has; most telling of all is one in which she mistakenly refers (in Chapter 12) to the Rashtriya Swayamsevak Sangh as the Jana Sangh, that came into being only in 1951. Also, in some passages, the text shifts to a 1970s' perspective; in Chapter 8, she says she 'still goes to Rajghat every year'.

In terms of language, the translation exercise has been one of some difficulty. Kidwai's lexicon is extremely rich, and in it Urdu, Hindi, Arabic, Persian, English and Awadhi words form complex relationships. In some cases, the choice of one particular synonym is sharply valued, in other cases it is not. In the former case, I have retained the non-English word. The latter choices go largely unrepresented, however. Although this loss is unfortunate—particularly because this multilinguality is an important aspect of the narrative voice that constitutes the text—it is the price that the translation of any such text into English exacts.

Further, and more important, translation has the potential of levelling the register shifts the choices of words and syntactic constructions entail. For example, if a Hindi or Urdu speaker were to read the chapter on Gandhi (Chapter 2) in Hindi/Urdu, she would intuitively grasp that the style is one used to narrate the sacred. While a translation into English can perhaps attempt to reflect its architectonics of a narration of fragmentary episodes, its other aspect—the use of the barest form of language—is not so effortlessly captured.

Similarly difficult is the issue of translating form with function. In a language with as free a word order as Urdu\Hindi, how one arranges words in a sentence adds another layer of meaning to the sentence itself. I have attempted to establish a correspondence between forms wherever possible, but benchmarks of felicity and readability ensure that at least some aspects of Anis Kidwai's style and intent must remain occluded from readers of this translation. For those among them who have access to either Hindi or Urdu, I can only hope that this translation will encourage them to read the book in either of the languages.

Although this is the first English translation of *Azadi*, selections from the text and citations of its insights have been available in English for two decades. Anis Kidwai would have liked me to express her gratitude to Gyanendra Pandey, Urvashi Butalia, Ritu Menon, Kamla Bhasin and Mushirul Hasan for generous references to the book in their published works on Partition. A particular word of thanks is owed to Urvashi Butalia for her endeavours to bring *Azadi* to a wider audience.

In conclusion, a few words of acknowledgement of my own are in order. Without the labours of Ania Loomba, Githa Hariharan, Madhu Sahni, Mazhar Hussain, Rajeev Sharma, Rahul Roy, and Subhashini Ali, the translation and the impressionistic sketch of Anis Kidwai's life that I have appended to it would not have seen the light of day. All these individuals have contributed substantially to my understanding of the book and its relevance, and I am deeply grateful to all of them for their extensive comments, critique, contrariness, and scepticism that I could get anything right at all. The fact that this project has been so whole-heartedly endorsed by my siblings, Rafiq, Sonia, Sabina and Atiya, and my cousins, Seema, Bobby and Kamal, means more to me than I have words to express.

Most of all, however, this book would have been impossible without my mother, Amina Kidwai, whose loving engagement with the process of this translation has also revealed to me the extent to which she is Anis Kidwai's true legatee. I am also in Arpita Singh's debt for the painting on the cover and for her (and Anjum's) unwavering belief in me. A word of gratitude also to Rekha Kidwai, my grandaunt, for her many kindnesses on my last trip to Masauli, but most of all for the efforts she has made to keep Anis Kidwai's Home for destitute women and children in our ancestral village alive and functioning. The royalties from this book will provide for the Home's upkeep.

Thanks also to Sabeena Gadihoke for interceding on the book's behalf with the inspirational photographer Homai Vyarawalla, and to Debatosh Sengupta of the Photo Division. The extensive use made in this book of these respective archives bears witness to the magnanimity of these two individuals. Thanks are also due to Halim Rahi and Maansi Sharma for their assistance in research.

Last, but by no means the least, I am also grateful to the New India Foundation for the fellowship I was awarded for this project. In particular, I thank Ramachandra Guha for his generous guidance. Had it not been for his sensitive and insightful comments—and later those of Ranjana Sengupta and Richa Burman at Penguin and Mudita Chauhan-Mubayi—Anis Kidwai's wish that her voice be heard in all four corners of the country would still be unfulfilled.

Author's Preface to the 1974 Edition

Chance can sometime play the oddest tricks, and circumstances can sometime take on such ludicrous aspects that one is left bewildered as to how what holds today ever came to·be. You may set out on an endeavour with a particular intent but what transpires is something else entirely. When I look back upon it all, I am amazed to think that all the aspiration I once had from life was to idle away the years, snuggled in some corner in the garden of books. Never in my wildest dreams could I have conceived that someone like me would have a role in the horrific drama that was to be played out on this nation's stage. Or that events would take such a turn as to set me down on the blazing scorching earth of Delhi, at a time when Delhiwalas themselves were all turning tail and running for their lives.

In 1857 as well, Delhi had suffered so much. In fact, even before this, the city changed places, was abandoned, settled, deserted, resettled, scores of times. In 1938, Lucknow All India Radio asked me to host a programme in its *Kya Se Kya* ('From What To What') series, on the advances in social, cultural and educational conditions that marked our times in comparison to those of 1857. So I struck up friendships with aged women of Lucknow and its surrounding villages, hoping to cull from their memories some anecdote about the way of life then, some account of the chaos of the Mutiny, some flavour of the colour and culture of the period, some saga of the changing political milieu.

My disappointment knew no bounds when all my queries were left unanswered and all my efforts came to naught. All the old ladies came up with, their toothless mouths chomping frenetically in the effort of speech, was this: 'At first, the king reigned. Then there were the English. In the middle, for some time, Nawabs ruled. And then the English came back again.' Or this: 'There was an attack on the village. In the city, the guns went boom-boom. The platoon of the whites attacked and all ran and hid in the wheat fields. And Allah preserve him, my Munne *miyan* was born.' (At such times, silver-haired Munne miyan would be standing by, one foot dangling in the grave, glorying in his mother's fervent prayers that he live as long as the earth continued to revolve.) Or this: 'He was saved by the village barber. And that man, he was hidden by the baniya in the granary.'

This was the sum of their knowledge of events, of history, of the world. It exasperated me. Did the women then live on another planet that the winds of time never touched them? Today, when I think back over what I saw and heard of what our nation underwent in its first two years, I am convinced that these women were not of this world; they lived in complete alienation from the world outside the home and from the politics that made our nation.

Perhaps this was also because the Hindustan that these women lived in was so different, inhabited by bold Pathans, brave Rajputs, learned brahmins and honourable Hindus and Muslims. Women belonged not to Hindus or Muslims, but were the collective honour of the community, the nation. A daughter from one's village was one's own daughter. A sister had full right to make a passer-by her rakhi-brother; he, in turn, would not hesitate in pledging his life to defend her.

Historical records attest that when Delhi's princesses and noble-women fled towards Gurgaon, Jhajjar and other places, then the bands of Gujjars who came to loot them comprised only women. No man laid a hand on their bodies. Moreover, when the Gujjar women robbed these noblewomen of their silken garments, they thoughtfully gave them their own shabby clothes in exchange. And after all the plunder, if someone gave a noblewoman sanctuary in his home, she was kept as an honoured guest. For months and years thereafter, she lived in the comfort, respect, freedom and happiness that she would have enjoyed in her own palace.

If, as historians corroborate, this was the atmosphere of the times, it is then not so surprising that the old women I spoke to did not know much of political upheaval; the home and the personal circumscribed the limits of their experience.

In 1938, I could not have imagined that soon I would have to witness such horrifying scenes and that, this time, moral and ethical values, humanity and respect would be plundered alongside riches. And that when the frightening time came upon us, Chance would thrust me forward and say, 'Behold! Witness this saga of misfortune, and if you have the courage, safeguard this narrative!'

In 1947, when I brought my wounded heart to Delhi, Gandhiji took charge of the most useless member of the family and entrusted her with a task whose importance is only now becoming manifest to me. I learnt a tremendous amount because of this responsibility and, in the process, became acquainted with both the face of humanity as well as that of bestiality. I had read this couplet by Iqbal many times before, but the time appointed for my gaining a true understanding was clearly this. And I became completely taken that, truly, as Iqbal says:

nigaah-e-mard-e-momin se badal jaati hain taqdeerein
Under the gaze of a true Muslim, destinies alter their course
                                                    Mohammed Iqbal

In the lakhs of people I encountered in Delhi, I saw no resemblance to their proud forebears, of the Hindustan of old. It was a new age, in which our valour was to find as much glory in murdering a small child as in worsting a treacherous enemy. In his crazed flight from the violence, when he found a hiding place, the prayers of gratitude that a Muslim would send up equalled those that he would utter had he conquered a new land. One would stab another in the back and dance with joy at having proved his mettle as a warrior. Charming young men with innocent faces left schools and colleges in search of matchsticks, kerosene, bricks and knives, as amassing these was more important than seeking knowledge. And then,

ghar jala saamne
aur ham-se bujhaya na gaya
The house was ablaze before our eyes
But we could not douse the flames

Mirza Ghalib

This was the India of 1947–48, and it is a portrait of this I wish to sketch for you. But not because I want readers to gaze upon these scenes in horrified fascination, but because:

taaza khwaahi dashtan gar daagh haye seena ra
gaahe gaahe baaz khwan en qissa-e-pareena ra
If you wish the scars in your heart to remain fresh
Then, from time to time, revisit this old tale afresh

Maulana Mohammad Ayyub Surti Qasmi in
Muqqadamah Tarikh-e-Gujarat

Another thought obliges me to lift my pen; just as I was driven by curiosity to pester the old women of my times, the day is not far that innocent faces will gaze upon mine with the same questions in their eyes. Perhaps one day, the youth of the future will seek in the exertions of my toothless mouth answers to their ill-phrased questions; perhaps, a historian will one day need to know not just dates but also inner states of minds and hearts of the people; perhaps one day, the brave warriors of my own times will choose to regard their own visages in the mirror.

As I stand on the fortieth rung of the ladder of my life and look down, my head spins—it is as if the whole world has come up alongside me! How can I choose what to consider, what to set aside? I have seen so much—all of us who have lived through this last decade have seen four times as much as what the people of earlier times saw over centuries. And what we bore witness to in those two evil years has as its background a story ranging over a century and a half! How can the circumscribed nature of my vision and the limitations of my knowledge ever integrate these aspects into a whole? This work must be the work of the new historian of the new India. Just like a master surgeon's scalpel cuts away layers of flesh to seek out a festering wound, the historian's pen will probe all the aspects of those two years to find out the true causes for what happened. All I am capable of is to move the veil a little and show you a few glimpses of those anarchic times, and that is all I aim to do, with the promise that I will show only that which was initiated before me, and report only that which my own ears heard.

The drama that I will show you had other parts of India as its theatre earlier and now, for the last time, was being played out in Delhi, the heart of India. If the design had succeeded, then on the map of India today, along with Pakistan, would have been many other contending principalities, large and small. The Congress would not have survived, nor democracy. These impetuses for a divided India had in the past always prevented India from being united. Now, once more, this epidemic had broken out; the demand for Pakistan and the aspirations for Sikhistan and Jatistan were its symptoms. If I put together the animosity for each other with the political strife and conspiracies to destabilize the government, and add to them the martyrdom of Gandhiji, then the true significance of the events I witnessed emerges—what happened was not just directed against the Muslims. On the basis of what I have experienced, I can say with conviction that the objective was to obliterate the Congress, to topple the government.

Contrary to what some people think, Mahatmaji's martyrdom was not because of his sympathy for the Muslims but because this man so worthy of our respect stood in the way of the design to establish a multiplicity of governments. This, together with the fact that he had arraigned himself against the brazen murder of humanity by self-proclaimed stakeholders of religion, made it necessary that this obstacle be removed from the path. Even today, who can safely assert whether these kings, capitalists and religious leaders have truly been defeated, or reject the idea that they may yet prove successful? I have witnessed some of their attempts and these too I wish to place before the world.

In those terrible times, circumstances were often so fraught that at times it proved difficult to stay rooted on the side of justice, impartiality and humanity. On many occasions, I too wavered. In those moments, I found myself thinking like a hard, unyielding Muslim and justifying it to myself by reasoning that:

> *dil hi to hai na sang-o-khisht*
> *dard-se bhar na aaye kyun?*
> It is only a heart, not the dead weight of stone or brick
> So why should it not fill with sorrow?
>
> Mirza Ghalib

Mercifully though, the effects of a contemplation of the first principles of true Islam and the grace of Gandhiji's blessings ensured that this was the extent of my deviation. At such moments, I would ask myself whether my heart had so turned to stone that it could not be moved in sympathy with another distressed human. Was I beginning to forget that all humans were brothers, and:

> *dard-e-dil, paas-e-wafa jazba-e-imaan hona*
> *hai yahi aadmiyat aur yahi insaan hona*
> A suffering heart, a regard for loyalty, an abiding faith
> This is what humanity is, and to be human is this
>
> Brij Narayan 'Chakbast'

And then I have always believed that 'Humanity is Islam' and 'Islam is Humanity'. If the bonds with humanity were severed, then I too would have to debase myself in the same sludge in which so many wallowed. I would cry out, 'My beloved Allah, spare me this humiliation!' All my meditations are before the readers in this text.

But, for the love of God, do not look to this book for intellectual discovery or analytical brilliance, as in these pages you will find neither maturity, depth of insight, nor heady flights of language. You may even discern some infelicity in expression. This is the narrative of a woman who has lived her life in villages and *qasbah*s, of a woman whose eyes opened in a closeted home and, for this reason, her narrative cannot transcend her immediate context. All this book embodies is a mother's endless torment, a sister's fervent appeal, a daughter's anguished cry. Are there any left who still wish to pay heed to these calls?

> *banakar faqeeron ka ham bhes Ghalib*
> *tamasha-e-aihl-e-karam dekhte hain*
> Donning the guise of a faqir, Ghalib
> We watch the spectacle that the charitable have mounted
>
> Mirza Ghalib

This torment, this appeal would have been stifled just as many thousand voices have been in the past but for the perseverance of Hayatullah Ansari sahab, editor of *Qaumi Awaz*. When I went to Lucknow in December 1948, Hayatullah sahab insisted that I take all the notes that I used to make in copybooks or on scraps—as memory aids or to record events that affected me—and make a book out of them and place it before the nation. Although I agreed that I would order and edit them, I myself was quite sceptical that I would ever fulfil my promise. My inherent indolence and innate irresponsibility, together with my poor memory and the many small distractions I was prone to, continued to waylay me, and I kept putting off the manuscript.

But Hayatullah sahab's demands didn't let up in the slightest; instead, soon, another personage joined him in weighing me down. This gentleman was Miyan Ibadat Barelvi. He once heard me read out a few pages of the text; from then, he too began to implore me to finish the manuscript at once. In the end, exasperated by the clamour and the daily petitions that these two gentlemen kept up, I gave in, and began to collate, edit and shape my scattered observations into this manuscript. This is now placed before you.

Begum Anis Kidwai
4 King Edward Road, New Delhi
November 1948

Author's Preface to the 1978 Edition

~

Bismillah ir-Rahman ir-Rahim
In the name of the Keeper of the world and the Giver of Life
Allah has designated a specific time for the commencement and the
bounds of each act. Much as one may strive, until the appointed
moment for the completion of a work arrives, all endeavour is doomed
to flounder. This book met with the same fate.

Just witness this: through 1947 and 1948, as I watched the drama
unfold, I jotted my impressions in a notebook. In 1949, I wove these
scattered leaves into a manuscript. It was only in 1974 though that the
opportunity to publish it as a book finally arrived. The manuscript was
quite dated by then, and because I lacked the courage to scan it again,
the publisher was left to cope with my poor handwriting. The result—
many transcription and printing errors marring the first edition. To
worsen matters, the first scribe took off one fine day, necessitating the
appointment of another one. The result—a manuscript of a double
'beauty', wherein two completely different transcriptions coexisted.
Nevertheless, I am grateful to QET and D.R. Goyal and Subhadra Joshi
for placing the book before an audience for the first time in such a
beautiful binding and pleasing cover.

This was not the only misfortune that this poor text has had to
encounter. Its first mishap was that, in his farsightedness, Hayatullah
sahab divided the text into sections. I didn't take kindly to his efforts
and returned at once to the aforementioned scattered leaves to restore
the manuscript to its original state.

Around the same time, I became acquainted with Ibadat Barelvi. I thought I would get the book published under his supervision. However, soon after I made this decision, he departed for Pakistan and the manuscript stayed unpublished and unread. Some time later, I met Saghar Nizami, who was then editing the journal *Asia* from Meerut. He took a chapter and published it and then requested me to hand him the manuscript. He said he would be happy to have it transcribed and printed.

I was enthused but my brother-in-law, the late Rafi Ahmad Kidwai, was sceptical. Citing the example of another writer whose record of similar upheaval was published fifty years after the time about which he wrote, Rafi *bhai* cautioned me against rushing in. He remarked that although such books are often written, they should not be published so soon after the events they recorded.

But I was determined, so Rafi bhai accepted my decision and even made a donation to help me realize my intention. Unfortunately, his support went in vain as, in the interim, Saghar sahab's financial difficulties became so grave that *Asia* had to be wound up. Two years later, the transcribed manuscript and printer's blocks were handed back to me with Saghar sahab's sincere regrets. When neither author nor publisher had money, how was the book ever to see the light of day?

After this, I showed some pages to the late Shafiq-ur-Rahman Kidwai and satisfied myself that the book was neither uninteresting in subject nor execrable in style. Before I could pursue the matter further, however, he passed away. Some years later, Rafi bhai also bade his final farewell and I lost all hope:

aan qadah bashikast o aan saqi na maand
The cup is smashed, and the Saqi too has departed
                                        Mohammed Iqbal

In truth, Rafi bhai's words had affected me deeply and I did not even look at the manuscript again for some years. Two or three years later, riffling through my papers, I chanced upon it again and decided that I wanted to get a discerning opinion on its worth. I submitted it to Dr Abid Hussain for his consideration. I will always be grateful that Abid sahab not only read every word but also corrected words that had been left out (or in) by mistake. He returned the manuscript to me with only one sentence deleted and the advice that no alteration or reorganization was needed—that it should be published exactly as it was.

Following this encouragement, I requested the manager of Maktab-e-Jamia, Ghulam Rabbani 'Taba' sahab, to accept it for publication. When he agreed, I dashed off the original manuscript, the transcribed copy, and the blocks to him, and began counting down to finally holding a published volume in my hands. But three years went by and, at the end, the original manuscript in my bad handwriting was returned to me. The transcribed copy and blocks had been mislaid; I guess I was to be thankful that at least the manuscript had survived!

I was now so dejected that I packed up and put away the manuscript, so I would never have to see it again and grieve. Then, in 1970, Shri Goyal and Subhadra Joshi visited me with the request that I give them something of what I wrote about those anarchic times for publication in QET's journal, *Secular Democracy*. I expressed my inability because what I had written was a lengthy, detailed report of the period that could not be extracted from. If they wanted, I said, they could publish a few incidents from it but I would be happier if it were left untouched for publication as a book. Perhaps one day, its time would come.

Goyal sahab took one look at the manuscript and immediately declared that he would publish it. He was very insistent so I gave in and, yet again, handed over the precious bundle. The book that resulted was exactly the same as the manuscript—good or bad. Its binding and cover made it a little more tolerable but never, not in my wildest dreams, had I imagined that the intellectuals of this country would hold it in such high regard, that people like Jagan Nath 'Azad', Maulana Abdul Majid (Dariyabadi), Reoti Saran Sharma, Qurrutalain Haider, Gopi Chand Narang, Dr Ausaf Kidwai (Editor, *Azaim*), Ishrat Ali Siddiqi (Editor, *Qaumi Awaz*) and Rizwan Ahmad (Editor, *Azeemabad*

Express) would review it, or that the Uttar Pradesh Urdu Akademi's literary establishment would consider it worthy of a prize. From the depths of my heart, I thank all these distinguished persons for applauding my effort. I give thanks also to the Almighty, whose name never left my lips as I wrote, in prayer that no word I wrote should be other than what was true.

I am aware that this book is not a systematic arrangement of history, its consequences and its narrative and is, at best, a haphazard collection of events. But it is written with the blood of my heart and will certainly reawaken in readers the memories of those poisonous times that we have excised from our hearts and minds.

In these twenty-eight years, these eyes have witnessed the massacres in Jabalpur, Aligarh, Chandausi, Meerut, Ahmedabad and Bangladesh, and the barbarity of Turkman Gate. I have seen the level of poison rise and dip. However, none of these incidents have made me waver from the conviction that a nation's life depends on both the preservation of moral and ethical mores as well as democracy and unity. Nor has the hope left me that:

shab gurezaan hogi akhir jalwa-e-khursheed se
In the end, it is the light of day that shall banish the night

Mohammed Iqbal

The call to humanity, the imperative of love for the nation, the foundations of world peace and the unity of the nation itself depend on the strength that moral and ethical values and religious tenets infuse into the new generation and the new world. The character of the populace is the character of its government; the latter's ethical decline stems from the former's debasement.

Our world and time is past. An epoch has drawn to a close. I, and many others of my generation, now sit in readiness to bid our final farewell (if we have not already done so). Through this book, I have just this to say:

dekho mujhe jo deeda-e-ibrat nigah ho
meri suno jo gosh-e-naseehat niyosh hai
Gaze upon me if you have the eyes of one who can take
    admonition
Listen to me, if your ears can bear to hear the truth

Mirza Ghalib

Makers of the new world! Save yourselves from the poison we drank of to commit suicide. If the monuments you construct stand on moral and ethical values, then fortitude, grandeur, dignity and steadfastness will be your reward.

I thank the NBT officials for publishing this book and translating it into different languages of the nation. I hope that in this way, my voice will not be a voice lost in the wilderness and will find its way to every corner of the country. Once more, heartfelt thanks.

supurdam ba to maya-e-khesh ra
tu dani hisaab-e-kam-o-besh ra
I entrust all what is mine to thee
You know best whether it is much or little

Nezami Ganjawi

Women performing a havan for Independence on 14 August 1947,
at the residence of Dr Rajendra Prasad in Delhi.

1

I gather once again
the pieces of my shattered heart

September 1947 arrived, bringing in its wake scores of anxieties
and tribulations.

Since its beginning, news of Hindu–Muslim riots had been
streaming in. Memories of the Direct Action in Calcutta and the heart-
wrenching tragedies of Noakhali, Bihar, Multan, Rawalpindi and
Garhmukteshwar were still fresh in our shattered hearts. Thousands
had fled to India, and the miles-long convoy of destitutes from India
was writhing slowly across the land, now almost in Pakistan.

Multan and Rawalpindi had seen the most terrible massacre of
Hindus and Sikhs. A Pakistani friend narrated the tale of his misfortune:

'When I reached Rawalpindi from London, I saw scores of corpses
hanging from trees by their hair. When I fled to Mussoorie, the riots

there forced me to languish in a camp for a month. Our first child was born there in fact. If Shafi Ahmad Kidwai had not looked after us, who knows what fate awaited us. And it was only with Rafi sahab's help that we could get out.'

I can still recall the glee with which votaries of both religions had greeted the news of the massacres. I remember how the brother of the famous Muslim League leader Chaudhary Khaliquzzaman had chortled, 'It is true that we faced defeat in Calcutta but in Noakhali, we taught them a lesson! These Hindus are such cowards! They simply fled, leaving their women behind. Best of all, these Sikhs, with all their swagger about bravery and valour, have been completely exposed! Their own obesity got them—the fat fellows couldn't hold their ground in the battle. Look how they are scurrying over to India, their tails between their legs!'

I gazed at him in horror, thinking what could become of a nation that gives birth to such heroic 'braves'! I said, 'Do not rejoice so in the destitution of others. If nothing else, bear in mind that for the two days of jubilation you had over Calcutta, you had to spend many more bemoaning what happened to the Muslims there. I suspect Multan and Rawalpindi too may well extract tears of blood from you. I still remember the wells brimming over with corpses in Noakhali, the children aflame in Bihar. How can you forget them?'

My old chacha, Chaudhary Muhammad Ali Ridaulvi, surprised me by exulting over sensational reports: 'Only 300 or 400 men were killed in Calcutta, but I hear that 4,000 women were welcomed into Islam as well . . . 4,000!' His face flushed with pride as he uttered these words.

I also remember the enraged words of a well-known journalist, castigating the government for its weakness: 'If it were left to me, I would ensure that not one Muslim survived! If we don't exact revenge for what has been done to us in Pakistan, we have achieved nothing! From now on, we too will make it impossible for these fellows to live here.' This gentleman had already begun to secretly support the Rashtriya Swayamsevak Sangh (RSS).

A strange bestiality was born in those days. Even those with the most delicate of temperaments today celebrated wildly the misfortunes of others. Even the well educated, the seemingly sensitive and sensible had enthusiastically joined those stoking the fires of retribution. To think that once we'd have had no hesitation in swearing by their reliability and level-headedness!

I would think—what would those mothers have gone through, as their children were torn from them and hurled into bonfires, when young girls were snatched from their parents, wives wrenched from husbands and made to change their religion? Those wives, those sisters, hollowed out by the agonies of their experiences, what Hindus or Muslims could they possibly make? May God's wrath rain on those who did this to them! Witnessing all this, I would yearn for the kind-hearted Indians of yore, who had lived in amity, albeit in utter subordination to the infamous British rule. At least on the face of it, they were decent and trustworthy and capable of respect for wives, daughters and daughters-in-law.

How things had changed, and so quickly. Until June 1947, Mussoorie had bustled with life. Cinemas and theatres stayed open till 2 a.m. Once, I recall, I had insisted on staying over with a friend, Begum Hayatullah Ansari, and at 2 a.m., we two women walked from Rivera to Charlesville Gate unescorted, without misgiving.

Those days, the Azad Hind Fauj Band used to play every evening at Mall Road, just below the Library. Thousands would gather to hear them—burqa-clad women, hurly-burly Sikhs, all would be there. Children would be entrusted to *pahadi* men, who would seat them in baskets and take them for long strolls, returning them unharmed to their parents a few hours later. Mussoorie was so safe then and the men who plied horses and rickshaws considered so trustworthy that it surprised nobody that a ten-year-old girl, holding the finger of her four-year-old brother, walked from Charlesville to Collectory Bazaar without any harm befalling them.

India's Partition had been decided by then. Whenever I thought of it, my heart would clutch with foreboding. People had already begun to whisper, 'Wait and watch, these newcomers (refugees) will surely foment trouble.'

Hindu–Muslim relations were already strained but life still flowed evenly. Our apprehension was that as soon as Partition took place, Britain would seize the opportunity to sow trouble. We were also afraid that such large-scale migration could result in great hardships. Anger mounted in our hearts against our leaders who had agreed to this division.

In June, during Bapu's prayer meeting in Delhi's Bhangi Basti, my sister Bilqees—whose passionate temperament always rendered her speech excitable—impetuously decided that she would march up to him to ask why he agreed to this division. If India was for everyone, and every one of us was to live and die here, why this Partition, this exchange of populations? How could any of us, those who had dreamt so long of a united, victorious, indomitable India, be satisfied with this fragment of a dream?

As soon as the prayers ended and Bapu rose, Bilqees was poised to dart through the crowd to accost him. But as she sprang forward, her husband Wirasat Ali Kidwai, held her back, saying, 'What are you doing? This is hardly the time. Just wait, another opportunity will arise.' By the time Bilqees could extricate herself from his restraining hand, Bapu had gone. To this day she regrets the fact that she failed in her mission to vent her feelings in full public view on that day.

I remember well that first 15 August—the designated day of liberation, rung in by the horrifying shrieks of terror resounding from Calcutta across to East and West Punjab. The day when the corpse of Delhi was being mangled underfoot, the day when women were being dishonoured. A day of freedom, yes, but a freedom slashed and streaked with blood. A day choked by smoke and fire.

The Government House echoed with the victims' moans and entreaties, yet we were happy. Or, truthfully, we forced ourselves to be happy. All else aside, the long years of struggle had borne fruit. Whatever else had happened, at least the yoke of slavery was undone. Perhaps with this freedom, the demons of communalism would also soon be exorcized. True, the nation was divided but even separate, the two parts could live in peace and prosperity.

But on this day, even this feeble consolation was not to be available to many of us and we were to experience again a sense of servitude, of alienation, of otherness. I went searching for happiness that day but everywhere I went—and Begum Hayatullah and I had scoured the best part of the city by foot, rickshaw, car—there was the same gloom, the pall of despair that stifled the hope we once nurtured.

The tricolour's flutter could not lift our hearts, nor the roars of '*Inquilab Zindabad!*', or celebratory slogans charge us with triumphant pride. Signboards and posters in Hindi seemed to mock us. Hearts and spirits benumbed, our blood was cold.

On that day, India took its first steps back into the past. Foreheads were being anointed with tilaks. Why were brahmins from Banaras being summoned? Why were there frenetic searches for *kari*s to enunciate the Quran? Why was *chandan* being prepared? Why were those long beards being carefully groomed? What could Buddhist *bhikshus* possibly have to do in the Government House? Were we to grow accustomed to the sound of wooden *khadau*s slapping its smooth floors?

Fretting and fuming, I made my way to the Government House that night. At the threshold, my head lifted with pride. This imposing entrance to this magnificent building, on which the tricolour proudly fluttered, was now to be the thoroughfare for all citizens—everything here was now ours, everyone who lived here, our comrade. Just as quickly though, the light in my heart was extinguished. The language being spoken around me was even more alien than English. As Josh said:

> *jisko dewon ke siwa koi samajh na sake*
> *zayr mashq ab hai wo andaz-e-bayaan, e saqi*
> That which can be comprehended by no one but the giants
> Is the tongue evidently in use these days, Saqi
>
> Josh Malihabadi

Seated all around on *chauki*s were Buddhist monks, brahmin priests, Muslim clerics, and God knows who else. Many languages

were spoken that day—English, Sanskrit, Arabic, difficult Hindi—
but not the sweet tongue that belongs to us all:

jiski har baat mein sau phool mehak uthte hain
In every expression of which a hundred flowers perfume the air
                                                    Josh Malihabadi

So much was said that day but none of us understood a word.
Like me, the many women seated around, gaped at the spectacle with
choked throats and incredulous eyes and, when it was over, returned
home feeling as if the ground had shifted beneath our feet. Despite
her best efforts, the first governor of independent India, Sarojini Naidu,
could not read out the oath of office correctly. All of us who listened
were stupefied. Truly, the new dhobi starches even the rags that come
his way.

All the years we had waited and struggled, were they all for this
moment? Who wanted to resurrect long-buried corpses of the past?
Or wanted self-proclaimed stakeholders of religion to reign instead of
democracy? Which fool could have aspired to a future in which the
past—fat Hindu priests and all—held sway, where a few padres and
karis were charged with consoling the minorities?

This was too painful. To witness this spectacle of Brahminism made
our hair stand on end. We had been shown a glimpse of the terrible
future. And those who had been cynical bystanders for the past twenty
years could now gleefully taunt us, 'Now you see it, don't you? Hadn't
we said that as soon as freedom is won, India would become a Hindu
rashtra? This is why Pakistan is necessary; in fact, it was this mindset
that gave birth to Pakistan in the first place!'

Chaudhary Ridaulvi gloated: 'It's all there in an article I wrote—
the brahmin has always been dominant in India. Buddhism prospered
but Brahminism ensured its ultimate obliteration. Islam shone only
briefly, soon losing its identity to be coloured in the same hues as
Brahminism. Christianity too bowed before Brahminism in the shape
of the Theosophical Society, which acknowledges brahmin supremacy.

Brahminism is hegemonic by nature. However much Gandhi may struggle, and all of you rant and rave, India will never be free of the Brahminical order.'

To listen to these taunts required great patience. We held our breath, waited, but no light shone through. Some of us wondered—what about ordinary people? The working classes, the poor, the farmers, the middle classes, how would they find a way out of this labyrinth? Those of us who willingly wore the burqa that the Congress gave us—only to be disappointed with the farce that was being enacted— felt that it was now our responsibility to lift this veil of deceit.

The wily had divined the direction of the wind and where these ominous clouds would unburden themselves. Soon the Muslim Leaguers had cause for celebration. New friends joined them and they were no longer alone in being shorn. On the other side the youth, particularly the headstrong young progressives, began to wrestle with the question: Will the old trusted hands of the struggle for freedom, who have just routed the British so convincingly, indeed prove useful in these changed circumstances? Should we strengthen their hands or discard them altogether? A new battle was now to be joined, not with foreigners but with our own; it would not be the struggle of the Indian masses but of a handful of the youth who, caked in blood and ashes, would build a new India. But who knew then that the greatest sacrifice would have to be made by the father of the nation?

And then September came. It had hardly been fifteen days since India had become free, when Delhi erupted in violence. The pristine tricolours that had proudly fluttered atop every house and shop, in every lane and street, were spattered with blood, as Delhi, like Dehra Dun and Mussoorie, was engulfed in the flood of suspicion, hatred and violence originating in Punjab. (Apparently, someone once remarked that it was as if a Ganga of riots was flowing through India. At which, Bapu remarked, 'Yes, but one whose Gangotri is in Punjab!' So true, as Punjab was indeed the source of this terrible carnage.)

Telephone lines down, the postal system in disarray, trains cancelled, bridges destroyed and streets filled with people writhing, crawling, being trampled underfoot, being looted and murdered, and dying, dying like flies, shunted from here to there by the unseen staff of the great Allah. God save us, this was perhaps the greatest butchery ever witnessed.

In old tales it is said that Bakht-e-Nasar (Nebuchadnezzar) had enslaved the whole population of Jerusalem and taken them to Babylon, that Moses had guided 40,000 Jews out of Egypt, and that Carthage had enslaved the populations of the territories it had conquered and set them to bake bricks. But how could this compare to the numbers of our times? While India had seen great wars like the Mahabharata and Nadir Shah's three-day siege of Delhi, even at the height of the cruelty, not more than 10,000–20,000 could have died. But these were old stories, from times when even a mere province was called a nation. No, what we witnessed could not have happened ever, from the very beginning of the world until now.

In Lucknow, distraught women, men and children would beg me to somehow get word of the safety of their loved ones from Delhi. 'Can you get our relatives out of Mussoorie?' 'We don't know whether any of ours are still alive in Dehra Dun, but if they are, in God's name, can you get us news of them?' And I would nag Rafi bhai with repeated phone calls and scores of letters.

It was my habit to take a mile-long walk along La Martiniere Road daily after the morning namaz. I always went alone—which other woman could be persuaded to accompany me at such an early hour? In any case, it was perfectly safe.

Until September. A current of tension now charged the early morning air. Now, small groups of men, four or five at most, would occasionally pass me by. Doctors, lawyers, students, farmers, they would usually be discussing events in Punjab and the rest of India, some ruing the tragedies, others engaging in heated debate. One day, walking sticks, staffs and umbrellas appeared in their hands. Their demeanour changed and the tenor of the conversations I overheard made me feel that truly the harmony of Lucknow was fraying. Earlier

I refused to heed my family's warnings but now, the palpable change in the atmosphere made me discontinue my walks.

Communal harmony committees were formed and meetings were held across the city. Concerned residents intensified efforts to ensure that violence did not break out; it was thanks to the joint efforts of Hindus and Muslims that Lucknow did not sully its traditions of principle and honourable conduct.

However, the worry of family was enough to rob one of all peace. My days were spent in a torment of anxiety, my nights measured out in feverish paces, in the grip of a dread that allowed me no rest. Although relatives in Delhi were assured of some security, anxiety about Mussoorie consumed me. My husband, Shafi Ahmad Kidwai, the administrator of the Mussoorie Municipal Board, was alone there, as I had come away to Lucknow to look after Abbajan, my father-in-law, who was seriously ill. I knew that Shafi sahab's characteristic stubbornness would never allow him to leave Mussoorie, and that any pressure would only make him more adamant to stay. Moreover, it was clear from his letters that he had devoted himself to providing relief to victims of the riots. He would never agree to come away.

Nevertheless, the family continued to ask him to return to Lucknow. His brothers were worried. We received news that he was to come to Lucknow on 21 September on official work. Then we heard that his visit was delayed, as he could not leave Mussoorie in those conditions. Thereafter, the date kept getting postponed.

He did write. Earlier, he was worried about the safety of his relatives, friends and employees in Dehra Dun, when riots engulfed it. But when riots broke out in Mussoorie, he was calm:

mushkilein mujh par padi itnee ki aasaan ho gayeen
So many were the troubles that beset me that they became
   my ease
                                                    Mirza Ghalib

He would not write about himself but would ask after the whole world. Once he wrote that he was missing our elder daughter, Azadi, who had recently been married. 'Send me her address, so I can write to her.' And he did send her a letter. Other letters were full of concern for my health, the children's well-being, the safety of others, as if we were in peril and he, alone in riot-torn Mussoorie, was safe.

One day, his letter spoke of what was happening around him: 'I am sitting in my office, writing to you. I hear from the road below the noise of the crowd, the sounds of gunfire, the shrieks of the suffering and the wounded. Houses are burning, shops are being looted, all in broad daylight, as the police just watch.'

Another letter: 'I've shut the office and am at home since three days. It is raining very hard. Even the poor men who ply horses and mules have not been spared. I have instructed the jamadars to cover their corpses with grass and leaves.'

The next letter came after the violence, written with a heavy heart: 'I have lived through much since 1921. I have seen a period of soul-stirring unity between Hindus and Muslims. Just as I have seen the brutality with which the British regime greeted the agitations organized by the Congress. I have experienced the turbulence of 1942, the inspired passionate struggle for freedom. I have witnessed the anarchic behaviour of the Muslim League in past elections. And today I see the egotistical madness of the majority. All days pass, these too shall, but I will always remember the callous and partisan conduct of the official machinery.'

A letter dated 27 September: 'Telegraph lines are down. An official telegram despatched on 17th reached here only on 24th, one dated 12th arrived on 22nd. I just cannot get through to Delhi. Four or five days ago, I thought of apprising Pantji [Govind Ballabh Pant, chief minister of the United Provinces] of the situation but the telephone would not connect. Now, there is neither telegraph nor telephone.'

On his way to his office, situated on a hill above Collectory Bazaar, he would often find corpses littering the path. Who else but he would bear the ritual responsibility of bathing them, clothing them in shrouds and burying them? He was himself the only Muslim still abroad on the streets of Mussoorie. With the help of the jamadars in his employ, he would have the bodies moved into ditches and covered with mud, stones and foliage, to save them from the depredations of the eagles and vultures circling overhead. After all, as administrator, it was also his duty to keep Mussoorie's air clean. Rarely would any other administrator of a municipal board have to fulfil such a terrible obligation!

Whenever I think of those moments, I want to take my own life. He had to do all this alone—I was safe in Lucknow. Why didn't I go to him? Why did I return that day when, panicking for his safety, I left the house secretly to board the train? Why did I listen to my younger brother, who caught up with me at Nazar Bagh and begged, 'Don't go! No trains reach Dehra Dun unharmed these days. Wait a little longer!' I should not have listened. I should have gone to him.

And he would write, 'Do not concern yourself about me. Save for one day when it was raining, I go to work every day.' This, despite the fact that all other Muslim employees were in camp and Hindu employees were also more absent than not. But he was determined. As soon as the riots stopped, he opened the office and worked every day. The office had to function as usual if relief work had to continue.

On 28 September, he wrote two long letters, quite similar in content, one to his brother and another to his friend. The letter addressed to Rafi bhai was mislaid soon after his martyrdom, as Rafi bhai sent it to the district magistrate to assist him in his investigations. It was never seen again and the investigation was never completed. Could that letter have been the reason why he had to postpone his inquiry? A question that only the district magistrate can answer.

I have, however, the letter to his friend before me: 'I go regularly to office, contrary to advice. If I had let fear overcome me, I would have become the victim of some mishap by now. And there are many who would desire such an "accident" to take place. The Muslims here have suffered great violence but their financial losses are even greater. They have been driven out of Landour and Kulri Bazaar and are now in a camp at Rampur House. If there had been a police guard at Imperial Bank or the building opposite it, so much looting could have been prevented. But the truth is that the plunder was instigated and sponsored, and its spoils have found their way into the homes of the servants of the people.'

In another letter: 'All my Muslim subordinates are in the camp. I have to arrange for money for their salaries and upkeep. I have ordered that until it is safe for them to be ferried to and fro, they shall be considered to be on leave. And that in view of the dire straits they find themselves in, not only their salaries but also money from their Provident Funds should be released.

'. . . The education superintendent is a Congressman and is working very hard on the relief front. Until the last breath leaves my body, I will serve them. The cruelties that they have suffered have caused me much pain. If only twenty-five policemen could have been persuaded to do their duty with sincerity, the entire Muslim population of Mussoorie would have been spared. But this was not what the responsible officials of the police and the administration desired.'

Since 1 October, no train had reached or left Dehra Dun. The traffic of motor lorries had also ceased: 'I used to listen to the radio but, for three days, it too has shunned my company.' Why so? The reason could not be found out. He could not speak to either Pantji in Lucknow or Rafi bhai in Delhi.

In a letter to my brother, and in the one to his friend, he writes, 'These are the moments when one comes to commune with one's God. Pray for me that I don't lose courage, that my resolve stays firm. Death has an appointed day. It is inevitable but just pray that God will fortify my heart, so that the fear of death does not deter me from doing what I believe to be right.'

In another place, he writes, 'No true friend, no companions are around me. It is God himself who gives me courage to face every new day.'

After 2 October, there were no more letters. He must have written; he used to write to me daily. It would not surprise me to learn that they were waylaid. He was being threatened every day, by phone and by anonymous notes—if he did not leave Mussoorie for Dehra Dun, he would be killed. We found one such letter in his papers later. Aziz Hayat Khan, a refugee in the camp, writes, 'Shafi sahab used to visit us in the camp every day on his way to, and back from, office. He would listen to our grievances and try to solve them. The day before his martyrdom, he said, "I have got another warning today." I asked him if he would be more careful and he laughed, "Oh no, and I'm certainly not leaving!"'

Around 3,000 people were then refugees in Rampur House. Of these, around 800 were Kashmiri and Balti workers, to whom Mussoorie municipality owed thousands of rupees. That very day, they begged Shafi sahab to get them their dues, so that they could return home. He promised he would do so the very next day. But, when the next day—that apocalyptic tomorrow—arrived, these poor workers were to beat their heads and bemoan their fate. All of them did make it safely out of Mussoorie, but they left in penury, perhaps to die of starvation.

Shafi sahab had arraigned himself against partisanship and dereliction of duty of the officials and against the section of the public engaged in hooliganism and rioting. Both sections were united in their desire for an event that would make this hindrance 'disappear'. He, on the other hand, believed it his duty to never surrender and to stand firm in combat with these forces. How could his actions ever have won the approval of those engaged in such acts? Besides, many were fearful of the public exposure he had the power to effect. There must also have been others who, in taking his life, wished to be celebrated as the guardians of their faith.

For many days, we had heard of his imminent return. He had written of this so many times. He had wanted to come home so much. But God willed otherwise, and who can challenge fate? The entreaties of friends in Dehra Dun, all of our letters, the anxiety at home, nothing, nobody could delay that appointed moment.

I often wonder whether I failed. Perhaps I did not insist enough that he come home. My brothers would rant: 'Why aren't you more persistent? It is as if you don't care!' But who knew his nature better than I? How could I pressurize him? In comparison to his bravery, I could only feel shame for my cowardice.

To flee from danger, to retreat in the face of opposition, to betray his conscience under the threat of bodily harm or any other adversity, stood in complete contradiction to his character. He believed that

India was his home, his nation, his *janambhoomi*. He had the same right to reside on this piece of land, the same freedom to roam across it, the same facility to undertake business and industry on it, as was invested in any other citizen. What was happening now marked enmity rather than fellow feeling and in this destruction of the nation lay his own downfall. He was entitled, he believed, to defend his birthright and his dignity. How could Shafi sahab then be expected to turn his back on those from whom these very rights were snatched away? He would never compromise on taking what he believed to be the correct course of action, and I had never tried to make him do so. On the contrary, I had myself written these words to him, 'I am of the opinion that at such a time, any responsible person must never yield his ground. It could be that because of him that a few poor people may live in security, the lives of some others be saved, and yet others benefit in some ways from his availability.'

But the truth was that all I really wished for was that he come away from Mussoorie. And if that was not to be, that I should somehow go to him. I wanted to burn with him in the inferno that was consuming him—but I could do nothing. Silently I lived in prayer. I didn't stop my brothers from telephoning him or prevent them from sending him telegrams. I myself wrote to him, many times: 'Everyone at home is very worried, and I don't know how to say this, but because it is also my own wish, I think it would be better if you came to Lucknow. If only people would let me, I would be with you by now . . .'

His letter of 2 October was in reply to mine: 'Anis, do not weaken me. I will not leave here. Let the turmoil subside, then I shall bring the miscreants to justice, but if that is not fated, so be it. Just pray to God that I may remain steadfast.'

His reply only increased my respect for him. He could have run away to save himself; in fact, we were asking him to do just that. But he believed that the greatest weapon and truest armour against brutality and domination was Gandhiji's ahimsa. Even if he were the sole person left to protest barbarism and injustice, he would battle on alone in that theatre of war. How could I even think of denting that resolve, when I myself was convinced of its rectitude?

I tried unsuccessfully to quieten my anxious heart. Only Allah can know the torment in which he spent the remaining four or five days of his life. Alone, all alone, surrounded by enemies, menacing telephone calls, threatening letters. Alone, and at every moment, the footfalls of approaching Death . . . dear God! I am reminded of how once, while bathing in Mussoorie, he had so angered me by repeating this couplet:

kisi munh se na nikla yeh mere dafan ke waqt
ki in pe khaq na dalo, ye hain nahaye hue
On the day of my burial, these words did not escape anyone's
    lips
'Do not throw dust on him, he has just bathed!'

Qamar Jalalwi

I protested his ominous words but he just laughed away my objections. His laughter annoyed me further. For the remaining part of my stay in Mussoorie, he did not recite the couplet before me ever again. It all comes rushing back to me now, all of it, even that which I do not wish to remember . . .

Without consulting him, his friends from Dehra Dun, Mr Khurshed Lal (president, Dehra Dun Congress Committee) and others had reserved a train seat for him on 8 October. Finally, he agreed to return to Lucknow that day. However, fate had decided otherwise and, on 7 October, just a day before, all hopes of his returning to Lucknow were dashed forever. Between 9 and 10 a.m., on his way to office, near Baharistan, he was martyred.

A chaprasi should have been with him. Who were the killers? Where did they come from? Why did the policeman whom his friends had arranged to protect him, on their own account, stay at home? Many such questions were posed, questions that neither the chaprasi nor we could answer. Nothing could ever be resolved.

And what about the pistol he had started carrying, on the insistence of Azad sahab (collector of Mussoorie) and Khurshed Lal sahab? In all our years together (since 1921), I had never seen him with a weapon. When his friends had made the suggestion, he had said that he did not see the point of carrying it, when he did not even know how to use it. So he was taught how to fire it and his friends insisted that he always carry it in his pocket. It did stay in his pocket forever, untouched even at the moment of his death. Clearly, he did not think it necessary to bring it out. Months later, the handkerchief from his pocket was given to us. Though it had been cleaned, the bloodstains were still visible. It was as if a brand of innocence had been etched on it in blood . . .

> *zindagani ki haqiqat Kohkan ke dil se poochh*
> *joo-e-shir-o-tisha-o-sang-e-giraan hai zindagi*
> It is Farhad whom you must ask about the truth about life
> It is as difficult as digging out a river of milk, as breaking heavy
>   stones

Mohammed Iqbal

He must be happy now, having sloughed off the stone of life. He lived a life of straitened circumstances and great worry. He would spend hardly a twentieth of his income on himself just so that others could live in comfort. Every day, in every moment of his life, he put others' needs, aspirations and desires before his own.

Now, when everything was over, my shattered heart imploded. For a moment, I was ablaze in a passion for vengeance but soon I regained control. Where thousands have lost their lives, he was just one. Was it not solace enough that he had died unsullied? He did not take another's life; he did not commit cruelty; he was not responsible for the destruction of another. Whatever God and faith asked of him, he submitted; whatever his dues in service of humanity, he settled.

Somebody once asked us, 'Why was there no demand from you or your family for a proper inquiry and a search for the murderers?' What could I possibly say? I no longer had any demands or desires. I could never regain what I had lost. There was no turning back the clock. The wound in my heart would fester forever and no spring would ever brighten the wilderness of my life.

By pressing for the murderer's capture, why should I be responsible for making his wife a widow, of depriving his children of their father? Why should it be I who becomes the cause of his mother's torment? Why should I not leave a decision on this matter to He who metes out reward and punishment to the whole world? In any case, how am I to know who the murderer is? Is it not the job of the government to take care of these matters of investigation and justice? Let alone the fact that he was its official; its own citizen had been murdered. If the government did not apprehend the culprit, it was a sign that it was weak, insensitive and incapable of governance. And neither the law nor authority needed either consultation with us or our sanction to proceed.

Even if I had insisted, what reason did I have to believe that my complaint would be pursued? Such terrible crimes had taken place in this period but had any steps been taken to apprehend those criminals? It was as if all provisions for penalties had been erased from the law. No, what had befallen me was nothing unusual. I was merely one of the tens of thousands in the grip of grief.

To regain some peace, to foster in myself a sense of resignation, such were the ways in which I tried to console myself! How I prayed to God that he would grant me some measure of the steadfastness that Shafi sahab had exhibited.

For a week after, I had no sense of what was going on around me. But till when could I mourn? I was alive, and even if it was only to meet the public gaze, I had to live out a human life. I began to compose myself and, after four days, decided that, all right, I could not go to Mussoorie but I would go to Delhi, and submerge my own sorrows into the misery flooding the city. I would go to Gandhiji in Delhi.

Gandhiji, that epitome of goodness; Delhi, whose bylanes are redolent with a sense of history, a city that has been resettled as many times as it has been destroyed, a city at times plundered by strangers, at times looted by its own, a city, to whose history, a new and bloody chapter was being added by the violence that had consumed it since 5 September 1947. I was going to this city to drown the greatest sorrow of my life, in the hope that in the deluge that washed over us, I would sight some distant shore upon which I may anchor my future.

> *jab kashti sabit-o-salim thi, sahil ki tamanna kisko thi*
> *ab aisi shikasta kashti par sahil ki tamanna kaun kare*
>
> When the craft was worthy and secure, who thought of the safety
>   of the shore,
> Now when the craft itself is riddled, who may aspire to a shore
>   at all?
>
> Moin Ahsan Jazbi

Mahatma Gandhi, or Bapu, at a prayer meeting.

2

In the presence of Gandhiji, the martyr of the nation

(October 1947–January 1948)

It had long been my dearest wish to spend some weeks at the feet of the most towering personage of our times. My heart ached that I had yet to profit from the teachings of that Good Samaritan, that great reformer of this century, that ideal of spirituality in this age of materialism. But every event has its own designated moment and then, as Ghalib says:

> *dete hain bada zarf-e-qadah khawar dekh kar*
> Wine is apportioned by the measure of the drinker's cup
>
> Mirza Ghalib

This measure was born in me by the greatest injury of my life, a wound after which neither grief nor pain could touch me again. I was being tried on that anvil of strength and subjected to the searing heat of that furnace of purity in which the entire country was being tested. God alone can say whether I passed but my resolve became so true that I could summon the courage to go to Bapu to offer my service.

My only regret is that this longed-for aspiration could be fulfilled when the measure of his days was nearly full. However, even for this, I am grateful to God—even if for a few moments only, the rays of this dying sun could thaw my frostbitten heart. I thank Him that I too was afforded a glimpse of this apogee of spiritualism and could, with my tattered resources, present myself at the court of this messiah.

I had telephoned that morning to ask for permission to visit Gandhiji. Birla House was teeming with people, its galleries choked by the incessant traffic. Everywhere a bustle but in Bapu's room, a profound calm. There, seated on a takht covered with a milk-white sheet was that apostle of amity, clad in white khaddar. His granddaughter Abha, his grandson's wife Manu and others sat nearby. I tried desperately to stay composed but, on seeing him, the dam broke. My tears flowed with the abandon of a distressed girl when she sees her mother approaching. I could not utter a single word.

Gandhiji was the first to speak, 'I understand. It is for her that I have been waiting since morning. Come, sit.'

A serene smile played on his face. Perhaps on a small stool beside him, a bowl of porridge and some vegetables were kept, which he ate slowly. Speaking softly, he said, 'Do not weep. He is not dead, he is alive. He was martyred while doing his duty. How many can hope for so fortunate a death? Such people never die.' I said, 'Bapu, custom dictates that I stay sequestered at home for many months but I have broken these shackles, as I hear that you will shortly leave for Pakistan. I too want to die serving the people, as Shafi sahab did. Before you go, please help me find purpose.'

Smiling, he said, 'How can I leave for Pakistan when there is so much to do here? Calcutta was simply a sport compared to Delhi, a mere dalliance. Until all this ends, until each Muslim child can leave his home and move about freely, how can I possibly leave? Such madness has possessed people these days!'

After talking to me for a while, he said, 'Go to Sushila and ask her for some work. She is working in the Muslim camp in the Purana Qila and she will tell you what to do. Meet her and then come once again to see me. To serve others is a good thing. There is no need for tears. Go, live a life of service and be happy.'

He must have said other things but I cannot recall what they were or even what the sequence of events was after my meeting with him. Perhaps I went straight to the camp from Birla House. After meeting Dr Sushila Nayyar, Gandhiji's disciple, I took on the responsibility of the food for the ill and wounded, learning from her the way in which it must be prepared and distributed.

I often wonder what would have become of me if I had not received Gandhiji's guidance at that perilous juncture of my life. I travelled readily down the new path he showed, hoping that I would one day find the thoroughfare that would take me straight to my destination. Had Bapu not supported me, I would still be standing distressed at the crossroads, unmoving, uncertain where to go.

By the time I met Gandhiji the second time, the tears had stopped and I was much calmer. He was in the company of Maniben Patel, Subhadra Dutt (later Subhadra Joshi) and some others I did not know. Subhadra was presenting the case of a Muslim officer. Maniben suggested, 'Why doesn't this man go and meet Sardar Patel and put the whole issue before him?' Subhadra said, 'But how can the poor man get to Sardar in the first place? He does not have the required connections in high places.'

Just then, Gandhiji caught sight of me. Seeing my altered demeanour, he smiled. I told him that the reason for this change was that I was now working with Sushila in the camp and feeling fulfilled. Gandhiji was happy, 'This is good news, then.'

I sat a little longer but then, thinking I should not impose on his valuable time, I left. In the days that followed, I attended the prayer meetings often, as they were held at a time when I would be at home. In the mornings I would be in a hurry to reach the camp and it would be 2 p.m. when I got free. If any exigency arose, I would of course take time out from my duties to go and meet Bapu; ordinarily, however,

I would send word to him via Brij Krishna Chandiwala (Gandhiji's secretary then) or Sushila. Although I would have liked to see him every day, I felt that the people with a greater right to share his time were those who had been associated with him for far longer. I did not want to trouble him unnecessarily with my unsolicited visits, fearing that he would resent the imposition. Though I soon came to understand that Bapu would never take umbrage, my timidity and respect for elders prevented me.

One day, I heard him telling Dr Zakir Hussain, 'Doctor sahab, some people came to say that they have managed to save some of the things that belonged to your school in Karol Bagh. Please go and collect them.' Clearly, the conversation had been under way for some time; I couldn't immediately understand the import of these words. Later I learnt that the riots had caused losses of several lakhs to Jamia School, Publication House and Library. Some good souls had managed to save some of the school's property and wanted Doctor sahab to inspect it. But Doctor sahab, despairing at the destruction of so many valuable books and priceless years of work, could not bring himself to visit the place.

As Gandhiji spoke on in hushed tones, my thoughts turned to the time I had first heard his name, twenty-seven years ago, when talk of the formation of a political party based on ahimsa, principles and conscience had led me to scrutinize my self, conscience and principles. Since 1921, how many hopes I had nurtured! And then my thoughts turned to an appreciation of Gandhiji's high ideals, his simple life, his sweet words—and the way he had been made the target of his opponents' ire and sarcasm. At times termed a naked fakir, at times a traitor, often abused as the arch-enemy of Muslims and equally the executioner of Hindus and yet venerated as the Mahatma. In the words of the poet:

rind kehta hai wali mujhko, wali rind mujhe
The drunk worships me as a saint; the holy man abuses me as
    a libertine

All these scenes played out before my eyes. This man, so puny, a bag of bones, but imbued with stupendous inner strength, patience and endurance, so tireless in his ability and desire to serve—where did he come from? And now, when twenty-seven years of work was perishing, when the edifice he had so painstakingly erected was crumbling, how could he continue to be a beacon in this pitch darkness? For how long? What would happen if this light of hope were extinguished, our source of comfort snatched away? Oh God! These thoughts deprived me of my sanity.

Dr Hussain left after a while. Next, Ramdas Daulat Ram addressed Bapu and presented the difficulties his food ministry was facing in procuring supplies. Bapu was softly making some suggestions when I got up to leave.

Delhi, in September and November that year, was a bloody corpse, over which eagles and vultures circled, waiting for a single lapse on the part of this old caretaker (or his removal from the scene), so that they may pounce on it and tear it to shreds.

No place was safe, no heart secure. All love had been wiped out and hatred reigned supreme. Here, Muslims were in peril—the ground hard, the horizon remote. There, caravan after caravan of Hindus streamed in, beaten and injured, looted without succour or hope. There was no peace to be had anywhere. In times like these, Bapu's room was the only sanctuary. Countless terrified desolate Muslims, impoverished Hindu refugees crazed with anger, destitute women, orphaned children, Sikhs with flowing beards, brahmins with tilak-adorned foreheads, Christians in long robes, sanyasis and ulemas, all found shelter there:

karishma daman-e-dil mee kashad ki ja een ja ast
Charisma tugs at the heart, come, this is your abode
                                                          Nazeeri Neshapuri

This was the sanctuary in which they were the most secure, where no one would intimidate them, where they would not be chastised or countered. After all, if one could not confide freely in one's father, who else could one turn to? Each felt that Bapu would gather him, his child, to his bosom and protect him from every hazard. Each one who confided in him felt that in the very act of telling him one's sorrows, a soothing balm for all care had been found; a difficult knot would be unravelled, a weight lifted. And this was true—a calm would miraculously descend upon us all in his august presence. From governors to beggars, there was not one who did not come to Bapu for his prayers and blessings.

Even today, the musical poetry of the Kalam-e-Pak, Ram Dhun and bhajans echoes in my ears. That pristine rag, that simple setting, that quiet gathering, with Bapu seated on his chauki, not uttering a word, eyes closed in devotion, lost to the world, still as a statue. The prayer meeting finishes and he starts, as if life is suddenly breathed into the sculpture. He opens his eyes and precious words scatter in the air. That sweet broken language from his toothless mouth, those simple words, never dramatic or fanciful, never poetic or rousing, but each successful in finding its aim in the listener's heart, each hammering in—oh, how I wish to God that everything he said were to become an eternal truth!

His discourses salved so many aching hearts but for others, were spurs towards hatred and enmity. For some his words were admonition, for others direction. (For three months, this noble staff tried to rouse Delhi but to no success—the deeply slumbering did not awaken!)

On many occasions, his words would move listeners to tears. Once, I looked up to see the old Sikh standing near me, weeping. When I touched my own cheek, there were tears there as well. I have always despised tears as marks of weakness. I did not want ever to cry but, at times, they became my only release. I would not cry for myself but it was impossible not to be moved by the plight of others, whose lives were in such greater disarray than mine. Yet, I was always ashamed of shedding tears in the presence of Gandhiji.

So many tall trees had been uprooted and the foundations of so many grand buildings shaken. Caught in the raging storm, so many boats had sunk. The vessel of new Hindustan was capsizing and its helmsman, uncaring of his own life, was trying desperately to steer the ship out of the maelstrom. Just a few believers gave him their whole-hearted assistance; others watched the spectacle from the safety of the shore. Would this damaged craft ever reach the further shore? This anxiety would strike me like lightning and, in that moment, all my peace and hope would turn to ashes.

Once, as a Congress worker narrated to me, Gandhiji addressed the workers: 'I have heard with sympathy the long tales of the terrible trials that Congress workers have had to face in dealing with this communal conflagration. Can you tell me how many people were killed?' On getting an estimate in reply, he asked, 'And how many of these were Congress workers?' The sheepish reply: 'To our knowledge, none.' Bapu responded, 'Then how can you say that you tried your utmost to stop the rioting? If not one Congress worker was killed, how can I believe that you tried at all?' Such were Bapu's lofty ideals, which he expected others to adhere to as well.

I went to Bapu's every three or four days, but soon my work in the camp and the emotional upheaval I had so recently suffered took its toll on my health and I fell ill. When I recovered, it had been many days since I had gone to that fount of wisdom and discipline. When I met him, I was still coughing. Hearing my hoarse voice, he said, 'You are not well. What happened?' I replied, 'I have been ill for a few days. I have not been able to go to camp and neither have I been well enough to visit you.'

With the customary smile playing across his lips, he said, 'That is bad. But why did you fall ill? Those whose life is devoted to service cannot afford this luxury! When one serves from the heart, then what can illness matter? Recover soon—a lot needs to be done!'

His words are etched on my heart. Even now, whenever I fall ill, the first thought that strikes me is that there must be some infirmity in my will to serve, or else why should ill-heath ever affect me?

On another day, he was spinning. I remarked, 'Oh the yarn you make is so beautiful! Mine was never so fine. Can you please give me some?' He asked, '*Was* never so fine? You no longer spin?' That was the truth, as to my utmost embarrassment, many days had passed since I had even touched the charkha. In fact, I had left it in Lucknow.

For various problems in the camp, I needed Gandhiji's guidance and intervention. Once, I took the secretary of the Paharganj Congress Committee to meet Bapu. Mohammed Ayub had lost everything in the violence that consumed Paharganj. Many Muslims from the area, including him, were in the camp, with most of their property now in the control of the newcomers. Mohammed Ayub belonged to the Thathera clan of brass and metal workers, and he and his family had battled for their lives with the rioters, using as weapons brass tubes stuffed with gunpowder and lotas stuffed with masala for firecrackers. Twelve of his family, and about half of the members of the whole clan, had lost their lives.

Given my usual reluctance to take up too much of Gandhiji's time, and thinking of my many other chores, I did not go in. Just sending word inside that Mohammed Ayub was waiting, I returned to the camp. I wasn't there when the two met, but just thinking of how Bapu must have felt seeing the sorry state of his Congress colleague brings tears to my eyes. How must that noble heart that contained limitless compassion even for the enemy and was so easily moved by the tiniest misfortune have suffered on hearing the travails of this poor man—his clothes in tatters, his face drawn from months of starvation, his spirit broken by the humiliation and the destruction of his family.

Later, Ayub sahab told me that as he narrated his saga, he broke down repeatedly and Bapu too was deeply moved. Although Bapu gave no assurances of a better future, Ayub sahab felt that his burden had been lightened. He had gone to meet Bapu for this succour alone and had returned feeling that he had gained a new fortitude.

On another occasion, I took Hindus and Muslims of a village to meet Bapu. They wanted to stay together but local authorities were hell-bent on clearing out the village to facilitate the entry of refugees. Though we knew that such incidents greatly distressed Bapu, he was our only hope to resolve these problems, as their ramifications were beyond our scope. He was the one leader who would listen to us. The prime minister was also a court of appeal but there is no real choice between talking to one's father and an administrator. With the latter, we would have to observe decorum but with the former, we could speak in however agitated a manner and emotional a language that our feelings dictated. Bapu was truly the chief source of support for thousands of sufferers.

News of the violence in Ajmer had reached us, and Bapu was grieving. Initially, our information was garnered through official reports but soon some Congressmen from Ajmer arrived and apprised Bapu of what had happened there. These people also escorted Pandit Nehru to Ajmer on 3 January. One day in January, when I went to meet Bapu, Mirza Abdul Qadir Baig from Ajmer was talking to him. The conversation had been going on for some time so I didn't learn all the facts about the riots until I myself visited Ajmer some months later, but I did hear his heart-rending account of the situation in Ajmer Sharif, the excesses of the police and security forces, the cruelty of the RSS, and the ineptness of the administration. He said that all the surviving Muslims were now in the dargah. Bapu asked, 'I've seen that space. How could all the Muslims possibly fit in there?' Mirza sahab replied, 'There is a lot of space actually; it can accommodate about 7,000–8,000 people.'

'But Ajmer's Muslim population is far greater, isn't it? Where did the others go?' said Bapu. 'Some went to Pakistan, some to Hyderabad, some were killed, others scattered. I hear that some went to Tonk as well.' Bapu said calmly, 'That is what I was enquiring about.'

And then, 12 January dawned. We had heard the night before that the fast would begin at 11 a.m., and early that morning the whole household left for Birla House. When we reached, we found people gathered, some on the veranda, others on the platform outside. A few were gazing in at the veranda where Mahatmaji was propped up against bolsters, on a takht shaded by a canopy. This was his usual winter routine—he would sun himself every morning, retreating indoors only for meals.

On one of the chairs placed around the takht was seated Sardar Patel. They were deep in conversation. The crowd slowly thickened.

As the conversation dragged on, the anxiety in the crowd became increasingly palpable. Gandhiji's young grandson, holding his mother's hand, watched with wonder.

At last, it was time for the meal. The grandson insisted on eating with his grandfather, despite his mother's attempts to restrain him. 'At the best of times,' she said, 'Bapu hardly eats anything, and whenever the little boy is present, he always ends up with a share of the few vegetables and oranges that Bapu does eat.'

Brij Krishnaji approached us, 'Everyone else has spoken. If any of you would like to speak to Bapu, come now.' I looked at the women around me and saw that all of us had but one plea in our hearts—'Please Bapu, do not undertake this fast unto death!' But no one could bring themselves to speak—we were equally bound into silence by the awe he inspired in us. With trepidation in my heart, I summoned the courage to step up to him. From a few yards away, I bowed my head in salaam. Bapu smiled and said, 'My sight does not really serve me well at this distance but from the manner of the salaam, I knew it was you.'

I said, 'Bapu, what we—all of us who work for you—want, what all of us beg of you, is just another fifteen days. If by then things do not improve, you can begin your fast. Things are already improving, as you can see. The city is peaceful now.' He teased, 'If I had asked you how things were before today, would you have given the same answer? Have you come to hoodwink me?'

'No, Bapu,' I said, 'This is the truth. The situation has really improved.' Gravely, he replied, 'What is the truth? Have all mosques been vacated of people hiding there? Do Muslims have the freedom to move freely? The news from Gujrat is bad. What if Delhi goes up in flames again?' A train full of refugees from Pakistan had been stopped by Pathans in Gujrat, Sindh, and hundreds of refugees brutally massacred. Scores of young girls were abducted and their relatives in Delhi were aggrieved and enraged. He added, 'And have you seen what has been done to the *mazar* of Hazrat Qutubuddin Bakhtiyar Kaki?'

I replied that I had never seen the place. 'Then go and have a look. Qutub sahab's dargah has been attacked and damaged. If a similar fate awaits Ajmer dargah, what is the point of my continuing to live? People have simply gone mad.'

Several others had entered the room, including Maulana Hifzur Rahman and Maulana Azad, who sat beside Bapu and said, 'This is what I also say. As soon as it becomes imperative that you take some action, I will personally come and inform you.'

'Maulana sahab, I know for certain that you will do no such thing.'

What Maulana Azad said in response I cannot recall. Shortly after, Gandhiji addressed us again, 'All right, it is time. All of you must leave now, for your respective duties. Throw yourself into your work even more wholeheartedly. There is no point in tears.'

I was crying as he spoke, 'No one has stayed on this earth forever and I, like everyone else, must die one day. In any case, what is the point of living in times like these . . .? What Sardar Patel said was not correct, but he is the home minister and the Muslims will have to go to him on future occasions as well.'

The reference was to Sardar Patel's speech in Lucknow, where he had said, 'Let the Muslims who are here, remain here. Why do you bother to kill them? The heat from the ground will eventually become unbearable and they will choose to leave on their own accord.' This had outraged the Muslims in general.

Addressing Maulana Hifzur Rahman, he added, 'I am quite close to Sardar Patel and I trust that there is no difference of opinion between him and me on the truth. So, Maulana sahab, be assured. Carry my message to the people and leave me to my fate.'

Innumerable anxious faces, eyes brimming over, were gathered around Bapu, hanging on to each word that escaped his lips. I was perhaps at my weakest then for I can recall only fragments of what was said—neither was all completely audible to me, nor could I commit everything to memory.

All of us stood behind the takht, our heads bowed. Abha, Manu, Sushila and his other trusted helpers came to his side and the prayer meeting began. As usual, the Quran, the Gita and the Bible were read and bhajans sung. Bapu's eyes were closed. Our hearts were thumping, our eyes moist. Spirituality was again battling materialism and this representative of the humane was staking his life in the war against bestiality, insanity, injustice, cruelty, conflict. This epitome of humanity had placed a thing as precious as his life at the feet of God, saying, 'Oh my master, if compassion, truth and charity have disappeared from this world, what will I gain by living? Or else, resurrect humanity! Oh God of limitless love, shower compassion on this world! Or else, remove me from this earth, so that I may not witness so terrible a time.'

Gandhiji was praying. Words of appeal and devotion were on our lips too. We felt, in that moment, that all Creation was joined with us in prayer.

How strange it was. When the mantle of silence lifted and we opened our eyes and looked at each other, our hearts were light, our anxiety replaced by equanimity. Standing next to me was Mr Mehra, the kind and honest police officer who had recently been seconded to Delhi, and for whose innate sense of justice I will be forever grateful. He had been at the meeting since the start, his visage clouded by disquiet. Now, he too was at peace. The pall of gloom had been lifted. It was as if we had shifted our entire burden to Bapu's shoulders.

The crowd slowly dispersed. From Birla House, we went straight to the city. For many of us, the next five days passed in roaming Delhi's streets, lanes and by-lanes to seek out and plead with everyone, old or young.

In the period of the fast unto death, I went to Birla House only once. Thousands crammed the house and the street outside, desiring a glimpse of Bapu, a single word. I went in and sat in a corner. Just then, Bapu emerged but to see his distraught face and sorrowful demeanour, to hear the frailty in his voice, was insupportable. I spoke to him briefly and left immediately. I did not go Birla House again until the fast was over. Why go there when it was our sins that had brought about this day? How could I face Bapu? And then there was his command to immerse ourselves in our work.

On the fifth day, 18 January, Bapu broke his fast. The news spread like wildfire: Bapu had taken a sip of from the glass of orange juice that Maulana Azad brought to his lips! Crazed with joy, thousands broke into a run towards Birla House.

The day the fast had begun, the city had been very tense and violent but today, an enduring calm prevailed. The black clouds of trouble had cleared, sunlight glinted through. Light now shimmered in hearts that had once been tarnished.

I reached Birla House when the prayer meeting had just begun. It had started raining, so Bapu was not in his usual place out in the open. He stayed inside but the crowd, uncaring of the rain, stood riveted, listening to the prayers and the address that he made in such a weakened voice.

I had been escorted into the house by an acquaintance. Once there, I requested him to help me get nearer to Bapu. Up close, I saw that Bapu was visibly tired by the exertions of speech. He was surrounded by people, milling around. In front of him was a glass of lemon juice and water. He had just taken a sip when Jawaharlalji arrived, and Bapu's face wreathed into a smile of such innocent delight, just like a child's upon finding a colourful toy. It was an unforgettable moment—Bapu holding the glass in his hand, his mouth open in delight on seeing this new visitor. People turned to each other and said happily, 'It would be better to leave them alone now.'

Bapu was debilitated by the fast. For many days after, he was very weak. His face was flushed and puffy, his skin hung off his frame. And then the date for the Urs of Hazrat Qutub sahab came along. Gandhiji and some people close to him were to go on the day of the Urs. Some of us others decided that we would reach Mehrauli a day earlier, to repair the dargah and make necessary arrangements. On my part, this was also necessary so that I could face Gandhiji at all—he had asked me to visit it when he had begun the fast, but I hadn't done so yet.

On the day of the Urs, volunteers from the Ahrar Party and the Red Shirts of Khan Abdul Ghaffar Khan lined the dargah's inner courtyard. From between them emerged Bapu, walking slowly, leaning on his staff. So many days had passed since he last participated in a gathering in which Hindus, Sikhs and Muslims stood shoulder to shoulder. This was surely the first such opportunity since 15 August. What joy he must have felt to be part of this scene of love, amity and unity!

That moment is still fresh in my mind when Gandhiji, surrounded by Hindus and Muslims, stepped up to the mazar, hands folded, face smiling. I whispered to my friend Savitry, 'A living saint has come to meet a dead one!' Everyone was smiling, happy. *Tabarruk* was distributed and, just like in the times gone by, everyone swarmed for it. No rancour or enmity.

As Mahatmaji reclined on the platform, the shower of flowers began. Although he was quite weak, he looked satisfied. Then, Hilal sahab, the sole representative of *sajjadanasheen*s and *khaddam*s of this shrine present there, rose to speak of Qutub sahab's life, times and death. Maulana Ahmad Saeed, the erudite and popular Congress leader addressed us next. He was an outstanding orator; the lucidity of his language and clarity of his thought made a deep impression on me. Then, Sardar Sant Singh, that truly saintly follower of Gandhi, spoke. And then Bapu himself said a few words.

All I can recall of Bapu's speech—I was lost again in my thoughts despite standing so close to him—was that he said that like Qutub sahab, his mission was love and discipline too. Qutub sahab must have also sought to soothe away bestiality and barbarism with the same love and sympathy as his. Perhaps history was repeating itself, or were the pages of history being flipped back? How much similarity there is between past and present! Down the ages, how many such scenes have been veiled from our eyes, so that we are not aware of the departed gazing at us from behind the screen? If only a lesson once learnt was never forgotten! As the qawwal says:

kushtgan-e-khanjar-e-tasleem ra
har zaman az ghaib jan deegar ast
For those pierced through by the dagger of belief
Every time from the Unseen there is new life

Sheikh Ahmed-e-Jam

Just as centuries ago, this couplet had inspired Hazrat Qutub sahab to surrender his life, it now served as a call to the greatest reformer of this age to proffer himself at the altar of truth, and chanting He Ram!

He Ram! sacrifice his life. A few days after this Bapu attained immortality.

hai kabhi jaan aur kabhi tasleem-e-jaan hai zindagi
Sometimes life, and sometimes the surrender of life, is
  this existence

                                       Mohammed Iqbal

Bapu left when the qawwali began. The performers included a Sikh pair, who performed both qawwalis and bhajans. I turned to Maulana Hifzur Rahman, whom Gandhiji had requested to organize this Urs, 'Maulana, this must be the first time you have heard a qawwali?'

He joked, 'Yes, and I will listen to it. After all, my attention is mandated both by Bapu's orders and my own political allegiances. I will have to stay till the bitter end!' When I glanced again at him later, he was visibly enjoying himself.

When we left the performance, I saw a volunteer of Ahrar Party holding up a red banner: 'The Khudai Khidmatgar of the Border want Hindu, Muslim and Sikh Unity'. In the makeshift restaurants nearby where we all had tea, Hindus were serving Muslims, and Muslims, Hindus.

On my arrival in Delhi, the mood was lighter. The air was fresher, as if a new season had arrived. My steps fell with renewed vigour. I breathed deeply in the open breeze, in which there was neither the stench of blood nor the heat of revenge. There was peace on faces all around. I could even see a few Muslims walking in ones and twos on the streets and, in the eyes of the refugees, I believed I could no longer see the fog of despair and the gleam of revenge.

However, while Bapu wasn't despairing, he wasn't elated either. He had the air of a doctor keeping close watch on a patient who had barely turned the corner. He was waiting for more positive signs of recovery before celebrating. When we told him, 'The world has changed—it is so peaceful that one can go wherever one wants. The mosques are emptying out,' all he said was, 'Yes'—exactly as a mother acknowledges, but puts no value by, the excited prattle of her young son. This 'yes' held a message: 'You children do not understand; I have my finger on the pulse of India, and I know that a return to good health is still far from certain.'

One day, I heard that he was to go to Pakistan soon. I said I'd like to go along. He smiled, 'You also want to go with me? Everyone is saying the same thing. At this rate, the whole train will be full of people accompanying me! . . . But how can I go, so much needs to be done here!' I sat with him for a while, then left. This was perhaps my last meeting with him.

Relief materials being distributed at a camp for Muslim refugees in Delhi.

3

The Purana Qila Muslim camp
(October–November 1947)

M uslim sanctuary seekers took shelter in two camps. I will speak of them separately, as I think there were stark differences between the two.

The Purana Qila camp had not begun as an official establishment; it was an area settled by the injured, ill, aged, children and women who had fled Paharganj, Karol Bagh, Multani Dhanda, Shidipura, Sabzi Mandi and nearby areas. Crazed with thirst and hunger, they reached the mazar of Matka Shah, a shrine where earthen pots were offered. It was perhaps for this day that the Creator had made devotees amass these pots. A half-crazy old man had looked after the mazar until 5 September, when he was killed. A few days earlier, this old caretaker had started to suspend these vessels from frames he erected on the hillock. Unmindful of derision by onlookers, the poor soul laboured until the mazar's stores were emptied of all the pots.

These earthenware vessels, generously handed out by the *mujavirs*, the caretakers of the graves at the mazar, proved to be priceless for the *panahguzeen*, the sanctuary seekers. A pot, when whole, could be used to drink water from; when ration was distributed, it could be broken, and the hollow used to cook khichdi; and then, that very piece could be used as a cup. If only one wants, how little is enough to satisfy one's needs!

Nawab Ali, a contractor, had stored wood worth lakhs of rupees in the Purana Qila. These beams of wood became houses for sanctuary seekers, as also firewood to fuel their kitchens and warm them when the air turned chilly. So abundant was this wood that even after three months of use, and then the camp's plunder by the police and the military, quite a lot was still left when the camp was wound up.

Four beams would mark out the four corners of a tent and a piece of gunny, a dupatta, or a sheet thrown across the frame would provide a serviceable shelter from sun, rain and dew. Add to this piles of leaves, twigs, brush and branches—and you had beds and takhts. Such were the homes and tents of the panahguzeen; these were what they had to be, and perhaps were, satisfied with. Just like Satan's intestines, the list of bare necessities may be extended infinitely, but it can also be attenuated to the point where next to nothing is a necessity.

In the ledges and cubbyholes built into the Purana Qila's walls could be found spaces for one to rest. In the fort's storerooms and in the mosque built by Babar, the more genteel sanctuary seekers took up residence. In the *dalan*, the enclosed space near the gateway, a dispensary was set up; in the ruined area above the stairs close by, dupattas were thrown across for women to retreat behind it in purdah.

Well before more robust shelters and medicines could arrive, before doctors and nurses could begin their visits, infants started arriving. A newborn, to celebrate whose arrival drums would have beaten for months in an overjoyed home; a child, without whom a kingdom becomes a wilderness and the flame of a lineage sputters out; an offspring, in the longing for which the dust of temples, mosques and dargahs would be churned, mountains of riches squandered, land and property divided—that child was now an unwanted guest, arriving every day in the camp unbidden. Even when there were no nurses or midwives, bawling infants would find their way into the world, in every day fifteen, in every night ten.

Mothers cried, fathers cursed their ancestors, midwives snapped in irritation and camp workers begged the heavens to end the incessant stream of births—but neither the concern of parents nor the sympathy of us onlookers could remedy this problem. Every day, our responsibilities increased and, in despair, we begged God for mercy. There was no one to look after these infants, to bathe them. As the midwife on night duty, cursing loudly, savagely severed the umbilical cord and dunked the child in water, mothers had to look on helplessly, hearts gripped by panic. Weak and helpless, these mothers would not get even a moment of rest.

Finally, doctors and midwives started visiting the camp. Mahatmaji had come to Delhi, so soon Sushila and her associates began regular visits. Medicines also arrived. However, the need was overwhelming and the efforts were as minuscule as a single seed of cumin in a camel's mouth.

From morning to afternoon, little girls with starving infants hanging off their shoulders, their faces telling tales of longing and hunger, stood for hours in queue after queue for two ounces of milk. Each mother wanted just a little extra so her chapped, aching breasts could get respite; each young child insisted for a trifle more for its starving belly. The volunteers, always alert and economical, had to sternly refuse—how else would the morning tea be prepared and dry rotis made moist enough to swallow?

Living the life of beasts, people would eat food off their hands or in pot-shards, which also served as griddles for baking blackened rotis made from mud-laced flour. These shards, and some leaves, were their only vessels, crockery, cups. Other bodily needs had to be met with two bricks; at other times, these very two bricks would be put together to serve as a kitchen stove.

Thirst and hunger, typhoid, cholera, dysentery, fever and many other diseases were widespread. Any shortfall in misery was made up by snakes, whose bites delivered scores from this tortured existence. The rains in September were manifestations of God's wrath and, under that roof of a grey sky, all the sanctuary seekers could do was to huddle in the knee-deep mud and await death.

The Pakistan embassy was responsible for the organization in the camp and its officials oversaw its daily functioning. They had appointed the camp commander and controlled the distribution of rations and other supplies. Although some Pakistani aid was sent directly, the bulk of the responsibility (based on Pakistan's recommendations) for actual supplies of food and medicines as well as arrangements for train and air transport, lay with the Indian government.

The commander and his staff lived in a small room near Sadar Darwaza. Though the only hope of succour in this wilderness, the commander was an acerbic fellow. His permission was necessary for admission into the camp but it was impossible for any poor person to meet him—or at least as difficult as it was for Farhad to bring Shireen the stream in which milk flowed, not water. His only redeeming feature was that he had set up the camp, motivated by a desire to serve the community. But such was his hurry now that all he wanted to do was wind up the camp, get a certificate that he had run it and leave for Pakistan immediately.

It was also in his power to sanction permits for Pakistan. Whenever a special train to Pakistan was announced, hundreds of supplicants would stand in long queues and wait like beggars, hoping to receive his benevolence. Many would be scolded, abused, turned away, and only a few would come away proud owners of that ticket to heaven.

In October, refugees in Purana Qila numbered about 60,000, down from the 80,000 they had apparently crossed in September. The larger dalans, platforms and open rooms were crammed with the ill and the wounded.

In one such space, four midwives always sat about, bickering. One would claim that she had slaved the hardest in the month and a half gone by but no one appreciated her. 'Fifty children delivered in a day but no one has the decency to get me my salary from the municipality! Even though I have the permit for Pakistan at last, how can I leave?' At this, another would bristle, 'Are you implying, Banno, that I've worked any less? For one whole week, I worked so hard that my arms were numb. Just ask the doctor! And I was absolutely alone, you had not even arrived!' This would get the third and fourth midwife going, and the litany of backbreaking labour and denial of just wages would rent the air.

One day I asked them, 'Will you all return to your jobs once the camp is disbanded?'

One replied, 'Of course not! We were better off without this freedom. All we want is our salary from the municipality. Once we get our money, we will leave for Pakistan.' Another complained, 'Have you seen the way these Hindu women look at us? Why do they come to the camp to laugh at us? To rub salt on our bleeding wounds?'

I rebuked her, 'I cannot believe that. You are certainly mistaken. I have never met any woman who can be so cruel as to rejoice in another's misfortune.' At my rebuke, the lament began afresh, 'You can never know what we have gone through. We never want to see their faces again—our plight is because of them!'

Soon after, the midwives got their salaries. Until they left for Pakistan, their slander of Hindus did not cease. Even though the camp's lady doctor was Hindu and its nurses either Hindu or Christian, why should the truth have mattered to them at all?

Care in the camp hospital was now provided by two nurses who came in for only two hours a day; for the rest of the day, one doctor, himself a sanctuary seeker, was on duty. One day, just after the nurses left, a woman in labour was brought in. Neither my colleague Jamila nor I were there. I had to go to the tents and Jamila was checking on patients in the city hospital. I had left my daughter in charge; on this woman's arrival, she summoned the doctor and ran to look for help but could find neither me, nor midwives, nor any other woman ready to assist in the birth. By the time she returned, the child was ready to emerge; it was not going to wait any longer for the reception committee to assemble!

As the tent resounded with the mother's wails and the baby's cries, my daughter panicked, much to the doctor's exasperation. But seasoned as he was, he soothed the wailing mother, speaking gently, and also calmed my daughter, guiding her, one step at a time, into her new vocation as midwife. Following his instructions, she managed to discharge her duties. When I reached, mother and child were at peace. But my daughter was very upset, 'Where did you disappear? I looked everywhere for you!' The doctor was smiling, 'You have a fine daughter. See how well she has assisted me!' I was glad that Kishwar had now learnt how to be of help to someone in need.

The camp's filth, slush and malodours were intolerable. The hospital was positioned on elevated ground; while this ensured greater security, the space was also used to store rations, medicine and other supplies. This was also where food was cooked; in the enclosed courtyard next to the store were the two stoves on which khichdi was cooked and milk boiled. To the right was a tent always full of hospital staff, midwives, helpers, cooks and of course, spectators. To the left was a bed on which an injured lieutenant named Hameed lay, talking nineteen to the dozen. In the corner sat the lady doctor's desk. The tent housing the labour room and nursery and four other tents pitched close together for the sick and the wounded were also nearby.

From the hospital, one had a vantage view of the entire camp. As far as the eye could see, tents and tin-roofed shelters were crowded together. In their midst was a ceaseless traffic of naked children, dishevelled women, bareheaded girls and men burning in defiance and humiliation.

On the first day that I had the hospital food prepared, the patients were delighted, remarking that the khichdi had a scent of *asli ghee* for the first time. When I quizzed the ration in-charge about this lapse, he denied any culpability. Later, I learnt that the patients were right—the little ghee there was usually found its way into the parathas made for the staff! Similar was the case with milk. Tins of powdered milk were reconstituted by adding water but, at every meal, the gallons always ran short. When I assigned the responsibility of distribution to a young Irani girl Mahgul (a sanctuary seeker), we found that not only was it possible to give every infant and young child a quart, but there was ample left over for their elder siblings! Sushila was pleased, and said that with me managing things, at least the patients would get their fair share.

I was told that some time before I arrived, the inmates had been so angered by the conditions in the camp that they had surrounded Mahatmaji's car when he visited. They raised slogans against him, uttered harsh words and the situation became quite volatile. Even today, people were furious. The most innocuous of observations would set off the women, 'You tell me, can what happened be called a fair fight? What kind of masculine valour is this? To stab someone in the back, then strut around as if this cowardice was courage! What bravery is this—get thrashed in Punjab, so become heroes by murdering innocent, unarmed people in Delhi?'

One such woman was Kajalbash Begum, usually found amidst a veritable mound of trunks and chests, screened off by a makeshift tent of sheets. Wearing silken clothes and exquisite jewellery, she would continually harangue, 'Look at these eunuchs pretending to be men! What heroes they have become after attacking women and children! Let them try it once more—let them confront us women! I will thrash them to an inch of their lives with these shoes. The earlier contest was unfair: they had kirpans, we were barehanded. Give us knives and watch a totally different outcome!'

I thought to myself, 'Only those who have suffered can understand the pain of others. You may fume but if you did not have all those trunks and chests around you, you could not afford to spend your time raging thus. Rather, you would spend your time doing what that woman in the nearby shack must do—beg us for two buttons to fasten her collar.'

That woman in the shack would sit all day doing nothing, her two daughters beside her, all three with their heads bare. I asked her once, 'Why don't you work to support yourself and your daughters?' Tearfully, she replied, 'How can we venture out in this state, when we don't even have dupattas to cover our heads? Our kurtas are threadbare . . . If only we could find some clothes . . .'

Barring a few who had found the time to carry their belongings, most refugees had left their homes with only the clothes on their backs. They had spent the past month and a half in the same soiled clothes. There was no soap anywhere.

Until the Christian nuns came. God bless them for bringing mercy, cleanliness and sympathy to the camp. Very soon, soap was made available—the missionaries sold it at half the price—and many reeking bodies were at last cleansed. Those who could afford it, paid; for those who couldn't, I bought as much as I could. As a result, for every thousand, fifty had clean clothes the next day.

In the enclosed spaces near the fort's wall, a large group of cattle grazers from the Sabzi Mandi had taken refuge. Some families had no young people left; only old and middle-aged men and women and very young children remained. Their property was looted, their sons killed, their young daughters abducted—the survivors were beside themselves with grief and anger. 'If only we'd got a chance to fight back! If only the government had called off the military police, we could have quenched this desire for revenge!' It was impossible to console these distraught people, who no longer cared for life itself.

No Congressi ever visited the camp; its leaders had stopped talking to these people. (Except of course Gandhiji's disciples who, motivated by a spirit of service, would visit regularly, listen to the people's complaints, look after the ill and the injured and do whatever they could to alleviate their suffering.) It was only the ulema of Jamiat-ul-Ulema and Ahrar Party workers who came daily, despite the criticism and abuse heaped on them. Each day they brought two *deg*s of cooked food and a limitless fund of patience; each day the very sight of them enraged the sanctuary seekers, who accused them of being traitors, cheats, slaves of Hindus. But they were undeterred.

And there were the Jamia students. Despite running another camp at Humayun's Tomb, and though the Muslim Leaguers who ran the camp did not care a whit for their involvement, some Jamia teachers (also Congress members) and students spent four hours a day doing whatever tasks they themselves determined as necessary.

Although most Muslim League leaders were already in Pakistan, the party still held sway all over the camp. The commander and his assistant were both Leaguers and kept busy by inciting the inmates and heaping abuse on other volunteers. The propaganda was about how Pakistan had established the camp, how Pakistan sent everything from rations to medicines to equipment, and how Pakistan had saved the lives of the inmates (who avowed that they were Pakistanis). This Hindu government had destroyed their lives and killed so many of them because Hindustan was for Hindus alone—only those Muslims that became Hindus would be allowed to stay on. Had Pakistan not been made, not even these many Muslims would have survived. Had the Pakistan government not helped, the government in India would have been happy to knock off the remaining by letting them starve.

I once heard that, before my time, the Pakistan government had despatched rotis to the camp by airplanes. I asked the inmates, 'So, those days must have been very comfortable for you?' They replied, 'Rubbish! The rotis were for sale, eight annas each. Only those who could afford them had a wonderful meal. We poor people stayed hungry as always!'

On the streets of Jama Masjid, gold was being sold at Rs 5 for 10 gm and plates at one rupee for a dozen. In the camp hospital, the ill and the injured were eating food off newspapers and drinking water from empty cigarette tins (I gathered them). Even when we did manage to buy the rupee-to-a-dozen plates, they ran short—each patient who left took the precious plate and tin along, leaving us to once more tear newspapers for the next patient!

Clothing and bedding were also in short supply. The Jamiat made sincere efforts to supplement them but whatever assistance trickled in was inadequate. Just then, a donation of a few thousand blankets arrived from Nawab Rampur, with a delegation of the kingdom's chief minister, Col Basheer Hussain Zaidi, and other officials. Rampuris in the camp welcomed the sight of both the officials and the gift; it was a sign that the realm had not forgotten them.

The officials decided to tour the camp to identify the neediest. As hospital duties beckoned me, my sister and daughter took on the responsibility of escorting them. After a while, sounds of an altercation reached me and I rushed there. A Rampuri Khan sahab was arguing fiercely with a cattle-grazer over the allotment of blankets. Khan sahab maintained that the blankets were reserved for Rampuris while the cattle-grazer argued that need should be the only deciding factor.

However much the cattle-grazer argued, this distinction between Rampuri and non-Rampuri pervaded in charitable Rampuri hearts until the cattle-grazer was reduced to tears, 'Have you no sympathy for the state that circumstances have brought me to? I was not always like this, begging for a mere blanket. Ask my wife—she will tell you that she never wore a shawl worth less than Rs 35.'

With great difficulty, tempers were cooled and an agreement reached—after each Rampuri got a blanket, the remaining would be distributed among the inmates from Delhi via a draw of lots.

Soon after, Jamiat's efforts at procuring clothes bore fruit and stacks of used clothes arrived from Bihar and the United Provinces (now Uttar Pradesh, or UP). My own appeal for help was also answered and a donation of a few hundred rupees and sacks of used clothes from Lucknow reached. Some Begums thoughtfully sent even shoes, coats and sheets. I had made the appeal with full confidence in the women of Lucknow; the generosity of their response justified my faith. Because of these efforts, a thousand out of two could be clothed.

In Lucknow earlier, I'd heard rumours that the Delhi riots were actually pitched battles fought with cannons, machine guns and rifles but the picture I got now was quite different. From the camp inmates, I heard no stories about these feats—where had the men manning cannons and guns in Sabzi Mandi and Paharganj gone? Hadn't they risen up in rebellion against the government? I found none who could verify these tales. All I learnt was that wherever a gun was fired, it was in self-defence, and that only licensed weapons had been used. Cattle-grazers said they had staffs and sickles, butchers had meat cleavers and sharp knives, and in battle, death and defeat, these were the only weapons used. All said they mounted fierce resistance, and had the police not fired at them and the army not trained its machine guns at them, their knives would have equalled the kirpans that assaulted them.

Workers of a metal factory told me, 'We had purchased empty cartridges left over from World War II to melt down and make pots and pans. Mixed up with them, perhaps due to oversight, were some live cartridges, which proved useful. Though we had only a few guns, we made some barrels to fire the cartridges. With these weapons, we fought in Paharganj for eight hours but then the police and the army cracked down on us with such force that we were wiped out.'

Of the 800 in this Thathera clan, only 300 made it to the camp; the rest were killed. Most of them were Congressis (including the Congress Committee secretary, Mohammed Ayub, of whom I have spoken earlier), and when they left the camp, hardly a handful went to Pakistan. Almost all of them settled in Tonk—but without their young daughters, who went missing. We never could find out whether they were alive or dead; at least I never encountered a single one of them.

Even at this height of their destitution and despair, the eyes of all the inmates flashed with a mixture of wounded self-respect and disgusted humiliation of living on charity. Only a month and a half had passed, and the regular influx of sanctuary seekers would not let the wounds close.

There was such anger in them—at Hindus, at the dearth of God's mercy, at the callousness of Auliya sahab, at the government's injustice. These were the topics of conversation and the counsel heard all over camp. The terrifying smile with which a person would greet another, the irony with which they would ask after his welfare, as if mocking life, death, Creation itself. And the reply—in a few stark words would be narrated the murder of his children, the destruction of his home and family. 'Miyan, why do you ask this?'

raha na khatka chori ka
dua deta hoon rehzan-ko
No more the fear of danger or burglary
My blessings to the robbers for this deliverance

— Mirza Ghalib

'I sleep in peace every night. There is no grief left.' And then that bleak laugh, leaving me trembling in horror.

When misfortune peaks, compassion and empathy falter, and this was true of the sanctuary seekers. Very few amongst all these Muslims felt any remorse for what they themselves had perpetrated. The noble feelings of tenderness and submission—the pride of a true Muslim— had yet to be awakened in them. The will to even help each other had deserted them, especially the women, who did nothing all day but sit around, weep and curse.

But for a few noble souls, some exceptional cases. I'd seen a young man holding a little girl in his arms visit the camp hospital. The girl would run to her mother, who was in the maternity tent with another infant at her side. I'd also often seen the man bring water for the young woman, and asked him one day how they were related. I learnt that they were, in fact, complete strangers, that pure human sympathy had drawn them together. All the relatives of the young woman had perished and she was alone at camp, with no one to look after her two-year-old daughter. So this decent young man had stepped up to help. Later, when the woman recovered, he willingly shouldered the burden of the whole family. It would be no surprise if these two destitutes, connected in grief, became life partners some day.

Another such case: a Mewati man would bring five children to visit a woman and her five-year-old son, both admitted in the hospital. The woman was on the road to recovery after ailing for two months but her son was seriously ill, and one day, the poor child passed away. Seeing the Mewati perform the last rites and console the mother, I assumed that he was the husband and the father but I learnt that they were strangers.

Of the five children in his care, only one girl was his—the rest of his own family had been killed. The woman had lost her husband and possibly her eldest son as well, a mill worker in East Punjab. Seeing her all alone, the Mewati took care of her children while she was ill; when she recovered, he welcomed them all into his tent.

Some days later, another girl reached the camp, having managed to escape the enemy. The Mewati took her in too. In this way, survivors of three families became one large clan and the source of support for each other.

By the end of October, most camp inmates who volunteered with us left for Pakistan. This had an adverse effect on the camp's functioning. Already, a constant feature of our days was the manner in which we had to treat the dead—overlook them, ignore them, devote all our energies to care for the living, but now matters worsened.

Caring for the dead was the responsibility of the Camp Relief Committee, a body instituted by a self-styled leader of Muslims. This committee had assumed the responsibility to distribute shrouds and dig graves. One day, I was surprised to see from a distance that a corpse had not been removed from the hospital and still lay on a bed next to a patient. Corpse removal was not part of our responsibilities; the committee or Jamiat usually bade final farewells to the departed.

My other duties in camp delayed me and I reached the hospital much later. The corpse still lay there. When I asked why arrangements for the burial had not been made, I was told that the dead man had no relatives in the camp save for the weeping young girl and her child sitting beside the corpse. I turned to Jamila and said that we had to find some Muslim men to carry out the rituals of bathing and burial. We set off together to find some men.

Our first stop was at the committee's tent, where we were made to wait a long time for an audience with Maulvi sahab. He was right there but we had to stand around like beggars. Long minutes passed and when he didn't even deign to look at us, I abandoned all deference to propriety and addressed him unsolicited—only to receive a dismissive reply: 'The gravediggers and bathers of the dead have left for Pakistan on the last train. What do you expect us to do?' We countered, 'But these are the sacred duties of any Muslim. You must have this man buried somehow.' Unfettered by any sense of responsibility, he replied, 'We cannot do anything. At most, we can give you a shroud.'

I insisted again, pointing out that the ulema were required to arrange for the burial of the dead. The only response I could provoke was that no one there knew how to dig graves and bathe the dead, so a burial was impossible.

One ugly scene later, in which Maulvi sahab's disaffection touched new heights, we found ourselves outside the Jamia tent. The boys were not there. Had they been around, we could have safely turned over the job to them, so reliable and committed were they. But they had just left and we had to look elsewhere.

We scanned the camp, begging God knows how many Muslims: 'In God's name, help us in giving this corpse a final resting place. We are women, we cannot bathe a male corpse, but we can help you dig the grave.' From everywhere the same reply: sorry, we don't know the rituals of bathing; sorry, we don't know how to dig a grave.

A mullah even chided us, 'I hope you know that not everyone can be entrusted with this ritual. There are procedures laid down by the Shari'a. If they are not followed, the ritual bath will be invalid.' Of course, Maulvi sahab could not bring himself to raise even a finger to ensure that this did not happen. In despair, we returned to the hospital to call the dead man's daughter, 'Come, we must ourselves bury him. Let's get to work.' However, that beloved subject of God refused to move; she sat by, shedding tears, and even forbade her thirteen-year-old son to assist us.

Just then, two old women came by. Gathering what had to be done, they said, 'We'll join you. We may not know the exact rituals but we can follow what we have heard of them. After all, this day will come for all of us—tomorrow may well be ours.'

As the women bathed the corpse, we set off to dig the grave. Jamila had barely begun when a few men arrived to help. Insisting that we move aside, they dug the grave, clothed the corpse in a shroud and completed the burial. Of the thousands of inmates, just this handful turned out to be humane. May God reward them for their kindnesses!

In early November, the group of Rampuris departed for Rampur, giving thanks all the way to their Nawab for arranging a special train for their return. After that, it was the turn of the small group of sanctuary seekers from Eastern Punjab. Then we heard that arrangements had been made for the safe transit of the Tonk group. The Delhi people thought wistfully: 'If only we were the subjects of some princely state . . .'

The hospital tents were crammed with patients. Their clothes spattered with dried blood, patients watched their injured bodies rot. For want of space, a twelve-year-old boy lay near the ration store, sidling slowly towards his grave; pus had entered the bone, all hope of recovery was lost. Scores of children had died of starvation and cholera. Filthy bodies, faces wizened like monkeys, spindles for limbs, bellies ballooning, these little frogs spent days lying in wait, yearning for that brief beautiful moment when the hunger whimpering in their stomachs would be hushed by a few drops of milk.

I implored everyone I could meet to help, sent word to Health Minister Rajkumari Amrit Kaur, confided in Bapu. Finally, two more nurses and a lady doctor who would stay all day were assigned to the hospital. Sushila would also visit every morning. Gradually, the outlook improved. Medicines also arrived but the scarcity was never fully remedied. I would supplement the stock from my own resources; fortuitously, there was always a supply of medicines at home, left over from Rafi bhai's frequent medical complaints and occasional illnesses of other members. I would also ask for doctors' prescriptions so I could purchase medicines. But a few drops of dew cannot ever quench thirst. I could never understand whether it was the lack of supplies or the corruption of officials, but this difficulty always dogged us.

As the numbers of volunteers declined, the responsibility of ration distribution fell to us. As expected, many of the genuinely deserving were too ashamed to claim their share; so, more often than not, the more brazen got more than their share. Kishwar's running quarrel with the camp commander was about the abiding complaint of the sanctuary seekers: though ghee, milk, sugar, ration and medicines were aplenty, none of it was ever available to them. Here too, they alleged the rich profited from distress and accused the officials of pilferage. I'd met the commander only a few times and could never determine the extent of truth in these allegations—the inmates could well be mistaken or misinformed—but Kishwar did not entertain the slightest doubt. Whenever she heard complaints, she would rush off to give him a piece of her mind, despite my attempts to restrain her. She fancied this advocacy of the poor and felt it her responsibility to regularly admonish the officials. The inmates were very happy with her because, through her, their complaints were carried to the higher authorities.

The patients in the hospital were not limited to actual residents of the camp. Some had been injured in Delhi and brought to us by relatives and friends; others were found lying injured on the streets and sent by the police or the army; on occasion, people thrown off trains would drag their battered bodies to us for care.

Actually, Muslims feared the fate that awaited them in the city's hospitals; the staff there, like in all other institutions, had demonstrated great callousness and insensitivity towards injured and dying Muslims. For them, a Muslim's life or death had no value and they refused to shoulder the responsibility of conveying them safely to relatives. From almost all hospitals, except for Irwin Hospital, patients disappeared. In fact, two hospitals were attacked and even seriously ill patients, drawing their last few breaths, were consigned to death by the valiants' swords. The upshot was that Jamila spent most of the day traversing the city in an ambulance, ferrying patients to and from city hospitals.

Jamila, a member of Sir Syed Ahmad Khan's family, had decided not to accompany her kin to Pakistan. A former medical supervisor of the municipality, her responsibility in the camp was to take the seriously ill to city hospitals and bring back those that had recovered. She worked in the camp until it was disbanded and lived in Sir Syed's house in Tiraha Behram Khan. As soon as a special train to Pakistan was announced, and people began to scramble for places, Jamila dealt with the relatives of the injured and diseased, who demanded that their ailing kin be brought back from hospitals at once. She was the sole source of information for families whose relatives were either lost or had perished; she always carried a list of the status of those hospitalized under the camp's supervision.

One morning, I accompanied Jamila. Our purpose was to initiate something for stray and orphaned children. For some days, we had been bothered by the frequent visits of Christian nuns to the camp, suspecting that they were there to gather children. Surely, we could ourselves make arrangements for the care of these innocents?

Whenever a train left for Pakistan, innumerable children would be lost. In many cases, parents would have boarded the train but their children, unable to embark, would be left behind. In other instances, the children would board but, in their excitement over the journey, refuse to get off, even when their parents were unable to board. Who knows what would have happened to those children in Pakistan? Did they ever meet their parents, or were they laid to waste on the train itself? I wanted that the children who loitered around looking for their parents, and whom we fed whenever they came by, be placed in a school—Jamia or any other that would have them. Though I had yet to talk to the Jamia administration, I had faith that they would welcome my proposal.

We got off at Irwin Hospital. We had barely looked around and noted the number of strays and orphans admitted there, when we saw that our visit timing was about to elapse. We decided to wait downstairs for the ambulance to return, when we heard another ambulance pull up and voices mount in anxiety, in confusion. We stepped out to enquire and were told that Paharganj's health officer, Dr Mufti, had been murdered during his customary round of the area. The ambulance contained his dismembered corpse.

I sank into a chair. The forgotten came back to me. Chills enveloped my body. Jamila, her head in her hands, moaned, 'They killed him! They can murder even an official of the Government of India! This is the height of cruelty, the limit of it all!' I stopped listening, my ears could take no more, I could not stay there any longer. I pleaded, 'Jamila, can you please telephone my home and ask them to send the car? God knows when the ambulance will come . . . I cannot stay here!'

In my distress, I couldn't even dial the number correctly, but finally the call was made. The car came and we left, but I couldn't bring myself to look up the children again for some time. And before I could summon the courage again, it struck the minds of my Muslim brethren that there might be no prospect of domestic help in the heavenly paradise that was Pakistan. Finding a use for what was available in enviable abundance around them—how could they, God-fearing Muslims, leave a Muslim child at the mercy of unbelievers in Kafiristan?—they bore away the children to Pakistan to be their domestic servants.

By end-November, despite the inmates' tears and entreaties, the camp was wound up. Trains ferried the panahguzeen to Pakistan. Everyone had to go—those eagerly waiting to cross over, those who did not want to set their eyes on it. Some laughed, 'Insha Allah, we will never return to Delhi again, even for a piss!' Others clung in tears to beloved doors and walls, cursing Jinnah and Pakistan.

The few that were left behind also departed, but only for the Humayun's Tomb camp. These included the hospital staff, that deserter of a lieutenant Hameed, Jamila Begum and Dr Siddiq, whose responsibilities to the Pakistan government meant that he could leave for Pakistan only after all the sanctuary seekers of the Purana Qila camp had reached there safely.

Humayun's Tomb camp was one of the last few places that remained secure for Muslims in Delhi.

4

The camp at Humayun's Tomb
(November–December 1947)

The camp at Humayun's Tomb was not very far from the one at Purana Qila. The truck carrying sanctuary seekers and my car reached there in a few minutes.

As I have remarked, the difference between the two camps was apparent at every level. For one, this camp had been established by the Indian government and was properly managed; Jamia volunteers looked after its daily functioning while the Indian government met its material needs. There were neither two orders in operation here, nor discord about India versus Pakistan.

Another difference was that everyone had tents. And yes, the cleanliness. The hospital was adequately staffed and its tents were well laid out—male and female patients housed separately, with adequate distance between the doctors' tents and the patients'. The kitchens were set away from the living quarters—as was the ration store, located at the entrance—and the food cooked here was reserved for the ailing and the aged. Further away, behind the living quarters, sanitation drains had been dug, so that a substantial number of people could relieve themselves at one time.

In September, the Purana Qila camp had housed 80,000–1,00,000 refugees. The Humayun's Tomb camp had peaked at around 60,000 then; by November, a much smaller number remained, the bulk having left for Pakistan or scattered into various districts of UP. The patients were mostly ill rather than injured and the camp residents were mainly poor rather than rich. A far cry indeed from the Purana Qila camp, where some inmates were simply biding time, clutching lakhs of rupees to their bosoms, until their train or flight to Pakistan. Dr Hussain told me later that among them was a man who had lived with a lakh of rupees tied to his body for many weeks. This fact came to light only when he was leaving and donated Rs 1,000 for refugee welfare. In contrast, most sanctuary seekers at Humayun's Tomb were desperately poor, with no idea of what to do or where to go.

Also, here, fewer hearts had turned away from worship and there were many more in which faith still had a home. Spaces had been enclosed using bricks and sticks for namaz and, on many mornings, I chanced upon women reading the Quran Sharif in their tents. Every few days, a group of Mewati Maulvis from Bangle Wali Masjid in Nizamuddin would come to teach the namaz and *kalma*s. There were fewer curses here, many more prayers; instead of anger, hearts were infused with compassion and the desire to help one another.

In neither camp, however, was Delhi's famed aristocracy—those nobles, their Begums, or their *nawabzada*s—to be found. I learnt that the cream of Delhi society, known for its genteel ways and refined tongue, had trickled away in ones and twos to Pakistan in September itself. Any visit they might have made to the camp had been for one or two days at most. The bulk of the camp population were always metalworkers, artisans, cattle-grazers and salaried workers—ordinary people awaiting their turn to leave for Pakistan.

In fact, the only commonality between the two camps was the belief that the Indian government wanted to throw them out of India. In all other respects they were diametrically opposed, and I often wondered what effected the stark differences? Was it the outcome of the commitment of Dr Hussain and his comrades? Or of prayer and namaz? Was the government more generous to this camp, or the volunteers more altruistic?

My first meeting with Dr Hussain happened around then. (I had an opportunity to make his acquaintance some years earlier too; he and his friends had visited Rafi bhai in Masauli but I couldn't meet him since I observed very strict purdah those days.) The day was Bakreed—the first Id after the bloodshed; this Id of Sacrifice, in the wake of the sacrifice of thousands of humans; an Id of joy, greeted by tears, groans, entreaties. In dirty clothes, faces gaunt with hunger, eyes tearful, bodies without limbs, men and women dragged themselves for an audience with God. There could be no need for words:

soorat ba been halatash maparz
Behold my face, but do not ask how I am

Kishwar was always keen on giving the children a treat; in the Purana Qila camp, she would often distribute lemon drops with milk. On this day too, she took a tin of sweets along and distributed them, with some *idi*, to the children there. A feast of pulao and sweets brought by the Jamiat and Ahrar Party followed. While in the Purana Qila camp, the distribution of any item would meet with pushing, shoving and grabbing, here the children were seated in rows, the task accomplished in no time.

The children were delighted but I found it too painful to look at the longing on those innocent faces, their eyes shining in eager anticipation. I had to move away. Just then, Dr Hussain walked up to introduce himself to me. He assured me that Jamia would ensure the safekeeping of however many stray, orphaned children I could send. In such few words, how great a difficulty was resolved! As we watched the happy children, I could see that Dr Hussain and his companions—

students he had so lovingly cast in his own mould—were quite overcome, eyes pricked by tears.

There was an unusual feature at the Humayun's Tomb camp hospital: the three special tents we erected exclusively for abandoned old women, weakened and crippled by age. This special provision was necessitated by the sharp increase in their numbers because when sanctuary seekers left for Pakistan, they couldn't be bothered to take their old mothers, *nani*s and *dadi*s with them. A heroic young man, knowing that blind old women linger long between life and death, had been pragmatic enough to dump his old grandmother at the graveyard on his way out! Nevertheless, just to breathe is life enough—the half-dead woman's cries attracted passers-by and she was soon rescued by volunteers and brought into the camp.

One day, I saw a truck being loaded with passengers and their belongings. A special train for Pakistan had been announced that day and a crowd of sanctuary seekers was clambering on to the truck, abandoning their old relatives who stood nearby, steadily chiming 'Pakistan for us too!' I demanded to know why they were being left behind. The reply was that they would be encumbrances—too old to even walk unassisted, let alone fend for themselves.

Something snapped in me. I admonished them, 'So only India has to be the recipient of these rotten old bodies? You will have to take your relatives along!' I asked the volunteers to help the aged relatives into the truck and only then allowed it to leave.

I had also forcibly reunited an old man with his relatives but, when the truck returned, Bade Miyan was still in it. His dear ones had prevailed ultimately and left him behind at the station. While the volunteers could foil similar attempts of the relatives of the three old women, they failed in this case; Bade Miyan was brought back to the camp hospital, to live in the special tents erected for old women.

This idea of special tents had been Kishwar's, because a large contingent of old women from Purana Qila had also come with us to Humayun's Tomb. Their welfare her main concern, Kishwar did all she could to make them comfortable. She arranged the bedding by pressing into service straw mattresses procured by Jamia workers. She ensured that the old women were clothed and fed and often, I saw the old women straining to hear her approach, as it was she who brought their food and water.

Seeing all this on his return from the station, Bade Miyan knew at once that this was his chance. True, he did not make it to Pakistan but this place wouldn't do too badly to put one's feet up! His face contorting in simulated agony, he took Kishwar in completely; minutes later, he was ensconced in a hospital bed under a pile of thick blankets. Seizing the opportunity, he snuggled in for a long period of rest.

And rest he certainly did, duping both Kishwar and the volunteers. Once I arrived at the hospital just in time to witness a volunteer Afsar, an intelligent boy studying for BSc, feeding Bade Miyan, who was according these efforts his full cooperation. Beholding Bade Miyan with his head inclined forward, mouth opened wide for the next morsel, I asked in surprise, 'What is this? Why are you feeding him? Is he ill?' Afsar replied, 'Yes, he has been lying in bed for many days. Thus far Kishwar has been feeding him, but seeing her so busy making beds, I offered to feed him today.'

I scolded Bade Miyan for his outrageous behaviour, 'You should be ashamed of yourself for taking advantage of these young people. If you hadn't found these boys and girls to fool, I wouldn't be surprised if you took to beggary! Come on, get out of bed!' However, all my scolding could accomplish was to get him to feed himself. He refused to relinquish the hospital bed, squatting in it until February.

Every day was busier than the last and, for days on end, I couldn't spare even a few minutes to go and meet Bapu. Some days I would go in the evening to the prayer meeting but, at those times, opportunities to talk to him were limited. Still, when my heart grew too heavy and my body too weary and I risked losing the spirit to carry on, I would run to Bapu. I would return much strengthened and ready to face the world again. What a great support he was!

At the camp one day I met a man who had lost half of his left arm. I asked him whether he was leaving for Pakistan on the train that day.

His reply, accompanied by a maniacal smile full of irony, was: 'What can I possibly have to do with Pakistan? Why should I go there? My wife and children have been murdered; my hand has been hacked off—why make the journey? I am just going to the city.' In his eyes a grim determination glinted and in his voice, a resolve that terrified me. I wondered, 'What has he to do in the city? The desire for revenge burns deep and steady in him—what devastation does he intend to wreak? How many will he strike with one hand?'

He reminded me of a young Sikh boy a friend had told me about. The young Sikh told her, 'Nineteen of my family were murdered. I, the twentieth, am still alive to avenge their deaths. I want to live only so I can kill as many of the murderers as possible; what happens after that is of little interest to me—I'll be hanged or I'll take my own life.'

But even amidst this horror there were some lighter moments. One day I found several people huddled on the ground near the camp workers' tent. I assumed they were another caravan of sanctuary seekers, when one of them handed me a piece of paper bearing about twenty signatures. It was a memorandum from the residents of a Shia orphanage stating that the refugees had captured their building, so they had come to the camp for sanctuary. They requested for tents, mattresses and rations. Immediately, I saw the perfect opportunity to take up Dr Hussain on his offer. I would send the young boys to him and house the older men in the camp. I asked the supervisor to identify the orphans in the group. He said that all the listed people were present but I could hardly see any young boys there. I suggested that the list be read out for verification.

The first name to be called elicited a response from a healthy young man of about eighteen, a moustache shadowing his lips. I said, 'My son, don't you think you're a little old to live in an orphanage? You are young and strong; support yourself by working. You may have grown up at the orphanage, which is why you are still with them, but perhaps you should be on your own now.'

The second and third names were answered by two boys aged twelve to thirteen years but the owner of the fourth name surprised us—a man in his thirties! My young companion snapped, 'Don't tell

me you are an orphan! Or are you the father of one?' The barb drew
the expected laughter, cutting the standing man to the quick, 'Of
course I'm not an orphan! We used to run the orphanage.' Looking at
the list afresh, I noticed that the names were not of orphans alone but
also of the orphanage workers. Of the twenty names, only eight or
nine turned out to be orphans.

Even these I could not send to Jamia and soon after, caretakers
and orphans both left for Lahore. The problem was that the caretakers
refused to hand the orphans over to me—they said the children
were the property of the Shia Imamiya Orphanage and could be
relinquished only to Shias. The alternative—to send the children to
the Shia orphanage in Lucknow—was also shot down. Unluckily
for me, there was no other like-minded Shia in the camp to whom
I could have turned for help in reasoning with the caretakers. So
fierce was their opposition to my proposals, it seemed that before I
would be allowed to even consider the orphans' welfare, I needed to
obtain a certificate of 'Shia-ness' from the Supreme Leader of the
Shia sect, the Majtahid!

Another interesting encounter comes to mind. Unlike at the Purana
Qila camp, here the procurement and distribution of shrouds was
done by the Jamiat and Jamia volunteers, not the relief committee;
the former arranged for the shrouds, the latter disbursed them. One
day, hearing a squabble between the heirs of a deceased gentleman
and the Jamia boys, I went over. The disagreement had arisen because
of a fatwa that the Pir of the deceased, also resident in the camp, had
issued regarding the appropriate length of the shroud so that it may
fully cover the corpse. The shrouds being distributed were shorter
than required, so the heirs were quarrelling for more. I tried to reason,
'Take the shroud being given, it will be of some use at least. I will
explain to Pir sahab, take me to him.'

Pir sahab was found outside his tent, seated cross-legged on two
thick straw mattresses, holding court for a few devotees kneeling
reverentially before him. In his service, I humbly submitted that since
the numbers of the dead were so great, it had become very difficult to
obtain cloth for shrouds. 'The situation has been even graver in these

past weeks; just a few days ago, we had to bury men and women in their own soiled clothes and dupattas or dirty sheets. We know there is a prescribed length for the shroud but these are difficult times that compel us to make do with whatever is available.'

Pir sahab flew into a rage, his devotees followed his cue, and once again, a quarrel with the Jamia boys broke out. I addressed the Pir again, 'May I ask why you live in the camp in such style? For years, your devotees have served you faithfully. Don't you think that in their time of need, it is your duty to serve them. Leave your corner and work with us—you will soon understand our challenges!' Of course, he paid no heed to my offer and bitter words were exchanged between our side and his. We finally left the place in disgust, leaving behind a Pir and his devotees spluttering in anger.

The next time I ran into Pir sahab was many days after this incident while I was helping distribute clothes. Sombre-faced, he observed, 'Baba Fakir is in need.' I taunted, 'After two thick mattresses and the flowing green gown, cummerbund and turban of an imam, what other need could you possibly have?'

'A blanket.'

'But aren't you a fakir, a servant of God and his subjects? Why would you need these worldly trappings? Why don't you immerse yourself in service and toil?' Pir sahab left in a huff. Our encounters after this fell into a pattern—he would be in queue for distribution of relief, I would taunt him, he would leave muttering and cursing. Every time he left, I would feel deep regret but, for some reason, I could not bring myself to give him anything at all. How he must still hate me, wherever he is now!

I remember another incident from December. Just as sanctuary seekers had begun to look for happiness, there was fresh news of violence in the city. A Jamiat volunteer (wearing a Congress badge) brought two women to the camp the very next morning after initial reports of renewed violence. Leaving them outside the tent, he said with characteristic agitation, '*Apa*, I cannot tell you how terrible yesterday was—not a minute of rest, the whole day spent running from here to there in Chandni Chowk!'

The camp at Humayun's Tomb witnessed a constant flux of Muslim refugees. The hustle-bustle led to some comic episodes even in those dark times.

I said, 'I guess we must be thankful that the violence lasted only a few hours.' 'Yes, but even in those few hours, I found these two burqa-clad ladies. I saw them walking and told them that they had better come with me immediately, or they would have to bid farewell to their lives, but—witness their imbecility—they insisted that I take them to the train station! I scolded them, said that they must come home with me for the night and I would bring them to the camp the next morning. So here they are—I'll just send them in to meet you.'

I was perhaps busy at that moment, so I waited for them to come in and didn't go out to receive them. In a while, the tent flap opened but instead of the women, a young sanctuary seeker entered. This young man was a member of the voluntary camp police and nephew of the camp commander. He respectfully addressed me, 'I have a humble request, Apa. I believe you know that I'm still unmarried?'

Smiling, I replied, 'Yes, I know. And therefore . . .?'

'And you must also know that my uncle, the camp commander, is a widower?'

'Yes, yes, but where is all this leading to?'

Shyly, he said, 'You know, those two women that have come . . .? Where do you plan to put them up?'

'I haven't thought about it yet. Why, is any tent vacant?'

Now the words came rushing out, 'Why, my own tent has space! If you think it proper, why don't you keep them there? The older of the two is expecting quite soon. We can keep her in hospital, look after her and, when the baby comes, get her married to my uncle, and . . .' I finished, 'And you marry the younger one, isn't it?'

Grinning, 'Yes, exactly. That's the thing. My uncle advised me to tell you of this plan now itself, so that you are kept informed.'

'But, my dear prince, I haven't even met the women! Let them meet me at least. Let me find out who they are, where they are from— these plans can wait, can't they?'

The women came into the tent a little later. I found out that they were not without attachments. One said her husband had died, the other said hers was missing; yet, puzzlingly, they both cited the search for their husbands as their reason for travelling from Calcutta to this inferno. I began to suspect that they were neither Bengalis nor bereaved. Nevertheless, I urged them to stay on and told them that, if they so wished, they could marry the two suitors waiting outside. To my surprise, this offer reduced them to a flood of tears, their sobs interspersed with pleas, 'Please let us go to the station. Nobody will hurt us. We will be safe. Let us go back to Calcutta, please!'

I calmed them down, got the workers' tent emptied out, had their boxes and bundles moved in and returned to my other duties. A few hours later, I remembered with a start that I had made no arrangements for their meals and rushed back to their tent.

The scene that greeted me was amusing to say the least. The uncle was standing by their side, the nephew kneeling at their feet, and the two women were seated and crying; on the *chatai* before them were offerings of a new book, an apple and some flowers! Thinking back now, I smile, but at the time, a wave of irritation rose within me. Seeing me approach, the uncle scrammed. When I snapped at the younger suitor, 'What work do you have here?' he retreated too. I tried to find out, again, who the women were and why they were crying, but in vain.

As was my custom, I completed my work for the day and left the camp by late afternoon. On my return the next morning I learnt that though no courtesy had been overlooked, no act of hospitality left untried, the two ladies remained inconsolable. Once they even made it to the gate with their belongings before being cajoled back into the tent; finally, in the wee hours, they escaped. Where they went, what became of them—no one could tell.

Another meeting between suitors and beloveds was destined, however. Returning from the Ittehad Conference in Lucknow, the uncle–nephew pair encountered the femme fatales again. Much was exchanged but ultimately, the widower stayed widower and the bachelor, bachelor. The poor prostitutes! They had thought that burqas would be good disguises but the ruse only intensified attention. How could these free-spirited gazelles, accustomed to prance and lope unfettered, welcome such incarceration?

The Jamia boys then told me that before I started working in the camp, it had been quite a den for such revelry. For these genteel sons of good families, even the simple task of distributing rations had not been without peril—they had to pick their way gingerly, saving themselves in this garden of burqa-clad thorns and the bickering that resounded through the camp!

The saddest creature of all, however, was a qawwal inmate. When he could take no more the tearful countenances, tear-filled tales, the weeping and wailing, he came to me: 'Begum sahiba, I can see you are free right now. May I submit something?'

'Yes, go ahead, tell me whatever you want.'

'No, no, not that. I want to present something before you.'

I still didn't catch on. 'Yes, yes, whatever you want.'

He said happily, 'Oh, so I have your permission. Shall I get the dholak now?'

'What nonsense! What do you mean "get the dholak"? Who are you? What do you want?'

Bowing low, 'Don't be upset my lady; I am a *mirasi*, a qawwal. I'll impose on you just one number, if you will give me your precious attention. I await your request.'

'Miyan, do something to bring yourself back to your senses. Music in this graveyard? When the dirges of death let up for a while, then there will be singing and other festivities. This is not the time, my friend.'

Crestfallen, he retreated. Truly, how difficult it was for singers of happy songs to survive in such times!

As the cold intensified, so did cruelty and bestiality. The numbers seeking sanctuary swelled. *Sharanarthis* from Punjab had banded together to grab their houses and property, rendering many insecure and homeless.

This word sharanarthi—'he who has gained refuge'—was a special gift of the times, and used for refugees from Pakistan. For days, we couldn't even pronounce it properly—such a fat, unwieldy word that it would simply fill up one's mouth—but just as we were getting used to it, Punjabi newspapers protested its use for the migrants from Punjab saying that they were not charity-seekers. They advocated the use of the word *purusharthi*—'he who labours'—in cognizance of the fact that the refugee's own labour rebuilt his life. Later, some also argued for the use of the word *muhajir*—'an emigrant'. I don't know which to use—the words panahguzeen and muhajir are Arabic and Farsi, and purusharthi smells vaguely of manual labour, so sharanarthi or refugee is what I use.

I had heard that the situation in the city was very bad, but hadn't been able to visit the troubled areas. An acquaintance, Savitry Bhargava (originally from Lucknow and working with the Central Relief Committee [CRC] for three months) had often offered to take me around Kalka but my responsibilities at the Muslim camp were so onerous that I could never take up her offer. Savitry was caring for the refugees in Kalka and Sheikh Sarai and spoke frequently of the dire situation there, of how it was unsafe to even walk by, of how one often saw bullets whizzing over one's motor car.

From the talk around me at the time, I had gathered that the

Muslims in the camps were being meted out unequal treatment compared to the refugees. While the latter were being rehabilitated, the former were being driven out of their homes. But it was also true that while the refugee youth were courageously striving to somehow tide over the crisis, pressing into service all their learning and self-discipline, the sanctuary seekers were a crowd of bickering illiterates, whose only exertions were towards the multiplication of their troubles.

The few refugees I'd met earlier had narrated their own heart-rending experiences, asking me to compare those with the stories from Delhi, 'Nothing really happened in Delhi. Mahatmaji is raising a hue and cry for nothing. Why is Panditji giving so much importance to what they say? If there had been a government truly committed to justice, it would have meted out the same treatment to the Muslims that we have suffered at their hands! They should be packed off to Pakistan immediately and their belongings and property handed over to us. But this government loves Muslims alone and is only interested in stopping them from leaving!'

From the other side the Muslims would cry, 'Stop those lies, you cheats! You did not suffer at the hands of any Muslim—you simply ran away! You have come here just to loot us. We know you have brought all your wealth—you think we don't notice your fancy clothes? And this Hindu government loves you and you alone—why else would its army and police fire at us—see how it helps you and kills us!'

These conflicting accounts had always made me want to see and judge for myself what was happening in the city, and now that I was at the Humayun's Tomb camp, I could also find the time. Neither my driver nor I was acquainted with the area, so I requested the young Jamia student Qaisar to accompany me to the affected areas. We set off one day on a tour of Paharganj, Karol Bagh, Multani Dhanda, Sabzi Mandi, Chandni Chowk and Chuna Mandi. We didn't alight from the car anywhere but wherever we looked, we saw burnt and dug-up houses, battered graves in graveyards that had caved in, mosques where idols had been installed. We saw no Muslims until we reached Jama Masjid, where hundreds of sanctuary seekers from Alwar and Patiala had taken shelter in the verandas and park.

So many different people had flowed into Delhi, but on each face was etched the same anxiety. Before this, who'd have ever thought of trying to determine whether a person on the street was Hindu or Muslim, but today, I was searching every visage for a sign of its religion, looking out for a skullcap or the distinct groomed beard that marked a Muslim man. When I found none in most parts of the city, my heart cried out, Almighty God! Have Muslims been so wronged and Your wrath at them so intense that they can only skulk around, hiding in shame? Is it that now:

> *le gaye taslees ke farzand miras-e-khaleel*
> *khisht-e-buniyad-e-kaleesa ban gayi khaq-e-hijaz*
> The legacy of the Prophet Ibrahim is the heritage of Christianity
> The soil of Arabia lies in bricks at the foundations of churches.
>
> Mohammed Iqbal

I have promised you honesty my readers, so you will discern that while I profess my search to be for humanity in this testament, at places my tears fall for Muslims alone. These are thoughts and emotions that I was unable to discipline, emerging as they did to the events and conditions that I witnessed.

But why was the majority of inhabitants of the Jama Masjid area still Muslim? Built by Shah Jahan, Jama Masjid was no Taj Mahal. No lore of love and loyalty was associated with it so why did rays of love, instead of the heat of hate, emanate from it? Why did poor innocents live in its shade, clinging to it for security? Was it because its foundations were permeated with the same love and longing as those of the Taj, or was the Taj's symbolism transformed into reality here? The Hindus and Muslims that lived here were still alive, still humane. Had humanity indeed survived in this land?

Just beyond Jama Masjid, Muslim workers hid in Dariba and Chawri Bazar and continued working for the Hindu traders who employed them. But after this, all the way to Mehrauli, the only sight of a visible Muslim population was in Humayun's Tomb area—on the narrow road leading to Nizamuddin, several Muslims could be seen walking about. The intervening areas—Connaught Circus, New Delhi, Karol Bagh—had been completely emptied of Muslims.

As we drove through, my guide, aged by experience to far beyond his twenty-four years, recounted what had happened there. He had witnessed arson and plunder of property in Karol Bagh and people's desperation to save themselves, hiding in the scrub and beneath boulders. He spoke of the attack on the Jamia school and publication house, in which Shafiq-ur Rahman Kidwai and some others had been trapped, death staring at their faces. Only when each one of his companions had escaped could Shafiq-ur Rahman sahab be persuaded to leave.

There were thus only two havens in the city, two symbols of love, two madrasas of amity, two paths to the righteous destination. Into these two sanctuaries, watered by springs of love and compassion, from villages, towns and principalities, the beleaguered and the besieged streamed, seeking asylum. In Jama Masjid, it was as if they were held in an embrace in the arms of its tall white minarets raised to the heavens in a proclamation of peace; in Nizamuddin, they were cradled in the unseen hands that reached down to gather up the scattered beads of a *tasbeeh*.

But wait—there was also a third! Birla House, the home of peace and of a vibrant living truth, where lived the father of India. His eyes filled with tears, he was battling for his children's lives, salving their sorrows, mending their broken hearts . . . With a jolt, my thoughts were interrupted—we were home, Qaisar was asking me to alight.

At Humayun's Tomb camp, only the commander was a government employee, the rest were honorary workers and volunteers. Work was done in shifts; some volunteers came in the morning, others at night. Besides this, there was the 'camp police'—the name given by the Jamia students to the group of camp inmates they had mobilized—who patrolled the camp day and night, alert for signs of a possible attack.

The workers' commitment had thus far ensured efficiency of functioning but greater challenges soon arose. In November and December came a deluge of sanctuary seekers, streaming in from neighbourhoods caught up in violence. From the villages, thousands of hefty rustic men, sturdy women, full-bodied robust youth in bullock-carts, lorries and army trucks bearing charpoys, chests, winnows, sieves and sacks of grain descended. From the city, men carrying their belongings in suitcases and boxes on their heads, their children holding their hands, their women clutching chests and *paandaans*, shuffled along in endless processions.

Very soon, the camp's cleanliness and order were things of the past. Makeshift tents mushroomed everywhere, anywhere. Our lives were made miserable by the never-ending requests for more permanent tents. The fact was that there were none available—the tents of the Purana Qila camp had already been given to the refugees.

Only those who spent night and day in the open, huddled under a mere sheet for a tent, in that bitter November and December, can tell of what they underwent. Pneumonia and influenza swept through the camp, everywhere bodies were racked by coughs, chests wheezed with congestion and the winds were so freezing that the cold cut through to one's bones. The situation was intolerable. In tears, I went to Dr Hussain for advice. He heard me out and said, 'But why are these people leaving their homes? Explain to them that they don't need to.'

'Believe me, I've tried but all my efforts to stem the tide have failed. My sister has also tried; just the other day, she patiently explained to them that it would be safer for them to gather courage and return home. She told them that given the sheer magnitude of the numbers bound for Pakistan, it was likely that they would starve there. Then there was the danger of perishing on the train itself. But her counsel only drove them into a towering rage, so much so that it was quite difficult for the boys to extricate her from the mob.'

A few days after this conversation, as if by a miracle, Dr Hussain sent us 200 tents. Thereafter, for weeks, we were busy distributing and erecting them. The problem was that no one knew exactly how to pitch a tent, and we were very short of hands. The same boys who distributed milk and rations also gave out blankets, and had to listen to complaints and abuses.

How could tents ever be enough to meet every need? The hospital was full of patients. I again approached Rajkumari Amrit Kaur, Sushila wrote official reports and doctors made official requests to garner new beds and medication. Another lady doctor (a very fine person indeed), two nurses and four midwives were assigned. However, the intense cold continued to plague the patients; there were simply not enough blankets. Although sixty blankets for the hospital had also been part of the consignment, only eighteen reached the patients. At most, a couple more may have been used elsewhere in the hospital; what became of the rest I cannot say. Perhaps they ended up in the safekeeping of the doctors or the camp commander.

Finally, I approached Bapu, 'The government is distributing thousands of blankets in the refugee camp. It is surely not so difficult to show some sympathy for people dying of pneumonia and fever, so why the difference in treatment? If the government behaves so partially, what is the difference between it and ordinary people?'

Bapu immediately called the secretary of the ministry concerned and asked him to deliver 200 blankets from the stock to the Humayun's Tomb camp. I returned and shared the good news. The delivery never arrived, however. I couldn't find the time to meet Bapu and request him to remind the secretary. In any case, how could one expect those in positions of authority to have a breadth of vision that would, at least in matters of charity, prevent them from discriminating between Hindu and Muslim? Unfortunately, Sushila was away then—perhaps in Punjab—and there was no one else whom I knew well enough to ask for help. Had she been there, she'd have followed up on the request and ensured that the blankets were delivered.

Ultimately the blankets did arrive but only because Doctor sahab bought them with the money he had received as a donation. My sister and my daughter appealed to the generosity of the Begums of Lucknow, Allahabad and Barabanki, and clothes and money arrived from there. Jamiat brought in clothes from Bihar and UP as well, and a student of Lucknow University sent new clothes and sweaters for orphaned children. All this added up to be enough to tide us over. God bless all those who helped us in the hour of need. Such was their generosity that I could give Jamia the large sum of money from Lucknow as well as Rs 500 and woollen clothes sent by Brigadier Usman, for the orphans in their care.

It would be terribly remiss of me if I continued this account without acknowledging the help we received at every step from that great man, the late Rafi Ahmad Kidwai. His unflinching support was the one reason why all of us could continue to share in the pain and grief of others. It was he who ensured that Subhadra and other workers did not lack for cars, jeeps and other material assistance. It was his generosity in providing me a car, a phone, domestic help and a home that enabled me to go wherever my work took me. Anyone in difficulty had the full liberty of exploiting his position in the government, and we certainly did so. In one such incident, I sought his help for a Sikh driver, beside himself with grief for his family trapped in Poonch, then under attack by Pashto-speaking Pathans. It was only he who could help; in just a few days, the Sikh driver's wife and five children were by his side, extricated from an extremely dangerous situation and flown to safety in Delhi on Rafi bhai's instructions.

Children of the refugee home for children at Ram Bagh, Delhi.

5

Children

(October–November 1947)

In October, I began visiting hospitals with Jamila to locate stray and orphaned children; otherwise, like scores of children being sent off to Pakistan, they would be too. To bring them to the camp was infeasible though; there were no proper arrangements for them to live or study. Jamila immediately proffered her Daryaganj house as a home for them. Her house was on Sir Syed Road, facing Kuche Chelan. It reminded me of Rashid-ul-Khairi, Asaf Ali and others. All houses in Kuche Chelan had been vacated, every building in the refugees' capture. Only Jamila's courage emboldened her to traverse the area every day.

Just then, a car full of bags drew up at the house opposite. Jamila remarked, 'It seems Masud sahab has arrived.' Masud sahab, formerly chief secretary to the Nawab of Rampur, had arrived in Delhi to serve as secretary to Maulana Abul Kalam Azad. To think that at a time when people were fleeing Delhi, he was bringing his wife and children into such peril! The house was his wife's ancestral property. I was gratified to see that there were still such courageous people left in this world.

Although Jamila's house was quite suitable, we would need some Muslim women to stay here and look after the children. But where would we find them? Moreover, we would need to request the police to guard the house to prevent refugees from taking control of it. I had no doubt that the deputy commissioner would promptly agree and make security arrangements but I also knew that after two or three days, the children would be found dead, and all the deputy commissioner would have to offer would be sincere regrets and a confession of helplessness. To even speculate on who the culprits could be, leave alone ensure punishment, would be a call beyond what his decency or discretion could afford.

However, now I knew Zakir sahab, who had promptly offered Jamia as a haven for these children. I visited the hospitals to check whether the children on my list compiled earlier had healed enough to be taken to Jamia.

In Irwin Hospital, the children sat together, sunning themselves on an upper veranda. Some had injured heads, others had broken legs, and on a tiny cot lay groaning a nine-month-old with wounded head and hands. A little girl's shoulder drooped because her forearm had been severed and a little boy was recovering from the wounds of a stomach split open. Mercifully, the wound had closed and the stitches were out. All the children were quite clearly under the care of a bright girl sitting and playing there.

Seeing her unharmed, I asked, 'You look well. Were you also hurt?' She laughed, 'Oh no! I came here with my *bua*. My parents are in Etawah.' I asked, 'And these other children?' Still smiling, she replied, 'These ones? This is Rasheed—all of his relatives died. That is Zainab— all of hers died too. And that is Nabu—his mother's throat was slit.'

She chattered on brightly—barely five but for her death was a sport, an interesting diversion. Everyone killed, mother's throat slit—such mundane events!

None of the children was older than eight. All of them lived in the hospital as one large family and each narrated to me another's story. One of the boys, whose stomach had been slashed, piped up, 'My two brothers died, but my father is alive, in Lucknow. We brothers had come from there—they killed them at the station itself. Please send me to Lucknow.' A smart boy, he gave me his home address. I found that only two children could be taken to Jamia. It was late and the nurse asked me to return the next day at 10 a.m. to get the doctor's permission for their release.

Just opposite the children's room was one allotted to wounded women and girls; the nurse took me there too. Eighteen-year-old Siddiqan's right leg had been hacked off. Next to her lay a dusky fourteen-year-old, whimpering in pain, her body covered with wounds; for two months, her agony hadn't let up. On another cot sat a beautiful young girl who came from Meerut to treat a cancerous tumour. Now, three months later, she wept for she didn't know if she had any relatives left to return to.

Perhaps the most horrifying case was that of the young woman who had lost both her hands—one arm hacked off at the wrist, the other at the elbow. Beside her lay her twelve-year-old daughter, swathed in bandages and splints, groaning, but that poor woman was bereft of her hands—hands with which she'd have caressed her daughter's head, stroked her back, moistened her parched mouth, soothed her pain. I will never ever be able to forget the helplessness of that woman's tears.

I glance at my notebook now and see 'bananas, *gajak, rewadi*' noted there. These three things always remind me of Rasheeda from Mehrauli. She could have been no more than sixteen, Rasheeda. She told me when the attack came, the men started to fight for their lives and most women held their Qurans to their breasts and leapt into the well. Some ran, however, like Rasheeda. But running did not mean escape—Rasheeda was caught and swords rent through each of her limbs.

Rasheeda said to me, 'Make me your daughter. I have no one left.' From then on, she called me Ammi and would wait for my visit. One day, I told her, 'Rasheeda, do you feel like eating something? Something special?' and she replied, 'Yes. When you come tomorrow, get me bananas, gajak, rewadi.' But in the following days, I'd go to the camp in the morning and return late in the evening, and in New Delhi, one could find neither gajak nor rewadi. The servants were too terrified to go into the city. I could not fulfil Rasheeda's wish, and these three words remain my shame. I preserve this battered notebook so that I may always be reminded of my lapses, my sloth.

I visited Lady Hardinge Hospital next.

When Faridabad was destroyed and its Muslims driven out to Pakistan, its famous rural poet, Syed Muttalwi—a staunch nationalist and a Congress leader famed for his rousing speeches—came to Delhi. His poetry and the children's literature authored by his son, Abu Tamayyam Faridabadi, were very popular. Syed Muttalwi's family was determined to stay on in India, despite losing all. I hear that it was only after Gandhiji's martyrdom that he and his family gave in, and left for Pakistan.

Syed Muttalwi spent his last few months in Delhi searching for the lost people of his nation. Through his efforts, many ill and injured were admitted to hospitals, though many more remained missing. I had gone earlier with Jamila to Lady Hardinge Hospital, where most of these people had been admitted on his request—'Please find out how our women from Faridabad are faring. Except from Irwin Hospital, I have no information about our patients. It is particularly impossible to get news out of Lady Hardinge.' I'd found many Faridabadi women and children there and noted their names. My report pleased Syed Muttalwi, 'One of the women in your list is someone I've been searching for many weeks. I'd be very grateful if you could bring her here.'

My mission today was in part to meet his request. However, when I reached the hospital, I found that the woman, along with her three children, had been discharged. Her relatives came to get her, said the nurse. We never could learn who took her away, when, and to where— she certainly wasn't brought to Purana Qila.

However, many patients, including children, were still admitted in the hospital. One sweet little girl of six had a head wound inflicted by a sword; it showed no signs of improving. The poor thing couldn't even tell me her father's name beyond 'he was called Munshiji in Paharganj'. In the veranda lay four children beside their mother, waiting for their relatives to fetch them. Where exactly home was, they couldn't say—just that it was a prosperous home amidst fields in a rural area near Mehrauli. Now that their wounds were healing, hope had brought smiles to their lips.

In another veranda, a young woman lay on a cot, her limbs bandaged and splinted. On her chest was a deep wound and the immense loss of blood had weakened her sight considerably. Immobile, her voice barely a whisper, she made me note down the names of her brothers, their wives, her nephews (some grown men, others mere boys). She asked me to send word to them that Bilqees from Paharganj is in Lady Hardinge Hospital, and that when they go to Pakistan, they should take her along.

Middle-aged Nooran stood nearby, narrating how she lost her husband and children and begging to be taken to her brother in Faizabad.

A Hindu nurse ushered me to a beautiful girl, saying, 'You must meet Farida Talat. She looks like she's from a good Muslim family, but nobody comes for her. She weeps for her family all day. She was admitted before the riots because she was ill, so she escaped injury, and has recovered now. I don't know why the authorities haven't informed her parents . . . Will you contact them?'

A young woman holding an infant was weeping inconsolably. Beside her, her three-year-old daughter was screaming in pain, the victim of some lion-hearted braves. The attack on her had been so savage that even thinking of it makes my hair stand—the pike had pierced through her private parts up to her stomach. As yards of medicated gauze were passed through that deep wound, no sentient being could bear her agonized shrieks or her mother's cries. 'They murdered everyone! They speared my child and hoisted her on the mace but left me alive to witness all this! What do I do? Where do I go?' Painful questions addressed to me—and the only answer I could give was to quake with her in torment.

A Bengali nurse signalled to me to come into her room. She told me of a little girl, three or four years old, who would soon recover from her minor wounds. Since she appeared to be a Muslim child, she asked me to take her away. The girl was brought, I asked her name.

'Sita and Haseena,' she replied. I asked her father's name and she uttered a Muslim name and a Hindu one. Same for her mother. The nurse interjected, 'Whatever she may say, she is Muslim. She says her father would spread out his hands in prayer, "My Allah, be merciful".' Other nurses disagreed, insisting that she was Hindu. Finding myself in a tight spot, I decided to take the girl to Birla House. Along with other children that I took away from the hospital, I requested for her. After the formalities, I took her straight to Bapu.

Luckily, I was granted a meeting immediately. When we entered, Bapu was spinning. With the customary smile playing on his lips, he asked, 'Where have you got hold of this little girl from now?'

'Bapu, she will cause a Hindu–Muslim quarrel! She gives both Hindu and Muslim names for herself and her parents. No matter how much I ask, I cannot find out why. What do I do now?' Bapu laughed and asked the girl, 'Child, what is your name?' With great composure, she replied, 'Haseena. Sita.' Bapu said, 'Achha, keep her with you for now. In a few days, she can be sent to the Kasturba Trust School in Mehrauli.' So, she stayed with me for over a week, after which I sent her to Mehrauli.

By end-November, I had hunted all hospitals in Delhi for children. Although several children were listed everywhere, they could not be found! Where they went was a mystery. Two children from Kalra were reunited with their parents in the camp but the rest—what happened to them? Perhaps, on recovering, they wandered off wherever their tiny feet took them. Perhaps they fell into the missionaries' hands. I could chastise only myself for not thinking of them earlier, for not acting when there was still time.

When the children in Irwin Hospital healed—overcoming ripped stomachs, split skulls, broken limbs—I took to Jamia's Okhla campus. When parting from the hospital staff that had tended to them for months, the feeble, limping children would be as emotionally wrought as if separating from their parents and siblings. The room with cots and mattresses piled together, the little benches in the veranda, it was their home, and their grief at bidding farewell to it was borne of a profound love. The world had beasts that hurt them but also some humane people, who saved their lives.

It proved possible for the girl from Meerut to be sent to the address she gave. Sir Mohammed Yamin Khan kindly helped, escorted her himself to her uncle's house.

When his stomach wound had healed, the boy from Lucknow was delivered to his family by Feroze Gandhi. I believe he proved quite a handful for Feroze sahab on the journey. First, he harangued him to tell him whether he (Feroze sahab) was Hindu or Muslim. Then, informing him that Hindus were bad people, he loudly voiced his suspicion of Feroze sahab's intentions in escorting him. He got off at a station to drink water but then changed his mind and returned, to order Feroze sahab—'Bring me a glass of water now. I won't get off. Too many Sikhs here, they will kill me!' For the rest of the journey, he kept chattering about the evilness of Hindus and Sikhs. Somehow, Feroze sahab managed to deliver him to his Lucknow home, where they found that the desperate father, unmindful of the danger to his life, had left for Delhi to find his three sons. How happy he would have been when he returned home—some joy in bleakness—that at least one son had survived!

The clever girl I'd met first at Irwin Hospital—Zarina—was the first to come with me. She chattered brightly at my side as we moved out, but when she saw a middle-aged Sikh approaching, she let go of my hand and rushed to hug him. He hugged her affectionately and asked her where she was going. I told him that she would live and study in Jamia till her relatives were traced. Delighted, he embraced her again, gave her some sweets and went on. Zarina didn't know his name or where he came from—to her and the other children, he was simply their beloved Baba, who brought them sweets, and in whose embrace they found love and laughter. This true representative of humanity didn't make distinctions based on religion even in these times of pain; he brought to the children their share of love. Alas! I couldn't even learn his name.

The next child to accompany me to Jamia was sweet little Babu. Throughout the journey, Babu cried for Kallu, his nine-month-old brother whom we had left in the hospital. It was just for a few more days, purely as precaution, but Babu was very upset. How little the two brothers resembled each other—Babu was wheatish, healthy, talkative whereas Kallu was ugly, dark, scrawny. No one knew whether they were children of the same parents, from one household, or strangers. Two wounded children were found by the military, loaded on to a truck, deposited at the hospital, and when Babu started calling Kallu his brother, people at the hospital followed suit.

Whenever I went to Jamia, Babu would throw himself into my arms, demanding sweets. If I took apples, he'd protest, 'Why not sweets?' When I went on a jeep, he complained, 'Why not a proper motor car? This is a bad car. I won't ride in it!' I teased, 'But who asked you to ride at all? I haven't come to take you away, have I?' He flew into a rage and snatched at me, whining that I take him to market to buy sweets.

Ikram sahab said that Babu often flew into rages, shouting and screaming, 'I will kill you, Ikram! I won't let you live! If only you'd die, Ikram, my life would be saved! Why don't you die, Ikram? Then I will die too . . .' And so on—always talk of murder, death.

One day, Ikram sahab telephoned me to tell me that provisions had to be bought. If I couldn't come myself, he'd be grateful if I sent the car to take him to Jama Masjid. Recognizing this as a good opportunity to take Babu for a little outing, I went myself.

When we set off, Babu was very excited and chattered non-stop, but, after a while, his mood darkened, as if forgotten memories had risen to the surface. Raising his hand to his throat, he dully said—as if talking in his sleep—'Blood came out of my Abba's throat. From this spot, right here, and he groaned. They killed my woman. My brother too. Then they picked me up, threw me down, hard. I sat on the tin pot and I cried all the time. Soldiers came and I sat in the car. Then I started living in a house.'

'Babu, which house was that?' Still staring sightlessly out of the car, in the same distant voice, 'In this house, where Miss sahab is, where Kallu is.' He fell quiet. A moment later, his hand caressing the car seat, he spoke again, 'I used to come with Abba to Jama Masjid in a motor car. For sweets and balloons. Toys too.' Then, in a sudden rage, 'I am going to kill Ikram.' This four-year old, why did he hate Ikram so? Still lisping, why did he rail against his 'Itram'? Why did he want to die? Why did he shriek 'Blood everywhere! Blood all around!'?

Rasheeda and Babu showed me the possible consequences of events around us, well before I began to reflect on it. Our ancestors were neither murderers nor bandits, so how could they have sown the seeds of such sin? What sinners we'd turned out to be! What, now, of these children, who at the age of just four could talk of blood, think of death and murder as mere play, await it so anxiously? At such a tender age, they ask, 'What are you? Hindu or Muslim?', live in fear that Hindus will slit their throats, and sagely advise, 'If you meet a Sikh, butcher him at once'—how will they turn out? Blood-filled psyches, stony hearts, children untouched by love—what would become of them? Which abyss of shame would Hindustan plumb along with them?

Troubled by these thoughts, I would find comfort in the wisdom of two Jamia boys, Shams and Qaisar. Sensing the impending peril and foreseeing our collective horrifying future, they had left the camp to work in the city—to catalyse constructive change. But me, I hadn't been alerted at all—I who was a mother didn't understand that it wasn't only the generations of today that were lost but that the future had been destroyed too. The coming generations would be even more blind and unfeeling, and if something weren't done now to restore balance, they would plummet into the deepest abyss of all. When there are no humans left, of what significance can Hinduism or Islam be? Religion, faith, rules, laws are for humans, and if humanity is lost . . . India will be gone, as will Hindus and Muslims.

Before all the needy or destitute women, I placed the offer of a job as the guardian of these abandoned children. Dr Hussain wanted to appoint a responsible woman, with an appropriate salary. But God knows what had happened to Muslim women in those days. They were first in line for charity but fled miles away at the very mention of paid employment. Some offered excuses, 'How can I possibly do this now? There isn't life enough in me after all I've suffered.' Others said, 'But I'm still mourning my own children. My heart is riddled with grief. Why does Allah miyan remain impassive while I suffer? Why doesn't He send me death? And you ask me to work, when all I long for is to cease?' Yet others would say, 'Just send me to Pakistan, please!' The rest would wrinkle their noses, 'For heaven's sake! How can you ask me to do this pissing–shitting routine when I'm in these circumstances?'

Totally demoralized, I asked Ikram sahab to manage on his own. As time went by, I saw that he was actually quite happy to be a housewife—the house was clean, the children's beds laid out neatly. The children were also happy, playing in the veranda all day. He would periodically call me to inform me of their progress—'Today, we'll go to the market to buy shoes,' or 'The children ask for you, why don't you visit?' Caring for the children and domestic arrangements clearly satisfied him.

On a visit to Lady Hardinge Hospital around this time, I learnt that Sakina, whom I'd seen on an earlier visit, had recovered. She had been separated from her family and I brought her to the camp to look for them, only to learn that her father, siblings, four daughters and husband had all left for Pakistan. After three days of witnessing her tears, I suggested that she come to Okhla. 'The children will distract you and if you help these parentless children, God will certainly be merciful towards you.'

That good woman agreed promptly and, for the next four months, cared for the children as if they were her own. Meanwhile, contact was established with her family via radio. Her four daughters were with her father in Karachi and her husband was in Agra. Discovering that she was in Okhla, her husband arrived almost immediately, but Sakina refused to go with him as it was still very unsafe to travel. However, when he came a second, then a third time, Sakina had to leave; they decided to first go to Karachi to bring back their daughters. The grief that she and the children felt at the parting was overwhelming, but how could she stay? Wherever she is, I hope she is happy. I will remain forever thankful to her for helping us when we needed it the most.

Ikram sahab was now a single parent again, but soon relatives of more and more children starting coming forward and the numbers of his charges started to dwindle. Zarina's uncle came to get her.

The last entrant to the Okhla home also left—a boy whose leg had been broken in several places. When he reached Okhla, his whole leg was plastered and we fretted that it would never rejoin. However, he improved rapidly, and when he was well enough to walk, he was taken, along with other children, to Jama Masjid to buy shoes. All the children clustered outside the shop choosing shoes, when suddenly, who should appear but the boy's father! That poor man's entire family had been wiped out but now, unexpectedly, he found that one reason for living had still been left for him—his precious child! To describe his joy is beyond the words I possess. The boy was equally overcome and, a few weeks later, I heard a voice call out to me in Kassabpura. It was the young boy again, happy at home again.

Siddiqan too left the hospital and I saw her in the camp one day. She could no longer walk and when I met her, this newlywed girl was in her husband's arms. He and his sister took turns to carry her around. Barely 'sweet sixteen' but one for whom youth was now only a dream, Siddiqan was still happy, basking in the love and concern her relatives were lavishing on her. For how long would this happiness last? Wouldn't this sympathy wane, and her youthful husband eventually tire of caring for a disabled wife? Was she fated to spend the rest of her days dragging herself on streets, begging for morsels? Who can foretell the future? My task was to look to the present. Soon, a curtain would fall over these events, making them a past I couldn't see.

In time, we decided that while the younger children would stay at Jamia, the older children for whom no one came would go to the Sunni Wakf Board orphanage, Bachchon Ka Ghar. Now that

Dr Hussain had been appointed a member of its board, it had become a true home for orphaned children.

In this group was a girl whose arm had been cut off. The wound had not healed but the loneliness pained her most now. She often asked, 'When will you take me away?' One day, she handed me a dirty pack of playing cards, saying in a sad voice laced equally with yearning and despair, 'Can you give this to Rasheed for me?'

Two innocent hearts were longing for each other, and this tiny little girl was expressing her love for her dear friend. Where the cards came from, who knows, but Rasheed and she used to play with them. Now that Rasheed had gone, what use had she for them? These love-laden gifts, the sole means of her amusement, this sum total of her wealth in her brief life, she now offered to her friend. This innocence won me over totally and the gift was conveyed to Rasheed immediately.

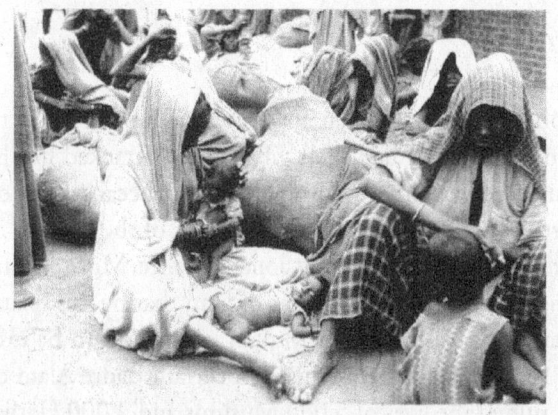

Refugees waiting for admission into a refugee camp.

6

The second wave
(December 1947–January 1948)

December 1947 saw two changes in the atmosphere of the Humayun's Tomb camp. The first was minor: for the first time, Congress members (other than Gandhiji's followers, who had been there from the beginning) were occasionally spotted visiting the camp. Once or twice, I even met members of the Congress Provincial Committee. A trifling change—they didn't do any work there—but a change nevertheless.

The second change was much more significant. New waves of sanctuary seekers began to arrive, including villagers of Tihar, arriving in a 5,000-strong contingent, with sacks of grain, cots and sieves laden on trucks and bullock carts. Women in their finery trooped behind strapping men in striking *pagdis*, with the majestic bearing of conquerors. We were all taken aback by this new breed of refugees. We found that neither had their village been attacked nor had they lost clan members, but they were off to Pakistan because of an exchange of property between landlords on either side of the border.

Apparently, the deputy commissioner of police, Mr M.S. Randhawa, had arranged for the 40,000 bighas of land that he, his relatives and friends had to leave behind in Multan and Sindh to be exchanged with the 13,000 bighas belonging to a certain Badre Alam of Tihar. This had ruined the lives of 5,000 Muslims and 2,000 Harijans who lived and worked on his land. The Muslims, having decided to follow their land, now trooped into Humayun's Tomb.

As usual, our first port of call was Bapu. He said he'd find out from the administration how this exchange had been allowed. He found that the official had permission from Sardar Patel, the home minister. Subhadra was incensed, 'But Bapu, how can an official facilitate exchange of property, when the governments of the two countries have yet to decide on the modalities? This official must be dismissed at once!'

Despairing, Bapu replied, 'You are right—he shouldn't have done so, yet he has. Your suggestion of removing him is perhaps not realistic either. Why do you expect that his replacement will be any angel? People have simply gone mad these days.'

This wasn't the first time that the case had been brought to Bapu's attention. On his orders, Subhadra had lived in this village, trying to counsel the Muslims to stay on. Bapu had also gone once, to reassure the Muslims of their safety. The prime minister's daughter, Indira, had also visited. Subhadra was furious with the Muslims, 'I stayed fifteen days, reasoning with them not to leave. Bapu did the same. Indira assured them that the government would do everything to help them. No other group received so many reassurances, yet they didn't have the will to resist!'

I reminded her of the sequence of events. On 11 October, an officer of the administration told the Muslims that they were in peril, that they should leave immediately. On 16 October, the deputy commissioner reiterated the advice. On 21 October, again, came this order; ultimately, a senior province officer despatched a truck to ferry the Muslims to the camp. Subhadra retorted, 'Whatever be the sequence, if they didn't have confidence in me, didn't trust Indira or Nehru, they should have had faith in Bapu's assurance. Why couldn't they hold on?'

When I reminded her of the socio-economic boycott they had been subjected to, she snapped, 'And these are the people celebrated for their valour? A clan, as famous for its outstanding soldiers as its fearsome dacoits, cowers with fear if one is beaten up, a bullock stolen, a petty sum snatched? Are these reasons enough for 5,000 fearless young men to flee? The fact is that fear settled in their hearts and overcame their reason. I, as a woman, had to run to the city to buy their rations while they shuddered with anxiety at taking a single step outside their homes!'

I wondered whether it wasn't God's vengeance being wreaked on the people. Was this state of affairs any different from that mentioned in the Kalam-e-Pak, where a people who have attracted God's wrath become subjugated to another more powerful one, and fear holds such sway over them that they are unable to battle their oppressors?

In December Subhadra learnt that 2,000 Harijans from that same Tihar village had also been thrown out; the Delhi administration had decided to settle refugees there. She said to me, 'You always have a jeep, don't you? Why don't we go and see for ourselves?' We decided to go the next morning.

Tihar village is ten miles outside Delhi. On the way, we saw an unusual camp, where squads of young men were exercising. I asked Subhadra whether she knew what it was. She replied that they were RSS activists, assembled for the rally the Sangh was holding in Delhi soon. Of course! The build-up for the rally had been enormous. Distinguished maharajas had descended on Delhi to participate; the Maharaja of Patiala (whose principality had seen the most barbarous slaughter) was to preside. (We later learnt that Sardar Patel graced the gathering and blessed the gathered heroes.)

Progressives in Delhi were astounded that the rally was being allowed at all. In spite of Bapu's presence in the city, despite a Congress government being in power, this organization of malevolents was being permitted to congregate in Delhi, where rivers of blood had flowed barely months ago. To what dastardly end were these new efforts directed? Why did the government not comprehend the danger, not react? Was it so incapable of distinguishing friend from foe that it was ready to have rioters and murderers as fellow travellers?

Discussing these things, Subhadra and I reached Tihar. Outside the village, we encountered three old men, gazing at their lost homeland with longing. One said, '*Behenji*, see what injustice is being done to us! Our houses and lands will be given to refugees. We aren't allowed to even enter the village. For one month, our cattle has been tied up in the neighbouring village. Our children and our cattle are dying in the cold! Today the village is being cleaned up and soon . . .' He burst into tears. Poor man, to have to witness all this in the winter of his life! We asked, 'Who is responsible for all this?' The answer: 'The government.'

I nearly laughed out loud. When I asked the Muslims, 'Why have all of you come here? Who was it that made you leave the village?' I invariably heard, 'The government.' When I asked the Hindus who forcibly converted Muslims, or the Muslims who were converted, 'Why did you force them to convert? And you, why did you give up your religion?' the reply always was, 'The government wanted it.' Both the persecutors and the ones they oppressed, both murderers and the ones they slaughtered, were killing and being killed in service of the government . . .

The old man narrated his tale of woe: 'Our village is the largest here, so the government made it into a camp and gathered all Muslims here. Soon, the population trebled. We exchanged sharp words with the new entrants whereas we had no conflict with our old Muslim neighbours. Then the government ordered all Muslims to be taken to the city camp. The *tehsildar* arrived with the police, the Muslims sold their ploughs and bullocks and were borne away in trucks. We hear they have been given land in Pakistan. Shortly after they left, we were evicted and, as you can see, it is now being prepared for refugees. All the houses are going to be handed over to them. We can't even enter— when they see us coming, they shout at us to leave.'

Touring the village, talking, I saw that it was quite large and fairly prosperous, with two-storeyed pakka houses and modest shacks. Hearing our footfalls, dogs peeped out from houses with pleading eyes—awaiting their masters. Their hollow stomachs, their wobbly legs spoke of how hunger had brought them to the brink of death.

Hailing a passing policeman, we asked for the custodian inspector. He took us to where the gentleman, seated on a bamboo stool under a shady tree, was overseeing men at work. Houses were being emptied, belongings being piled on to a raised platform outside a zamindar's house. Seeing us, he rose. Catching sight of the three old men with us, he snapped, 'What are you doing here? Leave at once!' I intervened, 'My brother, this is their village, their homes are being emptied, and you order them to leave? What violence is this!' He said, 'Madam, you don't understand. These fellows are all thieves—if I take my eyes off them for a second, they will nick something!' My intervention had bolstered the courage of our three old companions, but these words robbed them of their courage. The inspector scolded them again, 'Hurry up and get out! Don't loiter!' Wiping their tears, the poor old men started retracing their steps.

Deliberately not introducing ourselves, we drew up a charpoy and sat down to chat, 'So, you are having the village cleaned up? It would have been quite dirty, no? Are refugees going to be settled here?' The inspector replied, 'Yes, this village and all the lands that abut it have been allotted to them.' We enquired further, 'And all this is now with the Custodian of Evacuee Property, isn't it?'

'Yes, that's correct. It has also been decided that an agricultural college and its farm will be instituted here. There's a grand scheme in the works.' In a friendly tone, we asked, 'But, how can the property of a Hindu brother be classified as evacuee property?' Nonchalantly, he replied, 'Why, there's no problem. The Hindus have also fled.' We persisted, 'But we don't understand. While the Muslims will get the land and houses left behind by the Hindu refugees in Pakistan, what will the Hindu farmers do? Without their lands, they will starve.'

He replied indifferently, 'Why, they could be given some land in the farms that will be established here. At worst, they could find work on the refugees' lands.' Amazed, we asked, 'Do you see no injustice in this at all? Your plans will make someone who is a landowner in his own right a mere labourer on the very land that was once his?'

'Well, if he is desperate, that is what he will have to accept, won't he?' Angered, we now felt it necessary to interrogate him fully. We asked sternly, 'By whose order was this done? Whose decision was it? What is your name?'

The inspector was flustered, 'But you haven't told me who you are yet. I gather you have come from the city, but why?' We didn't answer and rose to leave. Panicking, he rattled off his name. I must say I quite enjoyed his obvious discomfiture.

As we walked back, he trailed us and, to impress us of his compassion, remarked, 'Madam, what really moves me is the state of these dogs. See how they start at every approaching footstep. Hunger has weakened them beyond words. We will really have to do something for their sustenance. I wonder how we can help them?' I could no longer restrain my laughter. 'You had no qualms in throwing out people from their homes, but are consumed with concern for the well-being of their dogs. Wonderful!'

Smiling sheepishly, he followed us to our car. A few feet away stood the three villagers, still wiping their tears. Wordlessly, they folded their hands before Subhadra in an urgent plea for help—they had now recognized who she was.

On the way back, Subhadra and I discussed our plan of action. She would go to Bapu and I was to try to meet the prime minister. Bapu was dismayed and said, 'It appears that I must die now!' Our hearts wept at hearing this. Quite frequently these days, Bapu would speak thus, 'I've been born here only to die,' 'I've staked my life,' 'I won't live for another ten years . . .'

The prime minister was equally distraught. He asked, 'But why did the villagers leave at all? My daughter and I had visited them and asked them to stay.' How was he to know that his officials didn't share his convictions? Two parallel administrations were in existence—the reins of one were in the hands of some divisive hooligans, of the other in Bapu's hallowed hands. Truth was weak, untruth powerful. That which Bapu sought to accomplish required patience but all that these merchants of terror, these adversaries of the nation, desired could be accomplished in a trice.

Nevertheless, Bapu and Nehru said that they would again ask the local government for an explanation. Bapu advised us to at once resettle the evicted in their homes. Subhadra left immediately, and by 10 p.m., cattle had been brought back to the village and tethered outside their owners' houses. 'This is Bapu's command—return to your houses. If anyone challenges you, don't pay attention. We will handle it.'

The inspector and his men left at night, and early the next day, 2,000 Hindus were restored their homes. As Subhadra was leaving, the villagers had another request, 'Can you perform another act of mercy? Please bring our Muslim brothers back as well.' Many also went to the camp to beg their Muslim brothers to return with them.

That which had been effected at Bapu's command, no one dared question. The prime minister announced that if the Muslims were ready to return from the camp, their property would be restored to them just as it had been to the Hindus. It was up to us to persuade the Muslims to return. Alas! We were unsuccessful. Things had come to such a delicate turn that it was apparent to one so astute as Gandhiji that unless serious efforts were made to dam this river, it would be impossible to stem its tide. This is why, a few days later,

be khatar kood pada aatish-e-namrood mein ishq
Undaunted, plunged Love into the bonfire of Nimrod

                                                        Mohammed Iqbal

The Muslims from Tihar stayed in Humayun's Tomb camp. Other newcomers soon joined them, from Jaitpur village. One day, the *nambardar* of Jaitpur, Ehsan—a straightforward, sober, sensible fellow—came to me. Speaking on behalf of the hundreds of his clanspeople in the camp, he said: 'If there was something we did to bring this upon us, we should be blamed; you can ask the *ziledar* of Madanpur, Trikha Ram. Just half a mile separates Jaitpur and Madanpur, so our families have lived next door for centuries. For all our lives, his family and mine have shared joys and sorrows. However, even that could not save us—nobody came when we needed help.

'And if anyone says that it was we who held wrong views, that's simply untrue. No party other than the Congress has ever been able to gain votes in our area! To think that we were ready to sacrifice our lives for the leaders in power today, when not one has bothered to enquire about us. We have been languishing in this camp for so many days . . . We were sought out only when our votes were needed. If you get the chance, you could perhaps request Pandit Nehruji Maharaj to honour us with his presence, even if just for the last time?'

Ehsan had just come back from Bulandshahar, impressed by the peace and security arrangements made by the UP government. Though UP was peaceful and his in-laws urged him to settle there, he was reluctant. If Jaitpur was to be left behind, why go to UP? Pakistan would now be his destination.

The next day, I went to Jaitpur with two colleagues—Shantaben, a disciple of Bapu, and another Muslim, Anis sahab. From his appearance, it was impossible to discern whether Anis sahab was Shia or Sunni; some even thought him a Hindu. Some believed him to be a communist, others a lapsed mullah. While his dress was Madrasi, his language was pure Urdu. He was a man of few words, but always smiling. This smile misled many into thinking that he was good-natured but those who had worked with him knew he had no sense of humour. He would often fly into a rage and the disaffection would last for weeks.

Trikha Ram received us very cordially, welcoming us with refreshing glasses of milk and water. Only then he asked us to introduce ourselves. I was about to reply when Anis sahab cut me short. He rattled off our names belligerently, as if throwing down the gauntlet to say, yes, these are Muslim names—what are you going to do about it? Gauntlet thrown, he shot me a triumphant glance and looked so ridiculous in the process that I could not restrain a smile.

Pretending as if nothing were amiss, Trikha Ram continued, 'Well, in any case, we are happy that you have graced us with your presence.

You see, the Jaitpur people are of our caste and *gotr*—our brethren. And you know how foolish and uneducated we villagers can be! How can we divine what the government really wants us to do? When the government announced that no Muslim was to live in India, we told our Muslim brothers, "Now that it has been decided that only Hindus can live in India, why don't you all become Hindus, so we don't lose each other?" Ehsan disagreed, "No, we cannot. If we lose our lives, that is our destiny. Let us leave for Pakistan."

'We all went to see them off till the village outskirts. At the orchard, we parted ways; our eyes were moist, as were Ehsan's. Now that you tell us that the government has given no such order, we are ready to do whatever Mahatmaji says. We will take our bullock carts to the camp and bring back all the families, including Ehsan's.'

When we went back to Ehsan with this news, he couldn't believe it. Sadly, he said, 'You have absolutely no idea of what we went through. Where is the option of return now?' I can now understand his predicament but we were less perceptive then. While his heart wanted nothing more than to return with his family and friends to Jaitpur, a deep sense of fear warned him against it. Whether deriving from mistaken beliefs or a lack of trust or the possibility of a forced conversion, he refused to return.

Some days later, I saw this respectable, proud landlord pleading with the camp commander to allow his wife to go to Nizamuddin for a few hours. She hadn't bathed or washed her hair for a month—her sense of privacy wouldn't allow her to wash herself in the open. However, the permission was not forthcoming.

Fed up of this miserable life, Ehsan was desperate to leave for Pakistan. Many of his friends had stayed in India—most of them relocating to different areas in UP—but that option was not available to him. He had sold all his farming equipment, and if he were to now return to his village or go to UP, it would take him at least six months to settle down. If he had to make a fresh beginning, why not in Pakistan? Many others thought the same but, as I shall narrate in later chapters, even this new beginning was not to be had so easily.

Besides the Jamia students, many young men were working in the camp. Among them was Zafar Khan. Assuming that he was from Jamia, I was ready to grant that he was a decent sort, though I didn't particularly like him as a person. Only later did I learn that he was in fact a sanctuary seeker who had slowly but surely inveigled himself into the camp's administration.

Around this time, the government began to suspect irregularities in the camp's functioning; ration supplies being consumed far exceeded the quantum expected, given the population. Suspecting that ration was being lifted by sanctuary seekers, in collusion with camp coordinators, the local administration conducted an inquiry. A magistrate, with several girls in tow, turned up to investigate. When I entered, the girls were in the tents and the magistrate outside, gathering statistics and tallying figures. It was only after I talked with him that I understood the ingenuity with which the inmates had defrauded the authorities, claiming rations for four inmates for every two. The three *chhatank*s of flour or rice distributed could not sate the healthy appetites of these strapping rustics. When volunteers, chaprasis and hospital staff kept a little extra for themselves, this was how they could meet their requirements.

The officials were brutal in their inspection, as if the inmates were criminals, as if they expected this merciless interrogation to bust a deep-seated conspiracy, unearth a cache of arms, detect a live bomb. How remote were sentiments like compassion and consideration in those days!

Zafar Khan, who had designated himself as ration in-charge, came to me fuming, 'This is completely beyond the pale! I've told the inmates that what is being done to you is unforgivable. We must refuse to take rations henceforth!' I thought he was blustering his way out of a tight spot and didn't pay further attention to his ranting. Little did I know that his intentions were mischievous and that this was just the preface to a strike that would assume alarming proportions in the days to come. On the brink of starvation, faces gaunt with hunger, their children listless, not one inmate accepted rations over the next three days. Jamia volunteers were desperate, unaware that this strike was the fruit of the misdeeds of one of their own colleagues.

Before my incredulous eyes, Zafar Khan grew to become the leader of the camp. Himself one of those who had stolen extra rations, he had become quite emboldened. (This Nawab without a realm was not so poor that he needed to live in the camp. Neither was his brother, who with his staff, had set up residence in a corner of the camp, for one reason alone—security.)

As the strike continued, the assistant commander, Ismail Patel, a diligent Jamia volunteer, sought the administration's assistance. The deputy commissioner was informed, the food ministry approached but no solution emerged, not one official responded with any sense of urgency. I made fresh attempts. I called Chief Commissioner Khursheed Ahmad Khan, to be told he was away. I rang Deputy Commissioner Randhawa, to learn he was resting. Called again later, when Sir was sunning himself. I telephoned the chief commissioner again and, wonder of wonders, got him at once. I apprised him of what had transpired. 'Really? Two days have gone by? I didn't even know this was happening.'

'Well, now you do. Please treat this as urgent or else deaths are inevitable.'

'Certainly, I will try for tomorrow itself.'

Morning came. The situation was unchanged. The secretary to the food minister was to come, but he couldn't find the time. The magistrate continued his investigation but hearing what had happened, left without further enquiry. The day went on. In the evening, when I could no longer ignore my anxiety, I ran to Bapu. Immediately, he had the food ministry notified and despatched Sushila with me. All this took some time and it was quite late before I could reach the camp. I found ration being measured out and distributed—in the interim, the food secretary had been to the camp and successfully persuaded the inmates to break their fast.

This incident convinced me that Zafar Khan was duplicitous but there was little I could do to exclude him. The problem was that the number of Jamia volunteers had shrunk. Some had left because college had reopened, some because of the monotonous work and some got involved in other voluntary work.

As December wore on, there were more newcomers, some in rather unusual circumstances. In all my forty-one years, I'd never had occasion to encounter the army or the police. The life I'd led had no part of the law or courts in it. Here, in the camp, I ran into both.

A man had been separated from his wife, because she was at her parents' when the attacks came. Now, all the Muslims in her village including her family, had been forcibly converted to Hinduism. Agitated by longing for her and spurred on by his parents and other villagers, he decided to wrest her back. He bribed the Dogra security guards to accompany him in a military truck to his wife's village to get her, as well as his brother's wife, back.

The deal was struck for Rs 200, and presently executed. However, just as the girls sat in the truck, the villagers found out and rushed to the spot, armed with lathis and spears. Two or three lathis found their mark, his brother's wife was snatched back, but the husband succeeded in carrying away his own wife.

All this was done with such stealth that none of us got any wind of it. So when the magistrate came looking for an abducted woman, we hadn't the faintest idea. The police also came, and a *thanedar* searched the camp. On the thanedar's second visit, he was accompanied by the girl's father, some zamindars and patwaris of the girl's village. He narrated the incident to me and said he was convinced that the girl was in the camp. All of us expressed ignorance, although we did ask whether this was really an issue that required involving the law. After all, which regulation forbade a husband from fetching his wife to be with him?

He replied, 'The girl is now a Hindu; her parents have converted. Her father reported the incident as abduction. Moreover, shots are reported to have been fired that night and that is certainly a law and order issue.'

'But how can a married daughter be considered to have changed her religion just because her father has? A father has no legal right to restrain his daughter thus. The girl's husband is a Muslim and though he kept asking his wife to come to him, the father did not let her go.' His reply was officious, 'But *janab*, the man went to get her in a military truck! That is a crime. And then he caused a riot and firing took place.'

Neither did I have complete details of the incident then, nor did I fathom the mischief that the police can get up to. Witness my imbecility—I was taken in so completely by thanedar sahab's assertions that I asked the inmates to produce the husband before the police. I told him, 'Now that you have involved me in these proceedings, I'll ensure that he is truthful. But you must also promise me that you will be lenient—these people have suffered tremendously.' He assured me, 'Of course, no question about that. Please summon him.'

I now realize that were it not for my intervention, thanedar sahab couldn't have ever laid his hands on the man. After hiding for a few days, he'd have been secretly sent off to Pakistan. Only in deference to me was the man produced at once. And on my reassurances, he confessed to everything—the money that changed hands, the blows that were exchanged—but vociferously disputed the involvement of guns. This was true—thanedar sahab had fabricated it to add weight to the charges.

I told the girl's father, 'Bade miyan, it is shameful that, at this venerable age, you tarnish your faith thus. Do you really want to compound this by sending your son-in-law to jail? How will you face Allah?' The old man began weeping copiously, tears of hopelessness and misery. The people of his clan and village kept up a steady stream of abuse at him. The daughter and her husband broke down too. The old man's tears revealed to us that the whole thing—police complaint, false reports of a shooting—was the mischief of the thanedar and *zila* administrator. Seeing the situation getting out of hand, the thanedar rose quickly, 'Come on, son, come with me.'

I said, 'What, surely you aren't going to arrest him now?'

'That is what the law requires.'

Furious, I burst out, 'And what an impressive system of law! Soldiers posted as security guards may leave their duty without permission, taking a military truck for unauthorized work, but your laws don't find them to be offenders. No, but the man who fetches his wife from her father's house is a criminal. You police officers intimidate the girl's father into making a false complaint about gunfire and rioting but neither you nor the people who attacked the couple are culprits! The husband took the guards along for his safety but the law doesn't accuse the soldiers who concealed this from their superiors! The person who pays them for their services is the only guilty party. All right, take him! I will see how you will prosecute him!'

The thanedar left with the boy. Tearfully, the girl's father told us how about fifty Muslims in his village, fearing for their lives, had started calling themselves Hindus. Within two days, I compiled a list of these people, and with the help of Police Superintendent Mr Button had them rescued and brought to the camp. Although the girl's father submitted that he had been pressurized to make a false complaint against his son-in-law, thanedar sahab succeeded in sending the husband to jail.

I interceded with a senior police officer, pleading for a resolution. He promised he would do so if the matter came before him, but I hadn't counted on the thanedar's pig-headedness—he kept the file with him for over a month. For that entire period, I had to bear the accusations of the man's wife and relatives. 'All this happened because of you,' they would cry, 'and you don't even care!' How were they to know how hard I tried, but the wily thanedar won, and I lost. Despondent, the family left for Pakistan shortly; as they left, they pleaded with me not to forget the man.

One day, news came that the thanedar had been shot dead. The man was released, stayed in camp for three months and left for Pakistan. The military people got away, no investigation was carried out. People continued to hire their services and trucks.

A completely different visitor to the camp was Majid, heir to a jeweller family of Paharganj, just back from Pakistan. A former Jamia student, Majid told me that he had returned in search of his family's riches. 'When we fled, we had to leave behind even the few possessions we had gathered in a hurry.' Two of his sisters were snatched—one was restored to them the very next day, thanks to Subhadra's efforts. The second sister was much more unfortunate; when her captors attempted to make her a Sikh, she committed suicide by shoving her head into an oven.

Although refugees now occupied this man's house, and most jewels and ornaments had been looted, there were still some secreted in a thieves' hole in a wall—he hoped to gain them through some ruse. Also safely stashed away somewhere else in the house were ornaments he himself had crafted for his sister.

This brave young man, clad in a khaddar *kurta-paijama*, denim bag on his shoulder, traipsed all over Paharganj and Karol Bagh in search of his family's former wealth. From the *pansari*s in the city lanes, he bought back his forebears' valuable jewellery designs, which had been earlier sold to them as scrap paper. In the dead of the night, he recovered his sister's jewellery from their former home. He didn't have the courage though to carry all these valuables to the airport by himself. He needed my help and I arranged for his safe transport. As he was leaving, I said, 'Seeing that you love Delhi so much, when things normalize, you will return, won't you?'

Sorrowfully, he shook his head, 'No, to return would be intolerable. In the 1857 rebellion, my ancestors were hanged at Khooni Darwaza. This time too, ten to twelve of my family perished. Our hardship will remain fresh in my memory for a long time. Luckily I had the time to slip some small packets of diamonds into my pocket else we would be staring at starvation. Those diamonds are my family's future—I will use them to make a set that will, I promise you, earn me the price of a shop.' I later learnt that this talented, artistic, industrious young man made his life in Karachi.

Then the carnage in princely states like Alwar, Patiala and Nabha began to send more sanctuary seekers into camps. I heard of the events from Alwar's sanctuary seekers in the camps in Gurgaon and Jama Masjid. They had only terrible tales to tell. All of them were like hunted animals. The ones in camps were the lucky few that escaped. The maharaja was the hunter, his army and the maddened *mobshi*s, predators. Together they snatched children from mothers' arms and hoisted them on pikes, dishonoured young girls before their parents, murdered husbands as wives looked on. In their barbarity, they spared nothing, nobody. Many members of the royal family, the ministers, the police and the army were all tainted; and who knows on how many backs the maharaja's hands paused in quiet encouragement:

rahi na tarz-e-sitam koi aasmaan ke liye
No manner of cruelty is left outstanding for the heavens
Mirza Ghalib

A girl from Alwar told me, 'When violence broke out, our maharaja addressed us, "You must not be afraid in the slightest. We promise we'll safeguard every person's honour, life and belongings. My only condition is that all of you hand over your weapons to my men." The people trusted him implicitly and surrendered even their knives. The next day, when mobs roamed the streets choosing victims to butcher, the maharaja left. There was no one to stop the killings, and looting continued for days on end.'

Pakistan has accused the Indian government of genocide, but as far as Delhi or other provinces of India are concerned, this is a false allegation. Jawaharlalji did everything he could to help the distressed. In fact, he was on the streets himself in those troubled days. With his associates and his daughter, he worked tirelessly for the victims' relief, rescue and safe transit. These were the people who condemned the violence, stopped the madness. And then there was Bapu, whose cries were heard the world over.

However, as far as princely states are concerned, undoubtedly genocide was attempted. In most families, all the men were slaughtered; even months-old boys were despatched. Girls were spared—how else would the men, from old widowers to adolescents, ever be wed, and the ancient custom of trafficking women be preserved? In the Garhmukteshwar riots, the massacring and looting were executed by mobs of youth from Punjab; the Muslim National Guard made rivers of blood flow in Rawalpindi and Multan; the 'feats of daring' that the young men of the RSS pulled off in East Punjab and in the principalities were all known to the government and the people; yet, only Allah can know why people did not come to their senses.

In the princely states, not only were common people murdered but also members of the council, highly ranked government officials, nobles and landowners. In Jind, the entire family of Bakhshi Suqutullah, adviser to the government, was massacred, save for a four-year-old girl. Why leave her alive? So that she could grow up and service the needs of some Sikh?

Fortunately, other officials of the Jind government managed to wrest her from the attackers and sent her to Delhi, where Lady Mountbatten and Rameshwari Nehru had her conveyed to her relative, Janab Khaleel Baghwale in Jama Masjid. The officials made the principality protect the child's inheritance and, some years later, Pandit Nehru himself had a sum of Rs 200 fixed as a monthly allowance for her. She must still receive the money.

Then came the Ajmer massacre. I'd heard Mirza Baig tell Bapu of the terrible events there, but got a fuller picture when I went myself in early January 1949. After journeying through the scorched villages and deserted areas of east Punjab and Alwar, Jaipur's tranquillity calmed my gaze. There was happiness here and light, and on every face, kindness and peace; in the way that people moved about, there was a freedom and joy, as if they had just celebrated a marriage. This city had been calm in December 1947 too, because of the maharaja's and *rajmata*'s efforts, and when waves of riots lapped at Ganganagar, just outside the borders, 'our Rajmata sat in her plane and flew over the town, asking us to seek shelter in her principality.' Now, in the whole principality, Hindus and Muslims lived in harmony.

But as soon as Jaipur was passed, from Kishangarh to Ajmer, again the same hushed landscape, the same emptiness, the same unease. In Ajmer, a full year after, humanity had yet to return. Every corner was crammed with people but once again, there were desecrated graveyards, ruined mosques, destroyed houses and the same fearful, cowering, insensible Muslims. Just a glimpse of Ajmer perturbed the beholder.

People I met in the city told me of the build-up to the riots of 25 December 1947—the quarrel that began over the gramophone on 5 December, the convention of wealthy and educated insurgents in Kishangarh a few days later, the partisanship of the officials, and then on 14 December, the burning of seven persons alive. The food supply and rationing department played a vital role; information about the city layout, accurate maps of the neighbourhoods where Muslims lived, their population and numbers of their men and women, even their names, were all provided by the rationing officer to the goons. This information proved crucial for the rioters to plan and sustain their assaults on a wider scale than elsewhere.

And then on 25 December, the massacre of 5,000 humans, the plunder of homes and belongings. I was told the mobs were really assault battalions, comprising inhabitants of seven villages each. Here too (like Delhi) was news that cannons had been used, but this time the rioters had pressed them into service. Here too, a wealthy landowner was said to have raised his sword and two large village communities forced to become Hindus. The fervour shown in these attacks by the brave Rajputs on these villages of 'Mughals' and 'Mirzais' befitted ancient battles. As did the cruelty—a landowner ordered the massacre of unarmed, captive Muslims, which was accomplished in a trice.

Talking to these people, seeing them quake with fear again, as they narrated these events and the train massacres at Narnaul, barely twenty kilometres from Ajmer, I was moved to pity. But that soon gave way to anger, when a young man told me how the Muslims lived in Ajmer today, more than a year later. After all this violence, the Muslims had shaved off their beards, cast aside their sherwanis. Policemen could ask them to remove their skullcaps whenever they wanted; the dargah was being starved, very rarely did goods intended for it reach it without interference.

'The limit of cowardice!' I exclaimed. 'How can you live in such humiliation? Delhi's Muslims still keep their beards, wear sherwanis and skullcaps too, whenever and wherever they wish to. Why have you people let yourself become so subjugated?'

The young man expressed his helplessness, yet I couldn't see him as a genuine claimant for sympathy. I can never believe that a human being can ever be so helpless. Neither am I well disposed to such subjection. No doubt that:

> *bandagi mein ghut ke reh jaati hai ik joo-e-kam aab*
> *aur azadi mein bahr-e-bekaraan hai zindagi*
> Constraint smothers the river of meagre water
> And in freedom is life an ocean without limits
>
> Mohammed Iqbal

It is we who search for—in fact are the progenitors of—this ocean without limits. In history, man has faced countless situations when he has had to eke out space to stand on paths narrower than the width of a single hair and sharper than the edge of a sword. If we are alive, and want to live, then whether someone accommodates us or not, we have to make a place for ourselves.

> *yaqeen muhkam, amal paiham, muhabbat fateh-e-alam*
> *jihad-e-zindagaani mein hain ye mardon ki shamsheerein*
> Unwavering faith, exemplary deeds, a love that conquers all
> In the jihad of life, these are the arms that Men bear
>
> Mohammed Iqbal

A corpse squad was especially deployed in Delhi during 1947–48 to pick up the corpses of riot victims littered around the city.

7

In the city
(December 1947–January 1948)

By end-December, a new problem was taking shape. If the first wave of Muslims fleeing Delhi had seen jewellers and cattle-grazers, numbers dwindled by massacres and murders, leave for Pakistan, it was now the turn of the silversmiths and artisans, who streamed into the camp. Every train that left carried away many more of them.

Delhi's businessmen fretted—if all craftsmen left, what would become of Delhi's famed handicraft industry? 'The workers who had washed the gold, laid the jewels, crafted such fine, delicate jewellery had all been Muslims. They made the jewellery, we sold it; that's how it was for centuries. They were also good tailors, and zardozi and *kamdani* embroidery was their skill. How can we ever supply the country as we used to?' Hoteliers and restaurateurs mourned their departed chefs, and the public finally noticed that most drivers and mechanics too had been from this community. Where Muslims were once seen as good-for-nothings, their worth was now coming to light.

The city's traders and businessmen also resented the Pakistani refugees, who had set up shacks on the footpath all along the market, hawking goods cheap. Shopkeepers of Chandni Chowk were incensed that the hawkers undercut them in prices. A shopkeeper once told me, 'Sahab, these Punjabis have completely destroyed our beautiful city. Unmannered, uncultured fellows! Until this day, kebabs were never sold in Chandni Chowk but look now, there are stalls selling them at every corner! At Fatehpuri and the Fountain, liquor is sold openly. These people stand around drinking brazenly and eating *chaat* and kebabs all day, and we have to pinch our noses when we pass by. Our women are imprisoned behind the strictest purdah and cannot move out at all. For a woman to go to the bazaar is to invite lewd remarks. What uncouth people they are!

'Just think of the effect on our children. You won't believe what I saw the other day—a comely young woman walking in Chandni Chowk, festooned with jewellery worth at least Rs 150–200, face shining with powder and lipstick plastered on, chewing on a long stick of sugarcane as she walked? Can there be any greater indecency?' His complaint was one generally heard from others of his ilk. These Jain traders, whose beliefs made them cover their mouths after 5 p.m. lest they harm even an insect, now had to live with these shameless carnivores in their midst. They could bear it no more.

The business community petitioned the government—do whatever is necessary, but stop this madness. One day, three gentlemen from the city honoured us with their presence. I didn't know any of them but hearing one introduce himself as '—of Berlin', I understood that this was the gentleman whose voice was recognized all over the world. The second was an aspiring Sajjada and the third a businessman. They sailed in and commanded us to summon representatives of the city and villages.

When the people gathered, the three began to harangue them boorishly about how they must return to the city. When one ill-humoured Hakim sahab raised his voice, 'Of Berlin' was enraged. No ordinary anger either—it displayed his entire oratory, punctuated by forceful hammerings of the table, and culminated in his marching off in disgust! There was much tension in the camp for a while after that.

The stream of people flowing into the camp would just not abate. The scarcity of tents, the ferocity of the winter and the sprightliness of pneumonia and small pox had rendered life intolerable; and the hospital was full. Outside the camp, there was constant commotion, thanks to the Dogra security guards, who demanded money of passers-by and took goods forcibly from shopkeepers without paying. As some inmates had set up small shops, buying goods with the little money they had and reselling them, the Dogras' antics were always a cause of tension.

Weary and dejected, I met Dr Hussain in Okhla and told him everything. He couldn't think of a solution either. The incoming were no longer the desperate, robbed, beaten, wounded, diseased destitutes of a few months earlier; these were people who had the time to sell their homes and gather their belongings before arriving at the camp. Neighbourhoods continued to empty out, and any talk of the possibility of returning to their homes was met with belligerence.

Dr Hussain said, 'I think it may be wiser for you to spend less time at the camp. There is no profit in exerting yourself so much for these people's comfort. Perhaps the inconveniences they will then experience may persuade them to return. Surely, that will be your greatest service to them.'

I spoke to Rafi bhai. He too said, 'If you can't bear to see it, don't. Why are these people coming at all? The government and administration ask them to stay, you suggest that they return, yet they come? They must fancy hardship.'

I persisted in my efforts. I knew it was the socio-economic boycott that Muslims faced in their homes and workplaces that had made their lives unliveable. I told Mahatmaji of the conditions in the camp, sent word to the health minister, asked the doctors to make urgent requests for additional beds and medicines and somehow managed to meet the deficits. At least there was enough for treatment to continue.

By this time, most Jamia boys I was close to had become disillusioned by the atmosphere of constant demand and complaint. Some returned to their studies; Shams and Qaisar went to the city, though they still visited the camp regularly. During one session, when they entertained me (and themselves) by recounting stories of their wilfulness, they suggested, 'Anis apa, we know that you too can no longer abide working here. Come to the city, work with us. Work is needed there, not here.'

Subhadra had been saying the same. While it's impossible to restore people to their homes from the camp, it is easier to prevent them from leaving, if we work in their neighbourhoods. Moreover, the greatest need is to keep the peace; without that, the camps will never close and stampedes to flee to Pakistan never stop.

I thought it over and decided that I should also start working in the city with Shams and Qaisar, who had set up base in a building in Bara Hindu Rao. By the end of December or early January, I began spending most of my time at the Bara and cut down my visits to the Humayun's Tomb camp to twice or three times a week. The base was in a building belonging to Rehmaniya School. Such a large place, with dozens of rooms, but its emptiness now keened a lament for both teachers and taught. Refugees circled the place, but Shams and Qaisar acted with great courage and determination. They shut themselves in and didn't stir out for weeks. Bands of refugees tried to break in, even a bomb was hurled, but nothing dented their steely resolve. Disciples of a mentor such as Dr Hussain, they would never give in, never retreat. They kept the door barred, drank copious amounts of tea to silence their growling stomachs, and stayed put.

Inspired by their courage, some other boys joined in, as did Jamia's scoutmaster, Ikhlas Ahmad Siddiqui. The first step was to gain the children's confidence. The Jamia boys joined in their street games, and to win over the children in no time at all was Ikhlas sahab's special talent and amusement. In four days, the number grew to twelve. The first time I went, Ikhlas was lounging on a chair watching them play. Though the locality's Muslims were too scared to venture out of their houses, though the refugees, who had settled in many houses all around, thought us enemies, the children came to our aid by sneaking out of their homes to play at ours.

The Jamia boys told me to spread the message of peace and harmony in the neighbourhood. 'Reassure the Muslims, gain the refugees' confidence. Make all of them send their children to us. When Hindu and Muslim children gather in one place, amity will naturally follow—the cycle of accusation and recriminations will be broken.' Following the counsel of these astute young men, I began my rounds of the locality, alone or with Subhadra. I met many people; I addressed them in small groups and urged them not to lose hope, to find the means to help themselves.

My appeals usually engendered an outraged uproar, particularly in the women. Their shouts of anger and protest would bring the house down. Some would pull down their veils and stomp out, muttering curses; others would quarrel: 'If it had happened to you, you would know! If your children had been killed, your family uprooted, your home looted, your husband killed, then you would know the pain!' But I no longer felt any anger at their words. I don't know where my rage and indignation went. At times, I was amazed at myself—I was never so calm and sensible before.

By mid-January, signboards announcing Bachchon ka Ghar (Children's Home), an orphanage, Markaz-e-Ittehad-o-Taraqqi (Centre for Unity and Progress), and Shanti Dal (Peace Corps) adorned Rehmaniya School's gate, and I came to spend the better part of my days in the activities of these three rooms.

On the initiative of the Congress labour section, all those working in the area for peace had joined to form Shanti Dal. Dominated by socialists, it used all means—baton, gun, impassioned appeal—to preserve amity. In these dangerous times, progressive young Hindu and Muslim men, setting aside issues of party loyalty and ideology, had united for a common objective. (Another such group was working in far more dangerous parts of the city, its members primarily communists and socialists and some heroes from the Kakori case and the armed forces. It had been active from the very beginning of the violence. In September and October I interacted with many of them and learned of the situation in the city from their eyewitness accounts. The late Chaudhary Basheer Jung was also in this group. When peace came, he dropped out of sight for long periods and surfaced once every one or two years.)

The Markaz-e-Ittehad-o-Taraqqi took birth in a congregation of Indian Muslims in Lucknow, under Maulana Azad's leadership. Formed to address the fear and disquiet plaguing Muslims, it planned to constitute units across the country. On Maulana sahab's instructions, its signboard was posted at the entrance of a large house near Jama Masjid; a famous writer and a former pro-Nazi orator were put in charge.

Where did the Markaz-e-Ittehad-o-Taraqqi implement its programme of action? Who were its other functionaries, leaders, volunteers? How successful was it? Not questions that I can answer. What I do know is that the two notables at the helm fell out over where the furniture was to be purchased from, which room allotted for which work. And the issue that caused the greatest discord was where the chaprasis would sleep at night—in the premises or in their homes? One a writer, the other an orator; one a Congressi, the other a Nazi—the battle of ethical beliefs was no less than a clash of world views and ended only when one of the two packed up bedding and flounced off!

The only place I know where the organization really worked was Bara Hindu Rao, where Jamia students adopted this cause as their own. For these young men, the fact that the prospects were unknown, the results uncertain mattered not in the slightest:

> kas na danist ki manzil gaah-e-mashooq kuja ast
> i kadar hast ki baang e jarse mee ayad
> Who can tell where the intended destination lies
> It is just the rumblings of a distant caravan that can be heard
>> Hafiz Shirazi

What they knew was that the present could not be borne. These young discontents did not want to shut out the moans that haunted them; rather, attending to them, they wished to bring succour. And they didn't rue the fall of so many tall, shady trees. Steering a route that left them unmarked by the heaving politics of the time, they sought and found a place of well-being to begin their work. These talented gardeners had resolved to plant saplings for a new tomorrow; these conscientious workers were determined to lay new bricks at the foundation of a new nation.

Temporary school at the refugee home for children at Ram Bagh, Delhi.

Readers might perceive their capture of Rehmaniya School headstrong and imprudent, but these were young men whose intent was to rent the darkness to draw the bright morning light to us all. They believed that the moribund social order must be trampled underfoot if a new world was to be ushered in. Laying blame on the British could never mitigate the reality of all that had occurred nor salve the wounds that had been inflicted. While political manipulations— these skilful manoeuvres of pieces on a chessboard— may well plaster and level this teetering wall of the nation, shore it up for a while, they would not fortify its sagging foundations forever.

Outside our building, the Markaz-e-Ittehad-o-Taraqqi signboard survived for two months and our work for unity and progress was carried out in its name. We soon found ourselves in a position to replace it with Markaz-e-Talim-o-Taraqqi (Centre for Education and Progress). This was an educational programme launched by Shafiq-ur-Rahman Kidwai, under the Jamia Millia, just before the violence. Although only one centre in Karol Bagh had been opened, the programme had been successful. Besides a school for children, the programme had done commendable work with neo-literates and prepared pedagogical literature.

Congress members will never acknowledge these young men's role in establishing peace. How could they? They were never around to witness what the boys accomplished. For all I know, the Congressis may have been in Birla House, Government House, even the Provincial Congress office—all I can say truthfully is that no Congressi was found in the troubled bylanes of Karol Bagh.

Except for Subhadra, who was then a member of the Congress Provincial Committee. That chit of a girl, blessed with an acute sensitivity to the horrors lying ahead was intent on ensuring lasting peace. This adoring disciple of Gandhiji (but whose heart rebelled against the notion of ahimsa) had roamed the city day and night since September in this effort. Dragging out old veterans of the struggle from their homes, she made them work in Shanti Dal. Such was the force of her personality that even the Sangh and the League were not spared. Their members had to join in to keep the peace; in fact, she would make them stand guard all night long in Muslim localities!

Although Subhadra was fully aware that this did not stop these individuals from clandestinely sowing trouble, she knew that they were the right people for the job. She laughed at their dissembling and exploited it. How ready man is to grovel before authority! How opportunistic! Just the fear that Subhadra had access to Bapu and the prime minister persuaded the most inflexible. Many others agreed because they could clearly see that the government was intent on saving Muslim lives, rationalizing that in these altered circumstances, they were needed to help. So even those whose hearts and minds were still reactionary joined Shanti Dal, as did those whose cowardice and selfishness had led them to be 'neutral' in September.

As December wore on, we were happy to see quite a few Muslims muster up the courage to visit us. They were emboldened by, quite incredibly, the spirit of their children, who would praise our efforts to their parents when they returned home.

Yet, horrific murders still took place every other day in the city. The Bara Hindu Rao neighbourhood was in the grip of another crisis— middle-class and affluent Muslims were steadily packing up and leaving. Selling or leasing out houses and shops, they fled, compounding the miseries of the poor. Every time a businessman sold his property or leased it out against thousands of rupees of surety, refugees took over. The new neighbour's aggression, high-handedness and muscle would force ten of his Muslim neighbours to quietly move out of their homes. And when bands of refugees laid siege to a neighbourhood, the remaining terrorized Muslim residents had to flee for fear of their lives. For many, this was a second displacement, as the September–October riots had driven them to the Muslim-majority neighbourhoods in the first place. In November, when Bapu and the prime minister were apprised, they had these neighbourhoods identified as 'Muslim Zones', where evacuee property could be handed over only to Muslims.

The Shanti Dal called for a large peace meeting in the neighbourhood. Only about 200 people showed up. Many of them spoke about the adversity they lived in, the economic difficulties caused by the closure of mills and workshops, and the constant dread that plagued them. Shams gave an impassioned speech, addressing the better-off sections of the crowd: 'Just give us a few weeks to try and turn things around. Peace is beginning to prevail. We will redouble our efforts and the situation will improve. You must do this for us!' With the general public, he pleaded, 'You also must let your children come to us. For many months, their studies have been interrupted, and they idle away their days loitering and quarrelling. We are drawing up a programme for their education and their play—send them to us!'

One gentleman rose to respond. After lambasting the Congress leadership and its workers, he said, 'All right, we are ready to wait for two weeks but only on the assurance that if peace is not established by then, Begum Kidwai and Maulana Azad will also leave with us for Pakistan. I state with complete confidence—the Muslim no longer has a place in this country. The government does not want him here any more. It wants Muslims out of Delhi, because its design is the establishment of a Hindu Raj. Well, we Muslims don't want to live here either!' A long tirade on the government's injustices ensued; he spoke of the brutality and partiality of the administration, the police and the army, and the hostility and violence that Muslims had faced in their neighbourhoods.

His demagoguery had struck a sympathetic chord in many embittered hearts, so I had to respond. 'My esteemed predecessor has spoken passionately, invoking the Quran and the Hadis, referring to the legacies of being Muslim in India, singing to the tune of "my father is the king" to make his point. All I ask now is this: Show me one line in the Quran Sharif that enjoins a Muslim to run, and keep on running, when someone throws him out of his home, plunders his belongings and attacks him? In my own humble understanding, no such divine injunction exists. On the contrary, whatever I have read and understood is that a Muslim must challenge the denial of his rights, be steadfast in battle and may seek the help of Allah in this struggle. So, my brother, if you can show me even a single line to the contrary, I will gladly leave for Pakistan!

'Regretfully, neither is my brother's wish that Maulana Azad—his fellow Muslim and India's minister—accompany him to Pakistan likely to be fulfilled. It is useless to nurture any hopes of that gentleman—he wants to live and die here, in his country and for its glory. And for what reason should he run? It isn't as if there is death only here, not elsewhere. His faith tells him that death will come at its appointed time in every narrative of this world.

'But all these are great people and perhaps lesser ones like myself would find it difficult to keep the faith with such conviction. But even I—and this is what my Pir Gandhiji has taught me—prefer a death with dignity in my own home a thousand times over to a death by cholera in the camp, or swords of marauders on the train carrying me to Pakistan, or by bullets of soldiers or policemen, or the lingering death brought about by starvation while begging on Lahore's streets.

'Moreover, I am not here to tell you that the government is on your side. You are right, my dear sir, there is death, danger. However, if you are a Muslim, trust in God, else do not utter the name of Islam. I call you not to life but to an honourable death; my invitation is not to violence and hatred, but to ahimsa and love. Won't you answer Bapu's call? Isn't this all God's vengeance? How can you hope to escape? Wherever you go, it will surround you. Far better to submit to Allah's will. If your time isn't up, no man can end it. Meet this misfortune with courage, with spirit.'

By God's grace, my words found a place in people's hearts and the disquiet abated. The reins of the neighbourhood passed into the hands of the Congress Committee, Shanti Dal and the Markaz. From then on, scores of problems were brought to us daily, dozens applied for help and our young men ran around attending to them. We were already short of hands—and hadn't made any inroads into the refugees yet, though many of their children, including some former students of Jamia School, came to play at the school.

I mentioned this dearth of volunteers to Dr Saifuddin Kitchlew, an important Congress leader from Punjab who had recently come to Delhi to meet Gandhiji. Forced to flee Amritsar after the violence, he had met with cruel treatment at the hands of Muslims in Lahore; now, tormented by his own and troubled by strangers, bereft of home and belongings, he was a guest in our home.

Although Dr Kitchlew had resolved to live a quiet life, this resolve would be broken often. He was still a beloved leader of Punjabis in Delhi and tens of young Sikh and Hindu visitors—many of them young men and women—visited him daily. Hearing my problem, he immediately promised help. Some days later, eight students from the International Students' Congress joined us. The Congress government had recently announced that any college student doing social service for three months would automatically be eligible to write the examinations, so their involvement was not going to hamper their studies. These young men and women worked hard at running the schools and as a result we could make inroads into the refugee population.

As January began, there was marked improvement in the acceptance of our efforts. In the front-facing room of the Markaz, where we kept newspapers and magazines, there was a constant traffic of people. Each of us was approached more often by people for help; it appeared that the question of community and religion was receding. Muslims would come to the Markaz with a greater air of cheer, trust and interest. The refugees happily enrolled their children and the women, in particular, would frequent our premises. They would speak frankly, it appeared that they now thought of us as their own.

At times, however, when they recounted what they had suffered, their faces would flush with anger and grief. To which I would always say, 'Those who did that to you are enemies of humanity, your enemies and my enemies, irrespective of religion. We see them as the primary adversary, for they have forsaken God, plundered the country and left it a wilderness, slain humanity so bestiality may thrive.' At this, the aggression would leave them and our interaction would revert to its friendly manner. When I shot an arrow of love into an embittered heart, and saw flushed faces relax into a smile, it was as if all the world's riches were mine!

A resolute young Sikh refugee, Trilok Singh, became very dear to us. He had lost his father in the violence but a purer heart could not have been found. Intelligent and energetic, he was soon entrusted with all the work that other volunteers were reluctant to do. Shams was a bit of a philosopher, so Trilok did the accounts, administration, planning, budgeting and implementation. Qaisar was a strangely uninhibited sort, wise in matters of work, but childlike in deportment. No wonder he was the most beloved teacher of all children—all riotous play, festivity and madcap activity was implemented in his sponsorship!

As Scoutmaster Ikhlas sahab had left for Pakistan, the training of the new teacher recruits was done by Jamia teachers and teacher-trainees from Okhla. The new recruits included many refugee girls, who had been studying for their intermediate, matriculation, or graduation before the violence. Trilok was a teacher too.

I can still see Mr Banarsi, his thin frame parked at the table, engaged in intellectual and political discussion, or in initialling diaries of his Congress party colleagues. He was the party secretary, and since the Congress had mandated that its members do relief work, his signatures were required. Not that his cronies did much work—every morning they would bathe, doll up and stroll over to our building. Occasionally, I would ask him to run across to a village on his cycle to check whether all was well; he would always return to announce that he had (once again) gotten into a fight.

The school's activities increased. Qaisar decided that wall newspapers, posters and children's newspapers should be added to our activities, and organized the children to do so. Harmesh, Jabbar and others would work under Qaisar's direction and when the items were ready, Shams would display the exhibits in an ordered fashion. He was the director and all children and volunteers his workers and chaprasis. And I? I was the mother to all of them.

One day, Savitry Bhargava and Sucheta Kripalani visited the school. Both were delighted by its functioning; Savitry was surprised to find refugee children studying with Muslim children. Feeling that this should be replicated, she suggested a further step—exchange of gifts and sweets between Hindu and Muslim children. It was a good idea, and Savitry and I decided to begin the very next day with the temporary camp set up for Hindu refugees at Wavell Canteen. We planned to take the children from our school with us; however, the conditions were so fraught with danger the next day that my heart simply didn't permit me to expose the children. We set off alone.

Wavell Canteen was a short-stay camp, where refugees coming off the trains were lodged for a few days before being moved into houses in the villages or the city. What we saw when we reached there was a jungle of thousands of destitute Hindu and Sikh men, women and children living on the ground. Hundreds of children, condemned to the life of drifters by unspeakable barbarity, were wandering all over this sorry place. How correct their mothers were when they said, 'Even slavery would have been better than this. At least we would have had a home to hide in, where our children would be safe! At least we would have a modicum of dignity! What freedom is this that condemns us to wander the streets?'

Savitry and I met the manager, who greeted our proposal with enthusiasm. He arranged at once for the children to be seated in rows, piled the fruit we had brought on to a table and asked us to distribute. I addressed the children first: 'I have come to you on behalf of those Muslim children who are sweet and innocent just like you, who don't want to quarrel with you. They have sent me to give you their love and to say that they want to be your friends. They have told me to say, "Your parents and our parents are horrid people—they quarrel, they

Children at meals at Lahore Shed displaced women's shelter.

beat each other, they expel us from our homes. But we are all children, and children are never Hindu or Muslim. We want to be united with you, to be children with you, to play with you!"' The children of Wavell Canteen surprised me with their happiness at my words. Overjoyed, they said, 'We too want to play with them. We want to meet them and make them our brothers.'

In December and January, I still went to the camp regularly every three or four days. The conditions were still bad, if not worse, and I was particularly struck by the lot of government and institutional employees found there. I simply could not understand how Muslims of every government department, every hospital could be so summarily asked to leave. Many inmates now had no desire to go to Pakistan— they were eager to return to their former jobs.

As soon as the riots had started, the Muslim staff of Lady Hardinge Hospital had been sent to the camp. Many of them were desperate to rejoin work, their salaries were due, their belongings were there. Dispensary superintendent of Zenana Medical College, Mohammed Hussain, had completed fifteen or sixteen years of service. At first, when he was sent away, he believed that his matron had done so out of concern for his safety and would recall him after the trouble was over. But that was four months ago. Having written scores of letters, without response, he was now fed up.

He requested me, 'Can you please intervene? I am just stuck here. If, as you say, there is no government order that says that Muslims must not be employed, then why aren't we being called back to our jobs? Why should I have to go to Pakistan?'

At the hospital, everyone knew him and said that he was a fine man, a trusted employee—yet no one had thought of recalling him. I asked Dr Sarwat Ara to intercede with the authorities but she expressed her helplessness, 'My intercession will be useless.' I then met the matron and gave her his greetings. Delighted, she asked with enthusiasm, 'Oh, Mohammed Hussain is still here? Hasn't he gone to Pakistan yet? Is he well?' I replied, 'He is very unhappy. He wants to return to the hospital. Will you permit him? His belongings are still here, so can he just come back to work.' Hastily, she replied, 'No, no! Just give him my regards. I will get his stuff out right away, so you can take it back with you.'

Ultimately, Mohammed Hussain had to accept Pakistan. The date of departure remained undecided for long; why should this government servant of so many years leave without his Provident Fund? Under the guidance of the camp commander and doctors, he wrote many letters but no reply ever came. Word was sent to the health minister and he himself postponed his departure repeatedly. Nothing worked and finally, in March, he left. Perhaps he received the money later.

In every profession, it was the same sorry tale. Those who had opted for Pakistan as their place of service naturally left, but even those who had asked for India were hounded out. I recall a gentleman, a sanctuary seeker in Okhla, who had been a high-ranked employee of the post and telegraph department. He stayed on for long, waiting for the day when he could return to work; I think he held nationalist views. But whenever he went for a walk in the neighbourhood, passers-by would taunt, 'Oh, you haven't gone to Pakistan yet? Come, we will send you.' Finally, he mustered up the courage and went to office one day. His boss spoke frankly, 'Things are still very bad. Please don't come to the office.'

Given this general atmosphere, we were surprised to hear the praises that Delhi Cloth Mill (DCM) workers heaped on their management. They came into the camp by the truckload but all of them were happy to go to Pakistan. Apparently, when two Muslim workers had been killed outside the mill gates, the management decided that all Muslim workers should be relocated to work in their Lyallpur mill in Pakistan. The Delhi manager accompanied the workers to the camp because the Muslims did not have the necessary papers for admission. A man of exemplary conduct, he told us that they planned to call the Hindu workers from Lyallpur to work in Delhi. It seemed like a good plan but I couldn't bring myself to trust him. To this day, I rue suspecting his intentions, but the times were such that we were inclined to be sceptical of anyone who professed good intentions.

Fifteen days passed, during which this latest group was forced to live in the courtyard because of shortage of space, and there was no sign of departure. The DCM workers were now at the end of their tether. Coincidentally, no one from the management had visited them for a few days. We had not been able to garner tents for them and made desperate by the squalid conditions—their children ill their women upset—the workers now began to be as suspicious as I was. Some days later, I mentioned the sorry state of these workers to Bapu; immediately, he asked his secretary to call up the DCM people. The very next day, I saw beaming faces. They told me that their manager had come and assured them that they would be off to Pakistan shortly.

This was perhaps the only convoy that bade farewell to India happily, without recrimination and with confidence, as they believed their future to be secure. On their lips were praise and prayers for the mill owners' generosity and prosperity.

How different from the sorry tale of Birla Mill employees. By now, all of Delhi knew how Birla Mill had been transformed into a slaughterhouse, a haven for murderers. The honourable behaviour of the DCM management was a lesson that there were still some decent people left in the world.

So many government employees—schoolteachers, police personnel, high-ranked officers—in January 1948 didn't know what to do next. There were deep differences in the Cabinet on the question of a secular Indian state, which is why official statements never came out clean on the matter. In this atmosphere of equivocal statements, obstructionist administration and inexplicable governance, it was only Bapu who reiterated, 'India is for everyone. All religions have a place here. If we don't think of every man as our brother, this country will never prosper.'

Gandhi's physician, Sushila Nayyar, grieving over his dead body.

8

Action and reaction
(December 1947–January 1948)

And then, Gandhiji began his fast. What a calamitous month January was! So much took place. All the forces that had been ground into submission by misfortune, all those that had bowed their heads before Evil, all those that had been straining for release from its stranglehold, burst forth into free expression. Where until then:

> *takhreeb ne parcham khole the*
> *dam tod raheen thi taamirein*
> Destruction had unfurled its pennants
> The edifices had begun to decay

Josh Malihabadi

Humanity began to struggle out from the debris, forces of reconstruction began to consolidate. Truth turned in every breast, anguished love rushed out and the goddess of peace broke free of the grip of the demon of hatred.

Although it has been just a year since the fast, people already ask, 'What did Gandhiji's fast accomplish? It made no difference and he lost his life in the bargain.' How was I to make those eyes see that didn't wish to perceive the truth? I witnessed the surge that cut through the city on the first day. When we left Birla House and reached the city, we saw the people's demeanour changed drastically—repentance in every bowed head, each eye moist, the only subject that Bapu was on a fast.

The worst off were our Congressi brothers; they had recently strayed far from Bapu's teachings. Their expressions of sympathy had been so false that the very foundations of honesty and compassion had been challenged. They first stoked the fires of retribution and their debasement caused Bapu the greatest grief. He had expected that these people he had so carefully nurtured, they would stay steadfast as mountains, their steps unfaltering, and, if need arose, they would dive into the tempestuous river to rescue humanity. But it was they who first strangled justice, truth, love. That noble boatman had to accept that those intent on sinking the ship were not only looters and lunatics but some of his own too. When Bapu undertook this fast, our Congressi friends realized what they had done. Stung by God, they lived in the fear that their names would be among those responsible for his death. The dead rose from the graves. Sluggish consciences reawoke. Each person stood up to be counted, leaving home to work on new schemes to stem the tide.

On the first day, on our way back from the prayer meeting, Subhadra and I decided to tour the city. Our hearts were still bleeding and we discussed what was to be done. Just as we drove past the Idgah on Kassabpura Road, we saw a truck full of people's belongings leaving. Another was being loaded, women and children about to get on. I remarked, 'Looks like yet another neighbourhood is being abandoned today.'

'Yes, unfortunately. Shall we try and stop them?'

'Certainly,' I said. There wasn't space for even a sesame seed in the camp! Thousands of rustics had made their way to it already and if another 3,000–4,000 landed up, there would be chaos. How many more could the camp sustain? Subhadra stopped the jeep. She was immediately recognized and the gathering approached us and told us that they had decided to leave India. 'For four months, we have been locked up in our homes, lived in great difficulties. None of us has work and we have exhausted all our savings. In desperation, we have decided to migrate to Pakistan. You see we sell cow and goat meat and skins for our livelihood. The atmosphere is so tense that we are prevented from selling goat meat, on the suspicion that it is beef. Two or three men from our community have been killed and refugees in the neighbourhood make it difficult for us to move around. We are prisoners in this lane.'

I thought to myself, so they are also coming to camp—to spend nights under a sheet for a tent, to be hemmed in by pneumonia and fever, half to die here, some more in the stampede to board the train, some to separate from children, some to lose wives. As for their belongings, some will be sold in the camp for sustenance, some snatched by the police, some looted by dacoits when the train passes through East Punjab. And when they reach Lahore, the same cold, sorrows, police, goons—the scenes played out before me. These healthy young men, sturdy women, old men of steadfast faith—they will all call for death in their torment and crave for each grain entering their mouths. Leaving their two-storeyed houses for tents, they will dog us like beggars, leave no way for us to move around, until we too succumb to exasperation and shoo them away.

We sincerely appealed to them to return to their homes. Reasoning with them, we said, 'He who cares the most for all the wronged, our beloved Bapu, is still alive. We have just come from Birla House, where Bapu has staked his life for the return of amity to Delhi. Help us maintain the peace. By fleeing your homes, you spread insecurity. Does Bapu's life not matter to you? Strengthen our hands so we can stand before him and say, "Delhi is peaceful now. The Muslims no longer flee their homes, neighbourhoods are at peace." You're a brave community, so be courageous and meet these adversities like men. Cowards die a thousand times, braves only once. We promise the situation will change soon. Believe us that the government does not want anybody to leave or be killed.'

Both Subhadra and I promised that arrangements for their security and assistance would be put in place. At this they softened, but pointed out that the first truck had already left. Their relatives needed to be informed immediately, lest they set off to Pakistan. We agreed though we knew it would be tough. Relying on Allah to get us out of this one, we promised to get them back that very day. They fetched their bundles, trunks and belongings off the truck, and walked back.

The Muslims we had persuaded lived in the heart of the area and refugees had settled in all three outward-facing rows of quarters. Unknown to us, they had followed the whole sequence of events closely. At first, we glimpsed some heads peeping out, heard some raised voices, but when the Muslims started walking back, the refugees could no longer contain their anger. Pouring into the street, they ran at us. The situation could quickly get out of hand—I said we should leave immediately. Hardly had Subhadra gripped the steering wheel that the crowd was upon us. Surrounded at once, we were worried—how to calm this maddened crowd? Subhadra had been in every conceivable tight spot before and had Gandhiji's training, so she was quite an old hand. However, for me, this was a first and I thank God for keeping me in my senses and my courage intact. We explained to them, Subhadra speaking in Punjabi, 'Don't think of what has happened here as enmity. Consider the depth of the grief you feel and measure the grief of others by it.'

We also urged them to think of Gandhiji. 'Don't do anything that will endanger his life. Work with us for a peace in which not only do you gain a house, but no house-owner is rendered homeless.' But they wouldn't listen. The men shouted loudly, the women cursed. Occasionally a man detached himself from the group and moved towards us threateningly, but then retreated. 'Let the old man die! What did he ever do for us? Didn't many of ours perish? What difference can one more make?'

Mistaking Subhadra for Jawaharlal's daughter, a shower of invectives was hurled at Panditji. Some asked me, 'Who are you?'

I said, 'An ordinary worker, a volunteer.'

'No, tell us your name.'

My reply—Mrs Shafi—struck them dumb. One thrust his head through the window, 'What, you are a Muslim?' I could only laugh as I confirmed their suspicion.

'How dare you come here? Your Pakistanis are the ones who tore apart our homes and our lives, killed our children, dishonoured our women!' Hearing the detested word Muslim had refreshed their ordeal.

I tried to reason, 'Dear sir, the Pakistanis were never mine, always yours—your neighbours, your friends, your companions over centuries. If there is any cruelty that my people here have committed on you, then accuse us. If any Hindu or Muslim from here has troubled you, then revenge yourself on us. Give us some time to sort things out—all your clamour won't let us even begin to solve the problem.'

But who was listening? The screaming continued. In hindsight, I am amazed that knives and kirpans weren't brandished. The situation was delicate and we had to calm things down somehow, establish civility. In the crowd, there was clearly one rabble-rouser, scurrying between groups of women and men to egg them on. Some distance away stood another Sikh, watching the mayhem, not participating. He looked educated and Subhadra cleverly drew him into the fray, 'Sardarji, you look like a very sensible person. These people won't understand us. Can we speak to you?'

He approached and I said, 'Please explain to them the stupidity of what they are doing. Whether Muslims stay or leave, how can this possibly alter the inhuman conditions you are living in? Wouldn't it be better for all of you to live as brothers, supporting each other through good times and bad? India is such a big country, it can easily contain both of us. We can coexist in peace and prosperity.

'Bapu has started his fast just today for this reason. It is a misperception if they think his fast is for Muslims alone; no, he is on a fast unto death so that man becomes man again, so that good days return. The sins that Hindus and Muslims have committed are truly shameful but do we want them repeated? Please make them understand!'

Flattered by our compliments, Sardarji immediately berated the crowd. Some young boys and girls approached me to talk. When I said that we were in search of young people who would help us build a new India full of peace and appealed to them to join, they readily agreed, 'That is exactly what we want to do. But who gives us the opportunity?' Happy at their willingness, I said, 'I'll come tomorrow to your houses, alone. If you wish, you can kill me, but I will come alone to prove that I think of you as neither my enemy nor aliens.' A young girl put her arms around me, 'What are you saying, Mataji? Why will we kill you? Please do come to our house!'

Meanwhile, Subhadra was dealing with the women, who were clutching at her sari, not letting her start the car. She reasoned and sympathized with them and once Sardarji intervened, I nudged her and Subhadra flew us away from the place.

However, we had one more thing to do before leaving—ensure a security presence in the neighbourhood, to prevent a clash between the groups. The Congress and Jamiat had arranged for a special police force for the security of residents; this force worked under the supervision of a small committee of special magistrates. We drove to a nearby neighbourhood and asked for two guards to accompany us back. Dropping them a few metres shy of the quarters, without tarrying for even a few minutes, we sped off towards Humayun's Tomb to catch up with the truck of departing Muslims.

The Humayun's Tomb camp was more populated than usual those days. We reached in time to catch the first truck of Kassabpura residents; they had set up camp under the open sky, clutching their belongings to their breasts. We told them what had transpired and urged them to return home where their friends and relatives waited for them. Many were hesitant and some downright terrified to return.

Disquiet pervaded the atmosphere. One Hakim sahab, clearly sympathetic to the Muslim League, rose to reprimand me, 'You can certainly tell people to return but will anyone raise a voice against the government, which has engineered the massacre of Muslims by its security forces? This India will perish! What place can a Muslim have in a Hindu Rashtra? Stay if you want, but you will have to become a Hindu. I certainly won't!'

I responded sharply; many bitter words were exchanged between us. Hakim sahab gave a long, angry speech, swaying over many. Some sanctuary seekers asked me about Bapu. On hearing that Bapu had vowed not to end his fast until peace prevailed, even at the cost of his life, eyes moistened. I appealed to them to return home and live in peace with the refugees; this would save Bapu's life—our nation's greatest wealth.

My words had a profound impact on many of the Kassabpura people. They said if Bapu was ready to make even the ultimate sacrifice, the least they could do was to return, whatever happened. Many shouldered their precious belongings and began to walk, some went off to look for lorries and *tanga*s. Ultimately, barring a handful, all of them returned home.

A process was thus initiated, though Delhi itself was hardly safe yet. Every day in Delhi, four to six persons would be marked for death by the blades of valiants; that day itself, three murders had been perpetrated. Just a few days ago, a particularly frightening incident had occurred: some people were returning home from the camp in a tanga, when they were ambushed by a gang of Sikhs. Not only were their possessions looted, but the people and the tangewala were stabbed repeatedly. With the tangewala too injured, the horse galloped back to camp, bearing the bodies bathed in blood.

Reports like these made the sanctuary seekers even more fearful of returning. The assurance of a police guard was no guarantee. In fact, in most cases, if a neighbourhood came under police watch, it was bound to become uninhabited very shortly. In these times, it would be victims' relatives rather than murderers' relatives, who would be arrested, and the person who reported the crime more likely to be behind bars. (But don't take this to indicate that the entire administration was equally compromised, or that this lawlessness was a reality for Muslims alone; this mulishness was equally arraigned against the Congress leadership and even Bapu himself.)

Such terrible circumstances—no assured egress, but no sanctuary either—and despair had people in its grip. But Bapu was on a fast, so sanctuary seekers were moved, and as they realized that they had no real options, they began to return to their homes.

Efforts to hasten the pace of return gathered force. Congress Provincial Committee members and other workers visited the camp regularly. Vehicles with loudspeakers toured the camp, exhorting people to return to their homes, much to the discomfiture of the officials, who had been congratulating themselves on the admirable progress in ridding Delhi of these loathsome '*mussalmantas*'! Complete victory had been so near—just one part of the city still infested—but then Gandhiji created this chaos.

Seeing things turn around so fast, the Muslim Leaguers were dumbfounded. They had so wanted to prove that India was intent on genocide, on giving final form to the vision of a Hindu Rashtra, so they could crow, 'All this talk of democracy is a sham! See, not even a single Muslim family is to be tolerated in this city of Delhi, the capital of "Hindu"-stan!' But now, alas, they could say nothing!

The day after the Kassabpura people returned home, Subhadra hired numerous tangas, pushcarts and lorries, gathered children from different neighbourhoods, piled them on to the vehicles (as usual Qaisar was their commander-in-chief) and despatched them to spread the message of peace far and wide. On every child's lips were slogans— 'Save Bapu', 'Hindus and Muslims are brothers', 'Hindus and Muslims unite'! Not an inch of the city was left uncovered. Through their songs and poems, Bapu's message jolted people—they arose at last!

The children's feat will remain in my memory forever. When peace, love and truth appeared to no longer have an abode in Delhi, and Bapu had to stake his life on this chessboard of human existence, Nature rushed to his aid in the form of these pure children. It was as if the earth and the heavens had yielded up children that day, thousands swarmed into the streets, shouting slogans, challenging evil, exhorting the city to preserve not Bapu's life but humans and humanity itself. Primordial innocence was seeking truth and honesty, and its quest was to gather again the threads of kindness and sympathy, to rent the curtain of darkness, to bring forth the sun's rays. Standing back, watching, I wondered—how did this innocence survive all the assaults?

Within three days, Delhi was transformed. After day two, the murders stopped. Not a person was even stabbed. No one ran, injured and clutching his belongings, into the Humayun's Tomb camp. On day four, a procession of women—mothers, sisters, wives—thronged Delhi's streets, organized by Hakim Khalil-ul-Rahman 'Nar', a good man who had been a great support to poor burqa-clad Muslim women.

A mother's love, a sister's affection, a wife's respect had come to plead for amity from those who laid claim to honour and humanity. The procession went through Jama Masjid, to Chandni Chowk and Lal Kuan. Bands of school- and college-going girls and throngs of mature women streamed by, numbering at least 10,000. There were burqas, saris and Punjabi shalwars too—traversing the very streets where humanity had been slaughtered, honour plundered and innocence strangled in broad daylight. But today there was no fear, all was calm. Hearts were no longer ablaze. In people's gaze could be glimpsed amiability and approval, not hatred and scorn, and from their words wafted the scent of decorum and truth.

Yet, a lorry would race past Birla House screaming, '*Death to the Mullah Gandhi! Mohammed Gandhi Murdabad!*' Today, on the third day of the fast, some DCM workers ambushed it. They gave the passengers a good hammering. After that, though the lorry continued to race by screaming its evils just beyond Birla House, it wouldn't stop anywhere.

Except perhaps that one time. I was passing through Lal Kuan and found it stationary at the crossing. A gentleman inside was speaking. Slogans of 'Throw the Muslims out now!', 'Blood will have blood!', 'Let Gandhi die!' resounded. How could anyone say this, on the fifth day of the fast?

We heard that an appeal with the signatures of one lakh government employees had been presented to Bapu. Government officials had made sincere promises. The police had taken solemn oaths. But I still couldn't summon the courage to visit Birla House. I went just once to the prayer meeting, and Bapu even addressed me feebly, but I

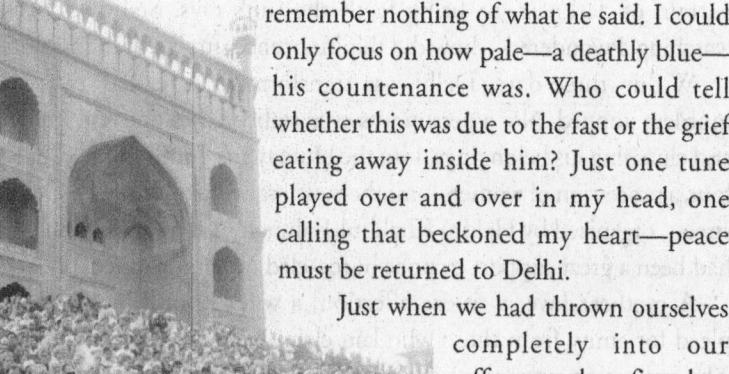

A public meeting at Jama Masjid in January 1948, being addressed by Maulana Abul Kalam Azad.

remember nothing of what he said. I could only focus on how pale—a deathly blue—his countenance was. Who could tell whether this was due to the fast or the grief eating away inside him? Just one tune played over and over in my head, one calling that beckoned my heart—peace must be returned to Delhi.

Just when we had thrown ourselves completely into our efforts—when five days of ceaseless activity had left the Congressis half-dead, the volunteers a pale shadow of themselves—we heard glad tidings: 'Bapu is going to break his fast!' Our lives were saved. A deluge of people ran towards Birla House.

After the fast, our work increased; we had to fulfil our promises. No programme of achieving them been drawn up, each of us did as we thought best but our efforts were directed at the same goal—enduring, resilient peace. The Congressis, making amends for past wrongs, had put their lives into the effort. As for the socialists, this is what they had done since September. The police's conduct also changed. Earlier our boys were brushed aside when they went to lodge complaints,

Maulana Azad speaking to the large crowd assembled at Jama Masjid.

now they were attended to with courtesy; earlier Muslims were shooed away from stations, not any more.

The number of peace lovers was still small though; there were those too who believed their dues had been paid once the fast was broken. They feigned reform but, behind the façade, were already plotting how to revisit their earlier mischief.

The college students ran eight schools for refugee children in different neighbourhoods. All the schools were temporary though; in many places, classes were held in the open. When the fast began, the need to bring together children of refugees and sanctuary seekers was felt deeply. On the third or fourth day, the children were gathered in Rehmaniya School under the Markaz's auspices. The house was tidied, mattresses laid out. All the young men who were friends of peace, all the young women who disseminated the lesson of love so diligently, all the architects of new India gathered, with over 400 children.

A grand function followed. Dr Hussain was invited to unfurl the tricolour in the courtyard, happy children played about and were photographed and treated to fruit, and Savitry behen made a delightful little speech of joy. Finally, Dr Hussain addressed the children and, in a fashion appropriate to their age and cognitive development, explained to them the current state of affairs and its consequences. The children embraced each other warmly and made promises of friendship and loyalty.

Once more, reason for optimism. I told Bapu the good news. He was pleased, but not as elated as I. There was something different about him these days; no genuine happiness in his smile, every utterance swathed in deep sorrow. He was often quiet and I would feel:

mai hoon apni shikast ki aawaaz
I am the utterance of my own defeat

Mirza Ghalib

Oh, why did I let so many days lapse between my visits? I hardly went to the prayer meetings these days. Why was I so irresponsible? I regret it so deeply now.

Those days, the Congress office at Bara Hindu Rao was quite the hub of attention. Although initially, the majority was with the indefatigable socialists, they distanced themselves after a while. The person who then took over was a meek gentleman, a believer in the politics of compromise. He wasn't alone; Congress was full of such of 'compromisers'. Convinced of this, the socialists openly charged the Congress of opportunism. But I didn't have anything to do with this quarrel.

Many of the sensible among the socialists were partners in our work. One introduced me to a few young men who worked in some of the city's most dangerous areas to bring relief to victims of violence, to spread the message of peace. The constituents of this small party were some surviving comrades of Bhagat Singh, communists, socialists and Seva Dal volunteers. Some members were good writers; wielding the pen as a mighty sword, they unleashed a fierce battle against the reactionary forces. In this struggle, in both India and Pakistan, each member of this party pressed into service all his time and wealth to continue the struggle.

Since September, not one in this group had not risked his own life to aid those who were in dire straits, yet the Congress condemned the rebellious exploits of many of them, considering them no better than goons. But when the nation was in trouble, it was they who worked for its rescue far more than the Congressis did. I was struck by the steadfastness of their convictions. Their hearts and minds were pure. While we could barely discern the future in the darkness enveloping us, they had an unparalleled clarity of intent and conception of the goal and how to attain it.

In January itself, Subhadra asked me to accompany her to a function, where she was to inaugurate a library. Thankful for some talk of knowledge at last, I went along. Syed Muttalwi was presiding, and refugees and local Muslims sat side by side as audience; here, the Shanti Dal's efforts had met with success. Syed Muttalwi insisted that I too say a few words. Despite my repeated requests to be excused, he wouldn't yield and so I gave the first speech of my life. My heart was beating so loudly that I couldn't even hear my own words; hastily I uttered a few disconnected sentences and sat down. The function concluded shortly, but I was mortified. Why couldn't I speak like Subhadra? Her speeches were just like her normal speech, long pauses and all, but the things she said were always so close to the mark. Then there was me, a completely useless old mare, who couldn't even string together two words sensibly! There and then, I resolved to remedy my shortcomings.

Just when I thought the situation was improving, I received a frantic call from Qaisar at 9 or 10 p.m. Two of our comrades had been carried off by a Sikh tangewala towards Karol Bagh, a very dangerous neighbourhood, from which no Muslim could ever hope to return alive. I panicked. The effect of Bapu's fast was diminishing—was a new beginning of violence to be made with our comrades? I asked, 'Did you report this to the police?' He said he was speaking from the Sadar Bazaar police station. 'But thanedar sahab refuses to pay heed. I've been asking him to depute two policemen to accompany me— neither does he agree, nor will he lodge a complaint!'

I made for the police station without any inkling of what I would do there. Arriving there, I was told that our two friends had happened to witness an accident—the tangewala had rammed his tanga into a cyclist. Such accidents were common these days, as tangas were being driven by amateurs, who had snatched the vehicle from some poor innocent; no one could stop them, as many months had passed by since they had stolen these vehicles. It was one such tangewala that our friends had seen crash into a cyclist. Helped by others, they captured the offender and insisted that he take the injured man to hospital. When he refused, the crowd urged, 'Let's take him to the police!' Our two friends boarded the tanga to take the injured man to hospital but the tangewala goaded the horse to gallop off to Karol Bagh. The horse was cantering along, the boys couldn't even jump off; moreover, some Sikh cyclists were riding along the careening vehicle.

Angrily, I turned to the thanedar, 'It's been so many hours and you are yet to write a report or send the police to look for our friends? What if the boys have been killed? Whose responsibility will that be?' I think the thanedar was significantly under the influence at the time.

He glanced at the guard who the family had sent with me as a precaution and said, 'No, no there is no fear of murder or violence.' I said sternly, 'That's what you believe but we anticipate exactly that. Provide me with two policemen immediately—we will search for our friends ourselves!' His voice slurring, he called out to two policemen. As they approached, I saw that they were armed with lathis, not rifles. Incensed, I raged, 'If this is all you can do, kindly keep your policemen!' Turning to the guard and Qaisar, I said, 'Come on, we three will have to make do. We don't want the police's help!'

Witness the guard's worthlessness; instead of following me, he went to the thanedar, and whispered something into his ear! All of a sudden, the thanedar's demeanour transformed. Perhaps he had been told that I had the same address as Rafi Ahmad Kidwai. Whatever it was, he was now alert, 'No, I'll accompany you with a full armed guard.' Rifles and machine guns materialized and he advised us to proceed.

After searching Shidipura and all adjacent areas in vain, we passed by the station again; the boys were there, unharmed. Two constables had managed to overpower the tangewala, resisted his bribe of Rs 50, arrested him and escorted him over. The boys were troubled that the tangewala would go to jail because of them but the thanedar was acting tough: 'Throw the rascal into lock-up!'

I had no doubt that once we left, the rascal would be happily on his way home! Such was the state of the police—scoundrels were free to strut cockily while poor Hindus and Muslims were thrashed and jailed. During and after the fast, we had been happy to hear that the police had made promises of good conduct in a petition to Bapu, but incidents like these demonstrated that the change was temporary. More effort and time were needed, if hearts were to truly change.

Even so, witnessing the effect my name had on the police, I thought that however much it may go against my conscience, Allah would perhaps forgive me if I pulled a little rank now and then to relieve those in trouble. Thereafter, I made shameless use of Rafi bhai's status; soon, I summoned the inspector-general of police to my home.

The case was this: a Christian padre from Palam came to deliver two young girls and four children to me. He had looked after them until then, but his strength was failing and his own life under threat. Besides, he was badly shaken by the fact that the children's mother, who had also been in his care, had gone missing some days earlier.

The family had comprised twelve people. The old mother had been murdered. Then, one son disappeared; the other cycled off to trace him but never returned. Then the police took away the father. One nephew was arrested on charges of conspiracy. Deeply moved, the padre gave the daughter-in-law and six children a home. One day, when he was out, an armyman came and asked the daughter-in-law to accompany him. 'Take all your money, I'll get your husband released from jail.' The needy woman went with him, never to be seen alive again.

Mr Mehra was the inspector-general. He had just arrived in Delhi from the frontier, himself a refugee. A decent and courageous man, he nursed no prejudices. Though there was no way that our first encounter could have ever dispelled the doubts I had about the intentions of any policeman, in time, my associates and I soon came to see him as trustworthy and committed. Through his sincere efforts, the two innocent men were let free and the daughter-in-law's body and jewellery were also recovered. The family stayed with us for many months, then perhaps left for Pakistan. Another good effect of the meeting at my home was that now my letters began to work; people at the police station were now instructed to heed our volunteers.

Then came the news that a bomb had gone off at the prayer meeting. The culprit was captured there and then. His name was Madan Lal but, as we know today, he wasn't alone; others were involved. They had all stood near our Father, aiming weapons at that heart so suffused with faith. But, when the moment came, their own hearts were struck with terror, and their trembling hands could not do the deed. Enemies to his left and right, the air around him hazy with bomb smoke, surrounded by panicking people, that tower of light stood, composed and calm, urging in a tranquil voice, 'Peace, my friends, peace!' My God, what flame glowed in that weakened body to dispel even a gloom such as this?

On the Urs of Qutub Sahib, we all went to Mehrauli. Some of us had earlier cleaned up the place. Walking amid the ravaged graves, the boys chanced upon a human hand first, then other body parts, and soon assembled a human shape, which they interred in an empty grave. When they told me what they had been up to, I was horrified, 'But how could you bring yourself to do such a terrible thing?' They laughed off my concern. Their hearts were strong—having laid scores of corpses to rest, how could the mere assembly of a skeleton disturb them?

Early on the morning of 30 January, receiving word of my father-in-law's (Imtiaz Ali Kidwai) deteriorating condition, I had to suddenly leave for Lucknow. On leaving the house, on boarding the train, on the way, many times, the thought that continually pricked me was that I was leaving without meeting Bapu. What guarantee was there for life or death? Why didn't I meet him yesterday? But it was 5 a.m. now, so there was no question of meeting him.

That evening, that golden orb of truth and peace sank into the horizon forever. Abbajan was in his final hours, when the news that Bapu had bidden us farewell reached us. For a while, I was stunned. Then, madly, impulsively, I called Rafi bhai to say that I was returning to Delhi. Flabbergasted, he replied, 'Leaving Miyan *jan* in this state?' I was mortified. Who was I going to meet? Who did I expect to see? The river of tranquillity had changed course; where would I find consolation? The manifold moans, tears, screams, pleas from pain-filled hearts thudded against the heavens, as Bapu's pure soul ascended to its heavenly abode.

Abbajan was breathing his last, but I had ears only for the radio. I heard Jawaharlalji's trembling voice narrate what had transpired; when I turned to Abbajan, I heard the Sura-e-Yaseen. The ground was hard, the horizon remote. And I? I'd taken my wounded heart to the greatest messiah of our times and somehow, as time passed, the mark had even lightened. But now this fresh blow, how would it ever heal?

As I watched Abbajan, the past rushed up at me. He was my father's elder brother and had raised me and my four siblings when we were orphaned as young children. He gave us five children more love than he gave his own. His many kindnesses, matchless love and extraordinary sacrifice were imprinted on my heart. But, even before my memories could run their course, the time came for me to bid him farewell. The father of the nation and my own father, both were lost to me forever in the space of two hours. Old wounds reopened; I grieved again.

Life itself seemed a burden. As if the day of judgement had arrived. The heavens would break apart and fall on us; the earth would split open, and from its cracks would spill out those that sleep within, rising to annihilate this sinful nation! Why, after all this, does this roof hold? Why isn't the world caught up in turmoil?

People said that even as Gandhiji's corpse lay inside the house, it was put abroad in the city that his assassin was a Muslim. My brother, Mustafa Kamil, who was in Delhi those days, himself saw a man moving about in the crowd at the prayer meeting saying this. He ran to tell Rafi bhai, who was standing in front. Rafi bhai immediately sent word to Jawaharlalji, who had already reached inside. Had Jawaharlalji and Sardar Patel not composed themselves so soon to make the radio announcement, who knows how many Muslim corpses would have fallen cold by the next morning! When they heard of the assassination, Muslims clasped their hearts, 'Most merciful God! Let it not be a Muslim! We will be annihilated. This curse will be on our heads until the Day of Judgement!' When the name was revealed, people were stunned. Sikhs sighed in relief, 'Vahe Guru is merciful! We were as good as dead if the murderer was Sikh.'

When a Nawab from Lucknow heard the news, he was inconsolable. When the funeral procession left that morning, he was there, bareheaded and barefoot, saying, 'I too am bound for the same place where Gandhiji has gone.' On the way, he fell, and restored his life to the One Who Gives Life to us all.

I returned to Delhi after a week, but I could see no present, no future. The calm after the hurricane, the quiet after the tempest. Wherever one went, the talk was about Bapu, stories about him,

rau mein hai raksh-e-umr, kahaan dekhiye thame
nae haath bagh par hai, na pa hai rakaab mein
Surging forward is the steed of life; who knows where it
    shall stop
The reins are not in my hands, nor are the spurs on my feet

                                                    Mirza Ghalib

Until the thirteenth-day ceremony, the *terhaveen*, I could do nothing but cry, my tears were for Gandhiji alone—who else did I have to weep for? I had come to spend the remainder of my life at his feet. I still go to Rajghat every year, to the samadhi of my guru to spend my tears; of what I got from him in life, I am bereft. I went to Birla House many times, to the place where walking the path of the true, the traveller fell asleep. There are still flowers scattered:

bar zamine ka nishane kaf-e-pa-e-to bood
salha sajda-e-sahab nazraan khwahad bood
The ground on which your hallowed footsteps fell
Will be venerated for years by your admirers

                                                    Hafiz Shirazi

I also touched my eyes to the takht Bapu used to sit on, the cloth that covered it. But there was no comfort, no solace, then or later. On the takht, leaning on the bolster was not Bapu but a large picture of him, but I couldn't summon the courage to look at it. In Iqbal's words:

zauq-e-huzoor dar jahaan rasm-e-sanamagri nihad
ishq fareb mi dihad jaan-e-ummeedwar ra
Pleasure in presence has established the practice of idolatry
Love deceives the desirous soul

                                                    Mohammed Iqbal

That same room, the same things, takht, pillows, all around the same books and, instead of Bapu, his smiling photograph—all the pleasures of beholding him in life could be gotten, but I was afraid. Fearing that I may begin to worship it, I didn't let my eyes stray in its direction. On a thousand other occasions I could have looked at it but in this setting, the sentiments it would engender in me would be altogether different. Like a true believer, I wept with my back turned to it. He who has departed may well return thus, but why should I bring him before these external eyes?

On the terhaveen, a gentleman insisted that I sit on the rath that this figure, laden with flowers, was being driven in. The scene was unbearable. Bapu's remains in front, the image behind. Death had the lead over life, and the eyes of the heavens could never have witnessed such a scene of mourning. All of India grieved for Bapu that day. Even Delhi had stopped, whose earth had just been drenched with the blood of the most complete human being of all time. Perhaps this was the sacrifice it had needed all along—that the unpolluted ashes of an innocent be mixed in its soil.

In the world, whenever cruelty has peaked, some exceptional personage has made the ultimate sacrifice, cooling the blazing furnace of sin with splashes of his own blood. People say Christ will rise again, that the twelfth imam of the Shias will return close to the Day of Judgement, that Krishna will be reincarnated. Only God is privy to his own intent, but I am convinced that all great men who will come will do the same as others who came before them. In Hussein's sacrifice of his sons at Karbala, in Jesus's embrace of his crucifixion, in all the others that gave their lives, there was but one motive—to keep Truth alive. What had happened before our eyes was the same.

I had often wondered what hands had raised Jesus to the cross. What unmoving hearts watched the Prophet's nephew Hussein achieve martyrdom, without food or water? Now, I understood. These same satanic hands tried to strangle compassion in our times. But compassion cannot die. Truth is immortal, it never perishes:

abr-e-raihmat tha ki thi ishq ki bijli ya rab
jal gayee mizra-e-hasti to uga dana-e-dil

Was it the mist of mercy or the lightning of love, my Lord?
That when the crop of life was reduced to ashes, a wise heart
    was born

Mohammed Iqbal

Behind the funeral procession, the portrait of Gandhiji's assassin was being sold amidst laughter. Just moments ago, these people had infiltrated the procession, clapping and laughing. But there had perhaps never been such a magnificent funeral march—each eye moist, each heart shattered by grief. Except for those enemies of humanity who were distributing sweets. These evil hands that had crucified so many until now, tormented the Prophet's heirs, put a bullet into Gandhiji—these hands believed that their work wasn't done and were confident of further success. My Lord, how much longer will You stay aloof?

All of India was shamed. Hearts changed, mindsets altered, and then we were all reformed. If only we had come to our senses earlier! But how were we to know that the gaze that could so effortlessly sweep from the past and the present across to the future was to be with us only for such a short while? If only I could have known that I would soon weep for the one who wiped away the tears of the whole world . . .

> *gham naseeb Iqbal ko baksha gaya maatam tera*
> *chun liya taqdeer ne wo dil ke tha maihraam tera*
> Sorrowing Iqbal was saved from mourning for you
> Fate chose instead the heart that was your confidant

Mohammed Iqbal

Girls recued by the recovery operation in a transit camp in Lahore.

9

Abducted women

(November 1947–February 1948)

A nother enormous problem that we were faced with in this period, and one that I have not yet mentioned, was that of 'abducted women'. This most shameful of the crimes was so widespread and undertaken so blatantly and with such cowardice that no parallel can be found in the world. We all knew that these sins committed by Hindus and Muslims had made Bapu's life unliveable, and so each patriotic section pressed itself into service to do anything that would bring a smile of satisfaction to Bapu's lips. Others felt the same and wanted to do something to relieve his burden.

Since the very beginning of my work in the camps, I'd heard the sanctuary seekers at Purana Qila and Humayun's Tomb weeping over their missing daughters and wives, either snatched from them or separated in their flight from violence. Although I maintained a meticulous record of these names, barring one or two, I hadn't been able to recover any of them.

I recall that day in November 1947 when a young man, weeping loudly, met me. Finally composing himself, he told me, 'My wife was abducted by Sikhs from Delhi. I have spent the last many weeks looking for her without success, but today when I was passing through Aliganj, I saw her standing in the flats there. Seeing me, she started to cry; I ran towards her but a whole gang of sword-wielding Sikhs rushed at me. I was unarmed, so all I could do was flee.' He said that hardly thirty minutes had passed since the incident. 'I came straight to you. Please help me, otherwise my wife . . .' He dissolved into tears once again.

I couldn't think of a way to help him. I didn't know many influential people yet; the only solution I could come up with was to take him with me to Birla House, where some remedy would be found. There, we told Brij Krishna Chandiwala the problem and he said, 'But this is a matter for the police.' But I didn't know anyone in the Delhi police! He suggested approaching Indira Gandhi. Just as he uttered these words, by the Mewati's good fortune, Indira walked in! Hearing us out, she said, 'Wait for a few minutes, I will return after meeting Bapu.' True to her word, she returned shortly and asked us to accompany her to Panditji's house. She telephoned the assistant commissioner of police.

Feeling that I was no longer needed, I left the Mewati in her charge. That didn't mean that I didn't think of the matter; I fretted over it until a few hours later, when I saw the Mewati approaching me, beaming. The assistant commissioner had gotten his wife back almost immediately, after searching the houses in the neighbourhood.

Similar was the case of the young Mewati Ausaf. He had been married only over a year, but his wife and two-month infant had gone missing. He spent all day searching for them, until he learnt that she'd been captured by a Jat named Mitthan, in a house in Bhogal. An old Chamari, moved by the girl's whimpers, had agreed to get the message to Ausaf. His wife asked the Chamari to get a 'phooter' (photo) of him for her. 'I had the photograph taken yesterday and sent it. The Chamari told me today that when my wife saw it, she burst into uncontrollable tears. She is absolutely crazed in her longing for me. That bloody Mitthan makes her toil in the fields all day. Some days, I hide there and gaze at her from afar. But I haven't been able to rescue her.'

He also told us that Mitthan accused his wife of being lazy and wanted to sell her—for Rs 200. 'Please take mercy! She will be in the fields near Okhla right now. Get the police to bring her.' Sushila had come back to the camp. Hearing Ausaf's entreaties, she said she would go herself. The day was ending, it would be evening by the time we reached. If I were alone, I'd have postponed the trip to the next morning. I said, 'Sushila, won't it be wise to take a policeman?' Sushila dismissed my suggestion, 'Where is the need for the police? Are you afraid?' I was ashamed to admit my apprehension. This skinny, smiling girl was so sober, so brave. Her self-assurance had given Sushila a special place in her friends' and colleagues' hearts.

By the time we reached, it was dark. But Sushila thrashed through the bushes, striding across the fields twenty paces ahead of me, and led us to Mitthan's village. On the way, we met many women but not Ausaf's beloved. Though we urged him to be patient, he rushed up to anyone we encountered and asked about her whereabouts. All we learnt was that she did come to the fields daily and had been there till late afternoon but had left early. She would be in the village now.

Bhogal was completely under refugee control by then, a Sangh stronghold. Only a few Muslims had been able to escape the carnage alive. But Sushila was undeterred, and when we reached the village, she barged into the first house demanding to know where Mitthan lived. I wondered what spirit Bapu had breathed into Sushila that she was so undaunted by thoughts of death, pain, harm. And I, who called myself a Muslim, was such a coward! Berating myself, I followed Sushila into Mitthan's house when we found it.

Ausaf was shouting, 'Jan *bi*, Jan bi.' No reply. Sushila scolded the family, 'If the girl is in your possession, hand her over at once. Or tell us where she is. I've come alone and if you produce her, I'll take her away and nothing will be done to you. Otherwise, the police will have to come and you will be treated as criminals.' But the girl was not produced and we left disappointed, reaching home only by 9 p.m.

A week later, I met Ausaf again, visibly elated. He said, 'Apaji, I've brought Jan bi back!' I was surprised, 'Where did you find her?' He said, 'I had to go really far to get her back. Jan bi tells me that when we were in Bhogal, she was locked in a hay store, as Mitthan had been forewarned. Her mouth was stuffed with cloth and her legs and hands bound. That very night Mitthan took her and ran to UP. On the way, they passed some Muslims reading namaz. Jan bi freed her hand and ran to them. As the Muslims outnumbered him, Mitthan had to run away. Meanwhile, I'd already started in the same direction, as I believed that Mitthan would flee. I'd been walking for a few days when I met the Muslims. I told them everything and they handed Jan bi to me. See, there she is, lying down in that tent. See how weak she has become!'

Jan bi was lying on a quilt, under a thick blanket. No more than fifteen, this frail girl lay listless, barely alive. Ausaf clasped her hand, 'Look, how thin her wrist has become! See what she has suffered—he killed our child!' They both wept. Laying her down gently on the soft bed, Ausaf squatted beside her. He had pressed all his resources into her relief; even his only jacket was draping her now. She told me how she didn't sleep for the first three nights, fearing that Mitthan would do something to her child. She clutched her child to her breast all the time. But on the fourth night, she dropped off for a while, and when she awoke, the child was gone. She was told, 'Oh, the child? It was eaten up by a cat.' The child was never seen again.

I watched in silence. Their first love, their first child, and what cruelty. Almighty, how much longer will You allow Man to dress in wolves' clothing?

Weeks passed and I made acquaintances in the police. I gave the officers the names of abducted women I had recorded in my notebook. More girls were recovered but our successes were insignificant in the light of the enormity of the problem. Mridula Sarabhai was one of the few alive to the urgency of this problem. She had come to Delhi with Gandhiji and lived in Constitution House. Mridula wanted to immediately implement a programme for the rescue of abducted women in India and Pakistan.

Delhi's courageous races, the Gujjars and the Jats, had long looted the province, but this plunder of its women had fallen their way for the first time. They embraced the opportunity with enthusiasm and brazen industry. Only the government got no wind of their activities. When officials excused themselves from

Gandhi with Mridula Sarabhai, a firebrand freedom fighter and activist, one of the few who were interested in recovering abducting women.

acting on reports, citing the difficulties of liaising with Pakistan and the provinces, it came to Mridula—blessed as she was with an extraordinary will to work and battle—to do something. In Bapu's lifetime itself, she went to Pakistan. Meeting officials in Lahore, Karachi and other places, she managed to quickly bring the two countries to an agreement that this brutality must not be condoned in any circumstances and that all abducted women must be restored to their relatives.

Very quickly, the Central Recovery Organization was constituted under the leadership of Lady Mountbatten and both governments began to rescue abducted women. Delhi was entrusted to the women's section of the rehabilitation ministry, with Mrs Rameshwari Nehru as in charge. Bapu had given Sushila the responsibility of the principalities. Following in the footsteps of Mridula, who made regular trips to Pakistan, Sushila went to Patiala first.

But the work had begun very late. When it did start, innumerable hurdles were placed—at times by officials, at times by disaffected individuals. Moreover, the inefficiency of the workers and lack of public cooperation troubled us constantly. The root cause was the fact that dogs don't eat dogs. Delhi's administration had been so compromised and was so complicit that not a single functionary could legitimately be called a law enforcer. And not only Delhi—after all, this crime had begun in Noakhali—it also held for other provinces in India and Pakistan.

Despite all this, Mridula's courage, Sushila's untiring labour and the efforts of many of our sisters in East and West Punjab brought results and thousands of girls were recovered. Groups of a few hundred each from Pakistan and thousands from India's provinces streamed in. (And these are figures for just fifteen months. The Central Recovery Organization worked until 1954, by the end of which 17,000 women were rescued from Pakistan and sent to India, and 20,000 Muslim women the other way.)

In Delhi, the number of recovered women didn't, I think, cross 200. Some were appropriated by social workers, some by Jamiat activists, some rescued by the police. A significant number was recovered by one man, working alone. This noble chamar rescued scores of abducted girls and secretly returned them to their homes. How I wish I could have learnt his name, but that remained forever a secret; all the girls would say was, 'An old Harijan brought me home.'

This number was far lower than the number of 1,500 missing I had gleaned from the camps and other sources. What had happened to the other women? I tried my utmost, searched all the villages, but could never find them. What I was certain of is that, barring one or two, they were no longer in Delhi. I learnt the addresses of a few in other provinces, but the number was insignificant.

Possibly, the number given at the outset was exaggerated. I say this on the basis of an experience. In my own reckoning, by March 1948, between fifteen and twenty girls had been recovered in Delhi. One day, a volunteer from United Relief congratulated me on having rescued 125 women—a figure he got from the women's section. Taken aback, I said, 'That's not true at all! Please don't repeat this falsehood to anyone. I could play along and enjoy the plaudits but what answer will I give to their relatives when they enquire about the missing women's whereabouts or when the Pakistan government holds me to a full accounting? We have recovered about fifteen or sixteen ourselves and another four were brought to us by the police.'

The stories of distressed girls from East Punjab and wrecked women from this side of the border were identical: the flight with family and neighbours from village to camp; on the police's orders, the beginning of the journey in a convoy to Pakistan; ambush on the way; abduction of all young women during the attack; division of these spoils among attackers, police and army. The conspiracy transcended borders.

Despite the violence, it was rare for any young girl to be killed, though they were injured at times. The 'hot stuff' would be distributed between army and police, the 'substandard' falling to the share of the attackers. Then these girls would be passed from one hand to a second to a third, so they would have been bought and sold four or five times by the time they came to be the pride of some hotel or reached a safehouse to be the dalliances of policemen.

As each girl was unaware of the conspiracy, she would think of this man, charging into the melee and gathering her into his strong arms, as her angel of mercy. When that good soul gently proffered his scarf to cover her body stripped bare by attackers, all ghastly memories of her mother's carcass with its throat slit open, her father's blood-bathed body, her husband's still-writhing corpse, would be driven from her mind, and she would be melt with gratitude for her saviour.

A long time would pass before she would understand that this man was not the blameless one among the looters or the decent one among the policemen, that all of them practised the same 'heroism'. Each one would have put his life on the line at least once to save a woman but equally, there would also be scores of women who, like her, cursed this valiant's mothers and sisters. By the time this secret was revealed, the waters would have risen above the head. It would be too late for her to run from him—she was going to be a mother, or she had already been sold to other men three or four times over. Having countenanced so many men, what face could India's daughter show her parents or her husband?

I can never forget the three adolescent girls from Najafgarh. One was rescued and sent to me by a Swami disciple of Bapu and Mr Nayyar, veteran Congressi and a member of the Provincial Committee. That proud daughter of a Pathan said, 'My two girlfriends were so lucky—Heaven gave them the chance and they finished the job. I didn't get the chance or I too would have done exactly the same.'

She narrated her tale: 'The three of us were taken to the same village. The other two girls were both with the same man, I was with another. Although a close watch was always kept on us, we managed to get a few moments together and then we would whisper to each other what we could do to free ourselves. One day, my two friends managed to secrete a sickle and later that night, when the Jat began to snore, they placed the sickle on his throat and pressed it down.'

Just imagine the scene: these pre-teen girls plot a murder, over many months; their hands aren't strong enough, so they press down on the sickle together with all their might. But at the loud gurgling sounds from the Jat's throat their control deserts them and they run for their lives. The sounds alert others in the house and they give chase. How far could those frail legs carry the girls? They are soon caught and fall prey to the maddened crowd. Yet, the only regret their friend has is that she couldn't do the same. As a woman, I can only pray that each one of India's and Pakistan's daughters is exactly like them.

In Bapu's lifetime itself, a deeper question had emerged—when these abducted women were brought back, would their relatives accept them? When Hindu women had been recovered from Pakistani Muslims, their relatives had refused to take them. When Mahatmaji learnt of this, he was deeply affected, and said, 'Those who refuse to take in these women in distress are the greatest sinners. These girls are chaste and unsullied and much more pure than I am. They have escaped evil, so how can they be faulted for the offences of others?'

From the three or four cases I was involved with in Jamia, I was relieved to find that in general Muslims did not display a similar outlook. They would search for their missing women themselves and happily make them their own again.

As recovery work went on, the greatest difficulty was not to facilitate acceptance—instead, we found that most abducted girls didn't want to return. Muslims seethed at these refusals, young men flushing at this ignominious disgrace of their community's honour. Fathers would rant, 'Shame on such daughters! This is why a father prays so hard for a son. At least a son will be a support to his father in his lifetime, and after his father's death, guard the family's honour!' As for the sons, the one sentiment that moved them was a desire for revenge and anger at their sisters. How could the immoral wantons want to live with those who had murdered their relatives!

Readers cannot comprehend what I, as a woman, suffered when such things were said. I would try to explain, 'Try to understand their psychological state. Try to see why they refuse to return.' But the ranting and raving would continue. Finally, I had to enquire about the reasons for refusal myself. The most common type was the fine and sensible girl, most eager to flee her captors. These girls' minds were alive to the dire situation they were trapped in and they spent every moment planning an escape. They wrote letters to their dear ones seeking rescue even when they had no idea where they were being held. In their hearts, love for kin, faith and dignity reigned supreme. But put these ones aside and consider, if you will, the others.

Take the young woman who had spent all her life behind the purdah, never seeing the face of any other man besides her brother or father. Today, this girl loathed herself as a wanton who had expended her dignity by being with strange men for months. This girl was being offered a return home and she wondered whether her parents, husband, society, would own her again. A deep sense of misgiving and a fear of rejection would drive her to refuse the offer.

There is no denying that there were also some girls to whose way of thinking this immodest life appealed. The egotism that was the mood of the times gave licence to self-indulgence; and once they had sampled the pleasurable nectar of sin, their hearts rebelled against a return to that staid, disciplined life. However vitiated the atmosphere was, it was still in consonance with their natures.

Also among those who refused were a few modern, educated girls who believed that the world's problems could never be solved without 'international' marriages. Even before the riots, they had spurned religion and society, seeking out opportunities to demonstrate their open-mindedness; now, they were making hay while the sun shone. How could social workers ever hope to reform such sophisticated sinners?

And there were also some married women, who believed their honourable husbands to be their companions until death rendered them asunder. They wondered how they could, tainted by infidelity and scandal as they were, ever face men as proud as them? Would their husbands tolerate such treachery? Would their gazes ever invest in them the same respect as before? These feelings would shackle their feet and they would say, 'What was written as our fate has come to pass. Leave us where we are to live out the rest of our days.'

There were also some girls whose eyes had opened in homes of great poverty, who had never eaten a full meal or clothed their bodies in anything but rags. But now, they were in the keep of such generous men, who brought them silken shalwars and dupattas, introduced them to the delectable taste of hot coffee and cold ice-cream, took them to see two shows at the movies in a single day. Why would such a girl want to leave such fine men to return to her amma and abba, to a life of rags and scraps to conceal her burgeoning youth, to days of toil in the fields under a sun hot enough to melt her brain? And even if she were to do it, even if she were to leave this splendid man, so handsome in his uniform, all the romance that her old life had in store for her was a mud-spattered uncouth rustic, clutching the staff hoisted on his shoulder, for a husband. She wanted to escape this terrible past and that frightening future; she wanted to be happy in the present that was hers.

And for all women, there was another reason for refusal. How was she to know whether her self-professed rescuer was friend or foe? What

if the rescuers were also traffickers? Until now, whichever strange man
had taken her, had sold her. The fact that the rescuer wore a police
uniform was no guarantee either. And even if it were not a uniform
but an ornamental pagdi with a shining tassel, how could she trust
that he was what he said, a man sent by her relatives? In almost all
cases of rescue, this was the woman's suspicion, so much so that the
rescuers would have to forcibly drag her away and her fears would be
allayed only after two or three days with them.

The question of religion and of conversion rarely crossed the minds
of such girls. After all, what was their religion to them? It was only
Muslim men who went to the mosque regularly to read the Friday
namaz and the Alvida namaz, only men who listened to the mullaji's
sermons. Mullaji wouldn't let women even stand in the mosque. Every
time he saw young girls, his eyes would redden, 'Get out! What do
you have to do here?' Their presence in the mosque would defile
the namaz; if they went to the dargah, there was the danger of a
commotion; if they attended a qawwali *mehfil*, then the Sufi was in
peril of straying from his contemplation of the One to thoughts of
more earthly pleasures. Women simply polluted sanctity.

In any case, what did these women know of Islam? They had never
been taught anything but a few kalmas and a little bit of the namaz.
What relevance did that have? They had learnt it by heart and recited
it by rote, but what connection did this prayer have with the soul?
Her name was Rahimat, her abba Ramzani and her husband Nawab
Idris. Besides a few Islamic names, what wealth of faith was hers that
she should give up her life to safeguard it? And if truth were to be
told, it was not as if the Almighty had kept her in such comfort. In
fact, the god that this new man had was much more bountiful, for at
least she was fed. No, it was better to let them rant on; she was certainly
not going to leave this new man, who had brought such colour to
her life.

I also met some young girls who angrily scorned the offer of return
to husbands who had proven so cowardly that they just turned tail
and ran, leaving the honour of their family, the mother of their children
at the mob's mercy. These women would go mad with anger, 'You ask

us to go back to those impotents? We kept on crying out to them to help us—In Allah's name, save us! Why are you running away? Why don't you strike these scoundrels? Wait! Take me along! But for each one, his life was most dear. There was no love for us. Why didn't they kill us with their own hands? We certainly don't want to ever see their faces again!'

It is primordial to a woman's nature to laud courage. She will pine for the husband who can give his life to save hers. She will sacrifice her all, faith and society, to preserve his memory. She will even worship a husband who puts a bullet in her. What her heart won't allow her is to forgive a husband who runs away.

Both educated and illiterate girls had another problem. When the police or activists came to rescue them, they would be paralysed by the question: Will my parents/husband accept this child in my womb? What if they make me kill it, in the name of honour? This fear would make them refuse to return.

Finally, there were a few victims of the strange games that Nature can play. Cupid's arrows had to strike just those hearts and love was born in these unusual circumstances. These were genuine cases, and it was impossible for me to think of the refusals to return as mere obstinacy.

What these varied reasons for refusal told us was that the issue was not as simple as we had assumed. The activists had to reassure the women, support them, build trust, and gently try to turn their hearts towards accepting the idea of return. But I'm sorry to report that we were all unequipped, incompetent. We lacked the right spirit, which had to be of the order of Christian missionaries. None of us had any understanding of psychology, nor did we try to gain it. We would just parrot the few catchphrases that were habitually used in such circumstances, and when they proved ineffectual (as they often did), we would berate the girls.

To worsen matters, the police's conduct was unnecessarily harsh towards the girls, and extraordinarily considerate towards their abductors. Furthermore, as our efforts raised questions about the police, its officers were constantly busy to somehow implicate the activists in some case and arrest them, or at least defame them as criminals. Then there was the blind, unfeeling public, who would forget that the girls they were so desperately to hold back were just twins of their sisters, who even today were in Pakistan, shedding tears at their fate and the deeds of their brothers.

In both India and Pakistan, very few educated girls were recovered. The overwhelming majority was always with the uneducated daughters of farmers, workers and middle classes, primarily from the rural areas. As far as I could find, this was because educated girls were usually killed quite soon after they were taken. The ones that survived were those in the keep of highly ranked police and army officers, administrators, or educated people. Instead of devoting their considerable talents to putting the looters and lumpens behind bars, able magistrates provided fake certificates to these people that they'd had civil marriages with their captives two or three years earlier. This crime was committed with clinical efficiency by courts everywhere.

Some girls managed to escape on their own. I remember one incident; one day, I received a phone call from one such girl. She had just begun talking when someone came, so she had to abruptly call off. Luckily, she had already told me her address, so I could send in the police to fetch her. In general, the educated girls that survived were initially treated well and, in some cases, even married to a captor. However, many could not bring themselves to list the way the wind blew, and when matters came to a head and they protested, they too were killed.

The governments of India and Pakistan had decided that any girl in the possession of the other religion had to be appropriated by the state; however, the administration's enforcement of this agreement meant that every such girl had to be presented before a magistrate to state whether she wanted to return (in which case she would be handed over to her relatives) or not (in which, she would be returned to the person in whose possession she was found). This was the procedure in place for a long period; as a result, many girls were restored to their captors. Moreover, camps to house recovered girls had yet to be instituted.

In the initial months of the recovery operation, there was no order. Consider a few instances of the chaos. It was reported that a police inspector recovered two abducted girls from a village; however, the girls never reached us. One day, I ran into the inspector enumerating his exploits in recovering women and sanitizing his area. I seized the moment and asked after the two girls. He replied, 'Oh, we left those two in Jama Masjid. They would have found their relatives and gone back.' Who they were, where they came from and went to—he had neither the leisure nor the compulsion to inform us. What was important for him was that their numbers had been registered.

Another time, this very inspector brought a recovered girl to us, with the message that she wanted to return to her captor. The girl was clinging to him and bawling loudly. I grasped her hand and drew her away, murmuring encouragingly. As soon as we were in a room, her tears stopped and she asked, 'Are you Hindu or Muslim?'

'What, you think me to be Hindu?'

'*Tauba!* My apologies. I thought he was handing me over to the Sikhs. Allah be praised! I'm among Muslims.' Incredible. Inspector sahab had not even bothered to tell her where she was being taken and why. She asked, 'If my in-laws are alive, will you send me to them?' I assured her I would, 'What else? That is precisely why I called you here.' This was enough to make her happy. She took off all the jewellery that her abductor had given her and sent it to the inspector to return, announcing that she would not leave the camp unless it was to go to her in-laws.

She had given the statement that she wanted to stay with her captor because she thought staying with that one man would be infinitely better than having to be with ten. Her statement was officially retracted and she was delivered to her in-laws and husband, who was also alive, the next day.

Inspector sahab was posted in an area where hundreds of abducted women were being held. It was even rumoured that two were being kept for him by a ziledar friend. As the government had issued strict orders, this policeman had to now cover up his past misdeeds and get a high-ranked government official to certify to his industry on this front. He therefore 'recovered' two more girls. They were produced before Mr Button, the Anglo-Indian police superintendent, and they said they didn't want to return to their parents. A signed statement to the effect, certified by a magistrate, was also produced. It so happened that Subhadra was with Mr Button when these girls were brought in and she recommended that the girls be sent to me. Inspector sahab was alarmed and blurted out, 'No, not to that lady! Once she gets the girls, she doesn't let them out.' Mr Button scolded him, 'No! Her decision will be the correct one. She will be able to counsel the girls.'

The distressed girls were brought to me and exactly what Inspector sahab had feared, transpired. I took leave for a night and took them to Purani Tehsil, near Red Fort. We found their relatives there; in fact, one saw her brother in Urdu Bazaar itself and started shouting to catch his attention.

Similarly, another inspector brought four girls. He appeared to be amiable, as he didn't even mention statements, or suggest a return to captors. I was happy that there was at least one good man in the force. The next day, though, I was in for a shock—a newspaper report praised him for recovering 400 women from his area!

But where were all the truly missing girls? Everyone knew, but who had the guts to apprehend the captors? In Delhi itself, everyone knew that a senior local government official had a few abducted girls in his possession, but who could touch him? A girl named Zubeida was even admitted in the cantonment hospital for many days but despite my best efforts, I failed to secure her release. To worsen matters, although government and police officials were reluctant to adopt and implement anything else that Gandhiji said, they zealously enforced Bapu's suggestion that nothing be done to the person from whom an abducted girl was recovered. Bapu's advice was made with my knowledge, in fact on our urging. We felt that if a person were seen to repent and return a girl without fear of punishment, it would encourage others. We were apprehensive that if punishment were meted out, then in every village from which a girl was recovered, the others would be slaughtered.

In March 1948, a young woman named Husn bi was brought from a policeman's house. As usual, she began reeling off the same old story of kindness and gratitude, but when I took her husband's name, her eyes filled with tears. She said, 'I'm sure he has been murdered. But if he is alive, or if my *chacha*, who is also my *devrani*'s father, can be found, I can go back to them; otherwise, I will not leave.' Our list indicated that Husn bi had a two-year-old daughter with her when

A woman and infant rescued from her abductors.

she was taken. I found out that the policeman had kept the child. No mention had been made of her to the magistrate either.

All day long, Husn bi pined for her daughter; by evening, she was beside herself with worry. My problem was that I didn't know where the child was being held and I had to leave for Allahabad the next morning. Husn bi was to be presented the next day before the police commissioner; before I left, I called Maulana Mohammed Miyan, a well-known writer and activist in the Jamiat office to say that Husn bi's statement should be recorded only after her child was in her arms. But that didn't happen. Tormented by a mother's love for her missing child, Husn bi said that she wanted to go back to the policeman—and this was the statement recorded. She is still with that man, despite all my efforts to get her out.

One last case. Two young girls were recovered from two Sikh policemen. Although the camp was fully functional, the girls were not brought there. Being favoured by the police, they were sent to a nursing home. Their policemen abductors were given special permission to meet them and deliver special food to them. One of the girls was about twenty years old and an errant rustic; the other was the very young and very beautiful daughter of a respectable family. Having staying together for fifteen days in the nursing home, the two became such fast friends that the elder managed to convince the younger one to refuse to return. She told her, 'We will both go on a hunger strike and get them to agree to our demands. If they won't listen to us, then all the arrangements for an escape are in place. Whatever you do, don't say yes!'

On my return from Allahabad, both girls were brought to me. Learning of the rudeness and shamelessness of the elder girl first-hand, and sensing a complete impossibility of reform, I immediately took her (against the hopes and wishes of the people who had brought her to me) and dropped her off in the camp. As for the younger one, I took her home with me for a couple of days so that I could counsel and comfort her. I was confident that once the effects of bad company waned, she would return to the right path once again. As I knew that her father was alive, I had word sent to them through the Jamiat.

Our house had a police guard, both in the front and the back. The front gate was manned by an armed policeman, but nevertheless, in the dead of the night, that fifteen-year-old girl managed to disappear. The police was summoned as soon as we found out, and although it looked as if they would peel the sky and tip over the earth in their frenetic search, a whole week passed without any news of her. And then one day, a Muslim lawyer informed me that the girl is to appear that afternoon in a magistrate's court and that she will be deposing under the assumed name of Kamla, declaring that she has become a Sikh.

Fresh efforts were made and the girl recovered again. This time, the policeman was also arrested. However, what could not be decided was where she should be kept—it was said that I would incite the girl to rebellion and the woman warden of the camp was too cruel a lady to look after her. Simultaneously, a senior officer ordered the release of the policeman, with the ultimate result that the girl was handed back to her captor, with the proviso that she must be produced whenever summoned.

I complained to a senior police officer, who directed me to have her father summoned immediately. He could do no more, he said. I did not do so, but within a few days, the girl's father and his brother's son arrived to drag the girl away. The next day, the prime minister received a report that the girl was taken back, bound hand and foot. Naturally, he was very displeased to hear this and an inquiry was ordered. But what had to happen had happened by then. The Muslims were adamant about not leaving the girl behind. I had myself told the police not to intervene, because the Muslims were bound to take it as an insult to the community, but the officers did not listen.

As time passed, some abducted women were returned voluntarily, but in general, the police and the administration were callous. Not one government official was suspended for a single day. What I could not comprehend was how the government expected to run an administration relying on the abilities of such sinners? How could those that worked against the interests of justice be trusted to impose laws on others?

As for the general public, many people were led astray or were simply uneducated—straws whipped any which way the wind blew. However, they were individuals and ultimately responsible for their own deeds. But those courts, magistrates, policemen, officers were not—when the guardians of the nation and arbiters of its nationhood placed their hand in blessing on the heads of sinners, when they became their accomplices and accessories, then where would the doers of justice come from, and who could be called a criminal?

This state of affairs made us frequently refer to the past, when the British government was in power. In the eyes of its law, whenever abduction happened, both the abductor and his accomplice were equally guilty, and both would be sentenced. Wasn't the same law in force today? New ones had not been made yet, then why this anarchy in which a teenaged girl is made to give a statement before a judge, and this statement overrides social norms, the interests of justice and the agreement between two countries? Hadn't the governments of India and Pakistan decided that if an abducted girl's relatives could not be found, she should be kept at the government camp? Instead of implementing this, officials on both sides undermined it. In a sense, this should not have surprised us—after all, the bureaucracy of both sides was manufactured in the same factory; on both sides, the moral turpitude of its functionaries had to be covered up in a hurry.

According to me, Gandhiji did not want us to take the law into our own hands, to eschew thoughts of personal vengeance. He wanted us to forgive those who did us harm. The reason was obvious—to do any of this would give birth to a cycle of revenge and reprisal. That is why he believed that the law was the only institution that could mete out punishment, even though he was deeply dismayed to see several government functionaries in the long line of offenders. This was a man who had even advised those accused of political crimes during the freedom struggle not to evade the law—in fact, he had made the famous freedom fighter, and later MP, H.V. Kamath surrender. This was a man who sought to weigh justice in the scales of the truth; his vision of Ram Rajya was a compassionate, courageous, equitable, just rule. This corrupt and lawless mayhem could in no way be a realization of Bapu's dreams.

That Bapu had ordained that the foundations of a Congress government must lie in faith, truth and ahimsa were forgotten. The country no longer remembered the words that the progenitor of this government and this freedom had uttered in the days of his last fast:

> Was it for this that those who are no longer with us endured so much suffering and gave up all the amenities of life? Did they make the ultimate sacrifice so that black, instead of white, looters and rioters come to rule? *(11 January 1948)*

> The fighters for freedom have today become free of all moral ethics and now work in cooperation with those that until recently had stood against the freedom struggle. *(12 January 1948, after the fast was broken)*

But I was neither a Congress leader nor a government official. As an ordinary citizen, what I saw and felt is all I record here. The truth was that we believed that if harm was done to us, we must take revenge. We were hardly the proprietors of all goodness—if they didn't, why should we? Both governments continued to encourage and applaud their functionaries' misdeeds. If things had stayed like this, worse could have happened; but mercifully the Congress government soon began to recall the lessons it had been taught.

By March 1948, many camps and homes for recovered women were established in Delhi. An empty school building in Daryaganj was one.

Troops—or more aptly, herds—of girls were brought from the provinces and crammed into the Daryaganj camp. At first Hindu girls from Pakistan and Muslim girls recovered from India were housed together. However, when bitter quarrels took place between the two groups, they were separated.

But the camp's young woman warden couldn't summon the motherly love needed then. Most of her time was spent in housekeeping or paperwork. In any case, she was a reserved sort, and there was the injunction that the girls should not be disturbed in any way, that no one should speak too much to them or quiz them.

The girls would bring with them grief-laden hearts and disturbed minds. There was no one here to vent one's feelings on, no one to unburden one's heart to, nothing to do. Besides aimlessly skipping around all day, bickering and weeping over their misfortune, these girls had nothing else to occupy them. As I had no formal connection with the camp, I went infrequently. Whenever I went though, I was advised at the reception itself to not speak too much to them. Rude girls, they always mouthed obscenities, I was told. I would take a silent round of the camp and return.

This treatment, I believe, had an adverse effect on the girls. They could not vent the fever in their hearts and their disaffection only mounted. No one comforted them, or gave them hope, their just due as humans. Even a straw is a source of support to one who is drowning but this straw too was not in their grasp. None of them was told what lay ahead. Those whose relatives came could go away happily (as many did), but there were also scores of others who were bundled off screaming and cursing to Pakistan, without any promise of light at the end of the tunnel.

Armed guards were posted at the camp entrance yet men constantly crowded about. These were the abductors, waiting for a chance to spirit the girls away. The girls would shout out messages to them and signal; at times, the men would send in sweets and fruit to them via the guards.

One day, a caravan of 1,100 Hindu and Sikh women and children from Pakistan arrived in Delhi. I don't know how many stayed, how many went to relatives—all I saw was that the numbers were enough for two camps. Educated Hindu and Sikh women volunteers were doing all they could to shoulder the burden of their community—the camps were clean, well-organized and there were arrangements for temporary schooling and instruction in handicrafts. Although here too came obstinate and disaffected volunteers, the effort was to sympathize and reason with them, to eradicate the unruliness.

One girl from Patiala had been imprisoned in the house of a Patiala minister, along with her mother and two sisters. A few days after she came to me, her mother was sent to cajole her into returning; she had been threatened that if she failed, she would be denied her property worth Rs 1.5 lakh and her other two youthful daughters would not be returned to her either. The greedy mother—who herself had been impregnated and therefore could not think of going to any relative for help—tricked the girl into returning. I don't know what became of them, but it must have been tragic; I heard later that the girl's husband had announced a reward of Rs 500 for information about her.

The constant crowd of abductors outside the camp became such a problem that the authorities decided to shift the camp to the barracks in the cantonment. It was difficult to reach the place and the crowd vanished, but the girls started showing signs of mental derangement. They would hit and bite each other, hurl abuses at the warden, rail against the volunteers. I tried to assert that the only solution was to listen to them patiently. If we heard out their complaints and sorrows with tolerance, we would be able to reassure them and bring them on the right track.

But we lacked the organizational strength to do this. The Jamiat ulemas often made enquiries about recovered women and rued, 'How can one hope for a Muslim woman to be recovered?' Not one of them ever had the courage to get their wives or sisters to join us in this task. The real weakness was the men's, they themselves were not ready. On even the faintest sign of agreement from them, their wives and sisters would have immediately set out to do this work, such was their mood.

Congress voting session for or against Partition. (Left) Jawaharlal Nehru voting for the motion. Dr Rajendra Prasad and Govind Ballabh Pant are in the background. (Right) Maulana Azad sitting with Rajaji, 'looking very dejected'.

10

Hope and despair
(February–March 1948)

By February 1948, refugees had spread into most parts of the city. Houses left by Muslims were all occupied, as were ruins of old buildings, gateways to older neighbourhoods, *maths*, *shivalaya*s and mosques. Government, municipal and private schools were still closed, as refugees lived in them. Children of both refugees and inhabitants loitered in the lanes, despite the best efforts of the youth who had started temporary schools in different areas, including camps.

Soon, however, schools started to open. Refugees were evicted to the army barracks in Anand Parbat, Wavell Canteen, Bela Road and Kingsway Camp. Visiting these areas, one wondered if even a single Hindu or Sikh had been left behind in Pakistan. I had established contacts with many refugees since January, when I had left the camp;

now, I met the children regularly and got acquainted with their parents. I visited their homes and saw first-hand the intolerable conditions they lived in, and heard of the unspeakable horrors they had faced.

When February began, the Jamia boys sought to extend the Markaz's activities, as all the schools in session were for refugee children. No one could have even dreamt of such an experiment by which the two bloodthirsty communities would be persuaded to send their children to the same school but the Jamia boys had, and its success had given us courage and hope. Now, we needed to expand activities to Kassabpura.

The Markaz was opened in the marketplace and Trilok was made in-charge. No doubt this first Sikh to enter a Muslim area must have felt anxiety—even if not as much as the area's Muslims did; their jaws dropped when they first saw him. However, as everyone in the area trusted our group implicitly, there was no objection. Within a month, Trilok had established such a rapport that with one call, he could gather the whole neighbourhood.

One day, a goatherd who used to take the neighbourhood goats to graze, returned alone. His explanation was incredible: he fell asleep, and when he awoke, the goats were gone! Someone must have taken them away, he said. The owners came to Trilok, 'Sixty goats disappearing in one night! We've lost everything. Please help us, quickly.' Trilok began the search immediately and returned with all the goats the next day. He found them in the neighbouring locality and brought them back without quarrel.

Trilok reported his success to me, his Punjabi accent emphasizing the 'k' in the Hindustani word for goat, *bakri*. 'Apaji, I searched all night and found them!' His colleagues were delighted with his prowess and clapped his back.

Thereafter, the Markaz made steady progress. A month later, another boy was made in-charge, two months later another. All the boys showed great maturity, and without getting involved in any disputes, strove for social and educational progress. Soon, a third Markaz could be started in Pul Bangash; the whole area was now included in our educational activities.

My own contact with refugee women grew through the Jamia Sewing Centre I started, to foster reconciliation between Hindu and Muslim women. With a small sum of money I'd put aside, I managed a sewing machine and a Congressi sister helped me get another plus two charkhas from the CRC. These, and whatever yarn was available at home, became my capital. I toured neighbourhoods and housing colonies in search of poor and widowed women who could come to the sewing centre for work.

In this process, I met women of every class and religion, and learnt a lot about the situation of refugee women. When these women found out that I was a Muslim, their eyes would cloud with suspicion, their tone would turn belligerent. After a while, however, they would begin to feel that perhaps this Muslim was a different beast altogether, and they would relent a little, agreeing to at least give my offer a trial.

Yet, despite extensive publicity in Muslim neighbourhoods, very few came forward. Muslim women just could not summon the courage to step out. Starving at home clad in rags, they wanted us to deliver work to them at home and fetch it when it was done. But, of course, wearing the burqa—so filthy that just to touch it made one retch— was indispensable. So what if it didn't cover their faces and draped only the back of the body from head to toe? Their only anxiety was the slur of immodesty.

After much cajoling, eight Muslim women promised to at least visit us once; only four signed up ultimately. How different from the response of our refugee sisters—eight to ten of them, both needy and well-to-do, showed up on the very first day and soon their number rose to twenty-five. It was up to us to select the genuinely deprived. Male volunteers from the Student Congress also enrolled their girl colleagues.

A Congressi sister's assistance ensured that the CRC sent us many bales of cloth, which we distributed to the women daily. The Jamia Sewing Centre had become a reality. While the Punjabi sisters would be back with stitched clothes almost every day and take away the payment, the Muslim women would return only after two or three days. Undoubtedly, their sewing was neater, more delicate and superior, but the time they took over it meant they were paid only once in two or three days.

Soon, all the cloth provided by the CRC had been tailored. Thus far, we had been paying the women from our own funds; now we sent them the bill with the clothes. However, the money never reached us. Even though after much running around we learnt that the payment had been approved, the centre incurred a loss of Rs 25 in the first month itself.

The camp for Muslim girls in Pataudi House, Daryaganj, had just been instituted. I visited it occasionally and found this former girls' school crammed with women and children, including many orphaned children who had been divided up as bounty among the attackers once their parents were killed. I noticed that most children still wore the clothes that they had been brought in. Though the young women had new clean clothes, little girls wore tattered *ghaghra-cholis*. The warden said that all the clothes the government sent had been of the same adult size, so the children's clothes had not been changed. I offered, 'We have many clothes ready for children at our sewing centre. If you want, we could send them across.'

'Most certainly. We feel terrible to see the children in this state, but what can we do?' The very next day, I took thirty pairs over and soon the children were newly outfitted. A Hindu sister, one of the camp administrators, expressed her happiness that I had made them look so clean and fresh. I asked the office in-charge whether I should send a bill for the clothes and he asked me to. When I did so the day after, the warden refused to pay up. 'You can't possibly expect payment! I thought you were giving us clothes of your own accord.' I replied, 'But I already said that these clothes had been made by the Jamia Sewing Centre. Their prices are fixed and entered in the stack of bills in front of you. Refugee women stitch these clothes; if they are not paid, they will starve.'

She raised her voice, 'I'm sorry, madam, the government cannot pay you right now! It will take months for the bill to be cleared. If you still want payment, you can take the clothes off the children and take them back.' I tried again, 'I don't care if it takes months. Aren't all the clothes that you use in the camp stitched somewhere? They must be stitched by refugee women of other sewing centres like mine.'

'I'm sorry madam, but I cannot allow this. The government cannot pay your bill. At the most, we can write to you, thanking you for your generosity. But money is out of the question.' I couldn't bear to continue. Bitterly, I said, 'Aren't there enough poor people in the villages and neighbourhoods for me to be charitable towards that I would waste my money on a government-run camp?' I left. I couldn't even think of taking the clothes off the children—we would just have to bear the losses.

It seemed that because the sewing centre was associated with Jamia and me, it didn't deserve assistance. That most women in the centre were Hindu was, of course, irrelevant. I didn't perceive any difference between Hindu and Muslim, and certainly did not discriminate—for me, all distressed woman were equal. As my Prophet says, 'The whole of Creation is Allah's family, and he who serves Allah's kin is the most beloved of all.' But why would these people concede this? This consideration never left their own minds, their only concern was to brand each thing Hindu or Muslim.

The centre's objective was to foster peace and unity, not to found an organization or make profits. No instructors were appointed, all the volunteers worked for free. However long I could manage to run it like that, I would. Resolving this, I digested the loss of Rs 80 or 90.

Before me, Hindu and Muslim women, who till yesterday had run from each others' shadows, sat side by side, speaking of their trials and the world's travails, crying and laughing. This was my greatest success. The first day that they had gathered, what glares and taunts were exchanged, but now they were friends. The college girls who visited us occasionally managed to convince them that each woman's grief was equal, that bias cannot find a home in stricken hearts. We turned their hearts towards thoughts of love, amity, unity. Now, they often came to me for consultation. Alas, I was never of any significant assistance, beyond finding remedies for small problems. I wasn't officially connected to either the CRC or the rehabilitation ministry, and the problems of these women were not so transient that they could be addressed easily.

From February to mid-April, I worked in the city thus. My routine at the camp also carried on. Gandhiji's martyrdom had brought about an appreciable change in the overall situation. Muslims could now walk about freely. Whatever be the thief in the officials' hearts, they were better behaved, at least superficially. After losing everything, people had finally come to their senses.

The Muslim League's propaganda had also become quite muted, though this was only because their numbers in India were now negligible. We were therefore surprised to see that, even now, the night before a train was scheduled to leave for Pakistan, hundreds of people would be camped in Isa Khan Maqbara (near Humayun's Tomb). We couldn't fathom how all these people got passes. There was no place in Humayun's Tomb for new entrants, so they could not have been allowed in there. The Pakistan Office distributed passes only to inmates, so how could these outsiders acquire them? And why did these newcomers invariably board the train, not the inmates who had been waiting for so long?

The conspiracy was exposed at the railway station. The camp was so short-staffed then that many Jamia boys, who had earlier worked in the camp, returned for a day to help out. When they arrived at the station, they saw passengers surreptitiously handing over their passes to the police and volunteers after boarding the train. They immediately intervened and retrieved hundreds of surrendered passes.

I was apprised, and we investigated. We learnt that the police and volunteers had conspired to sell the surrendered passes at Rs 5–10 each to other aspirants. The overwhelming majority of passengers on the next train would therefore be of their customers. If any camp inmates managed to board the train, it would only be because they were affluent enough to pay. No wonder no poor inmate could ever board the train. In fact, such a crowd thronged the station that day that there was a stampede and many were crushed to death.

Nizamuddin station was such a small one, it was impossible to accommodate those numbers.

I decided that it was necessary for me to meet the Pakistan High Commissioner, Zahid sahab, to remedy this terrible situation. To meet him was no easy matter, certainly tougher than getting an audience with the governor-general. It was said that the humour that ruled him was obstinacy, and he impatiently waited for the day he would be liberated from the onerous responsibilities of his high office. I'd had very little personal interaction with him—what help did I ever need from him—and he had seemed inoffensive.

Arriving there, I first met a passionate young man from UP, a staunch Muslim Leaguer, whose conviction that India was the abode of kafirs didn't allow him to stay here for a moment longer. He perhaps secretly nurtured the dream that as soon as they saw him approach, the High Commission officials would rush out in grand reception of this new crusader; when I met him though, he'd had a rude awakening. Despite days of fervent pleas and urgent entreaties, his sighs had not reached the High Commissioner. As I waited, he paced about, asking me what he could possibly do. I was amused:

ibtada-e-ishq hai rota hai kya
aage aage dekhiye hota hai kya
It is but the beginning of love and already this complaint?
Wait and watch, much more may lie ahead!

Mir Taqi Mir

A crowd of people always thronged the gates of the High Commissioner's residence. Tents had been erected in the courtyard to shelter permit aspirants. But their wait lasted many days, and many were finally sent off, without the High Commissioner even receiving the news that they had been there. Here too, money talked; silver could get you not one but as many passes as you wanted.

From what I could discern, Zahid sahab was upright and not unkind, but totally unsuited for that atmosphere and job. To him, his duties were insufferable, the mood of the times grim, and his nature rebelled. This too was the Muslims' misfortune that, in all their troubles, the only 'messiah' they had was an ailing one. The only mistake the poor man ever made was to sit by himself, desolate, refusing all meetings and calls. Even a few words of sympathy were beyond him, such was his despair.

Yet, I had to meet him. I was let in at the gate, but the staff caught me on the veranda. Extricating myself from their grasp, I fell into the hands of the deputy secretary, who insisted that I speak to him as the High Commissioner was too busy. After much negotiation, I got an appointment with the secretary. I had to wait long. The secretary would neither refuse nor acquiesce to the meeting. I was in a hurry, so when I was finally called, I thought it wiser not to insist on a meeting with the High Commissioner and made the secretary note the facts as well as permit numbers of eighty Humayun's Tomb inmates who were waiting to leave.

I berated him, 'Can you please investigate how permits from your office are sold in the city? This is the height of mismanagement! You tell us that we must prevent the Delhi people from leaving because there is no space left in Pakistan yet you give a single individual the permission to take eighty people along! As a result, the camp never empties. Your office cannot even bother to put in a date of expiry on the permits, or send someone to the station to destroy used passes, to end this scam.'

Secretary sahab nodded vigorously all through, 'I will definitely find out. Yes, this merits an inquiry . . .' but ultimately gave not one concrete assurance. The commerce of passes continued unhindered, ending only when the camps wound up.

I did make one last attempt, though, and again I could not meet the High Commissioner. Perhaps that was for the best as by then I was quite angry. Inevitably, the exchange would have been heated and I would have had to live with the shame that I had troubled him when he was enfeebled with illness, however insensitive a man he might have been.

Another weak, callous person I met was Delhi's chief commissioner, Khursheed Ahmad Khan. He could almost never be reached over the telephone, but even if one were lucky, no assistance was ever forthcoming, beyond 'Yes, yes' to everything one said. Neither did he come to the aid of Muslims in their hour of distress. People said, 'Poor Khursheed, what can he do? The government has given him so many responsibilities, but Randhawa sahab has made him helpless. Khursheed isn't even consulted and has no power to send a truck to rescue a Muslim family!'

But I detest this making of excuses for one's sins—in fact, that is a far greater sin. If such was Khursheed sahab's helplessness and humiliation, there was always a more honourable route open to him. Better than this murder of conscience would have been protest. No force can stand in the way of a person who sincerely wants to help others. Even a verbal protest would have become public but he couldn't bring himself to do even that.

In end-February, some villagers from Jheel Khuranja and Khureji in Shahadra came to tell us of their troubles. They were camped in a disused tehsil building, without arrangements for rations or necessities. We visited them and, deeply affected by their plight, decided it was time to take the first step—they had to be restored to their homes. The officials flatly rejected our suggestion, however. Neither were they unwilling to take responsibility, nor would they help us in any way. When we took the proposal to the Jamiat, Maulana Ahmad Saeed's response was, 'Dutta behen (as Subhadra was often called), do you want these people killed?'

But in our ears only Bapu's words echoed: until all the displaced returned home, he wouldn't find rest, the nation wouldn't be at peace. If we could only have managed it, we would have returned all the refugees to Pakistan at once, and resettled all the displaced back in their homes in East Punjab. If only we had the prerogative and the requisite numbers in our ranks! But the situation being what it was, the only place where we felt we had a right to do anything was Delhi. All our schemes and all that our hearts desired would have to be executed here. The sphere of our influence was limited, our powers of execution slight, but our hearts and minds were unconstrained and our strength had increased eightfold. In death, Bapu had shown us the way of life and fortified our resolve.

Relying on our values and colleagues, we set out for the village to meet the ziledar that very evening. It was still quite cold and the elders in the village *chaupal* were wrapped up in thick blankets. The hukkah was doing the rounds as they sat listening to the woes of a refugee from Dera Ismail Khan. We were warmly welcomed but once the purpose of our visit was revealed, the demeanour of our hosts changed.

When we requested that Muslims be allowed to return, a local pandit said, 'Sahab, if the government wants them to return, we won't stand in their way. We had no quarrel with them; they left because the thanedar said they must. All Muslims from neighbouring villages were gathered and sent to the qasbah just ahead; later they were all thrown out of there too. Then goons were sent to empty their houses. We did not do anything.' After talking to the villagers for a while and taking a round of the village, we thought to ourselves:

harche baadaa baad ma kashti dar aab andakhtem
Uncaring of the end, we will lower our boats into the river

Farsi proverb

Whether we lived or died, we were determined to resettle those fifty to sixty people in their homes. Trucks were rented and two volunteers delivered all of them to the village the very next day. Floods in the Yamuna—God's wrath upon the village!—had washed away all but one house; on our insistence, Jamia had to give us fifty tents. Ahrar Party footed the bill for transportation. Two tents were kept aside for Subhadra and the volunteers, while the rest were allocated to sanctuary seekers.

Our task was to bring rations and other necessities from the city for these people. The looters had cut down their standing crops and other villagers were now cultivating these fields. They were certainly not going to give grain or land to the rightful owners, unless pressurized. To feed so many people for a month was no easy task, but God's grace and the courage of my colleagues helped us. Some days,

Jamiat would send sacks of rations; on others, one of us would garner some. Occasionally, Subhadra would take a begging bowl to the city and return with enough for some days.

Over the next month, we held small meetings for truth and reconciliation. One large meeting was also organized and then a panchayat of twenty-four villages was called. Coincidentally, I had to leave for Allahabad that day and couldn't attend, but my colleagues told me that the general air was not hostile, although there was reluctance to let other Muslims return. Other villagers were afraid that the truth—that everyone had taken a share of the loot—would emerge. All old neighbours knew what the other had done, what had been taken, by whom. Suppose the sanctuary seekers' things were found in their possession?

Knowing that this was a village where Hindus had been inhospitable even to Hindu refugees, we announced that sanctuary seekers had returned only because they had faith in their brothers' love. They had come on their own initiative, without relying on the police or the administration, and sought only sympathy and assistance from their neighbours. If the villagers wanted to help them, either by returning what was theirs or by giving them a share of their own, the returnees would forever be in their debt. This announcement had a positive effect, the panchayat decided that the sanctuary seekers would be given half of the new crop when it was reaped. Meanwhile, the villagers would share the grain they had.

We sent word to the central government ministers that despite receiving no help from the local government, we had managed to resettle these people. None of them had ever wanted to go to Pakistan, and thinking that India had to give them a home, we returned them to their native land. Now they were in dire need of assistance. A responsible government functionary gave us Rs 600, which we used for new thatched roofs, doors, bamboo structures, etc. The returnees built the mud walls of the houses themselves. Eventually, all the returnees settled down. Word spread, and many others returned.

Then came the time for crop division and dissension began. The police incited the villagers, saying that no such order had come from the top. 'These outsiders just want to maximize their gains—why should you listen?'

Our volunteers had left by then. Some of the returnees came running to tell us of how the thanedar had provoked the other villagers, how there had already been a Muslim–Harijan spat. All that we had achieved could go to waste. And how were we to deal with the local police, as our relations with them were terrible? Before us, the Congress, and before that, the group of young people who worked here had to submit to the police's designs. We, too, could face defeat.

However, it was our good fortune that some honourable police officers were posted in Delhi then; they could appreciate both sides of any issue and were ready to work with us. The biggest obstacle was the thanedar. Were he not removed, the villages would remain wildernesses. So, we had no objection when the local government decided to reward our greatest opponent for his efficiency with a promotion and a transfer. Our objective was achieved: the villages were bereft of his ministrations and nationalist forces could take root.

This peaceful return of sanctuary seekers to their village and the successful fostering of amity was the Shanti Dal's greatest achievement and one we were very proud of. The number of returnees had climbed to ninety and letters from other aspirants poured in from Pakistan. We sternly forbade such requests and three of our colleagues decided to camp out in the village to monitor the situation. The four weeks they spent there were greatly enjoyable, even though conditions were hard. One of us would visit every few days and the local Congressis were extremely helpful. This month-long visit increased our influence in the nearby villages as well.

But woman, little knob of poison that she is, will always be the undoing! That month, two women were brought. One belonged to this village; it was her marital home and though some of her in-laws were here, her husband was in Pakistan. Where should she be kept until he returned? There was no doubt that he would return as soon as he heard from her, but to give him or her the right of residence in the village was neither our call nor our right. Yet, to help another woman once again lead a life of dignity was both our duty and our heartfelt desire. Putting aside questions of law, we followed the dictates of our conscience and the woman's desire. Provided the husband would take her back, the girl could stay and we'd keep this fact from the authorities.

The girl was housed with an old aunt. She started cooking for some government employees. Soon, the village was taken up with this sunny, clever girl, with her dancing, sparkling eyes. Many mothers offered their sons in marriage, many widowers embraced the thought of another nikah. Our assurances to each suitor that the husband was alive and would return soon went unheeded, and one day we learnt that the old aunt had been corrupted, that the girl had left for the city! Subhadra was furious, and her threats ensured that the girl was brought back. We were initially told that the girl had been married to another but our rage broke one witness. He confessed that it was a lie, told to dupe us.

The next day, the husband arrived and immediately taught everybody a lesson. The wife was slapped around, the adversaries wrestled with and all those who had conspired to appropriate his wife abused publicly. How could simple rural folk become so scheming, so immoral? Those who had once believed the daughters and daughters-in-law of their neighbours to be their own could not hide their moral debasement from their own community!

Then, a fire swept through Kingsway Camp. Nature, it seems, was bent upon destruction those days. The fire raged unhindered and within minutes, the little wealth that had been saved from the looting— earned by months of labour, gained as assistance from the government—was lapped up. When I reached, I saw the remains of burnt huts, charred clothes, pots and pans blackened with soot. Even angels would have been tormented by the children's wails, the mothers' moans, the helpless silence of the aged.

But Man is the cruellest. Even at this time, he displayed the blackness of his heart. A woman cried: 'It's all gone! The little jewellery I could save from those Pakistani *musalla*s has gone to those sinners!' I asked, 'Was it burnt in the fire?'

'Oh no! When the fire started, we gathered our things outside the huts. While we were running in and out, thieves robbed us!' Some lost utensils, others trunks; someone mourned the loss of jewellery, others clothing. The robbers were among them, residents of this camp. What person viewed even tragedy as opportunity?

One man sat weeping over the loss of Rs 10,000. The camp commander expressed surprise that he had possessed such a sum, as he had been taking ration from the government all this while. I thought to myself that perhaps he had gained the sum that night itself, just before robbers had visited a thief's house.

Many no longer had even a scrap of cloth to shelter under. They would have to toil the same long hours they had to three months earlier to get that one meal a day, to be able to wear that one set of clothes. When they had first arrived, it was only when they could afford roofs of hay, tin, or cement that they had gotten some shade; now, it was to be that same blazing sun all over again, the same scorching heat. It made my heart ache. My God! You are the most bountiful. Why aren't You moved to mercy? Who else can help these 24,000 people but You?

But the people were not asking for His mercy, in fact they were remonstrating with Him for his cruelty. It was not difficult to see why: the months of trial had robbed them of all forbearance. The future that presented itself had a terrible face and no ray of hope peeped out from among the dark clouds. Why should they not be anguished?

Soon after, all the inmates were moved to empty school buildings and houses across the city and began the long wait for things to improve. Slowly, tents were obtained, thatched roofs laid, walls built—Kingsway Camp was ready for the refugees' return. They were brought back and now their inner disaffection and outer disorderliness peaked. Only God knew how long this cycle would continue . . .

In February, two men escaped from Khirki village to Humayun's Tomb camp. Their shorn heads with chotis caused much consternation. Groups of Muslims would form around them, hear their story and disperse to recount it. Some old villagers finally brought them to me. I was told that in many villages in Mehrauli, Najafgarh and Narela, Muslims were being forcibly converted. Now pretending to be Hindus, they were biding their time for an opportunity to escape. The two men asked us to help the trapped Muslims: 'Have them brought out and send them to Pakistan, please.'

I said, 'My brothers, that would be wrong. I ask all of you not to leave, and you expect me to send them away? I can bring them to Delhi for a month or two until things normalize and they can return to their villages. Some houses in the Muslim Zone are empty, so they can stay there but they must return as soon as peace prevails.'

My inexperience had deluded me into believing this impossible scheme to be an easy solution. The two men, however, immediately agreed and left for the village. Shortly after, armed with security guards, the police and trucks, we began the programme of rescuing the terrified Muslims. The truth behind the conversions was that though Hindu brothers had no objections to Muslims of their own class, zamindars, or artisans leaving for Pakistan, when it came to skilled labourers— carpenters, blacksmiths, oilmen—then they felt it to be a question of their own survival. If these people left, how would their fields be ploughed? If these Muslims had been allowed to live in the city, they wouldn't have been without work. They would have been able to earn by their labour. However, once the trend of 'purification' of rural Muslims began, it spread like wildfire; Jamiat too received numerous requests for rescue; in some villages, hundreds of Muslims had been forced to convert.

On the one hand was the Muslims' insistence that not one 'purified' Muslim be left behind, on the other the government's injunction that no one be forced to leave and all assistance be accorded to the wronged. This order had been in existence for some time but was being implemented vigorously by the police and the administration now, under their own unique interpretation of it. The intent behind the order had been to enable those who wanted to stay to do so without fear of religious conversion or eviction, but the administration's implementation meant that in the presence of the collectorate officials, a panchayat of forty villages was held and two whole villages of Muslims converted to Hinduism. For this dedication to duty, they were applauded by the local government, which commended them for maintaining such peace that no person felt the need to flee to Pakistan!

I accompanied the rescue team to Khirki, where fifty to sixty Muslims were being forcibly held. There was some apprehension of trouble, so the police surrounded the village. On just one call, all the Muslims rushed out. Three said that they had been converted and did not want to leave either the village or the religion. We accepted their decision; we didn't want to take up cudgels on behalf of either religion, provided the conversion was voluntary. We would fight against what was unjust.

How wrong we had been to think that it would be easy to get the Muslims out! When we announced our decision to take them away, a barrage of objections arose. There was the question of the Muslims' houses, on which they had spent a lot—but how could one hope to rent out a house in rural areas? Then there was the issue of their land— if they left the village, how would they retain control? And what about their livestock—the price they were getting was a quarter of its worth!

On top of all of this was that eternal debt, the fate that a farmer of those times brought into the world and carried till his dying day. Each owed something to another and the *mahajan*s got their ledgers out at once, lest even a straw be left unaccounted for. Some clamoured for the settlement of other obligations; even wedding invitations were seen through the prism of indebtedness: 'I gave so much to your brother when he married. But you are leaving before there has even been any talk of a marriage in my house—so pay up your dues!'

Luckily, one of our companions was a Congressi lawyer, Mr Parkash; his legal acumen proved useful. He had the ledgers thrown open and his examination of dates and sums exposed the extortion. Many of the 'outstanding' sums had long been repaid. This gave the departing villagers some reprieve. Though property didn't hold any value at the time, he managed to at least thwart attempts to snatch away ploughs and cattle. Working in concert with the police—he through reasoning,

Mr Button through scolding—the departing farmers got some money after all. The matter of wedding 'debts' was dismissed too.

I had thought that ultimately these people would refuse to leave but they remained firm, even as the baniyas displayed their meanness. Meanwhile, all the children had jumped into the trucks, Hindus and Muslims together, laughing in excitement, as if they were off to a village fair. The moment of departure came. As aged Hindu and Muslim women clutched each other and wailed loudly, many young girls sobbed quietly in each other's arms. An old farmer gazed at his *chana* fields, wiping his tears, 'See that *keekar* tree over there, I planted it myself. Look how big it has grown, nearly ready now . . . Who will harvest it, I wonder?'

Caressing beloved walls and embracing doors one last time, the farmers left, and were scattered like fallen leaves all over city. I met some of them again but failed to soothe away their heartache. Some days later, I heard that love of the land drew them to Nizamuddin but there too, they were disappointed. This longing ultimately drove most of them to Pakistan, but who knows whether their desire was sated there, or indeed whether they survived at all.

I couldn't endure the farewell. I told the officer, 'This is terrible work. I won't be able to do this again. Please ask someone else to accompany you.' I did not go again.

But Anis sahab regularly accompanied the police enthusiastically, always sporting his irritating smile. Once he was sent to recover an abducted girl, and although neither I nor my colleagues could swallow the tales about his daring feats, he did return with a girl. It was not the same one he went to get, however—but after all, the one he recovered was also some man's wife! Of course, all the credit for the recovery went to the police superintendent, leaving him smiling like an idiot.

He was always lecturing us. Whenever we were exasperated with the inmates, he would bare his lips in a false grin and intone, 'Don't harden your hearts against those poor souls. They need your sympathy.' This counsel would make our blood boil! How could this man, who sailed around with a shawl draped decorously over his shoulders in all weathers, dare to remind us of our duties!

For the rest of us, the Khirki village experience taught us a great lesson. We had failed in making the villagers content in what they had. We couldn't stop them from going to Pakistan. We couldn't fulfil our promise of returning them to their villages after a month. We were the reason that a village was deserted. To this day, I am ashamed of this mistake but I also ask myself, what else could we have done?

Refugees with their household belongings, on their way into a refugee camp.

11

The difficulties of return

(January–March 1948)

By March 1948 Humayun's Tomb camp had become an unsolvable problem. How could it ever be wound up? People no longer wanted killings and hostility—they had done all of that already, and were now aware of the advantages of peace. Disaffection and hatred against the Sanghis was widespread and they too were on the retreat, as there was no profit in repeating failures.

But local government officials were determined that Delhi be rid of every last Muslim. To this end, it continued to make wide-ranging efforts so that the stream of Muslims coming to the camp didn't dry up. In these efforts, an alliance with the Muslim League and the services of some self-styled Muslim leaders was crucial. One such leader was the retired army lieutenant Hameed whom I'd first met in the Purana

Qila camp. An influential landlord, fluent in English, he was a firm favourite of many serving officials of the Delhi administration. He'd been instrumental in emptying numerous villages in the province of Muslims (in fact, he'd been the chief player in the exchange of land in Tihar for Mr Randhawa that I spoke of earlier). Also well-connected with the Pakistan Office, his intercessions could get one a permit for travel to Pakistan or facilitate an exchange of property between the two countries in a matter of minutes.

Why did this man behave so? Perhaps he was blinded by greed, or he genuinely believed that the safety and prosperity of his friends and family was at risk. Thinking the future to be even darker, he had chosen this strategy. Whatever be the case, people were deeply impressed by his influence. They said that the Pakistan government was in close touch with him; rumour had it that he'd been asked to send the best cultivators of the province to Pakistan. They also said that he was an important part of that government's efforts to show the world that all Muslims had left India. God knows whether this was true, or his close friendship with Mr Randhawa lay at the root of his conduct.

We obviously could not make these allegations openly—what proof did we have? But we spent hours in speculation. Some believed, rightly to an extent, that his conduct was due to pressure exerted by the bureaucracy. How else could he have emerged as friend and benefactor of two governments and peoples? In my understanding, he—or the many like him—was of no real consequence. Individuals like him were thrust forward to harm people like us, mount obstacles in our paths, thwart our efforts. In themselves, they were not the problem; the real struggle was against the unseen hands pulling their strings, the minds working covertly behind theirs.

One day I chanced upon him. I said, 'You mustn't come and incite the inmates. Just when they agree to return to their homes, you land up with some promise or instruction. You are destroying them. So many villages have been deserted because of you. Why don't you just let us be?' He replied, 'I don't deny that many Muslims have been evicted and brought to the camp. But wasn't that the best option? I saw no other for my friends and family. Now there's no question of return; the lands have been exchanged. When what was ours doesn't exist, how can we go there?'

'But on whose orders did the exchange take place? I've made enquiries, the government didn't give sanction. The prime minister doesn't even know of it.' His reply was, 'Everybody knows—the local government had it done.' It wasn't the will of the local government, however, but of its highly ranked official, Deputy Commissioner Mr Randhawa. I tried to get the papers that would give me the evidence to bring him to book, but to no avail. Nevertheless, this conversation did convince me that all that I'd heard from the villagers was true. I hadn't believed them when they had blamed the administration, but now its complicity was confirmed.

We didn't let up efforts to convince the villagers to return. Throughout January, Subhadra and I went to the camp every few days to persuade them to return to Tihar, Jaitpur, Chhatarpur, Gadaipur and other villages. Our efforts initially met with great resistance, led by the Tihar villagers, by far the greatest in number.

I recall the first such meeting in January. A large number of villagers came, among them, a gentleman in a fez cap, scurrying about to canvas against us. Three or four others were constantly heckling us, their discourses studded with the choicest of difficult words from Arabic and Persian, intent on impressing the audience with their superior intellect. I understood, for the first time, the extent of power that a village patwari and ziledar could wield, and how exceedingly dangerous it could be. The Tihar villagers said that the government explicitly ordered them to leave their villages. We disputed the existence of any such order and asked them to think back to the fact that Gandhiji and the prime minister had persuaded them not to leave.

'That's true,' they said. 'We were indeed looked after and requested not to leave. And we are particularly grateful to Subhadra behenji, who served us selflessly. But what could we do when repeatedly ordered by the administration, the tehsildar and the police to leave the village?' I noted down the dates on which they had been approached. 'On the assurances we received, we stayed on in the village for two or three months, but then the difficulties increased. Forty per cent of our numbers were in service and suddenly one day, they were struck off the employment rolls. No reason was ever given. Our firearms were taken away; the Hindus, a mere 20 per cent of the population, have fifty-six licences. A village panchayat was held and our neighbours were told to socially boycott us. Our livestock was also grabbed.'

I asked, 'How many livestock went missing?' 'One bull,' came the reply. Subhadra spoke with scorn, 'Didn't you also pilfer scores of livestock in the past? Don't tell me you ran away because one bull was stolen!' What Subhadra said was true. At the height of its ascendancy, this region had been inhabited by bandits and rebels. Much of the area's prosperity was the fruit of their lawless pursuits, though many denizens were also excellent craftsmen. Nowadays, however, the chief occupations in the area were craftwork and police or army service.

By the second or third meeting, however, we gained the villagers' confidence. Before Bapu's martyrdom, we had managed to convince 5,000 villagers across villages to return. Their only condition was that Bapu meet them and give them his word that they could stay on, that they would be safe. I went to Birla House and had an appointment fixed immediately, as we knew that the Tihar people were their leaders, and the numbers of others quite small. If the Tihar people agreed to return, others would follow suit. Unfortunately, the villagers chose Hameed as their representative. He returned to report that Bapu had said dejectedly, 'What can I possibly do?' In truth, no such meeting ever took place between the two.

We had returned to the camp on the day of the first meeting with Bapu. After much cajoling, we again convinced the villagers to meet Bapu the next day. That evening, we received word from the Jamia boys that the deputy commissioner had visited the villagers. He spoke to them for long and later the villagers declared that they no longer wished to meet Bapu or return to their homes. Subhadra and I went to the camp the next day. The agitated villagers told us, 'Sahab, just leave us alone. The decision has been made. The deputy commissioner is sending Hameed to Karachi by plane and he will return with permits for all of us.'

What made them change their minds? 'When Randhawa sahab came that evening, we asked him if it was safe to return. He replied, "If I speak to you as a government officer, I'll have to ask you to return to your homes. However, if I speak to you as a friend, then I can't advise a return with confidence—conditions are far from secure."'

That ended it all, and all talk of meeting Gandhiji and returning home came to an end. As expected, the Tihar villagers' refusal to return meant that no one was going back at all. We were left with no option but to retreat, crestfallen.

Four times through January we had tried to convince the Muslims to return, and in every instance, failed. Finally, exasperated, we summoned Zafar and the assistant commander and forbade new admissions to the camp.

Therefore, imagine my surprise, when I found that Hameed and his family were now resident in the camp. Zafar told me he'd had to admit him, as Hameed had a letter from Mr Kapur, the magistrate. The next day I was looking at the caravans from the city gathering at Isa Khan Maqbara, when Mr Kapur showed up. I asked, 'Has the Pakistan government allowed Delhi people to travel to Pakistan? I thought you said it didn't want so many people to be sent there!'

'No, the permission is not for the Delhi people. The permit I have is for the people from Punjab. It says that we are to arrange for the train for them.' The train was to leave the next day, so quite a crowd had gathered by now. Some of them inched close to us to listen to what he had to say. On hearing his words, one shouted, 'What? Are you saying that Delhi people are not allowed to go?' Mr Kapur replied, 'Yes. The agreement was for an exchange between East and West Punjab alone. So many people from other provinces have already reached—there is no space for more. How many can to fit into that strip of land they have?'

The Delhiwala snapped, 'Then those rascals should have thought over why they were making Pakistan at all, if it's too small to fit all of us!' The magistrate turned to me conspiratorially and said, voice dripping with contempt, 'All this is Hameed's fault. You must get rid of him—all this trouble is of his making.' That comment set me afire.

Was there no limit to deceit? To tell the thief to burgle away even as you warn the king to stay awake! 'If you remember, I'd refused him a pass to enter the camp, but you gave him permission to stay in perpetuity. Now you call him a scoundrel!' He spluttered sheepishly, 'Was it me . . . Do you mean . . .?' 'Yes, it was you! I have it from you in your own hand.' To cover for his embarrassment, magistrate sahab had no option but to turn away from me and strike up a conversation with some others.

By February, the Jamia students had virtually ceased coming to the camp; now Zafar's rule was the cause of all the trouble. As long as the Jamia boys were around, Zafar had feigned great compassion; as soon as they left, his demeanour altered completely.

A brother of Zafar's also lived in the camp. He would sit around in a tent all day, red shawl over his shoulders, *surma* in his eyes, grand *salimshahi jooti*s on his feet, always boasting how he spent the previous night without a wink of sleep as he stood guard. Apparently, he'd gathered a volunteer force to this end. I learnt only later that he was responsible for looting many sanctuary seekers of the little money they had, on the promise of executing various tasks they needed done. He never did any and, one day, simply vanished, perhaps to Pakistan. The sanctuary seekers were left cursing.

I asked Zafar about his missing brother. He of course feigned outrage, 'I don't know where he is, but I cannot wait to lay my hands on him!' In truth, he had been in with his brother all along and he had, in fact, arranged his escape.

One day in the camp office I found Zafar's court in session. On the table was a pile of jewellery; to a side lay some opened chests. Startled at noticing me, Zafar hastily collected himself enough to say, 'Just see, Apajan, so many people left their things behind at the station. All this silver and gold jewellery, all these clothes and utensils. What do you think we should do with them?' I voiced my displeasure, 'All this has been here for some time! I locked it up in the godown. Why did you take it out?'

'I thought I should have a look. Why keep all this locked up? I suggest you distribute this among the inmates. I've already started the process, why don't you complete it?' I said sternly, 'Zafar, you have no right to distribute these things. The owners could well write to us asking for them. Trains keep going and we can always send their property with other travellers. Tell me whom you have given these things to, I will take them back immediately.'

Embarrassed, he gave me some names, saying, 'What could I do, these people were so greedy! They just insisted on taking the things along.' Among the names were those of the hospital doctor, the godown caretaker, the ration in-charge, and other well-fed 'needy' camp functionaries. I went to each personally and, on my scolding, a couple returned the goods on the spot and another two promised to do so soon. But who knows how much Zafar himself had taken?

Whatever I could recover and whatever remained was locked up in each individual chest, and I told the volunteers that I would transport them that very evening to where the belongings of other sanctuary seekers were stored. As chance would have it, the car that came to pick me up that evening was small, so I had to postpone this task to the next day. That proved too late; though I kept up the requests for weeks, the boxes were never handed over to me. Only Allah knows the difficulties the poor owners faced without them.

Then one day came the news that bullets had been fired in the camp and one person had died. I rushed over to be told that Hameed had been addressing villagers in the grounds. The police surrounded them, and when a villager tried to escape (or so the police said), guns were fired. Zafar said, 'I was trying to counsel the villagers to walk the straight and narrow path, as you often ask us to. That rascal Hameed got wind of this and summoned the villagers. Fearing tension, I asked the police to surround the gathering and order it to disperse. But people didn't listen, or perhaps didn't understand, and one man broke the cordon—that's when the military fired.'

However, when I made my own enquiries, the facts turned out to be quite different. Consternation had gripped the camp for some weeks at the news that no permits for Pakistan were to be given. While the Tihar people had been allowed to travel due to Hameed's efforts (or so he claimed), Randhawa sahab's patronage and Colonel Noor Khan's munificence, other villagers wouldn't be permitted to leave.

The problem began when these other villagers, at the end of their tether after suffering months of hardship, declared that they would return to their villages. Hearing this, the Tihar villagers too began to waver, feeling the tug of community and clan loyalty. 'If you can't go, there's no point in us leaving either,' said they.

Quite naturally, this set off alarms among those who had arranged the exchange of property between Tihar and Lyallpur. Hameed rushed to meet Randhawa and then called a meeting in the camp. When he was urging the Tihar people to rethink their decision, the police arrived.

Why did Zafar call the police? Because he was excluded from the conspiracy perhaps. Indignant at this slight, he complained to the military that Hameed was inciting rebellion against the Indian government. A lie—but who would condemn it? Zafar himself escorted the army to the meeting, signalling to them to surround the gathering. In panic, the terrified villagers tried to flee. One managed to break out of the circle and, in a flash, he was felled. The army said it had to take extreme measures because the crowd confronted them, but when I reached, all I saw were petrified inmates, the women bemoaning their fate and cursing the government.

Others in the city had also heard of the firing and, by the time I reached the camp, the stream of ministers, officials and celebrities had just begun. Over the next two days, it didn't dry up. But they weren't of any real help—they all professed inability to arrange for compensation for the dead man's family.

Well-known Delhi lawyer Sultanyar Khan also came, as did a Mrs Haider, who made an important-sounding speech 'on behalf of the Indian government'. I was quite bemused that she had paid us a visit at all, six months after the camp had been set up. I certainly had never had the gumption to claim such authority; she must certainly be some highly ranked official. Just like the Muslim minister who once came to say, 'I am not here to consult or engage with you in any way. All I want to tell you is our government's position on the matter: We order you to return to your homes. We will ensure your security.' Some village leaders took umbrage at his tone and protested. But how could a poetic mind ever reconcile to polemics; he retorted, 'Well, if you will not go home, then go to hell for all I care!' and flounced off.

Right after the firing, Zafar had Hameed locked up in a garret. Hameed saw me passing by and shouted out, roaring like a lion enraged at being caged. A man approached him with food but he waved him away, growling, 'No need for this. I'm not going to eat anything.' Apparently, he had refused food the night before as well.

I found this odd: How could a mere camp commander have the power to incarcerate anybody? I asked Zafar how he had accomplished this. He said, 'The crime was one of rebellion, after all!' The eagerness in his eyes suggested that he expected me to compliment him, but all he got from me was rebuke.

Meanwhile, the sanctuary seekers were getting restless and angry, and the threat of violence loomed larger every day. The waters were past the danger mark; thanks to these two scoundrels, scores of distressed souls were suffering. It became necessary to inform higher authorities of this dire situation and its causes. However, when I went to the camp the next day, I found that Hameed had left for Pakistan. Apparently, Randhawa sahab had ordered his release and bought his plane ticket.

An important player of the conspiracy had eluded us. Subhadra was deeply saddened by this, 'That man will be responsible for the deaths of all the Tihar villagers. Just wait and see, he will have them all killed.' But Zafar was still here, though he knew that his days were numbered; we were determined to bring the conspiracy to light. Even as we hastily built a case against him, the announcement of a train to Pakistan thwarted our plans. The Tihar people left and some days later, Zafar disappeared. Then, two or three more trains left in quick succession so that by April, Humayun's Tomb camp was wound up. At last, we were free of that onerous responsibility.

Zafar's escape is an interesting story. After the firing, it was decided that the camp would be wound up, so trains to Pakistan became more frequent. Zafar would go to the station with departing sanctuary seekers but one day, he refused to take the two volunteers who usually went along. Instead, he asked them to stand guard outside a tent sheltering some women, saying that they were new to the camp and might need assistance. The volunteers stood outside patiently for four hours but when morning passed into noon and noon inched towards evening and they didn't hear even a cheep from within, the volunteers gave up and looked inside—there was not a soul there! They rushed to the station, where they found that Zafar had boarded the train himself and was now on his way to Pakistan.

Zafar had fooled us all and we were left clutching the charge sheet we had prepared against him and Hameed. Also undone was the case of conspiracy we were building against Randhawa, Hameed, Zafar and two or three powerful landlords of Delhi province, by which all the Muslims of Delhi's villages were to be chased off to Pakistan. The conspiracy had succeeded, we had lost.

In March 1948 I also got to know Chhote Khan, a Mewati who was usually in a terrible state of excitement, his words tumbling over each other. He would occasionally sidle up to me, whispering conspiratorially, 'More Mewatis have arrived. The camp is full of Mewatis now. Help them to return to their homes. Come and listen to what happened to them in Pakistan.'

Unlike the other inmates who were awaiting permits for Pakistan, the Mewatis were in the camp because they had returned from Pakistan and were waiting to be resettled in India. With Chhote Khan, I once met them and heard the tales of the broken-hearted, defeated farmers: 'When we reached, the Pakistani authorities settled us on the border. There, day after day, there was trouble with the Sikhs, in fear of whom we had left our native land. And we had again landed in their midst! We consulted each other and decided to return. Others are on their way back too. When we are destined to fight and die, why not fight and die for what is ours?'

In January and February, the Mewatis' return to their homes in Haryana was relatively easy; there was no permit system in place yet. All one had to do was convey them stealthily to Nuh Tehsil and no one would get wind of their return from Pakistan. Bapu had himself reassured the Mewatis and extracted a commitment from the government of East Punjab that the Mewatis who wanted to stay on would not be prevailed upon to leave. As a consequence, 60,000 Mewatis lived in a single tehsil of East Punjab.

By March, however, the permit system was in place. Although I certainly didn't want to do anything illegal, their condition moved me to pity. The Indian government was also more lenient with them as compared to others and sent a party of responsible Congressis to assist the returning Mewatis and those who had already settled in. One important Congress leader—not a member of the ministry— was appointed to oversee the resettlement operation. He despatched a few trucks full of Mewatis to Gurgaon.

Chhote Khan would often explain to me why they left their homes in the first place. 'You see, we belonged to the Praja Mandal and the Raja was opposed to us. We were always at odds with the government there, which was hell-bent on effacing any sign of the Congress or Praja Mandal from the land. It was his government, administration and police that attacked us and murdered so many of us.' Then invariably came the concluding request, 'Why don't you join our Tablighi Jamat?'

The Tablighi Jamat was an organization of preachers of the namaz and the kalma that had recently come into the public eye because of its activities in Mewat. I had heard of it in Lucknow and read the rousing writings of two of its zealous members but the first chance I got to see its activities was in Humayun's Tomb camp. Preachers lived in Bangla Wali Masjid and visited the camp regularly to impart religious instruction.

The Tablighis were all rural folk, who earned their living by their own toil and spread word of the faith in their own fashion. Although I was disappointed to find no scholarly individuals among them, their devotion to and passion for the teachings of their God and his Prophet made me respect them. The leaders urged me, 'If daughters like you joined us, our entire organization would profit.'

For them too, I had the same answer I had for the Ahraris, who had asked me to work with them on the restoration of mosques and mazars (an issue I'll speak more of later)—'Come, see how many of these graveyards, mosques and mazars have been almost razed to the ground! We have to save them now.' But my answer was simple: 'Your efforts must first be to save the ones who read the namaz, for if there are none of those left here, what use are these mosques? What will you get by hanging a big lock on their doors? In any case, I can't leave the camp now, perhaps later.'

I was simply not ready to join them. My heart told me that the mosques were being destroyed because God has no need of brick, lime, stone, or mortar—all He needs to see is your ardour, the brow that trembles to incline in His glory, your intent, your devotion. When all this is lost, then all that your hands have fashioned and all that you take such pride in vanishes before your eyes. This is God's will. Those mosques were mere shells, lacking soul. Made of dust, they were consigned to it once more.

When the Tablighis asked me to join them, I said, 'First save the existing Muslims, keep the word of Islam alive on this ground, before you think of making new ones. Thousands are dying, thousands being converted—they need your ministrations urgently.' They replied, 'Our task is to make Muslims firm in their own faith, we don't enter into debate or dispute with others.' What help could I offer them? I was not so unwavering a Muslim that I could hope to influence others. Until I myself reached the destination of true belief, how dare I assume that I could lead others there? And I had so many other tasks, all of them more urgent.

Chhote Khan would scurry about from day to night, motivated by the single burning desire to gather all his scattered people and restore them to their Mewat. If I ever tried to slip him money, he would refuse. His allegiance to the Tabligh played no small part in motivating him. Even as the group's ideology was limited to prayers and prayer books, these hard-working and stoic men of the faith also believed that food must be earned by the labour of one's own hands. Once, I saw scores of Mewatis streaming into the camp and asked, 'Chhote Khan, how do you feed so many?' He replied, 'Allah is most bountiful. He provides grain to the whole world.'

'That is undoubtedly true. But surely, you must always be in need of money?'

'Oh no! We only spend what we earn ourselves. We don't take money from others.' I thought this brave, industrious race was worthy of note by both the government and the Ulema. If they were provided the right opportunities for education and progress, they could well make our nation an unconquerable fortress. But, as Iqbal said:

Achha hai dil ke paas rahe paasbaan-e-akl
lekin kabhi kabhi ise tanha bhi chhod dein
It is good for the heart that the sentinel of the intellect keeps close,
But it must also be left on its own at times

This group had only a pure and brave heart, over which the intellect had no custody. While they could, in words without artifice, teach innocent farmers the tenets of faith, with what expressions could they counter educated reprobates? They were so simple; they believed they could take this Tabligh they had formed in their villages and go into the city to spread the word!

All the accounts we heard from both India and Pakistan made me realize that the conspiracy was being enacted on a much larger scale. The horrific stories narrated by the minorities in both countries resembled each other such that at times one was convinced that there had been one mastermind behind it. Although the events in Calcutta and Bihar were somewhat different (as were the methods employed), in Delhi and Punjab, the riots and the ends they were aimed at were identical.

In both places, there was first the propaganda of Hindu Raj and Muslim Self-Rule, in which officials of the local administration and the police took full part. In both cases, these activities were said to be at the behest of the governments, which had supposedly declared themselves unable to safeguard the minorities. Then, the minorities were terrorized into leaving their neighbourhoods and villages for a nearby camp. Inhabitants of minority-dominated villages would give

in and officials would offer to convey them, under their protection.
Friendless and alone, these dejected people would set out on foot,
bullock carts and carriages, carrying whatever little savings they
had. And then, just a few furlongs into the journey, the ambush
would occur. Thousands of monsters, armed with lathis, pikes, guns,
kirpans, would fall upon the caravans. By the time the policemen—
who had been there from the beginning of the journey but fallen back
inexplicably just then—and their officers, a thanedar or a DCP—who
had promised to be with them but was unexpectedly detained by a
last-minute emergency—arrived, everything would be over.

The refugees were plundered, even their clothes looted. Women
were stripped on the spot. The aged and the infants were slaughtered
like sheep, and the maddened survivors became targets of the police's
or the army's bullets. The army thundered in, horses straining at the
bit, and the soldiers saved one or two—enough for a warrant for
good conduct from senior officers. The injured were carried off to
hospital; the corpses laden on barrows and dumped into ditches or
rivers, or piled and consigned to flames. Young women and unwed
girls were divided up as loot among jawans. The officers also got a
share but, in this case, these priceless proceeds had to be kept in the
safekeeping of a ziledar, nambardar, or patwari to be enjoyed in
secret. And when the officers tired of the girls, the trustee sold her
off to line his pockets.

Whether all this happened spontaneously or was guided by an unseen
hand cannot be determined. But what was known was that trust had
been so completely broken that even Sardar Patel said to Bapu, 'I don't
trust the Muslims any more.' The administrative machinery in Delhi,
now treading with utmost caution, had acted with such eagerness just
six months ago. From September until Bapu's fast, senior police and
administration officers toured villages, striving to convince the populace
that the central government had ordered Muslims to leave for Pakistan.
'Brothers, what can we do?' they would say, 'We want to protect you
but the order is that only Hindus be allowed to live here. The two
religions have been given separate countries, and each will rule itself.
You had better leave the village now.'

The Hindus in Delhi's villages were told, 'You must understand that Hindu Raj prevails now. If your Muslim neighbours agree to become Hindus, you must accept them as your own. Doesn't Gandhiji want us to shed all taboos of untouchability? So you must "purify" your Muslim neighbours by converting them to your religion; then you can eat and drink together as one family.'

In Najafgarh, the Muslims of Roshanpur, Dinpura, Potkhurd and many other villages were converted in the presence of government officials. Some of these later told me, 'Many senior officials watched as Jats from forty villages made us all take a public pledge. We cannot go back on the agreement now—they will have us killed!' Only three months ago, the administration had given the RSS permission to hold a rally in Delhi in December. Who didn't know that it was the Sanghi youth that had bathed Delhi, north-eastern UP, Ajmer and Punjab in blood just months ago? Let alone the living, even the corpses of Muslims in the graveyards had not been spared. But the administration of this city, the capital of India, saw no reason to disallow the rally. Barely a month after this, Bapu fell to their bullets.

A well-known revolutionary—a comrade of Subhash Chandra Bose and an officer of the Indian National Army—told me how, in September, he was informed that Shahadra was in the grip of terrible violence. When he called the police, he was told, 'We have no such information. You are misinformed.' The revolutionary confirmed the veracity of the information and called back. This time the reply was, 'Yes, there has been some trouble there. One or two persons have been killed.'

Not trusting them, the revolutionary set out with his comrades for Shahadra. As they crossed the bridge, they saw a stationary police truck. When they looked in and saw its bloodstained floor, they held the truck back. The superintendent and other officers took long to appear. The revolutionary argued that the spatter pattern of the bloodstains indicated that the truck had been used to dump bodies in the river, but the policemen were unruffled. Even the confession by their subordinates in the truck had no effect on them. Let alone punishment, not even an inquiry was ordered.

Even today, even after so much had happened and so much known, both sides blamed each other for starting the violence. We were only taking revenge, they said. Some Muslims still lived in denial, asserting that the Hindus from Pakistan didn't face even a trifling hardship. A sister said, 'Believe me, they were in no danger at all. In Lahore they could move about freely, work, live happily. When they decided to leave, the government issued strict orders that no one should hinder them—see how they have brought even their own furniture along! In any case, a Muslim isn't capable of cruelty but those Hindus are! See what they did in eastern Punjab and the provinces!'

On the other hand, Hindus would challenge, 'What did the Muslims lose? They rule on both sides of the border—there they have the government, here they cannot be dislodged from their property. They have had no trouble, not one has been killed. And they were fully armed. Don't you know that they even used cannons in Pusa Road and Sabzi Mandi? Compare them to us—how much we suffered, and when we came to Delhi, scores more of our people were murdered!'

What an enormous error officials in charge of law and order committed when they left their commands at the mercy of such people, in whose hearts burned such fires of retribution! This happened in both India and Pakistan. In fact, the greatest anarchy was caused when government officials were themselves included in the exchanged populations. I believe that on both sides, it was officials themselves, and their masters the capitalists, who paid the goons to execute this entire carnage.

In the summer of 1947 I had become acquainted with a Muslim League family that had fled the riots in Calcutta and come to live with their relatives in Dehra Dun. The gentleman was ill; his wife said that he'd taken ill because he witnessed the carnage. They lived close to our house and our daughters were good friends.

One day talk turned to the events in Calcutta. The lady spoke simply, with pride and satisfaction, 'Sister, all trade and commerce had come to a standstill. The only activity was the distribution of knives. They were brought in large containers to the shop, doors were shut, and knives distributed to the Pathans lined up in the rear lane.'

'For what purpose?' I asked. 'To kill Hindus, of course. The Pathans pounded them to pulp, didn't they? They were very useful.'

By the time a Pathan had murdered seven or eight people, he would fall down in a stupor; so lorries and cars would follow, to spirit him away once he fell. He would have to be dunked in buckets of water and packed with ice; else the murderer would have turned on himself and taken his own life. I asked, 'Did this happen only in your area, or did others do this too?'

'Oh no, all the big factory owners and traders did this. On the other side, the Hindu mahajans, mill owners, moneylenders and traders did the same. We had to arrange to save ourselves.' No wonder, I thought to myself, the master of the house was stricken by illness— the disease must be the plague from his conscience.

Similarly, I remember being told in Lucknow about how a car manufacturer stored lathis mounted with sharp blades in his house. Later, he distributed them from a mandir or a gurudwara.

Now, nearly one year later, in end-March 1948, the state of mind of the people on both sides of the border and in Delhi had not changed much. They would neither believe in, nor sympathize with, the troubles of the other side. No real trust be placed in either the Delhi administration or its police—many old sinners were still powerful. And this is why, when we heard rumours that June would ring in a fresh wave of rioting, we knew we had to act immediately.

Anis Kidwai and Subhadra Joshi (to Anis's left) at a political meeting.

12

New challenges and a new Shanti Dal
(April–May 1948)

As April began, vicious rumours about a fresh round of communal riots started to circulate. Apparently, the riots would start on 15 June; the targets would be Muslims (to be hunted and slaughtered) as well as Hindus—to be made to repent their sin of not welcoming the refugees adequately. The Muslims were convinced of its truth; like the promise of 5 September as the appointed day for the first round of rioting in the Delhi province had been kept, this would be too.

The city was abuzz with the news. It also found its way to the Congress office and Government House. Activists from rural areas rushed to inform us how arms were being collected at various places. Volunteers reported RSS *shakha*s being held at several places. At one particular place, it was a nightly affair with a parade and games with spears and pikes. Another reported meetings being held every day in gurudwaras and temples.

An employee of the Telegraph Office said, 'Last night, as I was cycling home from work, a man behind me remarked, "Why haven't these bastards left for Pakistan yet? Why loitering around here?" His friend replied, "Let it go, my friend. Come 15 June and we will make the ultimate sacrifice for them!"'

Tension was rising in the city. One night, as we sat on our veranda, a terrifying scream rent the air from the direction of India Gate. In panic, we rushed to our feet. Two Sikhs ran by. The policeman near us gave pursuit. Soon, numerous others rushed too. Apparently, a government babu and his wife were walking to the grounds near India Gate around 8.30 p.m. Though the area was brightly lit, two Sikhs attacked them and tried to carry the wife away. When the babu fought back, one of the Sikhs shoved a finger into his mouth and yanked, tearing open the sides of his mouth. The scream we heard was his. But he managed to save his wife and his own injury was not too serious. However, the effect of this incident was longer lasting; for months after, women wouldn't go to India Gate in the evening.

A major cause for this rising tension was the strife over houses in Muslim zones, which were established on our request that until peace returned, no refugee be settled in Muslim neighbourhoods. We requested this because whenever a refugee settled among them, ten Muslim households would pack up and head to the camp. Some part of the fear of the refugees was a result of the Muslims' imagination, some created by the refugees' antics themselves. From the minute the refugees set foot in a locality, they devoted their energies to capturing the neighbourhood for friends and family, by hook or crook. Whether driven by need or vengeance or both, the result always was that the atmosphere got so charged that locals had to run for their lives.

The government-demarcated Muslim zones were large areas—Jama Masjid, Ballimaran and Bara Hindu Rao, and a fourth, the tiny area of Nizamuddin. Empty houses were to be given to Muslim refugees only. Of the four localities, however, only the last was full; in the rest, many houses were still vacant. We were keen to fill the empty houses with the troubled, embittered villagers. Where else could they find homes? They did not want to go to Pakistan and could no longer live in the villages under threat of conversion.

Nevertheless, even in April and May 1948, the shortage of homes for refugees meant continuing attacks on Muslim zones, though there was a qualitative difference in the way houses were forcibly occupied. Muslims would be continuously harried—by entreaties as well as threats—to rent out their houses to the more affluent refugees. Government officials made important people of the city intercede on their behalf and policemen wielded the power of their weapons to ensure that even the most bigoted Muslim agreed to give their friends or relatives a room to stay in. As soon as one was successful, ten more aspirants would pool in and lay siege. Some employed a new strategy; the men stayed behind and sent gangs of women and children into battle. They would swarm the lanes, locate a vacant house, capture it and start living there.

The problem was that a formal pronouncement did not underlie the institution of Muslim zones; the central government could not enact a law without an Assembly meeting. An ordinance was out of the question because that would amount to establishing a permanent emergency situation. Therefore, the Muslim zones had no legal status and remained an operational principle expected to be implemented by local governments. So, it was entirely up to local government officials to communicate the reality and necessity of the Muslim zone to its functionaries.

As the Delhi government's entire endeavour was to ensure that the communal quarrel did not subside, it averted its gaze from the public's troubles and was deaf to our entreaties. In May, four months after Muslim zones were established, we had made little progress in convincing Delhi's administration and police that they had to be safeguarded. We were destined to be called liars by them, over and over. Whenever we tried to stop a refugee siege with the assertion that this was a Muslim zone, a police officer would counter-whisper in their ears that no legal order backed up our claim. Just go and capture that house, they urged, no case can be filed against you. And our interlocutors would laugh at us and do as they wished. Neighbourhoods would be attacked, shops would lower their shutters and passers-by would scamper to the Congress office for sanctuary. Burglary and stoning of houses became common.

This misery was compounded ten times when the menace of 'pagdi' swept into India from Sindh. I'd never heard of it and, for a while, I couldn't fathom what it was until my colleagues explained to me its important role in economy and business. The system worked like this: When the rich left India or Pakistan, they took the precaution of safeguarding their property by stationing a poor friend, neighbour, relative, or servant as guardian. If the man was honest, the house would be safe until the end. If not, he would give the property to a refugee brother for a Rs 5,000–10,000 pagdi. I also heard stories of some rich Muslim businessmen who, although unaffected by the riots, decided not to stay back in India. Because they couldn't hope to sell their land and buildings for a reasonable price in these difficult times, they took thousands of rupees as pagdi and left for Pakistan, planning to come back and sell them off once normalcy returned.

But what of the refugees that were poor or middle class or more gentle mannered? Their agony was unbearable. They would plead, 'Please tell them. They will listen to you, you are a Muslim!' I would try but invariably fail. I'll always regret that I could not assist the gentle Mr Talwar and his young son. I took them to meet the in-charge of the Muslim zone; the Socialist Party had recommended their case, so we met the rehabilitation commissioner too. I also sent them to Jamiat with the request for shelter for their sixteen other relatives. But nothing came of all this—no one aided these needy people. Those who could give pagdi always found a house in the Muslim zone, as did those who could vault walls and capture buildings.

These poor homeless would not, I feel, have suffered as much as they did had their selfish leaders not instructed them, 'Go, drive the Muslims out of their houses and capture their land.' I cannot believe that the Muslims of UP and Delhi would have been so heartless to refuse to help fellow humans in distress. Also, many refugees were middle-class government employees and businessmen, who could afford the rent. It was not the first time that a Muslim would be renting out to a non-Muslim. I myself had seen a Muslim landlord rent out the four parts of his house to a Muslim, a Christian, a Hindu and a Sikh family. The false leaders compounded the refugees' ruin. Instead of helping them fight for what was rightfully theirs and to counter only those who harmed them, they told them to kill all the Muslims of Delhi and Punjab.

Further, it was false that all those who crossed into India came because they were driven out. There too were the same lies, false propaganda: 'No Hindu or Sikh can live in Pakistan. We must leave.' If the population transfer were done gradually, the situation may not have been so adverse. But people had been herded across like cattle. These rudderless people were unstable, having lost socio-ethical moorings. How I wish our elders hadn't been so eager to see an independent India and Pakistan. How I wish they had left this day for younger eyes to see!

Matters were worsened by the inexperience of the Congress government, which eagerly despatched trains and planes to bring Hindu and Sikhs to India. What it did not do was to despatch its army to the border to take on Pakistan; it let the murder of its subjects go unchallenged. It would have been a thousand times better were this madness limited to a clash of two crazed armies. We would have been spared this zest for revenge, these blood-spattered streets.

The greatest offenders were the educated, the bureaucracy, the leaders, the merchants of religion—the fighting sated their bloodlust. Just as educated supporters of the Muslim League were responsible for inciting the Muslim masses, educated Hindus too were responsible for the growth of the RSS and its divisive activities. No one side could be held entirely to blame. On both sides, this conflagration was not only the design of the leaders but a conspiracy by administrators, capitalists and rulers of princely states. Government offices became dens of the Muslim National Guard and RSS, directing the destruction, and these forces were trusted allies of both governments. The army, police and broadcasting services were co-opted into this deep-seated intrigue, which destroyed such a vital, industrious, well-to-do, valiant race of India, the Punjabis.

Muslims in India could have justifiably called themselves a minority, but how could the term be convincingly applied to Hindus in Pakistan? Their numbers were just short of the Muslims. If only they had launched a peaceful resistance against the cruelty committed against them in Pakistan and called upon their Hindu brothers in India for help, I'm sure even their Muslim brothers would have joined in to protest.

But I am no politician, so my opinions will perhaps always be irrelevant. I am just a woman, and my views do not rest easy in the rubric of a world defined by law and legality. My views are guided by emotion.

Since end-January, when I saw the bright faces of Punjabi and Sindhi children and youth in a meeting in Karol Bagh, I had wondered: for how much longer will the hot, dry winds that blow in this city allow the verdant green of this crop, so lovingly watered by five rivers, to flourish? Won't these flower-like faces wilt soon? Won't these upright, healthy youth become gaunt and stooped? In just a few days, Delhi's rocky soil would leech away Punjab's beauty. Already tales of Mahiya and Heer had left their lips, leaving only curses and abuses.

> *aan qudah bashikast o aan saqi na maand*
> The cup is smashed, and the Saqi too has departed
>
> Mohammed Iqbal

An experience we had with a refugee teacher demonstrates the grave impact this atmosphere of ruin and desire for revenge had on an individual level. In itself a trifling matter, but in the context of a growing moral and ethical decline, instructive.

Around February, the boys had rented out both top floor rooms of our Talimi Markaz to a refugee family. For a moment, I was apprehensive: could giving up an inch mean the ultimate loss of a mile? But they told me not to worry. So they moved in and shortly celebrated the marriage of their daughter. For days, there was a constant stream of guests and relatives, including a man who was very pleased to see a school running in the building. He remarked, 'We too had a private school in Rawalpindi. Wouldn't it be nice if I could also teach here?'

Of course, we leapt at the offer. We were constantly looking for such idealists, who ate and drank little, rested even less and worked twenty-four hours. We welcomed him and set aside two rooms on the ground floor for him and his family. Meanwhile, the refugee gentleman upstairs had taken ill shortly after the marriage. He was taken to hospital, where he passed away after a long stay. I reached the house when the body was being brought out of the ambulance, and went up to pay my respects.

The terrible scene shook me to the very core. Several men and women were beating their chests, wailing loudly. The widow had beaten herself virtually senseless; her breast was a glaring red, so fiercely was it pummelled. When she picked up a shoe and slapped it against her face, hard, I rushed to her and exhorted Masterji, 'Please calm her somehow. She'll die if she carries on.' But he did nothing, and kept wailing. No one else did either.

I was distraught. What horror was this? The wailing, the distress, the moans made me faint. Who hasn't seen death? Even that which befell me was a calamity so unexpected that I wonder why my heart continued to beat. But that the dead could be mourned thus I never knew. I'd read of the customs of an unlettered world but not in my wildest dreams could I have thought that in the twentieth century, a section of India would practise them with such devotion, even sophisticated men partaking of it. The mourning carried on for days, but I couldn't summon the courage to behold that spectacle again.

Shortly after, Masterji moved in with his wife and children. Concerned that they, accustomed to Rawalpindi's cooler climes, would find Delhi's June–July unbearable, the boys gave up the only room with a fan to them. Masterji was also appointed Headmaster and, on the boys' insistence—who themselves had made so many sacrifices—was given a salary twice theirs, so that the family could make ends meet.

And here's how Masterji paid them back! Some weeks before the final examination in April, Masterji told the children he was going to start his own school. He asked the Jamia boys for a few rooms in the house as a venue. Naturally, the boys refused, saying that the idea of running two schools under the same roof was ludicrous. Masterji declared that there was no way he would teach in the Jamia school unless he was given a raise. He wanted at least Rs 400, he had a large family, he said.

The boys pointed out the unreasonableness of his demands. Our means were so modest that no employee was paid even Rs 100, so how could he expect Rs 400? They reminded him that at the outset he had been warned not to nurture any hopes of material. But Masterji couldn't be reasoned with. He took his pique to his students and incited them, 'This school is only temporary and no other school will accept its certificates. It's a waste of your time to study here.' Naturally, anxiety gripped the students.

Some college girls, who taught in the school, approached us to say that they had applied for jobs as guides in the police and telephone departments, and believed that a certificate of social service from Jamia would vastly improve their chances of selection. Shafiq bhai immediately agreed. The girls got the certificates the next day, in the presence of Masterji. God knows what transpired in that room but the next thing I heard was that they emerged in a rage, tore the certificates to bits and marched off, saying that they didn't need us or our certificates!

The final examination had been put off for a week on account of the school fair, a brainchild of the Jamia boys. Preparations were in full swing; boards, maps and photographs were pasted; the general excitement was rising. Then Masterji had a word with students of the sixth standard. Suddenly, these students—older, and thus wiser, in the school—began to protest the postponement of the examination. They demanded that it be held immediately so they could apply for admission to other schools. No amount of reasoning could placate them.

The situation turned ugly. The older students barged into other classes and demanded that everybody leave, shouting that they would set the school on fire, they didn't want such a school. Hindu students left, the Muslims stayed put. A Hindu–Muslim riot was nearly upon us when the Jamia boys showed sense and declared school out for the day. By then, however, the maps had been torn down, the photographs shredded, the rooms turned upside-down, and the search for matches to set the school on fire had begun. Somehow the children were herded out, the rooms were padlocked and I was informed.

Naturally, when the children reached their homes, their parents were alarmed to hear of these events. Prof. Rajendra Nath Shaida, the respected socialist leader from Punjab and himself a refugee, rushed over but got only vague answers to his astonished questions, 'What happened? How can such trouble have broken out in Jamia School?' The boys were too embarrassed to blame their colleague. Ultimately, this wily socialist divined the truth and upbraided his old classfellow Masterji. As he left, Shaida sahab declared, 'Come what may, my children will study nowhere else but in this school.'

A steady stream of personages began to flow into the school: the secretary of the Socialist Party, the editor of a leading newspaper, a refugee professor, an important sardarji and many others. Hardly had this flow dwindled, when parents started to stream in, so it was nearly evening before we could leave. It was heartening that only a handful of parents came to fight with us; most conveyed their regrets and assured us of their support. Many observed that during the violence, it was Jamia School that had given them hope for their children's future. They vowed that they wouldn't let the school be shut down and would do everything to ensure that such an incident didn't recur. This support meant that the crisis was over. The examination began the very next day and, two weeks later, the school closed for a month.

Masterji was the clear and present danger. Our conscience wouldn't allow us to deny a refugee shelter but, if he stayed on, a conflagration was inevitable. He had to be told to leave; the boys cited their compassionate natures as an excuse and this duty fell my way. Masterji had already been told that since Jamia couldn't alleviate his financial situation, he should look for other employment. All I had to do now was to tell him, 'Since this is an official Jamia school now, we expect a significant increase in admissions in July. I'm afraid we're going to need the two rooms we gave you, so please look for alternative accommodation.' He replied that he had already started looking. Fifteen days later, I had to remind him again. He told me he had sent in another application.

A month later, he was still there. The school's strength had risen substantially—at 300 now—but so had the strength of his household; the visitors and relatives had doubled. Tension turned to open hostility and relations strained. To exacerbate matters, Masterji captured two more rooms, making it a total of six—four on the ground floor, two on the first—controlled by Masterji and relatives. The problem was that there was just a single entrance, for students, neighbours and the newspaper and magazine enthusiasts. Masterji's relatives also took to riding their bicycles in and out through this same door. One day, a minor accident caused a major scene that featured Masterji's bluster and threats quite prominently. We had to act immediately. First we arranged for rented accommodation—two rooms at the other end of the neighbourhood—for the widow and her children on the first floor; she always said, 'My friends, wherever you send me, I will happily go.' With her gone, those two rooms were available for the genuine inhabitants, the Jamia boys, to occupy.

Next, we had to evict the predatory Masterji. The Jamia boys appealed to the Shanti Dal, the Congress Committee and the Socialist Party. I wrote to the Custodian and asked Masterji to sign so I could try to get him a house. He clearly had different ideas, because he simply refused to sign. I think he had been encouraged to stay put and trouble us by his relative, a police officer. He had also understood that if he didn't yield, we would sit huddled in our cloaks of propriety and do nothing to dislodge him. But dislodge him we did, taking the matter right up to the deputy commissioner and then the chief commissioner. In August, Masterji finally moved out.

In Delhi's villages too, the situation changed by end-April. Thousands of villagers could no longer live in their homes because of the threat of conversion; an equal number were eager to return. At first, applications for help came from the people who had left their villages when the violence began and scattered across the nearby provinces but, as April wore on, villagers who had been evacuated to Delhi also joined them. By end-March, the practice of rescuing Muslims trapped in the villages had been discontinued. I was myself most opposed to it; whenever Jamiat sent me a list of any such villages, I quietly put it aside. I lived for the day when I could work to restore the love and respect that the villagers once had for each other. Now, rumours about 15 June made us think of the means by which the Shanti Dal's efforts for peace could be taken to the villages.

Whenever those hell-bent on restoring peace assembled, the possibility of fresh violence dominated all discussion; what could we do to prevent this catastrophe? Though Bapu's martyrdom had encouraged the more honourable officers in its administration and police, the root cause of Delhi government's paralysis had not yet been eliminated. The sinners that still infested it were bound to patronize our new enemy. We had lost every skirmish with these corrupt officials thus far, so how could we now hope to worst them in this most critical battle?

The sole solution was to consolidate all the progressive forces. Under which banner though? The first hurdle was that a Central Peace Committee already existed, comprising celebrities and respected individuals and headed by Rajendra Babu. What then was the point of another? But we knew that ordinary people had no access to this committee. I certainly had no knowledge of its pro-peace interventions. People in the most populated and riot-hit areas were entirely unaware of its existence or any work it was supposed to have done. Possibly, I'm being overly critical; perhaps it did stellar work in keeping the peace in New Delhi and Secretariat areas—that seemed to be the extent of its influence!

Moreover, known to be partisan, this committee wouldn't admit anyone who held different views from it. Even if all patriots of different hues got together to intervene in its work, the only thing that was guaranteed was a confrontation with the local administration at the very outset—the committee was packed with its supporters.

To formally work with the Congress was not an option. We felt that any confidence that the Congress would prepare itself in time to take on the riots was misplaced—could it stop the violence in September? It didn't have enough determined people; one could count right-minded Congressis on one's fingers. It was now stuffed with opportunists, who had presided over RSS gatherings when it served their interests and were now suddenly secular and peace-loving. Having served as the right-hand men of the local administration, what good could they do for the people? Having mocked Gandhiji's principles, what Gandhism could they practise? Moreover, if we went with the Congress, our youthful volunteers and the socialists would desert us.

The Congress's influence had also waned considerably. It had no control over the new population and had lost its prestige and authority over the older inhabitants. A section had moved to the socialists and the Muslims were now inclined towards Jamiat, which had come to their aid when they needed it most. In fact, most Muslims were bitter because in a city where Congressi Muslims had been brutally attacked and killed, not one of their party colleagues had come to their aid. Who could ever trust the Congress again? (The disappointment, however, was with the organization; Muslims did not overlook the good deeds of many individual Congressis.)

The blackest stain on the Congress was that despite being the party with the loftiest ideals, the strongest organization, the largest strength, it did nothing to help the distressed or control the mobs. Its members, seeing their neighbours being attacked and killed, would at best shut themselves in their houses or stuff their fingers in their ears and run to Government House; at worst, they would simply give in and join the rioters. True, many Congressis nursed hearts bitterly wounded in Punjab and were tormented by the painful memories of their friends and loved ones. They had seen those corpse-laden trains arriving in Delhi, Pakistani Punjab's gift to Jawaharlalji. They had witnessed the agony of those victims of the sword, whose only crime was that they were Hindus. Surely, the memory of that terrible past was a miasma that clouded their minds. But then, why was it, I wondered, that they were never equally affected by the trains packed with Muslim wounded and corpses that travelled from India to Pakistan? How could the scenes in Delhi of people writhing in ashes and blood be miraculously occluded from their vision?

Such is Man's nature—quick to clamour over his pain, quicker to mock others' grief. The seeds of division and hatred had been sown and nurtured for years; the first shoots had now emerged and, if they were to be watered afresh by rivers of blood, they would grow into tall, broad trees under whose shade all that lived would perish.

Fortunately, the same objections to working with the Congress did not extend to the Shanti Dal. Though formally a Congress organization, in truth and in practice, it was not affiliated to any party. Its only allies were Man and humanity. The socialists would go with it because they knew that if they made another committee, they would gain neither the government's nor the people's trust, most of whom had not even heard their name. In fact, they hardly had an organization to speak of yet and their volunteers were inexperienced.

Mridula Sarabhai called the first meeting in Constitution House. But who really liked Mridula? Congressis were wary of her, socialists apprehensive and communists kept safe distance—all in anticipation of a thorough tongue-lashing. But all three groups agreed that among all the famous women leaders at the time, she was the one whose fame was justified, as she had no parallel in work, purpose and determination.

I'd only seen her from a distance but always liked her immensely. She was such an extraordinary woman—defiant, truculent, ardently nationalist, a true Gandhian. True, she was sharp, but aren't persons with an intellect as keen as hers always a little eccentric? It is those eccentricities that help them accomplish the most difficult of missions, those madnesses that bestow on them immortal life and enviable death. Such were Mridula's quirks. She was seemingly unmoving as stone but those fortunate enough to be close to her knew her to be soft as melted wax on the inside. Albeit, this was no ordinary wax, ready to soften at the weakest of flames—at times a furnace was required, at others, the gentle warmth of the sun was enough.

Mridula said that the danger looming ahead didn't threaten a community or an individual. Every community, every individual had suffered immensely in the riots the year before. It was our bounden duty to strive for the nation's progress and if we worked together, we would lay the foundations for a better tomorrow. If we failed, then this freedom would remain a dream and seeds of division would take such deep roots that it would be impossible to weed them out.

The congregation that gathered at Mridula's call was not numerous, because it was a meeting of representatives of political parties. Two responsible leaders of the Provincial Congress, one each of the Socialist Party, Jamiat, Shanti Dal, and the secretary in-charge of the Seva Dal confirmed that the threat of violence on 15 June was real, that preparations were on, rumours were being fed and the public's mood was one of fear and insecurity. What was to be done now?

We were all agreed that the major tasks before us were to reassure the refugees as far as possible, establish good relations between them and the Muslims and prevent the threatened riots of 15 June. We decided that our peace initiative, under the banner of the Shanti Dal would be autonomous, though directed at helping both the people and the government. For this period, individual party propaganda would be put on hold. Our objective was lasting amity. We would do everything in our power to achieve it, be it through quarrelling with the administration, arguing with the public, or confronting the government. This resolve helped us become the great wall against which we dashed the hopes of those who sought to sow strife. Our numbers grew, as many right-minded young refugees joined us. Some Sikh brothers offered to pitch in and proved very useful in many ways.

The Shanti Dal was therefore reconstituted to function under the overall control of the Central Peace Committee and guidance of Rajendra Babu, and make use of the kind of resources that the Central

Peace Committee could garner when we ran into difficulties. Some responsible people went to meet Rajendra Babu and he consented.

An overall structure to strengthen the foundations was developed. Each party deputed two representatives each to an advisory board that oversaw the work of the various committees in charge of activist selection, propaganda and city/village activities. For the moment, an old Congressi was placed in-charge of the Central Office; he settled in at once. Subhadra was made party convenor and a young refugee took charge of the information department. Mridula assumed all other responsibilities regarding funds and organization, and all the running around and wrangling these entailed. She also had to take care of all of us, meet our demands and deal with our tantrums.

The Central Office, in Constitution House, designated responsible individuals as in-charge of various local offices. Shanti Dal offices were also opened in twelve areas outside the city, either in an independent building or in the Congress/Socialist Party office of the area. In one place, I recall, the Shanti Dal functioned out of a tent.

Apart from maintaining peace in its own area, the Central Office was also responsible for publicity and information, using various means. Badges were made, two jeeps garnered. The local government was coerced into footing our fuel bill. Posters, pamphlets, meetings, *mushaira*s, impromptu addresses, public announcements were all used; even a play was planned but ultimately couldn't be staged due to organizational difficulties.

Besides all these committees, there were two touring committees— one for the city, another for rural areas. The City Committee toured the city all day, monitored the various Shanti Dal committees in the neighbourhoods and reported progress to the Central Office. The Rural Committee established Shanti Dal committees in every village and monitored/aided their efforts.

Mindful that local government officials would flaunt the peace committees they had established in the first round of violence in September–October 1947, we decided to ask that a Shanti Dal person be included as a member of these. We wanted the Shanti Dal to have a presence across the province. Although we didn't expect the officials to help us—indeed, we feared the obstacles they would create—we felt that greater coordination was needed between the central and local governments.

I wasn't worthy of assuming such onerous responsibilities, however, having neither ability nor experience. So I took on the lighter burden; grasping the tail, I clambered up as the fifth horseman to join the Rural Committee, whose exploits I'll narrate soon. Pandit Jaidev Sharma, Lala Madan Lal and three others were my colleagues.

There were many other secrets, many initiatives, many clandestine interventions that I was party to then but can no longer recall or reconstruct, lacking the documents. All that must now be left to the historian who decides to research on that small organization called the Shanti Dal. Despite its fledgling strength, this group did so much to bring Delhi's house in order and to fortify its government: it insinuated itself into every nook and cranny in the government and the administration, sorted out pearls from the slime and somehow managed to make the forces of destruction and division admit defeat.

And there is no doubt that, in all this, the most important role was played by the zeal and intrepidity of Mridula; in fact, hers was the conception and intellect that defined the group. With one foot in India and the other in Pakistan, her enthusiasm for embroiling herself in as many disputes as possible was unparalleled! But never once did I see her discriminate between regions, religions, or sexes. In fact, on the rare occasions that we heard her try to assuage the feelings of women—'After all I'm a woman so there is no question of us not helping you!'—we would stare at each other in amazement. It was as if these were the words of a stranger.

A chaudhary from one of the villages near the rehabilitation colony, Nilokheri, speaking to a refugee.

13

The villages of Delhi: Return and refuge
(June–July 1948)

Delhi's villages must have once been prosperous and well populated but when we saw them in June 1948, they looked abysmal. Most villages we visited from 4 June onwards had large deserted sections, houses vandalized, fields barren, lanes abandoned. Everywhere we went, rumours of a fresh wave of rioting on 15 June preceded us; some even admitted secret preparations that were under way. The threat had made people fearful and displeased.

In every village, we saw children roaming wild, young men hard at work in the fields, and women loitering near their houses or swaying gently towards the well. Normally, only the old men would be gathered at the chaupal, playing dice. As soon as we reached, this activity would cease, at the scolding of the ziledar or nambardar who would rush to meet us. His raised voice would beckon the rest of the villagers to the chaupal. Initially, the cat always got all the tongues in the gathering; every question we asked was met with blank stares in the direction of the ziledar or nambardar. We wouldn't even be asked to sit until the village *chaudhary* arrived.

When we mentioned the deserted areas, they would feign non-chalance and beg off any complicity in evicting their Muslim neighbours. 'We had nothing to do with their going away! We were on such good terms with them—so and so nambardar was one of our intimates. How much we pleaded with them not to leave. But they wouldn't listen; and when they left, they took all their belongings. They were attacked outside the village.' When we mentioned the land, houses and fields those Muslims left behind, they would show surprise, as if the question were a bolt from the blue.

In many villages, though, a sense of regret was discernible. Dolefully, they recalled the happiness of earlier times, when their clans held sway over ten to twenty villages and local kings feted them at court. All that was past. Where once Muslim neighbours had seemed to be thorns in their flesh, they now keenly felt their absence, now that three-fourths of the village was deserted. That is why they were at pains to emphasize that all that had occurred was because the government organized it—they did no harm to the Muslims, nor the latter to them.

> *ki mire qatl ke baad usne jafaa se tauba*
> *hai, us zood pashemaan ka pashemaan hona*
> After my murder, this renunciation of oppression,
> So touching this instant penitence of the mortified
>
> Mirza Ghalib

One of our first visits was to a Mehrauli village, where the *sakka*s who traditionally supplied water to Qutub sahab had been converted to Hinduism. When Gandhiji visited the village, he asked the villagers to accept the injustice and make amends. He wanted the sakkas to continue in their traditional roles as Muslims at Qutub sahab. After

Gandhiji's martyrdom, Vinoba Bhave visited and said the same. However, as yet there was no resolution.

We had also received news from a village just a mile beyond that a large group of Mewatis had returned after many months. During the violence, these people had fled to Aligarh, Bulandshahar, Saharanpur and other places in UP but had now reoccupied their broken-down houses. In these straitened circumstances, they sought our help.

We felt it best to call a meeting of both villages to reconcile the sakkas, Mewatis and other villagers. We notified the Mehrauli Congress Committee and village leaders. On the appointed day, however, we were the only ones there. The local committee chairman wanted a postponement but, as this was the second time the meeting would be postponed, Subhadra said, 'Well, I'm going to sit and wait. I won't leave till this work is done!' After quite a while, people started gathering. The Mewatis also came. They thanked their neighbours that in the month they had been around, they had not encountered any hostility. Nevertheless, they did face difficulties. What struck me was the pain they took to reinforce their loyalty to the Indian nation. Why was this necessary, given that they hadn't gone anywhere near Pakistan? The demand for this justification had become such a norm then that it had to be stated. Every Hindu had the unspoken right to demand loyalty from a Muslim.

Jajuji, a Gandhian from Wardha, was with us. In simple words, he spoke of the need for brotherhood and decency, counselling the villagers, 'You must return whatever possessions the Mewatis had in their houses. What kind of adults will your children make, when they have seen their fathers and uncles grabbing others' belongings?' But Pandit Jaidev acted in haste, appealing also that the villagers should all undertake to give material assistance to the returnees. We tried to stop him—I felt the proposal was quite demeaning—but the words had been uttered and two or three villagers announced a donation of Rs 5–10 each.

Now, the question was not one of reconciliation but of who would be the treasurer for this fund, causing a bitter quarrel. With two men wielding pistols, we worried that an entirely different sort of trouble may erupt. We had insisted on this meeting; who would believe that our objective was peace, not fund-raising? How this man's foolishness had warped our initiative!

Meanwhile, the villagers screamed at the chairman, 'What do you mean that we looted these people? We didn't take a thing; in fact, when the goons were clearing out the village and looting their possessions, you had it all wrested from them, saying that you would send it to the government. Where did all that go?' From us they demanded, 'How you can have this man on your committee? After this misappropriation, how can he serve with you?'

The situation got uglier but Pandit Jaidev was delighted, 'Let it go on, this is all part of the "strategy"! This is how that truth will emerge.' New to this work, he didn't know that while lighting a fire took a few seconds, dousing the flames took for ever. I could restrain myself no longer and thrust myself into the crowd, 'We have not come to collect money for them or us. Our sole objective is to foster reconciliation.'

Subhadra joined me and with Jajuji—us two at the top of our voices, he in soothing tones of patient explanation—we managed to calm things down. Had we failed, this 'strategy' could well have engendered a riot that day.

The discussion now turned to the issue of loyalty. We were asked about Kashmir and Hyderabad. The Indian government had recently achieved a significant victory in Poonch; referring to this, Master Shanti Swaroop said, 'Can any Hindu claim to be a greater patriot than that Muslim Brigadier Usman, the commander of this offensive? If we don't call all those braves who died battling for India's freedom—and even today are in the line of fire in Kashmir—loyal, then who deserves this epithet?' A local zamindar spoke, 'If the government insists, we will allow the Muslims to stay, we won't harm them. But the Muslims must understand that the old way will no longer be allowed. If they want to stay on, they cannot look to Medina for everything.'

I flushed with the slight to my community and self-respect. My first impulse was to tell him some home truths to assuage my injured feelings, but experience had forged prudence in me. Choosing my words carefully, I said, 'When you go on a pilgrimage my dear sir, doesn't your heart call out to the land and the river you move towards? Why do you think that the call to Medina is anything but that? Why do you think that Muslims don't consider India their homeland and wish to give it up? They don't and you shouldn't utter these unkind words. If to praise Jamnaji and entertain thoughts of visiting Mahadev, Jagannathpuri and Mathura behoves you, they too have an equal right to look to Mecca and Medina, to cleanse their souls through a contemplation of their God and their Prophet.

'These people have returned to their homes; where is the question of you "allowing" them to stay or asking them to leave? You stay in your homes, they will live in their own. What we ask for is basic humanity and decency. Be good neighbours. Every religion teaches this and this is what elevates us above beasts.'

The situation improved thereafter and we came away satisfied. We had managed to reconcile the communities. The sakkas started going to Qutub sahab. We sent some assistance to the Mewatis. Soon, they were back on their feet and earning their livelihoods by the dint of the hard labour they put in quarrying and work.

Shortly, we went to Najafgarh, stopped by many villages along the way. It was a blistering June afternoon and, on reaching Najafgarh, we were so tired that the first thing we looked for was the shop of a relative of a Congressi with us. We repaired to the sitting room, directly over the shop, and rested gratefully. Word of our visit was sent to the chairman (also a minister) of the local Congress Committee and we waited for him. Our host invited some neighbours over and excused himself as his daughter's father-in-law was visiting.

Among the neighbours was a Lalaji. One of our party, putting his usual 'tact' into play, asked Lalaji, 'Tell me, bhai, now that the Muslims have gone, how are you getting along with these newcomers?'

'Just getting along, I would say. It's good that the miyans left, though.'

'Would you want them to return?'

Lalaji rushed to reply, 'Oh no, sahab, there's no place for those miyans here any longer.'

I intervened, 'Was there such a great quarrel between you?

'Not exactly a quarrel but they were so arrogant—they wanted to make this country the abode of Islam. They were so rich and ate so much; because of them, our cows were slaughtered. Mercifully, they are gone and Hindu brethren have come here.'

How did the Muslims leave, we asked. Lalaji said only three or four were killed, because the tehsildar ensured that most got out alive. 'We asked our Jat brothers to join hands and, as a result, Muslims in many surrounding villages were also purified.'

We asked, 'So, now you are happy? You get along well with the Punjabi newcomers?'

Lalaji replied, 'I don't think we get along well. These Hindus eat meat and Sikhs carry kirpans. They drink and brawl. We have running quarrels. One day, we must meet them blow for blow but the next day, go back to behaving as normal. This is the only way to make them agree to what we want.'

We asked about the Congress. Lalaji replied, 'What Congress is here to speak of? There might be two or three Congressis but no one heeds them. The Sangh and Hindu Mahasabha are dominant here, and the only political demand is for Jatistan.'

Lalaji had answered all our questions in exceedingly good humour. I sat quiet through all this—my colleagues had instructed me to exercise restraint and be friendly until we fully understood the situation. Or else, people would clam up.

The chairman never turned up but the secretary came and promised that he would try to organize a public meeting for us. Our benefactor Lalaji exclaimed, 'But everything is fine here! Why should there be a meeting?' The secretary stuck to his guns though he did warn us not to expect a large crowd as, in effect, there were only two Congressis in Najafgarh—himself and the chairman.

Two days later, we returned to the village with Pandit Sunderlal. The venue was deserted, save for the secretary and the chairman, dejected at their lack of influence. We waited and, after two hours, a handful of people straggled in and the meeting was finally convened. The chairman spoke about the events of the past year, with sincerity and passion. His pain shone through in his words and we were moved by the decent man's helplessness at being such a lone voice in the jungle. His neighbours had made his life a living hell but even so, and without any support from even outside the area, he had stood firm.

By now, the crowd had swelled; people watched from shops and houses too. Peasants from neighbouring areas also arrived. So Pandit Sunderlal began his address, which went on for over two hours. What a speech it was—not once did anyone feel provoked, not one slogan of protest arose. Spinning from side to side to address everyone in the audience, Panditji threw down the gauntlet before the RSS, Hindu Mahasabha, Muslim League and all those claiming to be custodians of faith. The audience watched mesmerized, as Panditji paced and spun, the fever of motion interrupted only so long as it took him to sip milk from his glass. By the time he ended, the crowd had grown to about 2,000 people, all listening in rapt attention.

We left successful. From then on, whichever village we visited in Najafgarh, we were welcome, and we publicized our mission without fear. Pandit Sunderlalji had shaken the somnolent from their slumber, leaving our adversaries wondering, 'But how did this happen?' Some villages asked us to return not once, but two or three times. We also went to a village in Narela, which had been resettled in Bapu's lifetime, by the efforts of some able Congress activists. Ruined in September, resettled in November; but even in June, it had received no help. The ashram run by Swamiji, a veteran Congressi and member of the All-India Congress Committee, was the sole sanctuary for the distressed. With Krishan Nayyar (a social activist from Delhi, later elected to Parliament) and some others, Swamiji devoted his efforts to rehabilitate the Muslims. He saved not only their lives, but also their hope, dignity and faith.

Swamiji got these Muslims their lands back. He arranged for legal representation for the cultivators, when the landlords' bigotry denied them their decades-old customary rights of cultivation. Swamiji also recorded numerous complaints of cruelty, force and fraud that he conveyed to us for further action; despite reporting them to the police and administration, no action had been taken. He too was extremely dismayed at the state of anarchy, of lawlessness.

In every respect, Swamiji was exemplary. Although completely unlettered, he was hard-working, principled, truly Gandhian and without parallel in his humanity. His little ashram in Narela was a sanctuary for every needy soul. At the height of the violence in September 1947, all the Muslims of the neighbouring village took his refuge. After keeping them there for several days, Swamiji suggested that they go to their relatives in UP until it was safe to return. With his associates, he conveyed them across the river, promising to arrange for their return at the earliest. As soon as October 1947 was past, Swamiji and his colleagues were impatient to fulfil their promise. Consulting with Bapu, they called back all the Muslims. For five months, Swamiji's aged shoulders bore their entire burden, without an ounce of assistance from anywhere.

We too proved to be of little real help. All we could get him was trifling material assistance and inconsequential support; he resolved all other problems himself. From this very ashram, Krishan Nayyar had brought an abducted girl to me, after hiding her for two months.

Refugee women spinning away at the charkha in the refugee rehabilitation colony in Nilokheri.

Even when surrounded by opponents, Swamiji's courage didn't wane; I learnt this when we toured the area together. I was enthralled by his speeches—be it on matters of law, politics, international affairs, or religion, through his rustic tongue would shine his innate intelligence. After meeting some fine Congressis like Swamiji, I often thought to myself that Man emerged once again in these rural areas. Bapu's deeds weren't in vain; he didn't leave this land as barren as we thought. He planted a few trees, under whose shade weary souls would find rest.

By 30 June 1948, we had visited twenty-seven villages, covering Mehrauli entirely and making significant progress in Najafgarh. We held large and small public meetings; on some occasions, Pandit Sunderlal was put to the trouble, on others Jajuji. This flurry of activity ensured that 15 June passed without incident, despite the fact that the administration and the government had yet to be purged of thorns and barbs. All of us activists, who had spent the last few months in a heightened state of readiness, heaved a sigh of relief as June ended.

One of our tasks was to resettle those Muslims that had fled to places within India in their villages of origin. We reasoned with the inhabitants—old residents, refugees and the few Muslim returnees of the villages we visited—that they should let bygones be bygones and rebuild their lives. Amity at any cost was the objective. No one was to demand the return of any possession, save for land and houses. If a resident Hindu brother had occupied a Muslim's house, we would certainly undertake to restore it to its rightful owner, but if a refugee had occupied it, it was not to be asked for at all. In this case, the Muslim should find another empty house in the village, however broken or burnt, and we would fund its repair. This strategy pre-empted so many disputes, that our opponents couldn't find even one incident to use against us.

We soon realized that facilitating Muslim resettlement was no mean task. First, there was the question of financial assistance and relief. The local government was entirely callous on this front. Public fund collection was impossible as Delhi's suffering people were in no shape to contribute. In truth, we ourselves were reluctant to approach our

Hindu brethren. Where were citizens' minds so free of rancour that they would, disregarding thoughts of Hindu and Muslim, rush to aid a person in distress?

Despairing, we would make the proverbial sprint of the mullah to the mosque, and land up at Jawaharlalji's door. Not once but three times, his personal purse doled out large sums for procuring wood, bamboo, thatching, doors and doorframes for Muslim sanctuary seekers. Luckily for me, Chance had made access to this great man easier—my call reached him a little sooner than others' through Bhai sahab's kind offices. This route, and he, never failed us.

We also recognized how vexed the relations between local Hindus and refugees were in the rural areas. Local Hindus detested the refugees so much that they would rather let the Muslims return instead. In most villages, no Punjabi refugee had set foot as yet. Earlier, in the summer, a handful of refugees had made enquiries about vacant land, and though the zamindars and ziledar had greeted them politely and plied them with lassi and sharbat, none had ever been given a place. 'The Muslims were so indigent,' they were told, 'that they had nothing, nothing at all for you to take over. All that you see here belongs to us Hindus.'

The irony was that the Muslims had been driven out to make space for the refugees, but greed had laid the effort to waste. The administration lacked the will and the means to forcibly settle the refugees there; if the Hindus rose in protest, the government would rule in the villagers' favour. Now the refugees had begun to pressurize the administration and the government that land and houses abandoned by the Muslims be handed over to them—thus the Muslims' former neighbours were up in arms. The refugees were no lily-livered opponents either, emboldened by the administration's support. The only remedy we could offer was to seek out three or four dependable individuals, organize them into committees and charge them with the responsibility of preventing a riot in their village.

Shanti Dal activists urged both villagers and refugees: 'Don't fight. Hand over your complaints to us; we will fight to redress your grievances.' The difficulty was that the villagers and the refugees wanted their grievances addressed individually, not jointly. This attitude produced immense callousness on either side towards the other's problems—each believed that they were unconnected, that their problems were far removed.

In one village, we witnessed an intense debate between villagers and refugees. The villagers had drawn a Muslim nambardar into their camp—the refugees complained that this person had no right to be there. They charged that the nambardar had been brought just to thwart the allotment of his and his relatives' land to the refugees. The land was in the refugees' possession and the volunteers wanted it back. A Hindu charged, 'Is justice dead? This man too has rights, doesn't he? We are only refusing to give up what is his and his family's. As it is, you control everything in this village and what a terrible mess you have made of our once peaceful village. Don't threaten us—you have already torched so many huts, what next?'

We intervened, and much cajoling and counselling finally made them all agree to form a Shanti Dal committee, commit a list of their disputes to paper and send it to our office. The Hindus forwarded the name of the lone Muslim as a member; this enraged the refugees, who demanded to know whom this gentleman represented what support he had, as one voice counts for nothing. But the local zamindars were insistent, 'He represents us and we have complete faith in him. In any case, other Muslims are also on the way back. There must be a Muslim representative.'

Some days later, we heard that the plough had been taken to the disputed land, forcibly, by resident Hindu friends of the nambardar— the land was now his. Though this caused further bad blood, the nambardar emerged 'victorious'. But five or six years later, I met him in Kalu Sarai—he then tended cattle and birds of various households for meagre wages. I was surprised to see him in such dire straits and learnt that the whole thing was a farce. The objective had been to block the refugees from capturing the land; once that was met, he too was sent packing. The local baniyas gobbled up the land.

In a few villages, we met refugees who now owned houses and land in both East Punjab and Delhi. Residents of East Punjab, these people had owned orchards in Pakistan; now that land was lost and the government had compensated them with land in Delhi province. In one village, 1,600 bighas of land had been distributed to the refugees. These people would descend on the village at harvest time, reap the fields, sell the grain, take the money and return to East Punjab. In another village, one individual from the central agriculture department had been allotted 800 bighas; recently, he had sold trees from the jungle for thousands of rupees and left.

On a visit to a qasbah across Shahadra Bridge, we were shocked to find that not only were the houses vandalized, even the walls had been dug up. At one end, refugees had set up camp and the original inhabitants lived at the other end. We asked, 'Were these houses blown up with explosives?'

'Oh no, there was no violence. There was a Muslim camp here, and no harm came to them before they left. It wasn't like Gandhinagar (just two or three furlongs away), where more than three-fourth of the Muslims were killed and the rest sent to Delhi.'

'So who dug up the houses?'

The answer from the Hindu residents: 'The refugees.'

Entirely untrue. The refugees were certainly not responsible for the destruction. Here, and elsewhere in Shahadra, the destruction had been perpetrated either by reactionaries like the RSS or the police, both so taken in by the propaganda about Hindu Raj and Jatistan that they had lost all humanity. It was fashionable to blame the refugees for every crime. Even in places where no refugee had reached, they were held responsible for the havoc; on this pretext, the enemies of peace gave free reign to their mischief. What fools the refugees were! Why didn't they protest?

Our inspection and enquiries revealed that the Muslim Gujjars of the qasbah had been very wealthy. Their cattle must have numbered 5,000 and their high-quality dairy produce from pedigreed cows and buffaloes was supplied to Delhi daily. We also learnt that they buried their gold and silver in the walls of their houses and in their lands— villagers who had lived as their neighbours for years knew this. While some refugees may have dug up the Muslims' houses later, I was quite sure that the thefts were carried out well before the refugees arrived. In fact, by the time they reached, doors, windows, even the roof fetters had been spirited away!

There is no gainsaying the fact that the refugees did commit arson, setting fire to three or four huts. After all, they had to douse the fires of retribution burning within them. Now, in a bid for shelter from Delhi's scorching heat and blistering winds, they repaired the houses vacated by Muslims. They had to go as far as the neighbouring villages to cut down trees for doors and windows; although they had asked for money from the government, no help ever came. Nearby, land owned by the Improvement Trust lay vacant. The refugees demanded these vacant plots to build their own houses. We reported this to the Improvement Trust headquarters, recommending that their request be acceded to soon.

By end-June, some Muslims started to return to the villages. In Sheikh Sarai in Mehrauli, all the Muslims had either perished or fled to Delhi. When we received their request for resettlement, we went to the village to take stock. Between 1,000–2,000 refugees had moved in and rehabilitation work was on in full swing. The refugees had been organized into a cooperative under the CRC's auspices; supervised by a member of the Provincial Congress Committee, the cooperative was preparing government lands for cultivation and construction.

We noticed some unoccupied hutments, roofless like elsewhere but otherwise not in too bad a shape. We immediately approached the committee member, suggesting that he include Muslim sanctuary seekers in this cooperative. I said, 'If the resident Hindus also want to join, that would be wonderful. But perhaps they won't want to lose their autonomy, so we suggest that you run the scheme together with Hindu refugees and Muslim sanctuary seekers. I will persuade the Muslims.' Quite pleased at this proposal, Member sahab agreed.

What stiff opposition both he and I faced! We reasoned with our associates—let us give this experiment a try, now that we have the opportunity. I even said (though not without trepidation) that even if there was a risk of unfavourable consequences for Muslims, I was willing to take it—if the work were done with hard work, honesty, enlightenment and without discrimination over region or religion, I didn't expect any concern about unfairness. It would certainly benefit both communities.

We spoke to the refugee who was the executive head of this project. He heard us sceptically and finally dismissed it. Our associates raised many doubts about its feasibility—some of which, I admit, were not baseless. Finally, it was clear that neither were the refugees ready to take the Muslims along, nor were the activists so liberal that they would perceive both sanctuary seekers and refugees in the same light. No one listened to me and, till today, the Muslims of Sheikh Sarai live in the city. In their fields and houses, others live, plough, sow, reap; they visit the village now and then, to gaze with longing at what they lost. They no longer want to return. Somehow, by working in the employ of city traders, they have managed to get by.

Shanti Dal's report on rural areas established that the rumours of the 15 June riots were true. Preparations were on and through secret meetings, posters, even children, word had been passed around, inciting people to violence. Like in the violence of the last year, three groups had been targeted.

The first target—the Jats. Here, the demand for Jatistan was used as a rallying cry from September 1947 onwards. As some Jat zamindars in Najafgarh said, 'The talk everywhere was in favour of Jat Raj. All the important people in our community gave the call that brothers, it is time for all Jats—Hindu or Muslim—to unite. Look around, some have taken Pakistan, others Hindustan. The Sikhs are asking for a part for themselves. Shouldn't Jats also have the right to rule themselves?' The second target—Thugs, Rajputs and Chauhans of Mehrauli and, in them, the propaganda for Hindu Raj. The third target—the Gujjars and Harijans under the auspices of the RSS.

All the groups were supplied with arms in the post-Partition violence. In a planned fashion, units were constituted and asked to attack neighbouring villages and qasbahs. All groups commanded support at all levels of the administration and security forces; for example, the Najafgarh Jats were assisted by the army in their attacks in Bharatpur. We were also told that in some places, the army joined these irregular soldiers in attacking border villages.

In these visits to Delhi's villages six months later, we glimpsed the real India and its true atlas. More than once, I despaired—it would take at least half a century for all this to be set right. No government could have all the medicine needed to treat such a raging epidemic. To make these people human, a whole industry of social and non-governmental initiatives was needed. Only the youth, and only the true among them, could catalyse the needed revolution. If only the thousands of college and university students could spend two months of their annual vacation in rural areas and fan out to work for these poor people. But—

u shekhtan gumast ki ra rahbari kunood
He who himself has strayed, what guide can he make?

Rural India hardly ever had the amenities of sanitation, education and medicine. Now, after this violence, even the little that had existed vanished. Hakims, *vaidh*s, midwives, surgeons, pustule-lancers were all gone—either to their graves or to Delhi. For miles, there was not a soul to answer a patient's call.

Unemployment was rife, fields lay untended. The government would know the exact quantum of damage inflicted and the losses it itself incurred in the collection of agricultural taxes in this period of strife. In our estimate, however, only half the total land yielded two crops that year—the government's income must have been less than half. We were keen to restore to the villages the people who would ready the new crop, but when the old system was in tatters and each person had captured something belonging to another, this was difficult. Our efforts to call these looters to account were unsuccessful. In front of the officials, these people (mostly Hindu zamindars) would flatly refuse to admit that they had taken anything at all; to us, they would assert that all they now owned was always theirs.

If the government had the will, an easy solution would have been the institution of group farming by an organization of the entire village, comprising Muslim sanctuary seekers, Punjabi refugees and local zamindars, if they agreed. If only the land left by the Muslims, instead of being allotted indiscriminately—1,000 bighas to one person, 10 bighas to another, 2 bighas to a third and a brush-off to a fourth—had been appropriated by the government to be farmed by a cooperative of village residents. This novel experiment would also have afforded the possibility of accommodating returning landowners, by simply absorbing them into the group.

I repeatedly asserted that this should be our demand. But on one side were the Custodian and rehabilitation people, adamant that land allotment be as 'transparent' as the current system was, and on the other side were my own associates, determined that neither refugees nor original landowners lose their land rights.

If I couldn't convince even my own, then what confidence of success could I have that the state would agree? I lacked both ability and education to tease out the exact economic implications, so I decided to leave matters of land ownership to more experienced people. They could resolve the disputes as they thought best. Truly, in the end, it was they who proved more successful than I would ever have; their zamindari outlook and hidebound attitudes accomplished so much while I sat useless, priding myself in my halo of progressive values!

In all these efforts, we were continuously plagued by the hostility of the local administration and the police. Why did we ever expect these officials to trust us? We certainly didn't trust them. At times, it felt as if we worked for one country, and they for another. We were motivated by the desire to establish peace and the objective to strengthen the hands of our government. We wanted to wipe out all that brought dishonour to our nation and harmed it; we also sought to cure the anarchy that infested our nation and remedy the distress of our people. In my understanding, this was what government officials wanted too. Yet, we both considered each other opponents and enemies. We would take pains to ensure that they got no whiff of what we were up to, they never consulted us either.

We wanted to work with the institutions responsible for relief and rehabilitation in spreading the word of amity and bringing benefit to the people. We expressed our willingness to take on the responsibility of educational propaganda for the district board, so that schools and madrasas could be reopened. We were ready to report to the health department on the actual condition of health services, so that they could be improved and social reform accompanied relief work. However, they didn't give us the time of day. Nor did we have the time to follow up on our proposals—they stayed confined to our imaginations and the scraps they were jotted on.

Despite all this, throughout July and August, people returned to the villages. Their condition was abject, to say the least. Through either our efforts at persuading local Hindus to return to the Muslims their captured property, or by the Muslims' own initiatives of recapturing the fields as soon as the crop was harvested, they got their land back. However, they still had no hoes, ploughs, or sickles to farm it with. Some of them sought loans to buy ploughs and bullocks, for which we had to make just arrangements. How welcoming were the mahajans to their old neighbours, with what love and concern they offered them money! If the government didn't intervene, then the loans and interest amounts that lay just up ahead, would mean the land soon being confiscated by these mahajans. These matters kept Shanti Dal activists busy and many of our volunteers spent most of their days preparing lists of Muslim-owned land, reclaiming property wrongly appropriated by the Custodian, resettling evicted Muslims and arranging for their return to cultivation.

A Pathan leader addressing a large number of his men, gathered at Pandit Jawaharlal Nehru's residence on 8 August 1949 to vent their anger at the conditions in the camp.

14

The villages of Delhi: Conversion and caste
(June–August 1948)

An important task before the Rural Committee was to address the issue of forced religious conversion. Jamiat brought many cases to our attention and we took them up. Brahmin or Rajput, Jat or Gujjar, the Muslims of these communities appeared not the least different in their lifestyles and customs. The Muslim Jat was no less than his Hindu counterpart in perverseness and irrationality. The uproar for religious conversion was answered by whole villages of Muslims capitulating and accepting purification. Faith was not their bulwark against the storm; in fact, most couldn't even read the kalma. Even if they had, I doubt that they would have had the intelligence to explain their meaning. These were all just good-hearted, robust rustics. Entirely lacking a middle class—owners of hundreds of bighas of land

233

and two-storeyed houses they may have been—most of these Jats had use only for their thumbs, most couldn't even write their names.

And if such was the state of men, what can we say about women? And when such was the state around the capital, what can we say about other parts of the country?

kayas kun ji gulistan-e-man bahar mira
From the state of my garden, divine the condition of my Spring

Mauja Ali's Muslims appealed to Jamiat that they were weary of a dishonourable life of living as Hindus and wanted to be rescued from their village. Jamiat asked us to intervene but we had sworn not to take that route to resolve the Muslims' problems. The onus was on us to find a solution without a Muslim exodus from the village.

Our party reached the village that evening. Among our colleagues, as usual, was the well-known brahmin zamindar Pandit Jaidev. A pure Delhiwala, he spoke a mix of the high language of Shahjahanabad, the Zubaan-e-Urdu-e-Mohalla, and the Karkhandaari dialect, and wrote in the Persianized variety. He worked to resettle and rehabilitate Muslims, which meant also resolving all the legal and procedural difficulties in proving them to be genuine claimants to their land. He hadn't been in the Congress for long and so was willing to use a few entreaties here, some wheeling-dealing there and bluster and coercion elsewhere—whatever suited the occasion and met the ends. And whenever my principles were opposed to his tactics, he would take great pleasure in educating me of the need for 'strategy' and 'tact'.

Always untiring, and very able and experienced in law and administration, he was an excellent colleague; except that, on the inside, he was all brahmin. He frequently listed to me the duties of a woman as per the Manu Smriti, beginning with, 'The world is full of sinners because women have moved away from the virtues of fidelity to their husbands' and concluding with a lecture on his wife's exemplary piety. All this, plus his driver's vociferous agreement to his pronouncements, would cut me to the quick and I would quarrel. But, come what may, he never took offence at what I said.

As usual, Pandit Jaidev's first request was for the hookah for the Gaur Brahmins—an opening gambit he had used in the past with some success. How could people refuse a pandit? The request was immediately met. When I once mocked the stratagem, Pandit Jaidev's reply was, 'If the result we seek is our sole objective, then accept what works in villages!' Then, more conciliatory, 'Apaji, too much is made of eating and drinking together. The real thing is mutual love. True, Hindus and Muslims have never eaten together but tell me, despite this, why has there been such little animosity between them?' I had no comeback. Truly, before this violence, Hindus and Muslims were fast friends, though the taboos remained inflexible as always. Both friends wouldn't take offence at these proscriptions, rather respect them as prescriptions of each other's faiths. Now that we were civilized, untouchability was eradicated and food and drink had become one, we were bent on destroying each other.

The Gaur Brahmin hookah arrived. At first, the chat was light-hearted but then, pitying the anxious faces and bewildered eyes around us, we asked the Muslims to speak. 'Did you change your religion under pressure or voluntarily? If it was the latter, why do you want to leave the village now?'

A young man said, 'There is no problem here. What was decreed in our fate, happened; whatever lies ahead, I certainly cannot leave this village now.' Others echoed his opinion. Just as we were about to leave, an old man spoke, his hands trembling, 'These people may do as they want but I sit with my feet dangling in the grave—I cannot possibly live with this dishonour any longer. Save me, please!'

Instantly, the congregation erupted. The zamindars and ziledars protested, the nambardar shouted, 'When there were riots everywhere, we saved these people's lives. Ask them if we harmed even a hair on their heads! We stood in front of them and guarded them—and this is what they give us in return?'

The old man retorted, '*You* saved us?' and burst into tears. 'To keep us here, you made us eat pig!' His body quivered as he disciplined his grief, 'I cannot live such a life any more.' The nambardar fumed, 'What of our religion? We ate and drank with you, shared the hookah, put aside all taboos. You made us commit sacrilege and now you say this? This is how you repay us? What injustice is this?'

Everyone joined in now and began arguing with each other. The Hindu youth were especially agitated, although the Muslims drew some comfort from our presence. I intervened: 'Brother, please forgive my bluntness but I must say that both of you are sinners. When the nambardar was speaking, I thought that these villagers are truly good, there was no quarrel here, everyone lived in harmony and kept each other safe. But now I hold another conclusion: both of you defrauded each other, lied to each other, sullied each other's faith. It is despicable that when a brave Rajput shelters another, he should also force the man to eat the dirty thing that his religion forbids him to. In doing so, he makes the refugee a sinner and himself commits a sin too . . . And you Pathans—blessed with the riches of talk and truth, ready to stake your lives on your oath—can you so easily tarnish your faith just for fear of death? One word on your lips, another in your heart! When you knew that you had not become Hindus in all sincerity, why did you eat and drink with them? Think of the sin you have committed by breaking their customs. None of you is worthy of facing God. Only one route is open to all of you— repentance. Apologize, first to each other and then to God, and return to live in the same harmony as earlier. If you can't, I will send a truck and take the Pathans away. The government belongs to both and is committed to keeping both; whatever your religion, you are equal before it. How can you throw away this freedom that you have waited and prayed for?'

I don't know what it was, perhaps the time was such, that both sides looked ashamed. They asked for three days to hold a panchayat meeting before reverting to us. The next day we told Vinoba Bhaveji what had transpired and requested him to send his people to educate the villagers about Bapu's ideals. We believed they were now receptive to such contact and that this guidance would contribute to a radical improvement of the situation. Two days later, we returned to Mauja Ali. The nambardar welcomed us, but requested us to wait, as the villagers had gathered again for a final meeting, before they answered us. We went to the old man's house to wait in his veranda, which was piled up with wood, hay and wood-cutting implements.

The old man's son approached me, 'Please come, I want to show you our house.' I saw that the house was prosperous. He took me to a room filled with sacks of grain and declared, 'Just look at this. How can I be expected to leave all this? If my father wants to leave, I'll also have to. I'm his only son and he won't let me stay. I'd rather live on here though, the Hindu that I've become. With no other woodworker in this village, I'm valued and don't lack work.'

True, if all woodworkers, carpenters, ironsmiths and agricultural labourers left, who would set right the ploughs and bullock carts? The villagers would certainly not allow refugees to replace them. In fact, by the villagers' own admission, no refugee had been allowed to stray beyond Kalka. Even the homes vacated by Ehsan nambardar and his group in Jaitpur, barely a mile away, remained empty still.

The aspirations of Youth, and its calculations of what would be in its best interests, were at variance with the preoccupations with the hereafter of Age. Both viewpoints, I felt, deserved respect; unlike a Maulvi sahab who once accompanied us to evacuate some villagers, I couldn't bring myself to declare, 'Between the world and the faith, choose one.' Who knew that a man who chose the faith wouldn't, when crazed with hunger, completely shun God? What value would his declarations of unshakeable faith and regularity of clandestine namaz have then?

Pondering over all this, I returned to my colleagues. As time passed, we suspected that we were being fobbed off. We decided to give up and leave, thinking we'd make arrangements for transport and security for the next day. But, just as we were about to step into the car, the nambardar appeared, followed by several others. He clasped the old man's hand, gathering him to his breast. He said, 'Behenji, we've been neighbours and companions all our lives. We cannot part like this. He can live as he wants, as long as he doesn't go. We won't let a single one of them go like this.' I said, 'But he wants to live here as a Muslim and you don't like that. He and his companions wish to go because they are no longer allowed to carry out their religious duties. I can't understand why though: if for centuries you have lived together like this, what harm does his remaining a Muslim do to you?' The nambardar promised, 'No one will object to them being Muslims. We just want them to stay. But we want only our villagers, not those who settled after the Gurgaon violence. They are not our own. They started the problems between us in the first place. Please take them away.'

The reconciliation was complete, we came away satisfied. We gave Vinobaji the good news that he didn't need to intervene, as the conflict had ended in an embrace. He was delighted. The next day, we housed forty people from that village in Nizamuddin. They wanted to return to Gurgaon, but the situation was not conducive as yet.

Some days later, the old man showed up again. He wasn't in very high spirits but he had the solace of reading the namaz in his own home. He asked, 'Behenji, Ramzan approaches. Shall I keep the fasts?' My colleagues said, 'Certainly, you must. If anyone objects, tell us.' The old man went away, still fearful but reassured. This experience

Pathans from the Faridabad camp called on Pandit Nehru at his residence in August 1949 to vent their grievances.

gave us confidence that we could successfully intervene in difficult issues. We resolved to extend our efforts to Najafgarh.

Throughout June and July, we responded to such appeals, which increased as the months passed. By August 1948, we were besieged. The Muslims' petitions for help to Jamiat and the Pakistan Office grew more persistent and we got exasperated, as all our activists were harried enough as it was in attending to the Muslims' property-related matters. I decided to ask the Jamiat people to depute a person of theirs to accompany me to meet these villagers; this gentleman took me to two villages in Najafgarh which, until some months ago, had been Muslim-dominated. Now, about 1,100 Muslims had been forcibly converted and many of them had written to the Pakistan Office asking for citizenship.

Having been to one of the villages once earlier, a conversation I had with the converted villagers was still on my mind. Coming upon a badly damaged mosque, I asked them who was responsible for its destruction. The nonchalant reply was, 'This happened after everything was over. We too joined the other Jats in breaking it.'

'Why?' I asked. 'Even if you didn't need it any longer, it could still have been of use to someone else!'

'There are no Muslims for miles around; no one will ever read the namaz there.'

I had then decided that I believed the villagers when they said, 'It was with our full consent and happiness that we became Hindus. We are Jats; we were Hindus earlier and have become so again.'

But fresh news of forced conversion made me revise my conclusion. We made our way to the village, accompanied by two local Congressis. (The Congress had recently made some inroads into the area and opened an office.) The villagers were strapping fellows of a rustic disposition. We finally found the men who had contacted Jamiat and asked them what had transpired. To our surprise, they vociferously denied it all. 'No, sahab, we didn't contact Jamiat. We don't want to go to Pakistan. We are Hindus now and happy to be so. It must have been someone else.' Their denials rung so true that I was again convinced that the Ulema had been fed misinformation.

On my return, I met Maulana Hifzur Rahman, who said, 'You took local Congressis along, so they must have been frightened. This time, go with the gentleman from our office who met these people when they came to us.' So, the next day, I went to the village for a third time, accompanied by Arabic scholar Maulvi Anees, secretary of Jamiat's office. Now, the story took on an entirely new colour. Recognizing the people we'd met the day before, Maulvi Anees asked them if they had approached Jamiat. They replied in the affirmative. 'Then why did you deny this yesterday?'

'We were scared! If anyone gets to know we did this, all hell will break loose.' They were adamant that we must somehow convey them to Pakistan. The atmosphere was so hostile that they could not live openly as Muslims.

To evacuate 1,100 people and send them to Pakistan was so impossible that even making the attempt was ridiculous. Moreover, only a small percentage actually wanted to leave the country. But then, even to resettle them elsewhere in India would be no mean task either.

We tried to explain this, and said, 'We'll make all the arrangements for your security and peace of mind, but don't think of fleeing the village. We will arrange a prayer meeting with Vinobaji; after that, no one will say another harsh word to you. Just agree to stay on and you will be able live as you once did.' A Bade Miyan spoke, 'We became Hindus before a panchayat of forty villages called by a tehsildar. He told us he had permission from his superior. We gave our word. Now if we stay here and go back on our word, how will we face all the panchayats again?

I was indignant. 'Bade Miyan, at such a venerable age, this is what you have to say? For sixty years, you were a Muslim but you had no problem going back on that promise and facing Maulvi Anees and myself. You have been Hindu for just a year, so why should you be afraid of facing other Hindus now?'

An educated young man, looking quite weary of the situation, said, 'Janab, whatever anyone else says, the fact is that I want to leave, as do some others. The ones that want to stay on are those who had no compunctions in joining the Jats in attacking the houses of fellow

Muslims.' He was met with outraged cries: 'What, *we* attacked Muslim houses? We went along with them but never attacked anyone. We had to accompany them—would you have us rebel against the dictates of our clan?' The youth replied, 'All right! What is relevant now is that you want to stay on as Hindus. So you do that. But those of us who have asked for evacuation should be taken out.'

The debate went on and on. Finally, I said, 'This debate has been going on for three hours. I have come here three times to persuade you to stay—my duty is done. You Jats are supposed to be valiant people but you lack even the courage to declare your religious ascriptions. Islam has no need for such Muslims. I can't be bothered to save you from the lie you live. I won't make any arrangements for you to go to Pakistan; if you stay here, we'll do everything we can to help you. The Indian government has no interest in your being Hindu or Muslim, it wants you to live as humans!'

I never asked after them again though I heard that for several days, a Pakistani truck made repeated trips to Najafgarh, ferrying away all those who wanted to leave. Who gave the orders to press this truck into service? The Pakistan government couldn't have imposed its will on Delhi's provincial government. I was so disgusted that I didn't even bother to find out.

I did visit another village in the area, from where the same truck had taken ten to twelve people. Outraged, our colleagues rushed there to scold and threaten the villagers. The next day, I was taken to reassure them.

Several converted Muslims there wanted to follow their compatriots to Pakistan. A few were ready to live on as Hindus. We met three such men, who narrated the story of how they became Hindus. Apparently, on the occasion of a marriage, Hindus and Muslims fell out; the Muslims, very upset, declared, 'You treat us this badly just because we are Muslims. Well, we'll become Hindus any time you say!' The Hindus promptly summoned the village barber, who gave the Muslims shaved heads with a tiny little pigtail hanging at the back. What could I possibly say to them? One day such people may give up the *bodi* and adopt the long tresses and beards of the Sikhs!

However, I did speak at length to the converted Muslims who wanted to go to Pakistan. Quite masterfully (even if I say so myself), I first drew out their opinions on various matters. Then, elaborating on the nationalist perspective and democratic governance, I told them that the two allegiances they professed were contradictory and that their hypocritical conduct was good neither for them nor for the government. They heard me patiently and I could see my words were making an impression. Ultimately, the villagers came round. They said they had converted only for fear of their lives, but if they could live on as Muslims, they would willingly do so.

I always sincerely regret that I managed to reach so few of these places, had such few opportunities to meet villagers and soothe away their disquiet. Among my own associates, there were some whose religious allegiances prevented them from helping me further in this agenda. I don't accuse them though. Had I been in Pakistan and made to ask converted Hindus to live as Hindus again, I may not have been able to.

Another problem emerged in these two months. In Delhi's rural areas, Harijans were legally prohibited from owning land, though they could cultivate it. Traditionally, they had worked on Muslim lands. Now that the Muslims' land was being allotted to refugees, Harijans were speedily deprived of this customary right. In every village, Harijan–refugee relations soured, the former emboldened by their role in the anti-Muslim riots. When morals and ethics degenerate, the distinction between what one owns and what belongs to another lapses. The hands that had snatched and torn at Muslims moved towards the refugees. Harijans, like Jats, were turning persecutors.

In our daily reports (which would be translated into English and sent up to the highest echelons of the government, usually to Pandit Nehru), we drew the government's attention to this alarming decline. If this trend weren't arrested, we warned, Delhi would house bullies and tyrants.

When a once Muslim-major village was deserted, castes with smaller populations—Harijans, but at times other Hindus too—also found other dwellings. However, when we tried to get the Muslims to return, these other Hindus came back too. And because the number of Muslims that eventually returned was much lower than their original population, refugees too were brought to occupy the vacant houses. Such a village did ultimately get resettled, but with three kinds of immigrants—all refugees, all desperate and indigent, all worthy of assistance. Muslims were looked after by the Shanti Dal, refugees by the relief and rehabilitation department, but who would the Hindus turn to? No organization was dedicated to their relief. We offered our services and were glad to facilitate ration supplies to all three at the same, cheap rates.

Locals were very suspicious of refugees, so far ahead the newcomers were in expertise, health, looks, industry. One community, the Sikhs, was even armed. The locals feared that the refugees would take over India one day—weren't they already appropriating trade in the area? Soon they would rule both government and country. So, the locals started fanning the flames of regional hatred, but the Shanti Dal was alert and intervened to reconcile the three groups of 'refugees'.

The Harijans remained a problem. Lacking a culture of moral elevation, and under the influence of a secret intrigue, they had become extraordinarily rebellious. Many had even been handed kirpans and asked to grow beards. For long, some even laboured under the mistaken belief that they were Sikhs—until the return of amity brought home to them that a Harijan in our society always remained a Harijan.

One such confrontation occurred during the repair of Chiragh Delhi dargah. We went to see it much after work began but the cement was still wet, the lime on the walls yet undried. A Public Works Department (PWD) inspector complained, 'Sahab, please tell the chamars here to behave. They insist on walking on the wet floor with their shoes on, laying waste all our efforts. When we stop them, they speak rudely!'

Just then, another man walked across the floor. When the overseer rebuked him, he lost his temper and an intense argument followed, downright abusive in parts. I looked on in amazement—the rich landlords had prompted these poor Harijans to behave this crudely to the Muslims, but today the Harijans had turned on them. They were ready to take on government officials now!

I remember another incident from Palam village. Pandit Sunderlal was with us. We reached to find the village very tense. Apparently, a dead buffalo had been lying around for three days but the Harijans refused to dispose of the carcass. We called the Harijans and they reiterated. As the arguments got more acrimonious, Pandit Sunderlal said, 'If they won't do it, why don't we do it ourselves? Help me lift the carcass now.' A brahmin touching an animal carcass! Even the brahmins in our own party recoiled. All the while Sunderlalji was cheerfully calling out for help, his hand resting on the beast. People stared at each other, taken aback.

Luckily, the 'strategy' worked. Pandit Jaidev jumped in and addressed the Harijans, 'Do you even know who this is, whom you are forcing to lift such a vile thing? This great sage, a maha-brahmin, your honoured guest! If Panditji picks up this buffalo, you will live in eternal shame!' The Harijans weren't so debased that they would insult a guest. They rushed towards Sunderlalji, urging him to stop, 'Leave it, Panditji, don't lay a hand on it! Our quarrel is with the villagers, not you.' But Panditji had none of it and continued to help them. He had become so used to dealing with brutality and malice that he could no longer sit idle.

In July and August, the events in Hyderabad and the situation with the razakars were uppermost in people's minds. In villages too, we had to answer why the government was giving such latitude to Hyderabad. On the other end, the Kashmir issue was on every child's lips. Why the issue roused such passion I can't say but we were constantly waylaid with questions about it, which led to others.

In a village, some youth asked me, 'Mataji, if two brothers quarrel and divide the property, each takes his inheritance and goes his separate way, never laying claim on the other's again. Isn't the Hindu–Muslim situation similar? The old times, when two brothers lived in one house, are over, the division is done, so they must go to what is theirs. Why should the Muslims stay on? When they have taken their one-fourth share, what right do they have on India any more?'

Such a straightforward question, it was on every Hindu's lips. The Muslims were silenced by it but not me—I had a reply and gave it, at length. I managed to bring around two of the young men; the others stayed belligerent.

This strategy of dialogue and debate that some Shanti Dal activists like myself employed used to make our more energetic colleagues impatient. They would hardly give their audience a chance to question them or to think, and thought us foolish for our using this mode. True, this style of communication did not befit either zamindars or bureaucrats, but we were not these, were we? If our own minds were in turmoil, how could we not prod and poke the minds of others? And how could I depart from the fundamental principles of the Congress in these democratic times and adopt the repressive and tyrannical attitude of a dictator? I wanted to see into these people's hearts and so I took great pleasure in excavating their opinions.

In a public meeting organized by Shanti Dal, I heard the same demand for loyalty made by a minister. I was in the audience, which numbered a few thousand. He said, 'If the Muslim cannot pledge his loyalty to the Indian government, he should go to Pakistan. There is space here only for good people.' Heads nodded in agreement. He expanded, 'There is conflict over Hyderabad. Kashmir too has seen battles. The Muslims will have to tell us which of the two nations they owe allegiance to. They will have to prove which they consider their land. They cannot sit on two chairs at once.' He went on in this vein. I listened, fuming.

The speech over, the minister departed. Another person spoke, reiterating the demand. Then the organizer asked me to address the gathering. I hesitated but finally gave in: 'It has become commonplace in such meetings to demand proof of loyalty from Muslims. From old to young, from senior leader to the most junior, everyone is anxious about the Muslims . . . If Muslims have harmed India by their disloyalty, so has the betrayal of the patriots. Our leaders accepted the proposal for the nation's partition, despite the unhappiness that both Hindus and Muslims, particularly nationalist Muslims, expressed. The Muslims who made Pakistan have mostly left; the ones that remain are either those who had expressly and intensely opposed its formation or those that had initially flocked blindly to that cause in the name of religion but soon saw their error. Today, the greatest harm is being done by those who *claim* to be loyal. Please don't utter words that wound the heart and make it turn away from loyalty. We are all sinners. Look at your own hands—they are also tainted with blood. Bapu's assassination has burdened us with an eternal guilt. Let us join and cleanse our hands and our hearts, and end this endless cycle of allegations, recriminations, apologies.'

I don't know what else I said, or what impact my words had, but my spirit felt lighter afterwards.

The Nizamuddin dargah, Delhi, as in January 1946.

15

Mosques and mazars
(June–August 1948)

B y June 1948, fear of the government had compelled divisive forces to stop attacking the living and to devote their energies to revenging themselves on the dead. By demolishing these marks of our past, they wished to create an atmosphere of anarchy again. Shanti Dal reported damages to mosques, dargahs and mazars to the Inkhala Masjid (Evacuee Mosques) Committee, instituted by Bapu and headed by Mehr Chand Khanna, with the secretary of the archaeological department and a representative of Ahrar Party as its other members. Through its sincere efforts, many mosques and mazars were repaired and restored to Muslims.

Touring Delhi's rural areas, we had seen extensive destruction of holy places, as well as numerous instances of their capture by refugees and local Hindus. In Chhatarpur, a large village near Mehrauli, the population—originally of prosperous cultivators—had grown eight-fold in recent months. There was thus a severe shortage of houses. Although many refugees had captured undamaged houses of the Muslims, many were also living in huts and shacks whose thatched roofs had been torched in the violence. The area's two grand mosques were also bursting at the seams.

Right next to Mehrauli was Chiragh Delhi, where too the holy place had met the same fate. Only the mazar of Hazrat Roshan Chiragh-i-Delhi, Allah's mercy be upon his soul, stood undamaged—everything else in the dargah was vandalized. When we surveyed it, some old men approached us, their distress evident, 'Sahab, this has always been a place of love and peace. A Hindu disciple of Hazrat Chiragh Delhi ascended the seat after him. This dargah, so venerated by us and our forebears, is where we have always come on pilgrimage, bearing new crop, new wife, new child—to proffer thanks and seek blessings. The whole village exists just to serve it.

'Earlier, no one but the caretakers of the graves, the mujavirs, and other servants lived inside the four walls of this little city. But in 1857, or perhaps at the time of Nadir Shah's massacre, large numbers from outside rushed here for sanctuary and Hindus and Muslims have lived here in peace since. But this time, when the violence began, the Sangh exerted such influence that the youth refused to listen to us. The miscreants were primarily locals with a handful of refugees who had recently arrived. These young men attacked the Muslims first, then set out to destroy the mazars and nearby monuments.'

However, despite their exertions, the mazar stood unharmed—the only success the attackers had was in parting the heavy marble slabs on the roof of the dome by a few inches. Exasperated, they vented their frustration on its floor, smashed all the tiles to bits and destroyed the mirrors and paintings on the beautifully calligraphed drape on the ceiling. They then turned on the other monuments in the complex and destroyed all the mirrorwork decorations, smashed other graves to pieces, tore out the fountains, reduced all of it to rubble.

Pandit Jaidev used to aver, 'Apaji, no child of a Hindu can ever lay a hand on a grave.' But today, witnessing all this, he lapsed into stunned silence.

The old men whispered that they had managed to save and secrete many valuable carpets, chandeliers, brocades and fans. They held them in trust but would turn them over to us. They also told us that locals had pilfered the dargah's 500-year-old brass door, gold pitcher and other valuables. But these goods had not left the area yet; if we tried, we could recover them from people's houses. We informed the police and after eight months, it recovered the property. Some things were found in raids in neighbouring villages, others were anonymously returned, perhaps because the thieves sensed the wind's new direction and were afraid of attracting the government's displeasure.

Calling on Pandit Sunderlal again, we arranged a public meeting, to which the editor of *Milap*, Khushhal Chand 'Khursand' (who became Mahatma Anand Swami after his renunciation) accompanied us. Pandit Sunderlal spoke first, for three hours, about politics, religion, custom, history and events in India and Pakistan. He asked his audience to face up to blunt truths. Initially, the audience was provoked into objections but soon, the tide turned and eyes—his and his audience's—moistened. But whenever tears threatened to break free, he would dart in with a quip or two and the weeping listeners would be moved to laughter despite themselves.

Next up was Jajuji, who began by cleverly lobbing a few aggravating questions. When the replies revealed the thief that lurked in listeners' hearts, he calmly explained the facts. He had such incredible patience, that man. His discourse had little flash or quickness of repartee. From start to end, there appeared to be a single tone to his delivery, but his eyes and ears were sensitive to even the smallest alteration in the mood of his audience, even the slightest twitch in their faces.

Our intervention in Chiragh Delhi ensured that the dargah's old caretaker, Niaz Ali, returned to live there alone again. There was also no protest or unrest when, on the Urs, lorries full of people from Delhi came to celebrate. Things improved so much that we could now ask some local residents to relinquish the houses they had captured—and they agreed.

But just as we had begun to gather all the Chiragh Delhi Muslims from UP and the city, we heard that refugees were being sent there by the administration. Some days later, we found that not even one or two people could any longer be accommodated, as every building between the houses we had vacated and the mosque was occupied. I wouldn't have felt any sorrow if this meant that, after months of living on footpaths and abandoned graves, the refugees had found roofs over their heads. But that wasn't what the officials intended and most refugees remained where they were. Once again, regional discrimination, favouritism and nepotism triumphed.

If only the officials had reposed faith in our good intentions, we would have recovered all the captured houses from local Hindus. After resettling the four or five Muslim families, we would have distributed the remaining houses to refugees. There were hardly any Muslims from the village left alive—how could they have used up so many houses? They would have had to live with the refugee neighbours we brought them and every living space would have been utilized.

On 4 July 1948, Hakim Syed Hussain, a Shanti Dal activist from Basti Nizamuddin informed us that for three or four days, some digging activities were going on in the grounds surrounding the settlement. There was a graveyard there and two or three graves had been defiled already. Apparently, the ground was being levelled to construct a technical institute. He also said that just as a minister arrived, the local Shanti Dal Committee in-charge drew his attention to the violation. The minister immediately had red flags posted to demarcate the graves. Nevertheless, Hussain sahab worried that this wouldn't prove enough to curtail the mischief.

The next day, in Basti Nizamuddin, I saw quite a few red flags. Many large trucks stood nearby and many people—some digging, some transporting soil—were busy levelling the ground. Officials of the CRC and the PWD were blatantly participating. I believe the deputy commissioner was also there, but I didn't see him; my colleagues told me that as soon as he heard of my arrival, he retreated into a tent nearby. Perhaps he did not want to meet me.

The section of the ground under work included a high mound of graves, yet untouched. My companion, Syed Mohammed Miyan Nizami pointed out that the officials had stopped work because of our protests. But looking at his map, he suspected that something was amiss. Summoning the engineer, he said that four of the seventeen flags that the minister had gotten posted had disappeared overnight. On our insistence, the four flags were restored. I calmed the locals gathered around. There was no reason to be so upset; a technical institute would only benefit them.

Hussain disagreed, 'But why build it in on the graveyard? All of Arab Sarai is empty. There are even rooms there that they could repair and make inhabitable, if they so want. What is in these graves that they are so keen to build here?' Meanwhile, inside the *basti*, Muslims were hoisting their bundles and bedding onto their backs—the Custodian had to choose just this moment to carry out a survey!

I spoke to Shankar Sharan sahab, Chief Custodian. Recently arrived on deputation from UP, he was new to the job and we had hopes from him after bitter confrontations with the old guard. I told him that the survey was not legitimate—all houses contiguous to the dargah were occupied. Some

Inscriptions seen inside the Nizamuddin dargah, Delhi, in January 1946.

housed Muslim sanctuary seekers, some were reserved for visitors, guests and fakirs and the rest were occupied by mujavirs. All the property belonged to the Wakf Board and it lay outside the domain of the Custodian. Why had he thought that the dargah and its neighbourhood were evacuee property? If Hazrat Nizamuddin Auliya, peace be upon his soul, was in no state to migrate to Pakistan, how could he be designated a muhajir? Shankar Sharan sahab expressed ignorance, saying he had given no such order for a survey in Nizamuddin Basti. I was puzzled. Why was all this happening then?

Another story connects to this one at this point. A few weeks earlier, a sahabzada came to Delhi to participate in the Goodwill Mission being taken by some Aligarh students to Pakistan. Before he could leave though, he fell seriously ill and ended up staying in our house for over a month. I think he was called Usmani. I learnt later that he had earlier been a member of the Muslim National Guard. Before he left our house to move into a room in Constitution House, I saw him furiously dialling the telephone and talking to many people. Intrigued, I asked, 'What are you up to now, my friend? Some new programme of action?' He replied, 'I'm thinking of going into business.' Some days later, he moved out.

At all times I saw him thereafter, he was surrounded by many boys and girls. Some would drop into the Shanti Dal office in Constitution House occasionally. For some reason, I didn't like either them or this habit of theirs. I berated the office staff for letting these suspicious characters loiter about, 'Something about this gang disquiets me. It would be better if we adopted the general rule that anyone not associated with us cannot sit and while away time in our office.'

Shortly after, I saw a thick crowd outside the sahabzada's room. Intrigued, I went over. A young Christian girl from Bombay told me, 'Interviews are being held today. People from various parties have gathered—we are choosing volunteers.' Scanning the crowd, I recognized the face of an Aligarh student, whom I knew to be a Muslim Leaguer. I was wondering what work had attracted one of the greatest troublemakers of Aligarh Muslim University, when I ran into the sahabzada. He declared self-importantly, 'The government simply can't find enough young people to do its work. I have scheduled these interviews for the Social Service League to fill this lacuna. A thousand refugee boys and girls have also agreed to come to the government's aid.' I stayed quiet but there was a catch in my heart—which house was this gang planning to set ablaze?

Some days after the events of 4 and 5 July, I met him again. I asked, 'Where is the organization you were building? Graveyards are being effaced but I haven't seen one of your youth volunteers around. Who are they supposed to help?' He replied, 'With respect, you are completely misinformed. The people digging in the basti are mine. We have saved the government a lot of money. Our volunteers charge just Rs 100–150 and work very quickly—in just two hours, they accomplish what a labourer would do in twelve. And no graves are being defiled; we are just levelling the ground.' I was astounded. 'So all this is your doing! All those you summoned by telegrams were just to enable you to launch a united front against Shanti Dal. You want to break us by organizing this league? What else could I have expected of someone like you?'

The next day, I saw the sahabzada and his cohorts at the grounds, presiding over bands of refugee youth at work. No one heeded our protests. For the next three days, I kept on trying. I would have the red flags planted on the graves but, as soon as I turned my back, they would be removed. My challenges would be met with denial: 'Really, how did this happen? Certainly not by our hands.'

Considering the dispute inside the basti and the trouble outside, it appeared that this Muslim neighbourhood would be short-lived—after all that we progressives had done to preserve it. Besides Jama Masjid, this was the only quarter where love had reigned and peace had held but now the people clinging to Nizamuddin Auliya were in tears—where were they to go?

Meanwhile, Hussain was left ruing the day he mentioned Arab Sarai. Three days later, the mausoleum of his ancestor was broken to make way for a water pipe and plans to build a toilet near the dome were on the anvil. Luckily, a minister was visiting the basti with me then, so I asked him to take a look. He did, and saw that the reports were true. Despite a minister's orders, officials were presiding over the process.

Since a few days, we had posted two boys on duty at the basti, consciously picking one Hindu and one Muslim, so that neither would get carried away in reporting. We were afraid that a Hindu–Muslim riot would erupt any moment, but luckily it didn't. The Muslims were so intimidated that they could not summon the gumption to do anything; besides, they had faith that we would somehow find a solution to this crisis. We had also strictly forbidden them from intervening in the matter.

A bitter confrontation with the officials ensued. Shanti Dal wrote a letter of strong protest but, by now, the scale of the project was so vast that it was impossible to monitor what was being pulled down where.

One day, a short while later, Chaudhary Abdul Sattar, a member of Ahrar Party, asked me to see what was being done to Dargah-e-Shah-e-Mardaa, also known as 'Old Karbala'.

In the magnificent gateway of this monument, wrought in the finest marble, refugees had set up residence. In small rooms lining the walls on either side too, people lived. Some had even settled into parts of the monument proper. The little plaques of marble once affixed to graves (*taveezes*) were now used as mosaic in courtyards and as tiles for bathing places.

The cemetery was full of centuries-old blocks of engraved marble, now wrenched from the ground and put aside for use. The courtyard of the exquisitely inlaid mausoleum still bore the footmarks of Hazrat Ali (may Allah have mercy on his soul) but almost everything else—door frames, thresholds, inlays, mirrors—had been broken. Coarse white gravel dusted the ground, as stone worth lakhs of rupees lay in shards. Such destruction could only have been wrought by the hard labour of scores of men over several weeks.

My companions told me that this was the most sacred of Delhi's Shia monuments. Every year during Muharram and other holy occasions, Shias from as far as Iran and Iraq would arrive on pilgrimage. Spotting a small black engraved stone, I bent to pick it up—it was a piece of a taveez of a sultan's grave. From this shard, I could not learn his name or his years, as this information must have been given below. Spotting another, I stooped again—was this beautifully calligraphed piece the remembrance of some pleasure-seeking prince? Or of a wise man rich with learning about the faith? Or of a fakir who had renounced the ways of the world?

All the fragments spoke, communicating to us the stories of imams, learned men, princes, fakirs. They too had once roamed a world like ours, alive and sentient. In a Delhi not so different from ours, their greatness had once been heralded and the foundations of their knowledge and morality firmed. In this very city, they had spent the heady days of their youth in pleasure and celebration, and some corner of this place may once have become a spot for piety and contemplation. And to all these people must have come others, in the quest for enlightenment of the spirit or the riches of the world; on occasion, they too would have made the supplicants a victim of their arrogance. And on this very land would also have been some that called to Allah and steered His wretched towards compassion. Today, hammers pounded at all these people's bones; in Aliganj, tractors drove across them. If any of them were to return today, how incredulous they would be to find that this desecration was not the handiwork of beasts but the work of educated, cultured men!

This is the way the world has always been. At times, the living are killed and graves made for them; at others, the dead are dug up to make way for monuments for the living. In the great circle of Creation, all this has the significance of a mere moment; but Man cannot comprehend this. In these beautiful words:

aaj diwana udata hai jo viraane ki khaq
kal udayega yun hi viraana diwane ki khaq
Today, the dreamer wildly churns the wilderness to dust
Tomorrow, this very wilderness will whip his dust in the wind

Safi Lucknowi

chalti chaaki dekh ke diya kabira roye
do paatan ke beech mein sabut bacha na koye
Seeing the mill grind moves Kabir to tears
Betwixt the two wheels, nothing is left whole

Kabir

After inspecting the monument, when we returned to the courtyard, we were surrounded by irate refugees. Some women stepped up to throw their children at my feet, 'Look at our children, dying, and you have no concern. We are rotting here and nobody even gets us a house.' Some shouted, 'And these Muslims trouble us night and day.' Surprised, I asked, 'Muslims? But my dear bibis, no Muslims are left for miles around. Where do they come from to trouble you?'

The reply: the 'Muslims' they referred to were snakes, which had bitten and killed many children and elders. I was incredulous. 'So, Muslims are snakes?' Then I explained that their own mistakes had led to this situation. 'By disturbing this monument and cemetery which is scores of years old, you have invited the snakes. These old structures must have been their homes. You dug up their homes, so they revenge themselves upon you.

'As for getting you houses, we will certainly help you. Approach the Shanti Dal, apply for help, we will give you all the assistance you need to tackle your difficulties. And just reflect on the appalling thing you have done. You needn't have destroyed the cemetery—what harm could graves do to you? You could have just left out that portion and lived in the monument.'

The crowd protested that it was not responsible for the destruction of the cemetery. They had arrived later, after truckloads of people had dug it up. My companion told me that until April 1948, the monument and the cemetery had been unharmed, which meant that the destruction took place in May–June 1948.

On the drive back, I saw that another graveyard and a mosque had once been on the way. We saw a tractor levelling the ground. The rubble of the dome and its foundations could be discerned and a few broken graves still remained. I thought it best to take this matter to Khannaji personally. The next day, he and an official from the archaeological department accompanied us to the place where the mosque and graveyard once stood. In an old map I obtained from the Secretariat, the mosque was clearly indicated but the only trace of its existence now was the levelled, cemented ground; all the graves had been completely effaced.

The PWD officials contested the charge. Khannaji and the official from the archaeological department reiterated that they had enough proof that a mosque and graveyard had existed there but the PWD people were intent on disputing every attestation, wanting to play a game of oneupmanship. Disgusted, we left—everything had been completely erased, what could we fight for?

My Ahrari friend, however, was undeterred. He insisted on taking us to see the state of the mosque in the courtyard of the jail near Khooni Darwaza. I was fed up and didn't want to go. I had always been reluctant to get involved in this work. So what was this unseen hand that kept pushing me back towards something I had no taste for? I had never even liked going to the family cemetery and these past few days had been spent exclusively in graveyards and graves. People could dig them all up for all I cared. These graves had become old, we would make new ones, ones that would make each of your stiff necks bow before them in respect and humility!

Little did I know then that just a few days later, this would become a reality, and Brigadier Usman would be martyred in a death so honourable that would be lauded even by the enemy! When the majestic funeral procession wound through the city into Okhla, a multitude of mourners had walked all the way on foot and each heart was full to bursting with respect and admiration.

In any case, I'd already seen the mosque that Sattar sahab wanted us to see. The entire structure had been virtually demolished; its walls were now barely a foot high and all that remained was the red sandstone floor inside. The delicate white outlines of prayer mats etched across this floor spoke of the many foreheads that had bowed so low in His devotion; it was as if their marks branded the floor. But no, that cannot be true—if the prostrations had truly been so devout, how could they ever be erased?

sabt ast bar jareed-e-alam dawam-e-ma
In the book of this world, its mark is indelible

Hafiz Shirazi

Whatever my thoughts, the fact was that the mosque was gone, save for the floor and an elevated platform. This was where the policemen had sat for many days. The poor things still had no idea how miscreants could have dug up a whole mosque under their noses— oh, the sightlessness of the seeing!

Khannaji consulted the map and found the mosque marked. Taking a round, we noted the remnants of the dome, pillars and floor. We read the *fateha* for the dead and came away.

In the third week of July, a meeting of senior functionaries of the administration, representatives of various political parties and social workers was held in the prime minister's office. The Shanti Dal's programme of action was presented to Panditji, who expressed his approval.

The meeting discussed the confrontation between Shanti Dal and the local administration. Scores of problems were raised, debated and thrashed out. The general secretary of the Provincial Congress Committee bluntly spelt out all the issues, citing many incidents and levelling charges of non-cooperation and hostility against the administration and the police. The police officials present tried to dismiss these charges but there were so many of us there to counter them and ultimately they could not refute them all.

The most senior official of the Delhi province was there throughout. A quiet man, he would neither get agitated himself nor let others. Although he never made promises—it was beyond his powers to get his officers to implement any undertaking—we gained his moral support. Like him, some other fine people in other departments also responded to our repeated appeals to their human goodness. As yet, however, we could not rely on their good offices because their numbers were small and most had only a trifling role in operational matters.

After a lengthy, frank discussion, a firm decision was made that all social workers would work within the ambit of the law and that all the officials who earlier used the law as an excuse to trouble us would now cooperate. A responsible official of Delhi said, 'The decision to vacate the mosques has been hasty, which is why the refugees are so disturbed. They should not be asked to leave until new houses are ready.' The secretary of the Socialist Party said, 'I agree, and I've opposed this move all along.'

I said, 'But don't you think you should have one rule for places of worship? How can these be places of residence? The only way to prevent the desecration and destruction that follows in the wake of the refugees is to adopt this as a principle. And then, the Muslims too become disaffected on seeing this.' An official replied, 'But the destruction happens only when the refugees are asked to leave.' The secretary endorsed this and grandly declared, 'The difference between you and me is that I work with the living, whereas you care for the dead.'

Truly a wonderful statement! If it had been some other time, I might have enjoyed this banter but then I felt very hurt. I thought of responding in kind, but it would have been inappropriate.

The meeting continued and many things were said. Then Mridula spoke, with all her natural frankness. As she laid everything out so plainly, we all exulted, and I realized for the first time that:

goya yeh bhi mere dil mein hai
That this one too lives in my heart

Mirza Ghalib

Within a week, Mridula called for a meeting of activists in Constitution House. Addressing it, she spoke of the negative propaganda that the destruction of mosques and dargahs had received in Islamic nations. In countries like Egypt and Iran, there was much concern

No. VI-(21) 56 Prop. II.,
Govt. of India,
Ministry of Rehabilitation,
New Delhi.

From: The 27th March, 1957.
    Sh. Kanwar Bahadur,
    Under Secretary to the Govt. of India,

To
    The Chief Audit Officer,
    Food Rehabilitation and supply,
    New Delhi.

Sub: Para 3 of the Audit inspection report for the
        period Oct. 1953, to March 1954 on the property
        accounts of the custodian of evacuee property.

Sir,

        I am directed to refer to your letter No. CAF - 3(10)-
40-11-1954, Dated the 1st November, 1956, and to state that
the properties belonging to peerzadas of Nizamuddin Aulia
Shrine Delhi were in the beginning treated an evacuee property
and were shown as such in the evacuee property Register
by the custodian of evacuee property Delhi. The question
regarding treatment of these properties was, however considered
subsequently and it was found that these properties, for
all practical purposes were essentially those of the Shrine
proper and were being used for religious purposes. Some
of these properties contained graves of character to which
sanctity is attached and some of them were reported to be
used for accomodating pilgrims during the Urs fair. It
was further learnt that their is no income of the Shrine
other than what is obtained in the nature of offerings from
the pilgrims. In view of this it was felt that if these
properties are allotted or not cause other than that of
the Shrine proper, there will be some amount of detraction
from the sanctity of the Shrine. It was, therefore, decided
that the custodian should not take any action whatsoever
whether by way of allotting these properties or recovery
of rent from the occupants therefore. The position theafore

The Nizamuddin dargah was finally freed from the clutches of the Custodian of Evacuee Property in March 1957, as this letter found in Anis Kidwai's papers reveals.

about the safety of the Kadam Sharif dargah. She posted one of our colleagues there and made him responsible for its repair and restoration, so that by Ramzan, Muslims could frequent the place again.

But we could do little to prevent the attacks. The secretary and other functionaries of the archaeological department would throw up their hands, 'We cannot possibly guard all monuments. In any case, the mischief is being done by the PWD.' I doubt that they ever shared this information with the elected government, perhaps because they themselves were not unblemished.

Whenever we heard of a mosque or mazar vandalized or forcibly occupied, we would alert Khannaji. He would arrange for it to be evacuated or write to the PWD chief commissioner, the institution entrusted with repair and construction of public buildings. This cycle of destruction, evacuation and repair had the same pace, precisely because the PWD was behind the destruction in the first place. Many of its officials were members of organizations who had carried out the destruction. Old Karbala, Shah-e-Mardan, Arab Sarai and other mosques and mazars today had the PWD to thank for their deserted, forlorn state.

Other government officials too abetted these demolitions. The police refused to even entertain the complaint that so-and-so deputy commissioner of a zila presided over the levelling of a Muslim graveyard, let alone register an FIR. In these activities, they were always assisted by resentful youth organized under names like Sevak Dal, Social Service League, etc. With such powerful hands of benediction resting on their back, why would they pay heed to our warnings and protests?

The outcome of our complaint wouldn't perturb them the slightest; indeed, it would go in their favour. Invariably, we would be forced by the callousness of officials to approach the highest ranks of the government hierarchy to get a hearing, and soon, an order for repair would wind down to their ranks. What an exquisite stratagem it was: not a moment's suffering due to remorse and one didn't have to look bad to the ones who were intent on digging up the mosques. And when the order for the repair arrived, they would set to its implementation with such alacrity that it would be hard to imagine more diligence and devotion to duty!

Meanwhile, blissfully unaware that it was imprisoned in the vice-like grip of its wily bureaucrats, the government was busy doling out money for both destruction and construction. It believed that the people responsible for this increased outlay were 'goons'. Though the image this word usually conjures up is of a young man with his hair slicked heavy with oil and combed out neatly with a centre-parting and masticating a juicy paan as he saunters on the street or loiters at the entrances of cinemas, leering at girls—that image is an anachronism. Times change. The goon now lives in houses, works in offices, sits in the judge's chair and can be the president of a university union, a leader of the people, a fiery orator at a public meeting.

It was only when I met Pandit Nehru and my report about the pressing problem of mosques and mazars was forwarded to him by the Shanti Dal with a note of support and recommendation, that this chapter was finally closed. I briefed Jawaharlalji in detail about events, current conditions and measures taken by nationalists. Panditji asked, 'Who is doing all this work from the nationalists' side?' I replied, 'Mridula.' He was quite surprised, 'Really? Is she very involved?' and when I told him that she was our leader and that she was everything to us and this cause, he fell quiet. I was surprised that he didn't know but not unhappy: this is the way real activists stay out of the limelight. No display, no swagger, even though they must have met nearly every day, Mridula had not even mentioned her activities to him.

If Panditji hadn't been apprised of the ground reality, we might well be sitting with our heads in our hands, mourning events of 15 July rather than 15 June. In the end:

raseeda bood balaye, vale bakhair guzasht
Difficulty was upon us but it passed with ease

Farsi proverb

Old women sewing at the displaced women's training centre at Bengali market, Delhi.

16

Shanti Dal activities in the city

(May–September 1948)

In June and July, the pace of relief and rehabilitation was so slow that the refugees were up in arms. The government had opened its coffers but the administration was afflicted by immense inertia. Had the CRC not been aided by non-governmental organizations, not even half the work accomplished thus far would have taken place, and the current disaffection would have lasted for another two years.

Our hearts were not yet moved by genuine pain for our nation, a devotion to duty, a will to rebuild what had been broken. After all, the administration comprised slothful, callous individuals from among us. Just like we were useless in our public lives, we demonstrated indiscipline and disorderliness in our roles as administrators. Nonchalant about the need for swift action, we gave no thought to how people were roasting in Delhi's heat. How long would the refugees bear it?

263

In all honesty, there was another thing. Over the centuries, we had lost the habit of governing ourselves. It was only by doing the deed now that we would learn how to; with experience, discipline would emerge and efficiency improve. The problem was that there was no respite for this learning to take place.

At its reconstitution, the new Shanti Dal had decided that as long as the government wished to maintain Muslim zones, we would preserve the original composition of these neighbourhoods—Muslim and old Hindu inhabitants—and prevent new entrants from settling. We had succeeded in Bara Hindu Rao. As expected, this goal didn't make us any friends among refugees; Shanti Dal volunteers were greeted with great hostility everywhere.

A specific Shanti Dal sub-committee was formed to seal houses in the Muslim zone and activists were enjoined to work in cooperation with the administration. On the latter's part, the recent accord meant that no one could openly oppose us, even though they didn't always extend the cooperation they had promised. On our part too, there were times when the interests of the government were at odds with that of the public and we felt duty-bound to take the people's side. So, we often set out to do one thing, but ended up doing another.

Preventing the refugees from taking over houses in Muslim zones was a terrible test, both for the Punjabi refugees and the Shanti Dal volunteers. On one side were bodies cracked and split by weeks in the burning sun, leaping eagerly towards empty houses that promised shelter and shade. On the other side were Shanti Dal workers, many of whom were refugees themselves. It is commendable that the workers largely held firm in these trying circumstances.

Despite all our efforts, however, sealing and allotting houses was not easy. Many problems were posed by the Muslims themselves. They were in a strange frame of mind, brimming over with malice and vengefulness. Rich Muslims in larger neighbourhoods would make the following proposal to their poorer neighbours: if the poor Muslims would leave their hutments in exchange for a room in the rich Muslims' big houses, their hutments could be given to the refugees on pagdi. The fools, driven by indigence, would agree. Some days later, the rich

Muslim would sell that very house by a *benami* transfer and depart for Pakistan, leaving the poor guy at the mercy of the new refugee owners.

I came to believe that a Muslim's word couldn't be relied on any longer. Once when a gentleman had reported to me that the court demanded that he present either one Hindu or two Muslims to corroborate his testimony, I was incensed. But the reality became evident to me soon. Even the word of four Muslims was less weighty than that of a Hindu—who knew when they would up and leave for Pakistan?

Shanti Dal volunteers and nationalist Muslims repeatedly interceded with the rich Muslims to pity their poor neighbours. But why would they accept our requests? Overnight, each affluent family would take thousands of rupees as pagdi and vanish. Before leaving, they would do us another favour—taking the volunteers standing guard on the neighbourhood as obstacles, they would make complaints against them to the police. In earlier months, the police was so irritated with us that it seized the opportunity to set into motion another case against Shanti Dal. After the July talks with the administration, at least cases weren't filed, though the police's hostility didn't abate.

Instead, we found ourselves increasingly in conflict with the Custodian department, even as a section of the Shanti Dal worked with it in sealing and allotting houses. We kept the assisting party and the fighting party separate; the fighting party consisted of Mridula and Subhadra. I remember one fight well. Some dishonest houseowners in the Muslim zone had hit upon a strategy to prevent their vacant houses from being sealed—they would import bogus people and plant them in their houses, saying they were residents. This strategy was known to the government by now, so when a minister was approached, he consulted the CRC and the Custodian. On their advice, he ordered the police to seal the houses that night.

The people in these houses were asleep when the police arrived; it hauled them out and started locking their doors. Whatever the true story about the owners, all these families were poor Muslim sanctuary seekers and, owing to the administration, were back on the streets. Shanti Dal volunteers tried desperately to tell the police; when they

129. *From Vallabhbhai Patel*

New Delhi
14th October 1948

My dear Rajenbabu,

Sometime ago I spoke to you about the activities of Mridula and the Shanti Dal. I have since referred the question of its future to the Chief Commissioner who has consulted the Inspector-General of Police and the Deputy Commissioner. The officers are all unanimously of the view that the activities of the Shanti Dal are leading to constant frictions, that the Shanti Dal has some very undesirable elements, that the present liaison arrangements between the Provincial Congress Committee and the Chief Commissioner are working satisfactorily, and that the continuance of Shanti Dal is neither necessary nor desirable; in fact, if the organisation is continued, it would accentuate present frictions and demoralisation in the administration. I am, in this connection, enclosing a copy of the letter which Mohanlal Saxena has written to Mridula.

I have no doubt in my mind that this organisation, which virtually aims at a parallel local administration and functions as such, should be wound up as soon as possible. I do hope you will issue instructions accordingly.

Yours sincerely,
Vallabhbhai Patel

The Hon'ble Dr. Rajendra Pd.
President, Indian National Congress
Pilani.

Enclosure:

(Copy of a D.O. letter dated 31 August 1948 from Mohanlal Saksena, Minister for Relief and Rehabilitation, to Mridula Sarabhai)

31 August 1948

You know I was given to believe that with the help of the Shanti Dal we shall be able to peacefully get possession of a large number of Muslim evacuee houses within a couple of weeks and it was with that object that I had agreed to certain police arrangements in the Mohallas concerned, as well as the allotment of houses so recovered. But unfortunately that hope has not so far materialised and I find that it is not possible for the Shanti Dal to keep out undesirable elements.

This exchange of letters between Rajendra Prasad and Sardar Vallabhbhai Patel demonstrates the extent of the friction between the Shanti Dal and the administration.

weren't heard, they called the Head Office. At once, Mridula and Subhadra descended on the scene and, on their heels, several government officials. Arguments continued till 3 a.m., until a government minister arrived. He felt so deeply about the mistake that he himself broke the locks and escorted the women and children back in, apologizing frankly all the while. By dawn, the people were back in their homes, the police in their thanas, the leaders in their houses, and the whole matter— caused by a few selfish individuals and corrupt government officials— was over.

Of course, our young volunteers made many mistakes in the sealing process. Many of them were well read and sensitive to the current state of affairs, but they lacked patience. Perhaps some errors of judgement were due to this but it would be unfair to lay all the blame at their door. At a time when the sentiment that every trace of Muslims be effaced from the map of India was at its apogee in the minds of the general public and officialdom, it was these few well-intentioned young people who sincerely wanted to end this anarchy. We had no option but to take the help of these novices, raw as they were.

Most volunteers were themselves refugees. Although they admired and respected Subhadra above all, some wavered. A few didn't know what ahimsa meant and, in the heat of the moment, were not loath in laying a few cane strikes on the fleeing attackers. Others, after going hungry for three meals in a day, chose not to risk their lives by starving a fourth time and would seek money as inducement from some poor desperate soul. Yet others, tired of standing guard at the gates of a Muslim enclave, would loathe even the sight of a Muslim, that ingrate who never showed any concern as they stood guard over his life for eight hours at a stretch, didn't even offer a cup of tea. Struck by the desire for revenge, they would succumb and sneak open the gates to let a refugee family slip in.

When Muslim zones were disbanded in August and houses allotted to refugees, some among the volunteers thought that the service they had rendered entitled them to the first option. Their colleagues agreed—it would be far better that they settled there, not some quarrelsome strangers. When things didn't go as they wished, many of these volunteers lapsed completely, took pagdi, and arranged for houses to be allotted to persons whose names were not on the original lists.

In this hour of our test, we made huge mistakes, mountainous ones. We scrambled to ensure that our own people were given houses first—socialists for socialists, Congressis for Congress, Shanti Dal for its volunteers—and the truly needy were left homeless. But all this happened not because we wanted it but because we were inexperienced, didn't pause to think. We didn't realize that many volunteers had joined us because they wanted material assistance from the CRC, or a government loan, or a house, or fame.

Subhadra was very sensible and many of our colleagues were very stable, but who could have divined the future? We were simply too trusting of all who worked with us; as a result, Subhadra was chastised by many Congress colleagues and the local government instituted court proceedings against many of our former volunteers.

But even with the Muslim zone houses added to the general pool, it was obvious that the administration had grossly underestimated refugee needs. In almost every department, officials from Punjab dominated, so when the allotment of houses vacated by Muslims and of newly constructed houses and shops took place, it was invariably Punjabis who topped the lists. This stepmotherly treatment had people from the North-West Frontier Provinces up in arms. The Sindhis too querulously demanded why they were pushed down the list.

In Kingsway Camp, 24,000 refugees still languished, besides thousands in camps like those in Kurukshetra and those in and around Delhi. The government and the CRC ordered the construction of new houses but even after thousands had been erected, countless families were left homeless to freeze in the approaching winter. Humayun's Tomb, Safdarjung's Tomb and the ruins of other old monuments were packed with refugees. If only proper living arrangements had been made there, the situation would have been less desperate, but no one could be bothered. Had it been explained to the refugees that these monuments were India's historical legacy and that they should care for them, they would have agreed to live there for a while. However, no one thought of it; neither did the archaeological department think of protecting the monuments in any way.

It was inexplicable that plots the Improvement Trust had readied for the refugees stood unoccupied for so long. The refugees told us, pleaded with the administration, begged for allotments. But deliberations and considerations took one whole year, and only by winter were a few people given some of these. If only the refugees had been given amenities—vacant land, construction materials, assistance of engineers—hundreds, if not thousands, of families would have made their own homes without any government intervention whatsoever.

Perhaps this proposal of mine was infeasible. I wasn't even the smallest cog in the wheel of government machinery, so how could I appreciate the impediments it faced? But many other members of the public thought like me. By end-August, our efforts had ensured that in almost all of Delhi's older neighbourhoods, the new populace was mixed. This gladdened my heart—only if people lived together would hatred and alienation end. Our work was to build a human brotherhood, not Muslim or Hindu ones.

The Muslim leaders didn't think like me. They were apprehensive (not without reason) and accepted mixed neighbourhoods with great reluctance. Their reluctance was partly due to the increasing influence of the Muslim League, some of whose members remained active in India and had managed to infiltrate Jamiat. These people were very stressed over the matter of houses. But even though nationalist Muslims and the Congress distanced themselves from them, and our activists refused to have any truck with them, these men hanging on the Ulema's coat-tails left no stone unturned to increase their influence on the government and administration. Their objectives—to expand their businesses; to get good prices for their property; to gain citizenship of both India and Pakistan.

Whenever any of the better connected of these gentlemen of the League came to Delhi, they made it a point to meet members of the Cabinet and the Assembly, the governor-general and even Congress leaders. Not once, however, did they make the effort to meet and hear out Muslim sanctuary seekers. The only reason these League fellows came was to feign acceptance of the Congress's perspective to get their work done. Obviously, they didn't need to hold their traditional sectarian and abhorrent attitudes in check for longer than was necessary.

One of these gentlemen even offered me, via the offices of a Congressi Muslim, a few thousand rupees and a house to establish offices of the Markaz-e-Ittehad-ul-Taraqqi in a Muslim neighbourhood, provided I got him appointed trade commissioner to Pakistan. What was more amazing was that the nationalist brother who conveyed the offer to me endorsed it enthusiastically. In his view, there was nothing wrong in accepting the bribe. We would get both a building and money, and our mission could be successful only when rich Muslims were in our control. The poor man was so crestfallen when I refused.

August also brought the first anniversary of our Independence. I cannot but marvel that our nascent government survived the myriad problems that had presented themselves. It must have been made of extremely strong stuff. Buffeted by storms, its ship not only bore all the lashings without capsizing, it even gathered speed as time wore on.

Delhi's administration, however, remained a thorn in our side. Although as a result of the July negotiations, some provincial administration officials had become allies, they would be pulled up by their seniors for assisting us. By August, Shanti Dal's more extremist section had had enough and pushed through the resolution that we should pressurize the government to overhaul the local administration. A dossier of complaints, charges, suspicions and proposals was prepared, our trusted generals apprised of every aspect, and it was sent up to the highest levels for action. Shanti Dal charged that the administration was intent on frustrating its every move. We warned the government that if the local administration weren't changed, all our activities would come to naught. The peace we desired would remain a pipe dream.

At long last, success was ours. We celebrated this victory—it was as if we had succeeded in weeding out one more root cause of the trouble. Everyone declared this our second biggest success. Once Delhi and its administration changed, both activists and the public found themselves in a new world. There was new hope in rural areas for relief and financial assistance from the government. The police began to recover the goods that had been stolen and offenders were increasingly apprehended.

But new problems soon engaged us. Just a few days after the administration changed, the new officials found themselves at odds with the refugees in Chandni Chowk who had set up little shacks on the footpath all along the market, to hawk goods at cheap rates. As more arrived, the rows of shacks increased. The shopkeepers were incensed, as the hawkers took away all their customers. The shopkeepers complained to the administration, which came to remove the shacks, to which the hawkers responded with an angry satyagraha.

The increase in stalls was matched by an increase in customers in all the city markets; Chandni Chowk, Connaught Place had all become filthy. Streets were littered with remains of street food like *chhola bhaturas*, alu chaat, *bhallas* and fruit peels. But why did residents of Lahore, a city reputedly as beautiful as Paris, behave thus? I was to get the answer soon, from Nawabganj and Kingsway Camp.

Refugee families living on pavements in Daryaganj, along Elgin Road.

In September, Subhadra told me to attend to the problems a refugee woman and her two daughters were causing in Nawabganj. Their neighbours complained that the daughters were so shameless that they would piss in the drains whenever they wanted to, wouldn't think twice about lying down in the street, in the midst of passers-by, would bathe at the public tap with all kinds of men gathered to watch.

I called for the mother and her two daughters; she arrived with one. I told them of the complaints, concluding, 'I'm surprised that despite your guiding presence, your daughters have gone astray. Why don't you restrain them?' The daughter burst into a flood of tears. The mother protested, 'All lies, falsehoods! This is just a ruse to get us out of here. My daughters do none of the things they say. The people of this neighbourhood are after them for no reason at all!' The girl cut her short, 'Mataji, why don't you come and see where we live first. Then we'll accept your decision.'

She took me to their 'house', a closet-sized *kothri* in a gateway at the entrance to the neighbourhood, one of four built for watchmen. In this space of four feet by two feet mother, father and daughters sat, ate, slept and spent their days and nights. Their only seating was a plank, which became their kitchen when they placed the *angithi* on it to cook. Their 'home' faced the road, bustling with passers-by. In tears, the girl said, 'Now tell me, how can four adults lie down together in this space? Two of us sit outside while the other two lie down. If I don't lie on the plank outside, how will I ever get any rest? As for water, there is just the public tap; if we don't bathe under it, where do we go? We have lived like this for a whole year—should we let our bodies rot unwashed instead?

'We try to relieve ourselves before daylight but the need can strike us in the day too, and then we have to sit at the drain. Will people stop coming to drink tea in the teashop out of concern for me? No, they will come, and the distance between us will always be the same two footsteps. What do I do if some people think that they come to see me? How am I guilty?'

I stood silent, searching for words, then spoke, 'Beti, can't you go to someone's house? Don't sit on the drain, it is immodest.' At this, she wept even more and said, 'Do you think anyone will let us enter his house? If I go a second time in a day to ask for drinking water, they abuse me!' The mother sighed, 'We too had a home in Punjab. We had dignity. We have come here to be humiliated. Please understand, we cannot live in this kothri and fulfil our daily requirements. People say what they want but it would be meaningful if they helped us.'

I had no words, again. Why should their neighbours have paid heed? They couldn't even summon sympathy when in front of a mother's eyes, in a father's lifetime, two innocent girls were being defamed in a public spectacle. In this gateway, it was not only the honour of this family being erased, it was also the dignity of our nation. With sorrowing heart and troubled mind, I went straight to Subhadra, 'If you don't get this family a house, it will be a sin before God.' She replied, 'I've already sent a request but that Custodian just won't accede. So many people have been given houses, it is only this family's number that never comes up for allotment.' I wished I could tear open the breasts of these legal luminaries and place the beating heart of a human inside. Perhaps then they would hear the cries of the poor.

After a month of ceaseless efforts, the family got a house. No doubt, the neighbourhood was satisfied to be rid of such 'wanton' girls; no doubt, also, that the louts who leered at them found such prey elsewhere.

A visit to Kingsway Camp in end-September, in the company of camp administrator Mr Shah, gave me another opportunity to understand the refugees' living conditions. The sun had set by the time we reached. We went first to the place where bales of thick white cotton, muslin and striped cloth were being cut and distributed to refugees. Someone was being handed over sixteen yards, someone else thirty, someone five, for their families.

Seeing the mounds of cloth, my thoughts turned to the tattered clothes that Muslim sanctuary seekers of Purani Tehsil and inhabitants of Muslim neighbourhoods were clad in. Hard as I tried, even a year later I had failed to persuade the government to give me even one pair of clothes for someone to cover his body. We had received so many requests but there was no official or institution we could approach on their behalf. All they got from us were personal donations.

The CRC couldn't help us because it was only for Hindu refugees. Thousands of poor rustics, who had fled their homes in Punjab and rural Delhi, were languishing in every corner of the city, unclothed and unfed. They had never gone to Pakistan, nor were they going to; yet, our democratic government continued to make such a distinction between those in distress. The only person who never disappointed us when we approached him with hands spread out was the prime minister. It was only because of him that activists like us had the courage to proclaim that our government was truly of the people, that it did not discriminate on the basis of religion, that it was for compassion and justice for all. It was only because of him that instead of dying on the streets, Muslims had a roof over their heads, under which they could struggle to make ends meet.

These thoughts occupied me briefly. The camp commander gave us a guided tour of some parts of the camp but, as it was getting dark, we requested to see the new quarters under construction. We saw the first near-complete batch of 800 well-apportioned houses, with kitchen, two rooms and veranda. Our 100 kaccha quarters were also being constructed; these had one room and a veranda, and there were plans to bring water and electricity to these as well.

We also passed the tents. Though there was no shortage of oil for lamps, the tents were pitch dark. The residents complained to us about a shortage of rations and milk for the children. They also cribbed that the officials in charge favoured their relatives and friends in tent distribution; the camp commander had two tents for his own family and some of his relatives had a double layer of tents to keep out the sun. Other inmates were forced to share tents—mostly two families lived in one tent, which didn't even shelter them from the rain.

Night fell and we had to leave. On the way back, we saw the Guru Granth Sahab being recited in a tent, with people seated all around. We stopped at the camp commander's office and spoke to him briefly about the conditions. I left a little earlier than my colleagues and sat in the car. As I waited, I heard whispers. Looking back, I saw three Sikhs standing behind the car. For an instant, I suspected their intentions—why hide behind the car? However, all they wanted to do was talk. One of them spoke through the car window, 'How would you introduce yourself?'

His voice was laced with sarcasm, and I was amused. I laughed, 'How can I do that? I cannot praise myself, can I?' Two or three others moved up as well. They asked again, 'What is your name?' Before I could reply, the camp commander and Shahji rushed in to stand between the Sikhs and my window. Angrily, they asked, 'What business is that of yours? Move aside, make way for our car.' Flanking the Sikhs, Shahji and the camp commander began shepherding them away. I thought this aggression would only worsen matters, so I told Shahji to let them approach again. I asked the Sikhs, 'What did you wish to ask me?' They asked my name again. Shahji bristled, 'She is Mrs Kidwai. What will you do about that?' One spoke, 'We want to know why you come here, sit and chat with the commander and then go off. Why don't you bother to talk to us, ask us what our troubles are?'

He went on in this vein and the others joined in. I cannot remember what was said. More Sikhs had gathered around the car meanwhile. I could see that Shahji and the camp commander wanted us to leave immediately. Nightfall, low light, embittered people—I was afraid but I knew that if I didn't engage with these Sikhs, nothing would have been gained by our visit. In a conciliatory tone, I said, 'My only intention in coming here was to talk to you, assess the conditions, hear your sorrows. But night has fallen. I promise to return the day after, to understand how we may help you.' My words calmed them and we left.

As our car pulled out, I noticed the camp commander whisper something to Shahji. I sensed that he was telling him to prevent me from returning the day after; so, when Shahji dropped me off, I reiterated, 'So, I will go to the camp the day after. I want to speak at length to the first Sikh who accosted me.'

I spent quite a few hours in the camp on my next visit. I kept beseeching my fellow travellers to take me to the Sikh tents but no one did. If I'd known the way, I'd have gone on my own. I couldn't meet that embittered soul—what did he want to tell me?

I saw a tent full of children; perhaps two or three families shared one tent. Seeing me, a mother cribbed, 'Do something for our children; they didn't even get milk today. The government sends tins of powdered milk but who knows whose stomachs they reach. All we get is this.' She fetched a dirty flour-like substance and mixed it with water. The powder stayed at the bottom, refusing to mix with the water. I took a sample from her, promising to take action.

As I exited their tent, another woman came running, brandishing a roti. I couldn't make out whether the roti was made of wheat or mud, so black it was. Perhaps it was some other grain entirely but experience suggested that the flour provided to these people could be half-flour, half-mud. I had seen it before.

In March I had visited a Gurgaon camp set up for sanctuary seekers from Alwar en route to Pakistan. Sweltering in a few inches of shade, the women would cook rotis that looked just like this one. The Muslim volunteers at the camp had said, 'See, Muslims in India aren't even given grain for a roti.' But today, Hindu refugees were eating the same rotis, even though the camp functionaries were Hindus, as were the relief providers. Greed does not discriminate.

In a clearing, I saw a scoutmaster leading children in a drill. They saluted us as we passed. I said to Shahji, 'Be careful—at this rate, they may catch the Sanghi chill that is in the air these days!' He laughed, 'No chance of that, I assure you. These are schoolchildren. A new school named Bal Niketan started here is worth seeing.' We agreed to visit it on our way back.

In the next row of tents, we took more samples of flour and milk powder. The powder of this second sample was different; in this, the water did turn white but a sediment stayed. We learnt that many children were falling ill across the camp, contracting diarrhoea after having milk prepared from the two powders. My suspicion was that this second sample was a mix of water, chestnut flour and milk powder, while the first contained soda, wheat flour and a third insoluble substance. We handed over all the samples to the Shanti Dal, to be sent for chemical analysis.

Many inhabitants in the camp were educated—once they were government officers, policemen, contractors, carpenters—and would use these skills to eke out livelihoods. At the same time, there were countless others—widows, elders, uneducated farmers, orphaned children—whose survival was entirely dependent on government rations of food and cloth. Everyone in the camp was equally entitled to ration and almost no one refused; yet the poor starved and the rich hogged; someone would get twenty yards of cloth, while another went naked.

A government that planned to equitably distribute the nation's wealth and invest all its money in people's welfare was making such mistakes even in a small camp! I cursed myself for thinking, just two days ago, that everything was being done for Hindu refugees and next to nothing for Muslim sanctuary seekers. Actually, everything was for the rich, and the poor received nothing. Hindus and Muslims were equally victims.

Today, I had beheld the soiled and terrible visages of some, their eyes shot through with the redness of insomnia, which spoke of frightening crimes, wounded souls and fevered minds. I had looked into the dejected faces of so many men and women, whose tear-filled eyes spoke volumes about their ordeals, and the half-dead faces of little children whose innocence had made them victims of hunger and barbarity. In all these were writ both the tales of 'Islamic purity' and valour in Western Punjab, as well the true bravery of its people, a people for whom:

The time is out of joint: O cursed spite,
That ever I was born to set it right!

William Shakespeare, *Hamlet*, Act I, Scene 5

I had heard them mourn their lost relatives, their abducted girls, their looted belongings but, most of all, the wretched life they led in the camp. The problem was that the refugees wanted immediate compensation. They said they had made sacrifices for India and demanded reparation for their losses. Whatever they did get, they deemed insignificant. When given stalls, they moaned that they had left behind such beautifully decorated shops. When given houses, they mourned their two-storeyed palaces. Money for their children's education, loans for college studies—none of these could sate the hunger in their hearts. Though given everything, they yearned for what was once theirs.

khaar-e-watan az sumbul-o-rehaan khushtar
The thorns of our native land are dearer than its flowers

Farsi maxim

I concluded that they couldn't be content until restored to their own place. This too:

khwab hai, khayal hai, aur shayad junoon bhi
There is desire, there is musing, and perhaps some madness too

There was no feeling of unity among them. One could easily be misled, by the fact that the tents that lined the camp stood in undivided rows, into believing that they were one people, but all one had to do was stand in a tent and ask who lived around. One would be told that while this one was a Multani's tent, the next belonged to a Rawalpindi person and the family in the facing tent had just arrived, looted and injured from Bannu. The fourth tent belonged to a Sindhi. And a neighbour of this Sindhi tent housed a family from Sargodha or Bahawalpur. And the person washing clothes over there, she is from Quetta. And so on . . .

None of these people had anything in common—appearance, food, lifestyle, behaviour, custom. They weren't relatives, friends, or neighbours; they often didn't understand each other's tongues. And the camp workers exacerbated these divisions. The Punjabis paid special attention to the needs of refugees from Punjab, the Sindhis helped the Sindhis; the worker from the NWFP held the Punjabis in contempt and the Baluchistani volunteer despised the Sindhis.

When these people were in their homes, considerations of clan, religion, or society would have held them back from committing many offences and sins—they had to follow the laws of these institutions. Today, however, they were unguided kites floating in the skies. Why should the Sindhi feel embarrassed before these Punjabi neighbours, whom he doesn't even know? Why should a Punjabi feel solicitous towards that man from the Frontier? What kinfolk did that Rawalpindi girl have that would discourage her from making eyes at that boy from Baluchistan? How long could one expect the middle-aged Sikh to wait for a woman—why shouldn't he take his pick from the many young girls without a relative to protect them? If on occasion, need should drive a Multani to pick the pocket of a rich Sindhi neighbour or whisk away a chest of valuables, who would ever accuse a refugee? Thievery would help him tide over these difficult times. All considerations of honour, shame and custom had deserted them, unfettered by any regard for others outside their families.

The bonds of this social order, this religion, this clan, this law—against which we flail so hopefully in our youth to break free, in mocking, reviling and contravening which lies our pleasure, but which can nevertheless reduce us to tears even in our old age—are the ties that bind us to humanity. A life unfettered by these bonds debases us, makes us beasts. When these Sindhis, Punjabis and Frontier people had been weighted by the burden of these bonds, they had been educated, dignified, prosperous, brave; today, free of restraints, all three had become dishonourable, insensitive, callous.

I had been aghast at the moral and ethical degeneration in the Muslim sanctuary seekers in the Humayun's Tomb camp; to see it once again made me tremble. The sullied honours, uprooted families were not the signifiers of the valour and ethical conduct of just a few Muslim Punjabis; no, in every tent, the barbarity of Muslim Punjabis did the dance of death. Witnessing this, the only conclusion that presented itself to me was that Man can be Man only if he lives in a community. Were he to live free of its chains, he would blunder around sightlessly, butting his horns at every object in his path and worst even animals in his bestiality.

It had yet to be decided how these three communities would be settled. Some suggested that populations from each zila should be settled in the same neighbourhood; others pressed for a province-or principality-wise settlement. Others objected that the second proposal would engender a new bigotry. They wanted the three communities to be mixed. But, as others pointed out, how would this prevent the same conflict that we had seen from holding in perpetuity? Some feared that if Sikh or Frontier populations were not mixed, a game of football was inevitable. Settling these communities together would only improve the possibility of a lasting amity—immediate and future demands would force them into dialogue.

I had become such an ardent votary of mixing the people of provinces and zilas that I couldn't entertain any other option for long. I was delighted to hear that the NWFP people were being settled together in Faridabad, the Bahawalpur people together in Rajpura and the Hazara people, also together, in one other place. I thought to myself that now at least, they could all become human again and be rid of this selfishness. I was convinced that one day, all these people—provided urgent steps towards moral and ethical reform were taken—would become valuable soldiers for our nation.

I also became convinced that Punjabi society itself must have been coloured by a strange hue. The things our society considers beyond the pale were normal for them. Perhaps there were no ethical norms in that province. Please don't think of everything in terms of Hindu and Muslim because society is constructed of all religions and castes. Both Hindu and Muslim Punjabis must have been of the same kind and had an identical conduct towards each other.

All that took place in Punjab was because the public's moral degeneration went unchecked until it plumbed the depths. This process couldn't have begun only a year ago and the origins of this despicable behaviour are what Punjabis and their neighbours must reflect upon. Were the foundations of that harmony they spoke of so much and that education system they had spread over the entire province strong enough to be measured by the metric of humanism? If yes, then why was this camaraderie so easily debased that all the teachings of religion deserted them, as did the dignity of humanity? Certainly, a brick must have been mislaid in this edifice. Something was definitely missing. Only if it is searched for will it be found and before one leaps to pick out the eyelash of someone else's eye, better to check one's own.

An abducted girl recovered from Gujrat, Pakistan, in October 1956.

17

The problems of abducted women
(April 1948–September 1949)

B etween August and September 1948, Shanti Dal undertook numerous tasks, ranging from specific ones like returning property to the more general one of preserving communal amity. In the specific tasks, our efforts may have met with as much success as failure but our crowning achievement will always be that despite the dire straits the city was in and the unrest among its denizens, Delhi remained peaceful.

After five months of tireless labour, some activists had wearied, others had turned their attention towards their own political parties, even idle people like me spoke wistfully of a period of rest. Others took longer to sidle off but I left for Lucknow as soon as September ended. When I returned in end-December, Shanti Dal's activities had become less frenetic and the bonds of this united front had relaxed greatly. All constituent parties had again started working on their own. The elections neared and the parties didn't want others to steal a march on them. And Delhi was peaceful. I became closely involved with the recovery of abducted women. My association with them lasted until 1955. I ran camps and homes and tried to provide as much relief as I could. Here, I speak of my experiences in 1948 and 1949.

I was never associated with the actual recovery operation—that was done by the staff of the Central Recovery Organization and Mridula, with army and police cooperation—so I cannot elaborate on that aspect. Moreover, I'm a woman and find it difficult to put down on paper for my readers all the obscenities committed upon women in both halves of the Punjab and the princely states. What will it accomplish? It was our dishonour and our own infamy, all done by our own hands.

But I can't leave the topic without saying that the reasons for this ethical and moral debasement couldn't have been only political and religious rage. There must have been other reasons, which the youth who wish to build a new India must investigate. The brutality, the regrettable incest put into play in this period—were these nurtured in our minds over centuries? How long had these germs infested our blood? As soon as the body weakened, the disease flowered and even the loftiest could not escape the contagion.

Which nation in the world has escaped war and strife? Only Allah knows how many skirmishes this Earth has seen in which the blood of humans has been let. But nothing of what our valiants undertook had ever been attempted. Such rules of war, such manoeuvres would have never struck the minds of any commander of any army anywhere in this world. Who thought them up? These bastard children on whom the burden of shame has been foisted for all time; these adolescent girls whose essence is now only carnal hunger; these deranged young women whose whole being is a fervent appeal—as long as they live, they will remember those malignant times.

Mridula led the rescue and rehabilitation of abducted girls. With her usual passion, she shuttled all over India and Pakistan, fervently appealing for cooperation from governments, administrations, peoples and maharajas (the latter took some effort). But Subhadra was not with us. As soon as we became embroiled in recovery work, Mridula's and my way parted from Subhadra's. Our activities were more social, whereas Subhadra's inclinations were more political.

From March through September, abducted girls were recovered from across India and sent to the camps and then handed over to relatives. By September, the only girls left in the camps were those whose relatives hadn't been found; soon, even these unclaimed girls were sent to Pakistan and the camp wound up. By then, I had left Delhi for three months.

In December 1948 I heard that another accord between the two governments was to be signed, by which any girl of one community found in the possession of the other had to, without exception, be recovered and handed over to the other side. The governments also decided that these girls would be sent to Jalandhar, where a tribunal appointed by both India and Pakistan would decide which girl was to be handed over to relatives in India, which to be sent to Pakistan.

For people from outside Delhi, the recovery operation would have to continue for years on end. People from Narnaul in Patiala told me that in Narnaul proper, 16,000 people were killed and about 1,500 girls abducted. Of these, around 500 girls had been recovered but no one could say if, or when, the other 1,000 would return.

In 1949 I witnessed the return of a girl who had been abducted eighteen months earlier. This girl was brought to the city from a respected government officer's house. This was itself remarkable, as in Delhi girls were usually rescued from less affluent homes. Who dared glance at highly ranked officials, ministers, rich men? Who had the gumption to raid mansions? For employees who so dared, these magnificent buildings could well become prisons. As Shakespeare says:

Plate sin with gold, And the strong lance of justice hurtless breaks;
Arm it in rags, a pygmy's straw does pierce it.

King Lear, Act IV, Scene VI

The girl told us her story. She and her family had taken their belongings and joined a caravan of a few thousand from Kapurthala, footing it to Ferozepur. A few miles later, the thanedar deputed to safeguard the caravan declared that the police's responsibility was only to convey the men to Pakistan and the women were not to proceed further. Naturally, this announcement elicited great consternation; people protested that they would rather die than abandon the women. A sum of Rs 6,000 was agreed upon as the bribe, but hardly had the caravan moved a few miles ahead that the thanedar again reiterated the injunction. This time, he accepted a further inducement of Rs 4,000.

When the caravan finally reached Ferozepur, the thanedar again refused to take the women to the train station (to board the train to Pakistan). Fresh negotiations began and people again delved deep into their purses for the last of their savings, now offering another Rs 6,000. Thanedar sahab graciously accepted, the caravan moved. The station was now just a few miles away and people had already begun to thank the heavens that the ordeal would be over soon—their savings were exhausted but their honour was untarnished—when disaster struck.

The thanedar had secretly informed the mobs that he would escort a Muslim caravan into Ferozepur. Even before the caravan reached the station, it was surrounded and attacked. Many were killed, many thrown into the stream and about 1,200 girls snatched. Only a few middle-aged women, some men and a few children boarded the train, in service of thanedar sahab's aspirations for a decoration for bravery.

Some girls died trying to escape. Others were luckier, like this girl. She ran into the stream, flailed around in the water for some time, found firm ground and walked across to the other side. She ran for three days, until she reached Ferozepur, where a kind officer took her in. She took care of his children and did housework and was paid a respectable amount for her labour.

A year and a half later, the police brought her to Delhi. She was educated, so I asked, 'If you can write, why didn't you write to your relatives?' She said she did. 'They should have replied. Perhaps they did and my employer hid the letters . . . He didn't want me to leave the job.' Now, she hoped to reunite with her husband, who was alive in Pakistan. But her child wasn't. The water had claimed him.

aadmiyat yahi hai aur yahi insaan hona
This is humanity, and to be human is this

Brij Narayan 'Chakbast'

How different this employer was from that old Jat in Mehrauli. When faith's stakeholders were bombing each other's homes and lining up women and children at death's door, this old Jat found a young Mewati girl weeping behind some rocks. She didn't know if any of her relatives were alive. Mehrauli had been emptied of Muslims. (Not that those Muslims were innocent either. They had used their weapons, their gunpowder and their bombs to blow up their opponents' houses and shops—in return, the Hindus had razed their homes to the ground.) Nevertheless, the old Jat took the girl home. He tried but couldn't locate any of her relatives. He told her, 'Beti, you're the child of my conscience, my *dharambeti*. No harm will come to you here.'

Many months later, with the consent of the two, he married this girl to his nephew, according to Hindu rites. As the weeks passed, this father-by-conscience was happy to see the ease the couple enjoyed in their conjugal life. By this time, the first wave of rioting had abated and Bapu's cries urging the slumbering to awake and repent could at last be heard. They reached the ears of the Mehrauli thanedar as well and he began running around in a frenetic search. One day, he laid his hands on this girl. Her name had been on the list I had handed over to the police in end-1947. Her father, now in Meerut, had asked me to seek her. As a consequence, the police brought her to me and I promised that I'd send her to her father within a day or two.

The next day, however, a large group of villagers surrounded the house, demanding the girl back. The police barred them but they were adamant. I told the police to let in only one person: the old Jat who had been the girl's father for many months. He had only one request, 'Just let me look at her once, that's all!' His tears melted my heart and I brought the girl forward. Both man and girl wept. The old Jat raised a trembling hand to her head and quaked, 'My dear child, you are my dharambeti. Because you were there, there was light in my life. This bibi says that your father is coming to get you and I think: when your *dharmpita* is so overcome at losing you, what torments your real father must have endured! If he comes, go with him my child, and keep me in your thoughts. But if he doesn't, then remember that till I live and my three sons breathe, our doors will always be open to you, regardless of whether your husband accepts you or not. Don't hesitate, just come and I shall keep you like a princess.'

What noble thoughts! What exalted ideals! Such love! Such humanity! I was so deeply affected by his words that I impulsively promised that if her relatives did not come, I'd send the girl to him. Even if the Muslims wanted to shoot me, I declared, I couldn't separate such a loving father from his daughter. But God willed otherwise; the next day the girl's father arrived from Meerut and the girl went with him happily.

Humanity survived even the massacre on the train from Gujrat, Sindh. Barely a handful of passengers were left alive, among them the wife of a rich man, the mother of adult children, who had hidden her jewellery and money in her clothes and boarded the train with her husband and relatives. The train was hijacked and she saw her husband, relatives and almost all other passengers being murdered.

Can we even conceive of what this fifty-year-old woman lived through as bodies writhing in agony piled up around her and she was taken off and stripped by the Pathans? She pleaded for a few scraps to cover herself; at first they didn't relent, but then one managed to convince the others to give her a few scraps to cover her nakedness. The Pathans then dragged her off towards the villages.

Such a terrible event, thousands massacred, how could the Pakistan police not have heard of it? They must have arrived on the scene but could neither catch the criminals, nor prevent the dishonouring of women. Mother India was being dishonoured in the streets at the hands of her own sons. Now, she was to be sold. At this age, she was being ruined in her own land, her wounded breast and unclothed body, bound hand and foot, was being mercilessly yanked across its farmlands. Her captors, those criminal Pathans, took her from village to village, to scores of houses, amidst catcalls. 'Who will buy this old hag?' they asked, unmoved by the old woman's plaintive cries. A mother's love implored but decency did not stir in these breasts of stone.

The Pathans didn't get their money, however. Increasingly irritated, they would have killed her had the world indeed been deserted by good humans. Three poor farmers were watching this scene. They approached the Pathans, 'Brothers, why are you humiliating this old woman? Take whatever money we have and let her go.' The Pathans quoted Rs 20 but even that measly sum was beyond the three's means. Pooling together all their riches, they could gather barely Rs 15—which the Pathans refused. The three villagers raised the rest by loan and donation and, after a while, managed to pry the poor victim loose from the Pathans' grip. A release enjoined upon every Muslim in the Quran (I.177):

wa-atal mala ala hubbihi zavil-qurba wal-yatama wal-masakin wabnis-sabil wasailina wa firriquab
And give away wealth out of love for Him to the near of kin and the orphans and the needy and the wayfarer and the beggars and for (the emancipation of) the captives

Among so many, just three truly good men and good Muslims—together they saved the honour of humanity. The distressed woman was nearly unconscious from hunger, pain, grief, exhaustion. For three days, those true subjects of God cared for her; on the fourth, they took her to Wagah border and handed her over to the Indian police. Bidding farewell, they slipped a handful of rupees to her, saying regretfully, 'We are so sorry that this is all we have.' The police brought her to Delhi, where she found some relatives, and which is where I met her. I have neither added to nor omitted from what she told me. I offer this account to all those friends of mine who are doubting Thomases—if they have the will to seek the truth, they will find that there exists a distinction between man and beast.

My thoughts turn to little Akhtari bi, a beautiful child of barely thirteen, whom an old villager found in some bushes, lying injured.

He took her home, tended to her wounds, fed her fresh pure milk and restored her to health. When she recovered, he married his fifteen-year-old son to her. Two children thus became partners for life. Their love grew more profound by the day, until seven months later, such was their devotion that they couldn't bear to spend even a moment apart.

Then began recoveries and arrests. Akhtari bi too was recovered. But unlike the others, this frail girl wept all day, refusing food. However much I counselled and consoled, her tears just wouldn't stop. She wouldn't take even a sip of water, wouldn't bathe, wouldn't change clothes—she just wept all day, and then all night. I was told that she would take something from her *anchal*, put it in her mouth and go to the tap for a drink of water. After much pleading, she accepted that she had indeed eaten something but refused to say what. But that day she did eat and drink a little. By late afternoon on the third day, her condition improved a little; the tears still flowed but not in floods. She told us that when people arrived to recover her, her husband stood there, weeping. As she passed, he tied a ball of ghee into her anchal and sobbed, 'When you get hungry, eat this. And never forget me!' Saying this, the girl dissolved into tears again.

I was in a terrible state. I was a social activist, an aged mother, a Muslim woman but also, the heart of a litterateur beat in my breast. I had a heart that could feel and a mind that teemed with imagination. This naïve, vestal, first love was to me as delicate as dew. But it was in my fate to trample it, to efface it, to wrench apart two love-filled hearts. My sense of duty amputated my hands and feet and good sense and thoughts of the hereafter rendered me powerless to act otherwise.

I had encountered girls so crazed by the burden of carnal desire that they would curse us for imprisoning them. I had also come up against three or four educated ones who would stump us with their citations of law and religion in favour of their desire to be free. But it was this frail little girl—who was like that mountain in which a spring had just been born—who truly made me regret our actions. She was the tiny raindrop that escapes the thick rain clouds; she was the bud about to smile in the first flutter of the morning breeze. And at my hands, this beautiful heart came to be destroyed.

What else could I do? Her tears had stemmed by the third day, replaced by a stoic resignation. I intimated her father. Of the whole family, only he and she had been left alive. His reply arrived and Akhtari was sent off with the other girls bound for Pakistan. Her tears fell like pearls to the ground and I could do nothing.

I even said to the police officer, 'My heart so wants to honour this sacred love, by returning her to him.' He laughed, 'What is this I hear? *You* uttering these words? Unbelievable!' But I couldn't have possibly done what my heart wanted. There would have been outrage, and the hell that the father raised over his only daughter may have escalated into an issue between the two governments. In any case, what right did I have to hand a minor girl over to anybody but her relatives? So when the time came for her to leave, I too had to become a Muslim. Her eyes wept, my heart did too, but I had to send her. I pray to God that she is happy, untainted by memories of the past.

Many readers will cry out in disgust, 'Is there no end to the cruelty you women committed?' In 1949 this question was thrown at us everywhere, as there was much propaganda against us. People asked, 'Why is all this being done to these girls? They have found their place in society, why uproot them? Making them homeless again is madness! To make a woman who is now a respected wife and mother of children return to her parents is not a favour but a sin! Forget who was taken from India and who from Pakistan, leave the women be—they are content and at peace.'

But we had no reason to believe this. Unfortunately, we never kept systematic records in the beginning, so we cannot estimate how many abducted women actually became respected wives and mothers and how many are even today without a place to call their own. But the facts we gathered in later months have formed my opinions.

Of all the girls were brought to us, or to the Tribunal, only a few ever made any equivocal statements about their religion. Those who did were mostly women who had fallen into theatre troupes and *tawaif* dens, or were wayward in general. They were admittedly a problem for us; they had so luxuriated in a life of hedonism that it was difficult to discern their religion, community, nationality and, at times, indeed even their sex! Luckily, their numbers were insignificant.

After this propaganda came the accusations—by the newspapers and the public—that recovered girls and women were being bundled off to their relatives without their consent, and despite the fact that they liked their new milieu. They charged that families of the general public were being shattered just to please women activists in India and Pakistan.

It was up to the government to respond to these allegations. What we did was because of an accord between the governments. How could implementers be held guilty? We appealed to every section, community, political party, even our Congressi brothers, for help, but let alone the public, even responsible leaders and personalities did not respond.

Perhaps we shouldn't have been so crestfallen at the desertion by these political personages. Quite frankly, they were incapable of understanding the psychological impact of the terrible crisis the abducted women were in. We should have realized that this was too much to expect of people who had never bothered to think about the psychology of their own wives and daughters.

But we did understand, we did care. All of us who worked on this front were women and could empathize with the abducted women. Only a woman can understand what is in another woman's heart, the problems that beset her at home, how the trials of her life play on her state of mind. No man can ever understand the mind of that woman who, in such bitter circumstances, bears a new generation, a new nation.

People perhaps forget that for a man to break free of the bonds of brotherhood for the sake of making an alien woman his own is against India's ancient traditions—community pride will never tolerate such an affront. The young may err all they wish, but they cannot compel the girl's parents, rooted in this social order, to wed their child to them, nor coerce their own families to give her the respect due to a married woman. Good or bad, this mindset is the reality, and it holds in almost every part of India. It will take at least twenty-five years before these attitudes change.

All of us workers were mothers and sisters and knew from personal experience that if husband and wife clash, then the offspring usually become idle, dim-witted wastrels. If there is imbalance in family life, the child is directly affected. A mother's vexed mind makes the child physically or mentally incompetent.

We had all seen the incredible damage that prostitutes incurred for their aberrations from the natural order. So swiftly their actions trample the flower of their youth, so much so that most become incapable of bearing enough children. Often their lives are marred by dirty, sexual diseases.

I'm reminded of an eleven- or twelve-year-old girl recovered from a middle-aged man in a Delhi village. I wondered what I could possibly ask the innocent child. God knows what horrors her fragile body had suffered! Imagine my surprise when she spoke belligerently, 'I was underage, wasn't I? I'd cook for my husband and take care of his health and entertainment. Whenever my daughter came, we would both make little sweet cakes of flour and ghee, for my husband to take to the fields. My husband would always say, "Grow up quickly, my little one."'

This child was the lady of the house and spent her time serving a middle-aged man. She was laughing and playing now but we all knew the consequences of child marriage. Ninety-five per cent of the girls wed before the age of fifteen were susceptible to anaemia, tuberculosis and other internal diseases, and lived the rest of their lives crippled by these conditions. And we had also seen in the streets of villages and cities such adolescent girls that these extraordinary circumstances had driven into poverty or into traps laid by evil people, who had lost forever their femininity, shame, natural virtues. For the rest of their lives, they were defined by lust and carnal need alone.

gandum az gandum barawid jau az jau
Wheat from wheat, and from barley springs barley alone
Maulana Rumi

We were mothers and our experiences told us how perilous it was for the child still in the womb, if the mother had to endure such great physical and spiritual torment. A mother with such a painful past, such a bleak future could never produce a child of healthy mind. The mother's mental agony could well be transmogrified into foisting a brutal monster, a bloodthirsty murderer upon the world. Such a child would always be a problem child. These bastard children of vagrant,

Pandit Nehru and Indira Gandhi visited a refugee camp in Jalandhar in 1948. A young girl rushed up to Pandit Nehru to tell him of her suffering.

rootless women gone astray could only become burglars and bandits, tricksters and mischief-makers beyond reform or remedy. Besides, such children would prove sexually incompetent or maniacal.

Another reason why we believed that such women should not be left with their abductors was that 75 per cent of them had been sold at least once and were still passed from hand to hand. Very young, minor girls never settled in one place and remained on the market for many years to come. Their youth was priced in thousands, and the greedy men who took them enjoyed them for a few days, then looked about to sell them again. Women between twenty and thirty years, on the other hand, mostly settled down quite quickly. Whether because of strictures on their movements or on their own initiatives or because they had borne children, these women had managed to find a foothold in some household somehow and struck roots. But very young girls were always sold, even if they were pregnant, and someone's child would be born in another's house. Readers should exercise sensitivity and imagine the emotional state of such a mother. How often would such a mother—in the uncertainty and despondency that her defencelessness had brought her to—consider taking her own life? And how can such terrible things not affect a child?

Both men and women want children. To perpetuate family and race, both need a new human that springs from them. For this, a woman bears all the trouble. To agree to this union on the promise made by a pair of love-filled eyes is in her nature. If there is no companion, she will make do with the memory of one but if reflecting on the past is horrifying, how will she bear this great burden alone?

While there is no doubt that birthing, rearing, loving a child is a woman's natural proclivity, it is still a huge burden—one that she has never had to bear alone. Indeed, if such an intolerable situation is foisted upon her, she hands it to someone else and skips town. Many abducted girls were no different; often, almost as soon as they arrived, they said, 'Send these children off to their fathers. We don't want them.' No doubt that behind these words lay fear of society and shame at their unwed status, but the way they spoke did not indicate that an abiding love underlay it. They would wrap their arms around the child, weep, and push him at us, 'Give him away, I can't keep him. Or you take him. He will survive, and when he grows up, he will meet me.'

I remember those two young girls, one seventeen and the other barely fourteen. The older one had been bought by two men in partnership and been the object of their joint amusement. The younger one had been taken two years earlier, when she was twelve. She sat beside me a silent question mark, her petrified eyes asking of me and every other human—who am I? She had no words left, no ambition in her heart, no vigour in her limbs, no obstinacy of adolescence, no loveliness of youth. Can my readers tell me what transgression we committed in bringing these two back? Would leaving them there not have been a sin?

True that Akhtari and others like her often knocked at our conscience. But such girls were merely a handful of the many I met. How could we have executed the desires of these teenagers, when their parents were still alive? No law would permit us. Besides, in light of past events and our milieu, what other option did we have? Should we have instead tried to erase these crimes? If we did so, this bad habit would only grow and, instead of preying on the other community, dishonour its own.

In fact, hasn't this ill already taken root in our society? Scores of abducted girls, all Hindus, continue to be brought to us from the railway station, where they were sold into prostitution. The camps also frequently witnessed incidents where one man shamelessly made away with another's daughter. It was our duty—as much as it was that of the government and political leaders—to end this situation quickly. We all felt that women could play a large role in these efforts. If they reformed their own families, the knotted branches would smoothen out by themselves.

In 1949 we observed that many abducted girls and women were besieged by dangerous, dirty diseases, as also tuberculosis, mental disorders and other conditions. It was vital to cure them urgently, however enormous an effort it took, because India's future could not be destroyed like this. We felt that these girls' lives could be further improved if special attention to their treatment was paid in government hospitals. It was also necessary to establish institutions like schools, sewing centres and home-based handicraft set-ups so that, after training for a year or two, they would be able to provide for their own selves. Education in care, nursing and domestic work was also imperative so that they may live their lives with dignity. In the following years, the Indian government started many homes for these girls, facilitated the hospitalization and treatment of scores of diseased girls (some needed injections for up to two years) and established institutions for their education and training.

I have no reliable information whether the Pakistan government took similar measures. They must have. In fact, I don't even know what happened to the girls we sent to Pakistan. I was always anxious for news of them. The strangest thing was something the denizens of India and Pakistan shared: when both left their countries, they seemed to have pledged that from the moment they stepped on alien land, they would speak only untruth and nothing but untruth!

A half-mad young girl comes to mind. She was brought to us by the police from some part of UP but she would also mention Bombay, Ahmedabad, Amritsar and, smiling meaningfully, scatter her narrative across these cities. She had a silken kerchief she would wrap around her head now, around her neck then; at times she used it to wipe her face, at others hid it in her bosom; when she had a headache, she wore it as a bandanna. I asked once, 'Gulab Bano, where did you get this kerchief from?' Gulab stared at me with large, round eyes, smiled and said, 'Niadar gave it to me.' Niadar who? The question always made her lower her eyes and whisper 'that one', as if to say—'Niadar, my love, who else?' Weeks of questioning could only establish that Niadar was the man who brought her from Bombay and married her. Whether the ceremony was Hindu or Muslim or both, we never found out.

In any case, after this marriage, riots began and she fell into the hands of others. After being passed from hand to hand for over a year and a half, she ended up in UP. This adolescent couldn't bear this torment and upheaval and lost her mental balance. Even the name Gulab wasn't fully hers; at times she gave herself other names.

Niadar's kerchief, the memento of a first love, was wreathed around her neck—all else was lost. Within a year, so many men came into her life, but none was Niadar. All she wished for was him. With great equanimity, she would narrate: 'Niadar said, "Lalli, why do you roam about so? Come to my home and I will marry you."' He got her new shoes, fine clothes and then they were wed. When she was sick, Niadar took care of her. But soon something else would come over her and a string of names would spew from her lips, but all sequence and coherence would vanish.

Gulab, and all the other half-mad girls, who smile and laugh all the time, do they perhaps laugh at all of us, this nation and its denizens, this religion and its standard-bearers, this government, its laws, its pomp? Who knows what amuses them so?

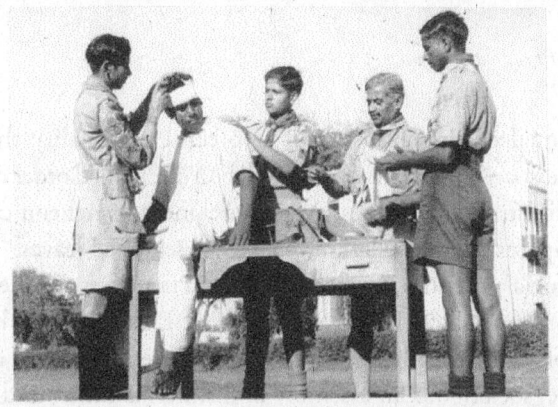

A squad of boy scouts who rendered first aid at the Purana Qila camp.

18

Man can never die

Zindagi kya hai anaasir mein zahoor-e-tarteeb
Maut kya hai inhin ajzaa ka pareshan hona
What is life but a manifest arrangement of the elements?
What is death but a scattering of these particles?

Brij Narayan 'Chakbast'

How pithily Chakbast has expressed the basic truths of life and death!

But this couplet isn't a commentary on just the being and nothingness of Man—the lives of communities and nations are also subject to this truth. Both are the unifications of scattered constituents; though these parts may appear distinct, a unifying principle always connects each to the other to form a whole that the world perceives to be one community, one nation, one society. This unifier may be religious or civilizational or the charisma of a forceful personality threading together disparate elements; it may well be a disciplined order of justice and administration; at times, even a foreigner's truncheon can serve as the impetus for the collation of all these scattered leaves.

The social order that unified India lay in tatters, as did the ancient framework on which it was constructed. There used to be some immutable principles then. Even though different races and religions lived here, society was an assembly of distinct identities and, for the world, everyone that lived here was a 'Hindi', however much they differed in terms of world view, religion, culture. This social order was founded on an accord about the basic rights that must accrue to each constituent of a human brotherhood, moral and ethical standards of civility and shared cultural practices. The aspirations that drove this unusual social order were the sacred goals of fellow feeling, humanity and compassion. In pursuit of these goals, all the constituents of this society devoted themselves to the common good, and the service of humans and moral and ethical conduct was considered the route to attaining Allah or Ishwar.

But today this social order is in ruins. No institution, section, home has escaped the adverse consequences of recent events. Just as in the season of cholera, all things, water and air become poisoned, the entire nation is afflicted, culture and religion assaulted, the old social order destroyed. In one sense, it is for the good, for how long could it be perpetuated, but the tragedy is that the new, upcoming society will likely be a jungle—the brotherhood of man is has turned into a pack of predators.

I had always heard it said that whenever a revolution reaches a nation, a conflict is inevitable, when the old order clashes with the new, Youth contends with Age, creation battles with destruction. But as the revolution ends, Youth must strike peace with Age and its experience, judiciousness and the sobriety of its order. Only after this can a democratic order, a progressive society and happiness and freedom emerge.

For months, some progressives had been proclaiming that the revolution was on its way. The communists were waving the red flag all over and the Congress sang hymns to democracy and sermonized about spirituality and moral values. But was what happened in these two years truly a revolution?

In revolution, there is life, but in this anarchy, there was more death than life. Revolution is Youth, with all its passion, energy, progressiveness, but all that was visible here was the spinelessness, the hidebound nature of Age. How would we make sense of it?

koi batlaaye ki ham batlaayein kya
Will someone tell me what I should tell?

Mirza Ghalib

Today, so many of us have heaved a sigh of relief, 'Whatever it was, thankfully it's over and we can live in peace again!' I fear this is self-delusion. We may not be free of that cycle of action and reaction. We also have to serve the sentence for our crimes. The bitterness in the hearts and minds of our offspring has upset the peace of their families; if we aren't careful, this generation may raze even the ruins of humanity that still stand. If we don't appreciate the urgency of addressing this degeneration, if we don't act immediately, then the thorns we have sown will continue to rend the fabric of humanity for years.

From the affluent to the middle class, there has been an inescapable change in outlook and conduct. It has struck at the very foundations of the psyche, right where the foundations of religion are laid, where humanity and compassion emerge. Both muhajirs and refugees no longer have any compunction in adopting the same behaviour with their own people that they meted out to their enemies. The injuries their friends and neighbours gave them have spawned such barbarity.

In normal times, while ethical and moral norms do change from age to age, such change doesn't undo the basic framework on which these norms are erected. This is no longer true and even fundamental truths are now falsified. The wrangle between zamindar and farmer, worker and capitalist, rich and poor is not new to India, or to the world, but praise be to this new India and its high ideals as even women and girls are today the objects of this strife.

And women too had incited passions. On the city streets, I met many sisters—both Hindu and Muslim—who were adamant that whatever happened was for the good. In fact, more of the same should take place. If only we could lay our hands on some weapons, then a war would be the best way! How did such cruelty find its home in women? It could have been the manifestation of their natural proclivity towards extremes or a call from the fires of retribution burning in them—whatever the cause, women were quite reluctant to let this situation end.

> *man az biganegan hargez nanalam*
> *ki ba man har che kard aan ashena kard*
> I do not complain of others' wrongs to me
> Because the deeds were done to me by my friends
>
> Hafiz Shirazi

This is no speculation, I assure you. I have concluded this from my experiences in the lanes and bylanes of Delhi and its ruined towns and villages, from the sagas I heard from victims, the passengers I met on trains, the women I met in their houses and the children I gently questioned in neighbourhoods. I may err somewhat but it is impossible to refute the basic veracity of these impressions. Many examples of the extent of the public's ethical and moral degeneration have been illustrated; it will not be inappropriate for me to now add some more.

In December 1947 I first sensed the beginning of the decline. Near Ajmeri Gate, I saw some children standing in a circle, brandishing sticks. I peered out of the car window, trying to figure out their new game. To my dismay, I saw that the children had surrounded an imaginary object and were beating it, shouting, 'Hit it! Kill it! Come on, finish it off now! Burn it!' and so on.

Scores of people were going about their business but no one gave the children a second glance. My sensitive heart and penetrating gaze led me to see in the scene before me something else altogether. It was not the children crying out 'Kill it! Burn it!'—the voices were of their fathers, brothers, relatives who were all engaged in these very activities those days; the innocent little minds were merely mimicking them.

Take another story from six months later. You will recall that many young men volunteered as social workers with Shanti Dal. One such youth, who worked for many months with us, was a refugee. His friends told me that his father perished in the violence and he himself escaped with great difficulty. Leaving behind his substantial inheritance, he hoisted his two young sisters onto his shoulders and crossed the river into India, where he lived in great penury. This eighteen-year-old appeared diligent and hard-working, with sensible views. His best friend was a Muslim and both of them got deeply involved in our work. When the Nizamuddin office began functioning, they managed it between themselves for the first three weeks.

One day, the boy confided in me that the uncle who had kept him for so long now wanted him to leave at once. He had no income, nowhere to go. Naturally, we promptly arranged financial assistance for him, as well as two tuitions and a room. Imagine my shock when one day a woman came to me to say that she was this boy's mother! 'I've been telling my son for so long to bring me to you, so I could ask you to get him a permanent job. But he keeps putting it off so I came on my own.' I asked in amazement, 'You are his mother? But he hasn't even mentioned you! Whom do you stay with?'

'With my brother. My husband, I, this boy and my other young children all stay with him. What else could we do, behen? Our orchard in Lyallpur is gone. It would be a great help, behenji, if you put our boy to some use. I tell him every day, ask Apaji to get you a job, but he doesn't listen. My brother says the same but the boy gets angry. We can't educate him any more. It costs a lot more beyond the tenth standard.' She prattled on, but I was only half listening. The deceit of it all! His father killed in the riots, he swimming across the river with two young girls on his back, now living with his uncle who says I can't bear your burden any more . . .

After a while, the mother bade farewell and after that day, the boy never showed up again. Perhaps he was ashamed but who can say there wasn't another reason behind his disappearance.

Consider another incident from ten months after August 1947— a time when the world believed that Delhi was at peace and when the government was satisfied that its administration was functioning properly. A new chief commissioner and a new deputy commissioner had just assumed charge.

As readers will recall, any attempt to contact the earlier chief or deputy commissioner was always abortive. Their chaprasis would say that they were sleeping (at 6 p.m.!) or sunning themselves at home (at 11 a.m.!), especially when they heard a Muslim name at the other end of the line.

In June 1948 an urgent matter necessitated me to call the chief commissioner. So I called his office in the hope that the new incumbent would not be as fond of beauty sleep.

The chaprasi said that the chief commissioner was out but would be back soon. I called back in an hour, the same man asked who was calling and like a fool I replied, 'Begum Shafi.' He said, 'Just wait,' and put me on hold. Fifteen minutes passed and no one appeared, so I dialled again. The same chaprasi said that the chief commissioner was resting. I said, 'At least tell him that there is a call for him.' This time he made me wait for twenty-five minutes and never returned.

I needed to raise the matter that very day, so I refused to be cowed down. After an hour, I called again. The same voice demanded that I should tell him what the matter was. I asked, 'And who are you?' The reply was, 'The chief commissioner's orderly.' I was extremely irritated but restraining myself, said, 'How can I speak of the matter to you? Don't waste my time and give him the phone immediately.'

I'd hardly finished when he let fly a string of abuses in Punjabi and Urdu. I didn't even understand most, but hearing such obscene abuses made my ears burn with humiliation. My body shook, my hands trembled. This was the first time in my life that such stones had collided with my ears. I banged down the receiver and sat there, shocked. It took me twenty minutes to recompose myself.

It had become all the more necessary to speak to the chief commissioner. This time, I called from the house of the union minister for telecommunications and then, of course, no excuses were made. The chief commissioner came on the line. I told him all, adding that such abuses weren't aberrations and that he needed to mend this shameful situation and teach his staff some civility. Mortified, he apologized and asked me not to take offence. He assured me he'd take all employees to task.

What else could I demand, especially since the standards of civility among our own chaprasis were far from what they should have been. Let alone a salute or greeting, they wouldn't even stand to welcome someone. I let such behaviour go unchecked, but my sister's daughter berated them. As a result, their conduct improved somewhat.

I don't know what transpired after my complaint but, after this, I didn't hear any complaint about impoliteness by either these two officers or their staff. I was always spoken to politely, the deputy was miraculously cured of his habit of sunning himself during office hours and the chief was no longer plagued by somnolence!

The reason I make so much of this incident is that this poor orderly is a mere representative of society and its mindset. From what I heard, even the prime minister was exasperated by the conduct of his chaprasis and had to caution them. When the whole edifice is shaky, why cry over one brick? In government offices, rudeness had become fashionable—whether a chaprasi or an official, he had to humiliate the members of the public that approached him. In hospitals too, people were always treated like beggars, and the staff had full right to take anyone, even the most dignified of supplicants, by the scruff of his neck and boot him out, abuse him and denigrate him. Humiliating individuals has become the new norm of public behaviour.

The Hindu–Sikh quarrels in East Punjab, bogus train permits, allegations of bribery and inducement—what were they but links of the same chain strung two years ago, the fruit of a tree planted at the same time. Brambles don't yield mangos, do they? Just pick the *Pratap* or *Milap* for any day, and god save me from untruth, you will find at least ten news stories about fraud, graft, abduction, murder, burglary and rape in Amritsar, Jalandhar, Bhatinda, Ludhiana and other cities.

Even schools and colleges weren't spared the evil influences of this mindset. Students do not flinch from making fun of their teachers, agitating against them, being rude to them in class. Professors too have no compunction in mocking their students, injuring their self-respect and humiliating them. In home or school, India has never made any interventions towards moral and ethical reform, to engender values of humanism. Masters abet the children in their indiscipline, family members are not the slightest bit ashamed of their indulgence in corruption. Mothers, sisters, wives speak with great gratification about the income 'on the side'. Openly, a man from one community insults, vilifies, or brings material/bodily harm to one from the other community with the encouragement of family and friends.

We tried to banish these prejudices from children's minds, but mindsets don't alter so quickly. All the efforts we put in at school would be laid to waste by the parents within a few minutes at home. Once, the proud Indian father would have been so conscious of his and his daughter's honour that were some louts to leer at her, he would forbid her from ever going that way again. And though he may well have joined a fair-sized war with the harassers on the matter, he would have been careful to be discreet, lest his neighbours get a whiff of what was going on.

Today, however, girls are foisted as a plague on the nation. All around, the harassment of girls causes conflict between Hindus and Muslims. Some such incident occurs every day and immediately, members of her proud community gather. The shameless harasser also mobilizes his community. The culprit is locked up, the girl and her good-for-nothing witnesses march to court, and so on, until I pray that all mothers be given such a medicine that no woman is born in this country for the next century!

The situation in Pakistan was not very different. In 1948 returning Muslims said that all was peaceful there; the Hindus were happy and their businesses were thriving. The true picture emerged when the father-in-law of a famous revolutionary visited Pakistan to recover some important documents and valuables. His Lahore house was still unoccupied—though damaged—and he could enter and search it. But when he emerged, he found the house mobbed, and he was shot at. Some days later, his wound untreated, he was flown to Delhi, where he was operated on. The tough man pulled through, mercifully.

In June 1948 some friends of the Jamia boys came to Bara Hindu Rao School, just a day after returning from Pakistan. They had gone with the intention of staying on but the situation was so unfavourable that they decided never to go back. A story they told me: a gentleman from Delhi lived with his wife and two daughters in a house he had, like other muhajirs, captured in Karachi. He guarded it fiercely, refusing to share the house with others. One day, two men visited and introduced themselves as Pakistan government officers, sent to ask him to vacate the house and move into another one allotted to him. The muhajir had no objection to the exchange and immediately accompanied the officers to see the new house. Shortly, the car returned with the message that the muhajir was satisfied, but wanted his wife and daughters to take a look as well. The three women got into the car and left. When the muhajir returned, he found that his family had disappeared. He found the wife ultimately but the daughters went missing. The muhajir was left weeping over his misfortune—it would have been better to die in India!

Read Pakistani newspapers today, and you'll see that they have also travelled the same path. Witness the state of Woltan camp, pay attention to the mehfils of dance and music, drink and kebabs, read the listings for entertainment programmes in Meena Bazar . . . Consider the evictions of Hindus and Sikhs from their homes, spare a thought for the abducted girls recovered from the crusaders of Islam . . . What shines through is a culture of hooliganism.

A Pakistani newspaper (*Aghaz*, 7 July 1948) remarked: 'The ethical and moral standards of a backward people have been so wrung out that whorishness is born among them, called "Zanan-e-Bazari" or "women of the streets".' It goes on to blame the 'disaster of East Punjab' as the progenitor of this state of affairs, and though it cannot summon the courage to include western Punjab in its discussion more fully, it cannot put the topic aside without saying this: 'The termites of sin had begun eating away at those honourable families.'

The article also sketches Lahore's conditions: 'The ethical and moral decline has been so extreme that Khan Mamdot himself has said: "The sale of alcohol has tripled. Deplorably, moral debasement and ethical decline have become so rife that the question is no longer simply limited to the removal of whorehouses, as public life in Lahore and its cultural norms have themselves adopted the garb of whores. The poison of sin has so riddled every aspect of our social life that the difference between whores and us is now only an issue of form and social rank, and not of substance.'"

In childhood, I'd heard the distinction between *gunah-e-Kabeera* (mortal sin) and *gunah-e-Sagheera* (venal sin), but had neither seen the difference demonstrated nor listened to respectable people debate the correct interpretation of the distinction. But today, wherever one turns, the air is rife with the story of Sagheer and Kabeer. Each side underplays its own sins and exaggerates the other's.

When Muslim girls were recovered from Punjabi Hindu men, they had the names of their rapists dug into their flesh. Even accepting that Hindu men did this in part out of revenge, in part in anger, in part to pass them off as Hindu women, how is one to explain why the Hindu girls recovered from Pakistan arrived in Delhi with names of the mujahideens and the dates of the crimes scratched into their hands? In fact, the spirited Punjabis tried to outdo each other—girls recovered from Delhi had 'Om' and designs of flowers and vines dug into their hands; those from Punjab and the princely states had the sinners' names engraved into their private parts and 'Pakistan Zindabad' branded on their chests.

Other parts of the country had seen riots and destruction at the same time as our much-mourned Delhi and the two Punjabs; for instance, Mussoorie, Dehra Dun, Saharanpur, Agra, Kanpur and Ajmer. While hostilities in other places were scattered and short-lived, the massacres and looting in Mussoorie, Dehra Dun and Ajmer were so large-scale that the Muslim population had to flee. Yet, even in Ajmer, which saw the most horrific violence, not one abduction took place, women weren't paraded naked and no woman was looted as the shops were. Not were there were any reports of large-scale abduction or dishonouring of women in Dehra Dun and Mussoorie. In all these places, a handful of brave Congressis emerged from their houses, confronted the rioters and saved lives and women's honour.

In Mussoorie, I heard of only one case in which a young woman and her infant daughter went missing. Although her relatives feared abduction, when the year-and-a-half-long search didn't yield any sign of her being alive, I figured she must have lost her life. In Dehra Dun too, I saw only one instance of abduction—a young girl, whose parents had been killed, was caught by a brahmin and sold to a Muslim. That man married her to his brother, with permission from the Ulema and magistrate. The girl looked at peace and, except for her parents' murder, had no tale of dishonour or violence to tell.

In Punjab and Delhi, however, Hindus and Muslims carried out exactly the same crimes, though there was a minor difference in the levels of vice exhibited at a regional level. In Punjab, it was usual for a woman to be used by three or four men at the same time but in Delhi, we didn't find any woman purchased with money put up by more than one man. A woman here was an individual man's investment and property, whom he could resell at a marginal profit.

My Punjabi brothers must forgive me; my intention is not to spread regional discord or boost regional arrogance. With great sorrow, I acknowledge that the extent of moral and ethical degradation that the two Punjabs demonstrated was unparalleled. As for Delhi, well, the poor thing has always been a cowbell of Punjab. Even if a kettledrum is played in Punjab, the sound echoes in Delhi. The city has always been a wreck in the love of Punjab.

Yet, even as I recall the multitudinous tales of human callousness, I also remember the stories of kind neighbours and true friends and the acts of extraordinary humanity. Though many neighbours were the first to strike their neighbours and snatch their young daughters, this does not negate the compassion and bravery of the few that defended their friends or looked after their children.

Even in the darkest hours, love shone through occasionally. At first, love emanated from the sun that shone in Birla House and rent the darkness wherever its rays radiated. When that flame was snuffed out, the light shone on in Gandhiji's disciples like Pandit Sunderlal, Jajuji and the Swamiji of Narela.

And that other man, who worked in some of Delhi's most

dangerous areas. Disguised as a peddler, vegetable vendor, or bangle seller, this dedicated Congressi sought, found and restored scores of abducted girls to their families. To my great shame, I was never of any great assistance to him. Once he asked me to recommend a Muslim woman who would help him in his efforts. Even knowing that this was beyond me—a Muslim woman and the desire to work are two mutually exclusive things—I looked but couldn't come up with even one such woman who would be ready to approach the work with the right humane, progressive attitude.

Had I not toured urban and rural areas, I'd have never believed that pure blood still coursed through this nation's veins. Had the numbers of these men been multiplied, this injection of fresh, healthy blood would have been the antidote to the poison raging within. Among such good men were two friends, whom we met while visiting hospitals in search of patients who paid the price for the bravery of their brothers in this great nation. In Cholera Hospital, a doctor approached me, 'Are you a Muslim?' When I nodded, he said, 'Then please take that patient over there away with you. He has recovered fully but cannot leave because of the situation in the city. Every evening I have to stay back to protect him. Visiting hours are between 3 p.m. and 6 p.m., and I fear that a refugee patient's visitor may seize the chance to kill him because he is a Muslim.'

I agreed at once and the patient was brought to the car. Just when I was marvelling at his luck in getting such a kind doctor, I learnt that he had been even luckier in having a friend called Mr Gupta. Apparently, this Muslim gentleman from Shimla had opted to go to Pakistan. When riots overtook his hometown, he came to stay with his old friend Gupta in Delhi, with his family and belongings. He intended to leave for Pakistan, or at least send his wife and children to stay with relatives in UP, as soon as the situation improved.

Barely a few days after they landed in Delhi, fires engulfed this city too. Gupta lived in one of the city's most dangerous areas; the Muslim family was trapped and uncertain about what to do. If they tried to flee, death was inevitable; if they stayed, retribution would surely claim them. But Gupta was clear—he told his friend that they should all stay on with his family. All they had to do was change their names, lie low and not meet anybody. Which is what they did. And though Gupta's house was often targeted over the following weeks, and he and his family threatened, he didn't betray them. But misfortune refused to relent and the Muslim soon contracted cholera. He was admitted to hospital, but his family stayed hidden at Gupta's, who spared no effort in safeguarding the precious people that his friend had entrusted to him.

The Muslim gentleman insisted on returning to Gupta's house. We had to agree, but we also told him that it was foolhardy. I suggested that he come to my house with his family. After dropping him, Qaisar was apprehensive, 'I don't know if any of these people will be alive tomorrow. I saw Gupta's neighbours looking at us as we dropped that gentleman off. How long can Gupta keep them hidden? I suggest that you get me a police guard, I'll go and pick them up tonight.' I was also alarmed and the family was brought to our home that very night. Later we learnt that if the Muslim family had indeed stayed on, even Gupta and his family would not have been spared by the next morning.

But the next evening, Gupta was at our doorstep, complaining, 'Yaar, why are you staying here? You have hurt me. But I forgive you. Get your things and come back to my place.' But this time, we didn't give in; even in October 1948, there was no real reason for anyone to shrink from murder. We managed to get the two friends to agree to separate and the Muslim gentleman stayed with us for many days. Later, he moved into Sher Shah Mess with family; they must be in Pakistan now.

Another such friend was Asha Ram. One day, he came to me with the name of a village and the name of a girl, asking me to rescue her. 'She's the daughter of my close friend, a clerk like me. He is Muslim, and though I could help save him and his family and send them to Pakistan, one of his daughters was snatched. My friend's last words to me were that I shouldn't forget her and I promised that I wouldn't rest till I restored his daughter to him. Now I've found that she is being held in this village in East Punjab.' He didn't know the name of her captor though and I told him that I'd be unable to help him without that information.

Some days later, Asha Ram was back with the information we needed. I forwarded it to the Women's Section. Two months passed. Asha Ram's friend's letters pleading for action didn't let up; Asha Ram's exertions continued. Finally, I had to take him to meet Mrs Nehru personally, to apprise her of the case. She initiated the process immediately and, shortly, Asha Ram himself went with the police to recover the girl and put her on the plane to Pakistan. Some days after this, Asha Ram wrote me, enclosing a letter from his friend. The girl was safe in her father's care, and the two friends lived on either side of the border, bound by bonds of love.

And then there were the Khudai Khidmatgar. Most refugees from the NWFP remembered with great fondness and gratitude their Muslim friends and neighbours and the Red Shirts from the Frontier provinces, responsible for saving their lives and their honour and bringing them safely to India. Almost all the refugees from there told the same tale—of how their neighbours stood by them in the hour of their greatest need.

Once, a group of these refugees came to Constitution House to ask Mridula to get them licences for their firearms. Surprised, I asked, 'But I heard that you people caught the flights with just the clothes on your back. So where did you get these guns from?' They replied, 'We could have left everything, but not our weapons. Our Muslim Pathans understood that to bear arms is a question of a Pathan's dignity. So they helped us bring them out.'

For these Pathans then, their Muslim compatriots had saved the two greatest riches a Pathan can ever possess—his honour and his weapons. Even now, after so much had happened, these Hindu Pathans wept in the memory of their Khan Badshah, Khan Abdul Ghaffar Khan. Even now, love writhed in torment in their hearts. These old memories had become the foundations of their lives, so much so that building house and setting up shop was secondary to getting licences for their guns. Soon, all Pathans banded together to form a Red Shirt organization in Delhi, led by Akbar Khan, and with Kanhaiyalal Khutak, Nagina Sahab and Khan Gazi as prominent members.

We also had reason to be reassured by the youth who helped us in our efforts to restore peace to Delhi. Their enthusiasm and diligence erased some of the dejection we often felt about the new crop. None of our work in the camps, schools, or the relief committee would have been possible in design or execution without these young people.

No, I'm convinced that 'Man did not die. He can never die!' Man is the cornerstone of Creation—the day he dies, Creation will cease to be. True, down the ages there have been attempts galore to kill Man, and there will be many more. True, Evil has always arraigned itself against Humanity, and the ferocity and scale of the assault we have witnessed is far greater than ever before. But just like, at other times, noble men standing for the just and the true have refused to submit to Evil, in this age too, a worshipper of Truth gave his life in defence of Humanity, so that Truth may dawn.

Somehow, that evil time is now past. A bloody saga has been writ on the pages of history, a terrible tale that will beckon the youth to it hereafter. The government, political leaders and intelligentsia ask us to let bygones be bygones, but I cannot understand how people can escape these memories when all around them are strewn the signs of what took place.

Should we be satisfied by the absence of conflict? Don't we wish to move beyond? True, the beads of the tasbeeh lie scattered and the one who would have gathered them and strung them together again is gone . . . But mustn't we continue the struggle to keep Man alive? Mustn't we strive to apply spiritual and ethical conduct to this moribund social order? The bonds of love can be rebuilt, provided we have the courage to do so.

Shouldn't we strive to sensitize our government? Or are we ready to accept that its administrative machinery will always comprise dumb, unfeeling cogs? Shouldn't the search be for sensitive, disciplined humans? True governance is possible only by people alive to the values of humanity. Those who make, implement, respect laws cannot be predators. If the government of a free India has to preserve its democratic and progressive character, if India is not to be enslaved once more, then we need something more than what we have.

A new synthesis is vital—of modern social, cultural, ethical values and the principles of humanity with the ancient Indian values of spirituality—so that a new way of life is born. This new social order must be built on the foundation of humanity; its development must be in the light of new knowledge and learning. Moreover, the edifice must be firmly grounded in earthly reality and not aspire to a world in the heavens. For how long can we allow those who dream of the glory of ancient Bharat or of a bygone Islamic age to deny the coming of a new world?

If one does not appreciate the nature and reality of different faiths, both an enlightened soul and peace of mind will be denied to contemporary man. And without a soul, flesh has no existence. This soulless society, this culture of thievery, these minds that dream of a unique culture and a unique nation—all these will have to be levelled in the soil of new India, to make it fertile.

But how? Only new minds can conceive it. Only youth can move beyond, frolicking amidst boulders in this difficult terrain. And only youth can

ishq badosh mi kashad een homa kohsor ra
Lift up this mountain of love onto its shoulders

Mohammed Iqbal

We old people! Our lives, good or bad, are past. We have already witnessed the fruits that our deeds have borne. Our old, defeated minds now move towards the final rest. The lamp flickers, the night is at an end; in no time, the gust of the morning breeze will extinguish it forever. But

kar-e-duniya kaise tamam na kard
No one has ended the work of the world

And before these new young hands lift this burden, this book must reach them. So that before they lower their crafts into the river, they are able to divine the direction of the wind and understand where the rocks and the whirlpools lie. So that their craft does not flounder midstream, like ours did, and be destroyed.

kashti shikastganaim ai bade-shart barkhez
bashad ke baz benaim deedare ashna ra
The craft is damaged; blow ye favourable wind, blow
That we might perhaps be with our beloved once more.

Hafiz Shirazi

Anis Kidwai receiving the Sahitya Kala Parishad Award in 1981.

Begum Anis Kidwai: Fragments of a life

A nis Kidwai was my paternal grandmother. I was fifteen when she passed away—too young to really know her. Translating *Azadi* has therefore been a process of a growth of understanding for me, as her words have given life and intellect to the beloved Apa (like my father and his sisters, we all called her 'elder sister') of my girlhood memories. I am now closer to comprehending the Apa who puzzled me when I was a child. I now understand why she was convinced by my ten-year-old self's protestations that I should not be made to learn the Quran by rote. I would learn Arabic when I grew up and then read it, I said, but I refused to let a maulvi sahab make me memorize it without my understanding a word. And I also now know that she was sincere when she told my journalist cousin Seema—who asked

315

for her permission to live in and report from the PLO camps in Beirut for a few weeks in 1982—that had she been younger, she'd have done so herself.

While this growth in understanding may be sufficient for a granddaughter but to be her biographer, my task must also be to find Anis. Despite the fact that the Kidwai part of her name is fairly well-documented, the search for Anis has not been easy. In all such accounts, Anis occupies very little print space. Most references to her remain anchored to the first chapter of her book *Azadi*, to the murder of her husband in October 1947 and to the terrible events of the Partition which she witnessed. So much so that even in a book that traces the careers of the Masauli Kidwais in the twentieth century,[1] she is the subject of just a couple of pages.[2] Here too, she emerges as a tragic figure encountered only after her bereavement, individuated by 'stoicism and fortitude' and a courage that came from her 'deep commitment to the family values she inherited and cherished all her life'.[3]

At the most basic level, the invisibility of Anis is symptomatic of how histories of political families are written, where a narrative of the careers of the men subordinates, even suborns, the narratives of 'their' women. At another level, however, this characterization of Anis as being born at the moment of her widowhood is also her own creation. This 'truth' that she begins *Azadi* with—wherein it is grief alone that propels this unconfident, politically inexperienced but sensitive and humane *qasbati* woman into 'a role in the horrific drama played out on this nation's stage'—is the one that now colours all depictions of her. However, there are other Anises too, in her earlier and later writings, most notably her unfinished autobiography—*Ghubar-e-Karwaan*,[4] where she is a stubborn little girl, a rebellious, politically committed young woman, as well as a sensitive literary critic.

Frustratingly, none of these selves of *Azadi* and *Ghubar* is easily recoverable from family memories. Perhaps because most of those who really noticed Anis—her children Azadi, Kishwar and Taufiq, her brother-in-law Rafi, her brother Jamal and his wife Shakuntala, and her friends Mridula Sarabhai and Subhadra Joshi—are no longer alive. Or, perhaps, these Anises were so personal to her that they were safely revealed only to the whole world; in the world of the family, the weight of their sensibility could not be borne by a *khala ammi*, *phuphijan*, or even an apa. Anis can therefore be found only through the words she used to inscribe herself into the world.

> Whenever my heart felt heavy, I wrote. It was my only route to escape the harsh realities of life—only writing brought peace to my troubled heart. There can be no better way for one to stay happy: smile at others, laugh at oneself, aim the barbs of fun and wit at oneself and others. And then relish the moment when you feel the sweet pain of injury.[5]

For me, to get to know this Anis has been the experience of truly discovering my Apa—a privilege I shared with my mother Amina, who patiently helped me negotiate through the minefield that the Perso-Arabic script has been for me. In the hours we spent together trying to decipher the few scattered pages of unpublished autobiographical notes and letters that Apa left behind, we have constructed an Anis whose story must be told. This narrative is perhaps not entirely the story Apa herself would recount, refracted as it is through my eyes, but I'm sure that the fact that I cannot dissemble objectivity is something that she—who could never tell a story without revealing her own location within it—would empathize with.

The first part of Anis apa's story is reconstructed from her unfinished autobiography *Ghubar*, supplemented by family information in Hasan (2004). The two accounts differ considerably, and understandably so. Anis apa is writing about her antecedents rather than her history, and specifically in the search of family values that freed her (and Rafi and Shafi) to become the forward-looking secular nationalist Muslim she was, uncontaminated by ties to the land and a moribund social order.

In Anis apa's telling, the Kidwais were Muslim *taluqdar*s and zamindars of Barabanki district, tracing their ancestry to the last decade of the twelfth century when Qazi Kidwa, a Turkish-born missionary, arrived in India from Medina in the wake of Shahbuddin Ghori's invasions (1191–92). Anis apa's story of Qazi Kidwa and his descendants is not that of the historian—where a conclusion that he was at best an adventurer is inescapable and the decline in his descendants' fortune expected by virtue of their being subjects of history. Rather, hers is a saga of spiritual and moral decline, a descent into feudalism from the spiritual heights that the progenitor scaled.

For Anis apa, Qazi Kidwa was a learned mystic. When he reached Delhi with Khwaja Moinuddin Chishti, the saint of Ajmer, he was received with full honours by Ghori himself and appointed chief justice of the Delhi Sultanate. But soon (c. AD 1201, according to Hasan 2004), Qazi Kidwa was in Awadh, where after a series of skirmishes, he made a place for himself and his cohorts (by capturing fifty-two villages from Bhor Raja of Jaggaur).[6] Although his immediate descendants consolidated his gains and spread to various parts of the kingdom, the subsequent centuries saw the area of the Kidwai influence circumscribed to Barabanki, and their traditions of spirituality and learning were lost almost forever.

By the late nineteenth century, reports Anis apa, the Kidwai clan comprised only petty zamindars and cultivators, for whom the claim to a glorious past and a pure Arab descent was of great value. But not for Anis apa, because she saw concealed within this obsession with 'purity', the practice of exclusion. Among the Kidwais she knew:

The Kidwai ancestral home in Masauli, Barabanki district. The front section was rebuilt in 1935 and was occupied by the male elders of the household. Women, including young Anis Kidwai, lived in the inner house, beech ghar, *which had a large central courtyard with rooms on three sides. After Rafi's demise, Anis Kidwai and her daughter Kishwar occupied the front section of the house in the months that they visited Masauli.*

Most had married into the Siddiquis, Alwis, Farooqis and Sadats. However, there were also other relatives who they disowned because they were Mughals, Pathans and Iranis. So rigid were they that they would break all ties with any clan member who married into these groups and deny them any share in the ancestral property. Hindustan's air had clearly erased from their memory that our Prophet married his daughter, Hazrat Zainab, to a slave. And for all their glorying in the purity of their Arab lineage, their shameful reality was that they denied their daughters their rights under the Shari'a. Even in the matter of widow remarriage, the Islamic Shari'at was forgotten.[7]

By the time Anis apa was born in 1906, the Kidwais were in a state of decline. Their ancestors' qualities of 'a spiritual inclination to renunciation, sacrifice, acceptance and resignation . . . as a legacy from the soldiering dervish who was the founder of their line' and strength of character marked by an 'Arab hospitality, munificence, bravery, generosity, humility' had been all but erased. If any vestiges of these graces were still to be found, they were in the few Kidwai families that had married into Sheikh families that still maintained the old traditions of learning and religiosity. It is to these few families that Anis apa lets us know she belongs (though she is careful not to be too direct), and equally through the descent of her mother, a Sheikh daughter of the ulemas of Farangi Mahal, as of her father, Wilayat Ali 'Bambooque'. Because of the forward-looking attitudes of *both* her parents and grandparents, Anis apa's entry into the world is located firmly at the cusp of modernity:

The twentieth century had moved forward hardly six years when an incident caused pandemonium in two time-honouring, conservative families of Awadh. The cause of mayhem was the arrival of a Christian lady doctor to assist in the birth of a dark-skinned puny little girl.

Surely, lakhs of children must have been born into the Kidwai clan before this, but what could one say to the grandparents of this little girl, who despite every objection, would not reverse their decision. They were determined to avail of the advantages of modern medicine to save the life of their beloved daughter and daughter-in-law. They would not abandon her at death's door by persisting with the ignorant, uninformed customs of old. This answer silenced most of their opponents, who said that well, of course, they have the right to do whatever they want to their own child.

But behind the purdah, the household's old bibis smote their foreheads at the sheer impudence of this lady doctor. 'What an outrage! To think that this woman, who walks about in full public view, laughs with strange men and shakes their hands, can so brazenly sail into the house of respectable ladies. And with the blessings of our own daughter, who finds nothing wrong in welcoming this disreputable woman! Even if every iota of shame has deserted her and all regard for decency fled her thoughts, for us she is nothing short of a man!'

As a result, all the old ladies retreated behind the purdah in disgust. To add insult to injury, that lady doctor barred the entry of anyone but her nurse and compounder. The girl's mother was also allowed to stay. After a while, the parents of the sixteen-year-old mother heaved a long sigh of relief. They were happy, but other relatives were still seized by the forwardness of that fat lady doctor. They called her a liar: 'How could she, as soon as she arrived, announce that the case was not normal?' But the lady doctor was all smiles, beaming with pride. Were it not for her sure hands and new instruments, this obstinate little girl could not have been persuaded to leave her mother's womb.

This was my birth, which thus became a historical landmark. Soon, this 'wanton' Christian lady doctor, clad in Victorian long black skirt and ruffled white lace blouse and large white hat, was espied visiting the houses of every gentleman of means in the zila.

This little scene is indicative of the events and characters that shaped Anis apa's early life. To begin with, there was the socio-historical context in which her parents became adults, where the limits of their world were being extended. In this new world, both education and politicization had increasing value, as old feudal relations were being recast. This outer world—with the burgeoning anti-colonial movements of the Congress and the Muslim League and Sir Syed

Ahmad Khan's socio-educational reforms, its Hindi versus Urdu and Hindu versus Muslim tensions, its Khilafat movements and World Wars—regularly entered Anis apa's home, through magazines like the *Awadh Punch*, *Comrade* and *Ismat*, and in the persons of the bailiffs the British sent to seize the property of zamindari families demonstrating disobedience.

But this isn't all that fashioned Anis apa as the older women, muttering disapprovingly behind the purdah, were by no means a spent force. Although the politicization of the men of the household promised to usher in a new permeability between the home and the world for its women, the winds of change hadn't yet gathered momentum. Anis apa also had to live in this old world and heed its strictures and admonitions.

Quite naturally, Anis apa's story cannot be the same as that of the Kidwai men; her antecedents lay both behind the purdah and beyond. Anis apa's narrative in *Ghubar* is unique because she shows us that while the histories and cultures of those inside and outside the purdah are differentiated, ultimately they are made of the same stuff—abiding social wisdom, respect for difference and non-sectarian social conduct.

Both my paternal and maternal grandparents were Kidwais, but there was such a great difference between the two households. Perhaps this was because of my maternal grandmother, my nani, whom we all called ammijan. She was a *sheikhzadee* from Lucknow . . .

In the way she lived and dressed, one could find all the elegance, orderliness and sophistication of Lucknow's culture. Knowledgeable in the prescriptions of the Shari'a and ever mindful of the sin of heresy, she was an orthodox Muslim; at the same time, she was also entirely without prejudice and capable of extraordinary compassion.

My paternal family, on the other hand, despite all their education and learning, were pure villagers in essence. They had cordial relations with Rajputs, accorded the highest respect to pandits, and in every custom they practised, pure 'Hindustaniyat' shone through . . . From the great prestige they accorded to pirs and their disciples, and the devotion with which they participated in the Urs of such holy men, one could see that they were inclined towards the mystical. They loved the festivals and rituals of Hindustan and their language was usually Awadhi alone.

At my paternal grandparents' home, Muharram was celebrated with great enthusiasm (even though Kidwais are Sunnis). *Nauha*s and *marsiya*s would be sung all day and my *nana* would fast for all ten days. Id and Bakreed [Id-ul-Zuha] were of course our festivals, but Basant and Holi would also pass by in celebration.

In deference to the beliefs of Hindu subjects, cows would never be sacrificed. Sweets distributed at any celebration would be made by both Hindu and Muslim *halwai*s so that none had difficulty accepting them. And contrary to the practice of other zamindars, the only tax they exacted from tenants was rent for the land.

At her maternal grandparents'—another Kidwai village called Bhayara—zamindari practices still flourished. Whenever Anis apa visited, she was struck by the evidence—from grain to green *chana*s to laddoos—of the demands zamindars could make as *nazrana* from their tenants. The Harijans among the tenants were also required to perform forced labour (*begar*). This was absent in Masauli—she was told the difference was because of her paternal grandfather Mumtaz Ali Kidwai. He had exempted cultivators from all extra taxes beyond the jaggery they paid as land rent. He had also proscribed begar; all labour done in his home was remunerated.

Indeed, Mumtaz Ali was progressive; he not only educated his two sons, Wilayat Ali and Imtiaz Ali, but also his daughter. Unusual for the times and Kidwai custom, she was married out of the clan. But the later Kidwais, from Bhayara and Masauli, did not follow his example; Kidwai women were 'illiterate and ignorant, and silly customs like superstitious rituals of wearing amulets to ward off the evil eye and offerings at mazars were rife'. Though Muslim girls were generally taught to read, writing skills were almost never imparted to them; it was feared they would misuse the skill to pen love letters! One such woman, who could read but not write, was Anis apa's nani (we don't know her name), well educated because of her Farangi Mahal antecedents:

> My nani spoke such exquisite and difficult Urdu. In a simple conversation, she would utter phrases like *dast-e-bakhair* [fortuitously], *farz kardam* [suppose that], *lihaza* [consequently], *goya* [that is tantamount to] . . . With what felicity she read the Milad Sharif! She could recall from memory so many remedies, be it the cure of medicine or of prayer. In every way, her organizational skills and her intelligence placed her the highest among all women of the household.

For the first five or six years of Anis apa's life, her nani was the most important influence. Her mother did not have much time for her eldest child:

> Fresh and beautiful as a bloom, my mother had already given birth to two other charming children. Perhaps this was why she paid no attention to the dark-skinned, quarrelsome, obstinate little girl that I was. But quite possibly this distance was also because only sixteen years separated me from her. The maternal love that was to be mine in later years had perhaps yet to be born in her. Moreover, how could such a young mother be expected to cope with three little children?

As Anis apa grew up, she felt the Bhayara–Masauli divide more personally. In Bhayara, a girl was sequestered in purdah by the time she was five:

> One was not permitted to even stir a couple of steps in public without a palanquin or some other form of transport, but here in Masauli, one just had to throw on a chadar and do the rounds of the neighbourhood in the day (and the whole village, at night). There, one had to observe the purdah with even your father's brother's sons; here even the most distant relatives could, calling out to their *chachi*s, *bhabhi*s and *mumani*s, walk right into the women's quarters.

Whether its source was religion or custom, says Anis apa, girls and women were subjected to great excesses in the name of purdah. Denied freedom of movement, women of upper-class households in Awadh villages had great difficulty in even undertaking visits to friends and relatives living close by. The use of the burqa as a mobile purdah was not yet popular. Instead, a curious practice was adopted:

> Maidservants would flank the path that ladies of the household would take to their intended destinations, holding up as screens sheets through which the ladies could pass, occluded from a stranger's gaze.

But this method was not without hazard, Anis apa recalls:

> On one such day, one such sheet slipped from the maidservant's hand, just as the ladies were passing through *and* some unfortunate wayfarer was passing by. The other ladies scampered away quickly, but my poor mother was left stranded. Being no Noor Jahan, she couldn't whip out a pistol and fire at the offender; instead, she stood rooted to the spot, her gaze lowered in humiliation, shivers racking her body. I wonder whether this shame was authentic or just a fiction? Could it have been fear, pure and simple? After years of living shut up in a cage like a bird with clipped wings, had she simply lost the power of flight?

Notwithstanding the difference between Bhayara and Masauli, little Anis was perhaps unusually 'immodest'. For most of her early years, she remembers being chided by her nani, dadi and other relatives for her unruliness. Fortunately, after age five, she started school and had to listen to this scolding only in the summer vacation. In Barabanki, where her parents lived, purdah was not imposed until she was perhaps nine or ten. Her parents, she says, 'heard out all the complaints that our relatives had against me' and would 'patiently explain to me that I must mend my ways'.

Anis apa's father, Wilayat Ali, had moved to practise law in Barabanki just a few months before her birth, a fresh graduate of Aligarh's M.A.O. Eton College. At the time, it was rare to educate daughters, but because of his and his wife's respect for learning, Anis too entered the classroom where boys of the household studied. Himself something of 'a freak in a family that had showed few traces of intellectual talent in the present or earlier generations (Hasan 2004: 102)', Wilayat Ali was also a well-known satirist in English and Urdu and regularly published in *Comrade* and *New Era*. His wife, family legend has it, was something of a poetess herself. At the time of her marriage, she brought with her a bank account, books and subscriptions to various journals, like *Tehzeeb-e-Niswaan*, the popular women's magazine from Aligarh.

Anis Kidwai's father and well-known satirist, Wilayat Ali 'Bambooque.'

In an age when the only instruction that both Hindu and Muslim girls received was religious, Anis apa received a rigorous education, learning Arabic (her mother wanted her to *read* the Quran, not learn it by heart), Farsi and arithmetic. She read in the same schoolroom that the boys (brothers, cousins, sons of friends and neighbours) studied in until they were eligible for admission to Barabanki High School. This government school admitted boys in the third standard, and until then schoolrooms at home were the norm for boys for lessons in Urdu, Farsi and the Quran. A retired maulvi had been employed, at Rs 5 a month, to teach them. For long, the only two girls in the schoolroom were Anis apa and Ram Kali, the daughter of Wilayat Ali's good friend and fellow lawyer. Later, another girl of the family, Zubeida, joined them.

> What a glorious schoolroom it was! Not a word could be understood in the clamour. At one end, a tall boy, his long neck oscillating like a camel without a bridle, swayed and recited, '*Ma qimaan kue dildarehm, nikhe ba duniya wadi nami aram*'; from the other corner, another called out, '*kareema babukhshai bur hale ma, ke hastam aseere kamande hawa.*' Ram Kali chanted, '*Jako rakhe saiyaan, mar sake na koye.*' And as another intoned, '*Alif zabar aa, be zabar baaaa*,' Maulvi sahab would be exasperated, 'For Heaven's sake, why are you stretching the *a* out so, it is only a zabar!' From another side, a voice recited, '*Quliya al qafiroon*,' as my little brother asked, 'But Maulvi sahab, *how* did the lion get into the sack?' And that chatterbox Zubeida, who just refused to concentrate, whispered to me, 'My abba has brought a fan that runs by itself. I'll show you.' And I moved on to the next page of the Third Reader of *Anjuman-e-Hayat-e-Islam* that I was studying.

Anis apa and Ram Kali were fast friends. Ram Kali would often take Anis apa to her home to savour her kitchen's delights but she wouldn't touch a morsel in Anis apa's home. Ram Kali's education soon ended but Anis apa's continued till her father lived. Unfortunately for her, it was only at home, though school education for girls had

become an option by the time she was six. In 1912, Saiyyid Karamat
Hussain started a school for Muslim girls in Lucknow; however, Anis
apa's father refused to admit her there, despite the fact that his good
friend, Chaudhary Mohammed Ali, had enrolled all his four daughters:

> No one gave any thought to my pain. Allah, what torments I suffered.
> The hours that I spent thinking of what life in school would be like!
> I who thought myself so much smarter than Kajjan Baji and
> Chhabban Baji was doomed, thanks to the conservatism of my family,
> to attend school and college only in my imagination. Brimming over
> with envy, I listened enraptured to their stories. What was it like
> when the bell rang and all the girls trooped into class? And when
> they gathered, chattering away, at the dinner table? What fun it must
> have been to play football and badminton in the evenings!
>
> I could only conjure up these scenes in my head, because the
> dream of going to school was never to become my reality. My mother
> was not so opposed, but I don't know what had come over my father.
> Such an enlightened man in every respect, he was adamant in his
> refusal. For me, the fact that the other elders were also up in arms
> was not of consequence, but my father's intransigence hurt. He
> believed that he would give such a complete education that no school
> or college would ever be able to match it.

And a fine education it was, though short-lived. When a visiting
relative asked Anis apa what she was studying some time later,
the information she supplied led him to ask her mother caustically
whether she was planning to make Apa seek employment once she
was old enough.

Anis apa's Barabanki home was always crammed full of people.
The women's quarters, the zenana, brimmed over with women,
maidservants, nannies and all their children. The other two parts of
the house were also full; the men's quarters, the *mardana*, were occupied
by Anis apa's immediate kin (including Rafi and Shafi) as well as a
host of cousins, while the guestrooms saw a never-ending stream of

visitors. This portion also housed her father's friends' children, who studied in Barabanki's schools.

> Two such boys were the sons of Patwariji. Being Hindu, they had set up their own *rasoi* [kitchen] in a corner. One day, I was suddenly beset by concern for their culinary arrangements. Poor Lala Kamta Prasad, who must have been in the seventh standard, was just about to put the first morsel of the half-cooked roti he had inexpertly made into his mouth, when I appeared. Sliding one foot just across the threshold, I asked brightly, 'Lala, what are you eating?' The more he raised his voice in admonition at my infiltration, the less I paid heed. Finally, irritated beyond words, he broke off a piece of the roti and threw it at me, 'Take this and get out!' Flushing with humiliation and anger, I picked up the roti and threw it right back into his rasoi. 'Am I a dog? I just came here to see how you were.'
>
> This one action was enough to pollute poor Lala's rasoi for the night. Crying, he threw aside his cooking pots and went straight to my father to complain. That day was the first time my ears were twisted with such brutality that the pain lingered for many days after. Even then, I couldn't understand why it was my fault. As far as I was concerned, the crime and the insult were all from Lala's side. It was only later that I understood this whole business of pollution and untouchability.

In the zenana, in Masauli or in Barabanki, both linguistic and religious identities were more protean than in the world outside. The unlettered nature of most of its Hindu and Muslim women inhabitants made the culture primarily oral: all song and story was in Awadhi. The Awadhi they spoke, Anis apa says, contained words from a variety of sources including Sanskrit and Farsi, but so distorted as to be almost unrecognizable.

In terms of religion too, particularly in Masauli, the communities of practice that women of the zenana made, bound them in the celebration of marriages and festivals. In Basant, all women wore yellow, and in Sawan, all young girls and women draped new dupattas and took turns at the swings strung up in the courtyard. Every Diwali, the Masauli house would be freshly painted and lit up with diyas. Though the celebration of Holi was officially frowned upon, young boys and girls always managed to find a corner where they could surprise the new bride in the house and paint her in all the colours of this syncretic world.

Hindu and Muslim celebrations differed only in that the Hindu women working in the household would do pujas in their homes, because their Muslim counterparts had 'made these festivals full of colour, swings, delicacies, mehndi, bangles and folk songs, completely their own'. Even as their Hindu sisters celebrated the triumph of good over evil in the burning of Holika, Muslim women would have black *masoor* dal and mutton cooked and offer up prayers in memory of Abraham's emerging unscathed from the bonfire set by the idolatrous Nimrod. While religious ascription differentiated, it did not divide; in the practice of faith, there was no segregation:

A beautiful synthesis of Hindu customs and the Muslim Shari'at was to be found . . . When the new bride came down from the palanquin and set foot in her new home for the first time, along with the beautifully painted *handi*, a fish would also be laid at the threshold. In marriages and at the arrival of a new child, all our songs were about Nand Lal; to these were added songs of Amina's Lal. Bhajans of Kabir, Surdas and Mira were sung all the time . . .

And all the bibis were simply crazy about that Awadhi folksong *Apne saiyyaan ko poojan piya, ayee hoon guiyyaan main to* [To worship the lord of my heart, I have come!] Just as many eyes would moisten when that heart-rending *Kya leke jaayen gauna hamre ram?* [What do I take along to my husband's home?] rung out as a desperate lament . . . Ram and Rahim, Ali and Fatima were so exquisitely yoked together in this imagination that the hearts of us ignoramuses would just thrill. Those 'uneducated' but wise bibis were far freer of sectarian feelings than us educated people.[8]

Such was the syncretic nature of women's beliefs that even the practice of religion had been indelibly marked by the customs of faith:

> In the qasbahs of Awadh, the bibis of the household would go to the mosque laden with sweetmeats, place them in a niche in the *mehrab*, and tell the imam, 'There you go! Now please read us the fateha for Allah Miyan.' Even at that young age, I would be puzzled—what does it mean to read the fateha for Allah Miyan? The fateha is recited for humans, not God!
>
> On giving the matter deep thought, I have concluded that the Hindu wives of our ancestors must have found it impossible to yield up their old customs of ritual offerings (*bhog*) before Hindu gods and goddesses, so they offered bhog to Allah Miyan in the mosque (may Allah forgive me for this heresy!). To keep their beloved wives happy, their husbands must have allowed this practice.
>
> If children did not survive their birth, then besides the remedies offered by pirs, prophets, *mannat*s, magic and *taweez*es, a *roza* for Hazrat Ibrahim or Hazrat Daniyal could be kept. Or else, a corner of the field be marked out with garlands of flowers and the space filled in with laddoos, gur, ghee. Such were the 'Islamic' practices by which a woman could beseech Dharti Mata to preserve the greenness of her womb.[9]

But even in the real world—just beyond this shared culture in which the edges of religion blur and gender is elided from the genealogies sketched by history—women's religious affiliations were less immutable than men's. In particular, when a woman was abandoned by her family, her religious affiliation could change, depending on who took her in as lover, husband, or philanthropist.

Anis apa understands this first through the story of her Bua, her brother's wet nurse and her own nanny. A child widow, this 'fair-skinned girl in a lehnga and white dupatta' was disowned by her family for her defiance of the Hindu proscription on widow remarriage. As a girl, she fell in love with a local Muslim Pathan, much older and already married. Yet Bua married him, despite the social ostracism of her family and community this entailed. Though the Pathan died shortly, Bua had found a family—the Pathan's son from his earlier marriage loved her dearly. In fact, whenever Bua and Anis apa's mother had a disagreement and Bua flounced off in a huff (not before all the Kidwai children in her care were loaded into the cart with her!), it was to this stepson's house that she headed. In Bua's life and the practice of her (now Muslim) faith, Brahminical customs and traditions left their imprint:

> Bua knew all the stories of the Hindu Devmala by heart. Every night as we lay in bed, she would narrate them. With tales from the Ramayana and the Mahabharata, we learnt from her the sagas of Sati–Savitri and Shakuntala–Dushyant, months in the agricultural calendar and all the proverbs about the seasons. And Bua never touched beef. Diwali, Sawan, Dussehra, Muharram—in fact, all gatherings to celebrate the sacred or the profane—gave her great joy. In Muslim festivals, her favourites were the rozas and Id. She kept all the fasts and often read the namaz (or what she knew of it).

Bua's achievement of this happy synthesis of Hinduism and Islam and a life of love was unique, as Anis apa's experience taught her through her encounter with Nargis when she was about ten years old. One day, when Anis apa was out for a walk with Bua and her brother, she saw a pile of rags lying in the way. Anis apa the tomboy couldn't resist kicking the bundle, and was immediately scolded, 'Can't you see it's a chilc,' The bundle untangled itself and from it emerged a young girl, gr my and febrile. Bua brought her home:

> Bathed and wearing a borrowed kurta–paijama and pink odhni, that pitch-black bundle of rags was transformed into a doe-eyed golden-skinned beauty. A few days of regular meals and care made her even more exquisite. Within a month, this girl was laughing and flirting with the other servants. We named her Nargis. One day, she followed

me into the part of the house where the cousins studying in Barabanki stayed. And then I didn't quite understand what happened. Little pebbles started flying about. Giggles and peals of laughter bubbled in the air. I had no option but to report to my mother that Nargis was throwing pebbles at the boys. The next thing I saw was Nargis being administered four slaps and a stern warning not to take that particular route ever again.

Shortly after, Nargis was sent to my nani's house in Bhayara for education and training. When she returned a year later, clad in a brightly printed gharara with a red dupatta covering her head, she was a newly married woman. A rapidly blinking young man was by her side; he was immediately taken on as a servant for Rafi bhai and sent off to Aligarh.

But Nargis didn't want to go to her husband. She couldn't abide him and had eyes only for the majestically turbaned servant who worked for Anis apa's father. And one night, she vanished. The family has no further news of her until:

Three years later, Nargis returned. We all embraced her. These days, she wore skirts and swore by the Heavenly Father. The Christian missionaries had been successful in finding a place for her in the good Lord Jesus' sheep, and in teaching her to say, 'Thy will be done, on earth as it is in heaven. Give us our daily bread.' We brothers and sisters insisted, 'Nargis, please come back to us!' So she agreed to stay. But now her conduct had become completely shameless. This time she was with us for at most a year, in which she displayed the most wanton behaviour, and finally decamped with the same majestically turbaned servant of my father whom she had first fancied.

This time, Nargis was gone forever, though a year later her husband was spotted in the Dewa mela wearing the orange robes of an ascetic. No news of Nargis ever came. While for others, she was another forgotten case, for Anis apa:

Her memory remained in my heart. Today, when I am involved in looking to the sustenance, education and reform of the girls of the Women's Service Home, I often regret the fact that we did not provide her with any such facilities. If we had, perhaps her life would have improved.

But these thoughts struck Anis apa only later; at ten, all she felt was impatience with this women's world that forced her into purdah, that too at a time when the world was undergoing such upheaval. Her father's political engagements in the build-up to the Lucknow pact between the Muslim League and the Congress had transformed their home. The household was constantly animated about the events reported in the newspapers every evening. Her father's friends and contemporaries would gather to discuss their efforts to bring the Muslim League and the Congress closer. But Anis apa was not allowed to join in; by 1914, her purdah had begun.

All she could do was watch glasses of *phalsa* sherbet make their way to the mardana and dream of slipping with them out of the zenana. When the soon-to-be famous Ali brothers, Mohammed and Shaukat, visited her home, Anis apa could only listen to the sounds of great things going on, burning up in 'resentment that the boys are allowed to mingle freely in the gathering', and she was not. As yet, she could still manage to sneak out to the passage leading to the zenana and, swallowing her pride, ask those boys for a badge to pin it to her odhni.

By 1917, the purdah was impregnable, so much so that when early in the year, her mother went to Lucknow for treatment, her father wouldn't let Anis apa accompany her. Finally, her nani managed to persuade Wilayat Ali. After spending three glorious months in Lucknow, amidst a milieu of literature and refined conversation, Anis apa and her mother returned to Barabanki in good health and good cheer. But that was not to last more than a few weeks. Soon, Anis apa's thirty-three-year-old father contracted cholera. As he lay dying, Anis apa, for the first time, came to an adult understanding of the cruelty of the practice of purdah:

My mother watched him from afar. My dadi could caress her hands on his head; my phuphi could rest her head on his chest; but the wife, who was losing her all at that moment, had to stand far away, stifling her cries and strangling her emotions.

When Wilayat Ali passed, Anis apa's mother was only twenty-eight. And only after his death did eleven-year-old Anis, nine-year-old Wajahat, seven-year-old Midhat, five-year-old Bilqees and two-year-old Jamal understand his large-heartedness:

That night—when our ruined caravan wound its way back [to Masauli] with a multitude trailing the white carriage drawn by two horses bearing our desolate little family—is imprinted in my mind forever. That night we came to understand that this was the funeral procession of a person so esteemed that for all the nine miles between Barabanki and Masauli, his corpse was carried by his mourners on their shoulders. On the way lay many small villages and, as we passed, villagers spilled out of their homes and joined in. Many in the mourners were children . . .

When the letters began to arrive, we learnt of the many wildernesses where the departed had tried to light the lamp of happiness. One letter told us how, besides extending daily financial aid to his late friend's wife and children, he had also taken out an insurance policy for his late friend's little daughter so that there would be no difficulties when she had to be married.

Anis apa's family moved to Masauli permanently. The following decade was the cruellest span in her life, one in which the beloved Masauli of childhood was transformed forever. The customs that were a child's delight took on a grimmer aspect.

For the forty days after his demise, every evening, my dadi would take my father's name and wail. All the relatives from villages and adjoining areas would have descended upon the house by then and the fateha would be read. This went on for an hour every day. For forty days, not a scrap of food was cooked in the house . . . and the stream of visitors would not end. And Ammijan sat holding her grief-stricken daughter. As far as she could, she would protect her from the assault of visitors, but the difficulty was that the widow's bed could not be moved until the iddat period was over. She could also not visit her natal home for a whole year.

Now that she was a young woman in the eyes of the world, the Masauli she had toured so extensively in the past was denied to her. Gradually the love and cosseting of the first few months gave way to nitpicking:

The loudness of my laugh, the way I chuckled, the familiar manner with which I interacted with my cousins (as if they were my real brothers), the habits I had, the way I dressed, the time I spent in reading or in playing carrom, ludo, or cards with the boys were all the target of their objections. But I had absolutely no interest in housework, cooking, etc. In Barabanki, I never set foot in the kitchen; my father never even asked me to fetch a glass of water; as a consequence, I was a complete stranger to the sentiment of living in the service of men.

In this new Masauli, she found that men demanded this service from the women of the household. Her education came to an abrupt halt, never to be resumed. The only escape left to her was to run over to her friend Farida's house, where the two girls would spend hours reading books and reciting poetry.

Though her uncle Imtiaz Ali gave his nieces and nephews the love of a father, the straitened circumstances of the Masauli household prevented him from affording them the comforts they were used to. After Wilayat Ali's death, the truth about the abysmal financial condition of the zamindari was revealed. Half of the land Wilayat Ali owned had to be sold to settle his debts. Imtiaz Ali mortgaged his own land to cover outstandings, so that his brother's children had some inheritance to speak of.

In the following years, matters became much worse, as both Rafi and Shafi were still studying (they had not appeared for the annual examination in 1918, losing a year). Rafi had been married in 1917, just six months after Wilayat Ali's death, to Majidun Nisa (Farida's sister) on his grandmother's insistence that it was her dead son's dearest wish. In end-1919, when Anis apa's dadi was on her deathbed, the family decided that her own wish must be fulfilled before she breathes her last:

> I think I was the first girl in the entire family to be asked whether I was agreeable to the proposal (accompanied with the statement that the match had been my father's intention and my dying grandmother's desire). What else could a fourteen-year-old girl like me say but 'As you think best. But if you can wait two years then it would be better'. But who was going to pay any attention to this proposition?

Mercifully for Anis apa, the ceremony was simple; Rafi's spartan marriage months earlier had set the tone for weddings. She was not forced to wear 'tonnes of jewellery' and 'heavily embroidered silken ghararas' that brides were burdened with at the time; within two or three days, Anis apa was back to her normal loose kurta-paijamas.

Though the marriage of any girl as young as Anis apa is a tragedy, it was this alliance that eventually sprung her free of her not so-gilded cage three decades later. But even at the time, her marriage to Shafi (and her closeness to Rafi) opened the doors for her into a world where the cause of political emancipation was prime, where allegiances were based not on kinship or patronage but on ideology and struggle.

In Barabanki, Anis apa had spent her childhood looking up to the two brothers, both groomed by Wilayat Ali in nationalist politics. They were much older to her, Shafi by ten years, Rafi by twelve, and had left to study in Aligarh while she was still a child. She was old enough though to divine the great difference in temperament between the two—Shafi was hot-tempered and outspoken, Rafi shy but genial; Rafi was brilliant, Shafi industrious. But both brothers were similar enough to empathize with her political leanings.

In 1920 Shafi returned to Masauli after his graduation, having given up his plans for higher education to take care of the household and the zamindari. His father Imtiaz Ali asked his English employers for a favour and an interview for Shafi for the position of zila deputy collector was arranged. Shafi failed to secure the position as he refused to display the requisite sycophancy to the British. Although he did get the position of cooperative assistant registrar a few months later, he quit in 1921 to join the Congress (with Anis apa's full approval). Rafi, who had stayed back in Aligarh to pursue a degree in law and was by then a prominent youth leader of the Congress, also returned to Barabanki to mobilize people to join the struggle.

When the two brothers went to jail in the civil disobedience movement of 1921 (along with ten or twelve other men of the Masauli family), Imtiaz Ali was repeatedly summoned to be warned by the colonial authorities that he must restrain his sons from these insurrectionary activities. Family lore has it that when he refused to give any assurances on his sons' behalf, the British sought reprisal by exerting pressure on the debt-ridden zamindari. But Imtiaz Ali's career was apparently left untouched, as he rose from naib tehsildar to the rank of manager of the court of wards and was accorded the title of Khan Bahadur.

Imtiaz Ali was deeply disappointed by his sons' irresponsibility towards the family fortunes, yet he didn't prevent them from following their chosen path. Anis apa's own growing political commitment was not similarly welcomed. Though Shafi endorsed her passion, he was not radical enough to free Anis apa from the bonds that imprisoned her within the home. Anis apa recalls how, when the two brothers were incarcerated in Lucknow, it was only Rafi who agreed to see the women of the household who went to meet him. Shafi refused and Anis apa was incensed: 'Did he think I would burst into tears when I saw him? Did he have the gall to believe that he was the only patriot in the house?' The real reason for his refusal to meet the women, she felt, was that he couldn't sufficiently question the tradition of purdah and didn't wish to be seen encouraging the women in their recklessness in contravening it.

Nevertheless, for a while in 1920, Anis apa succeeded in finding political expression. In a liberation movement that had by now drawn in rural women, she was able to set up a Congress Mahila Committee in Masauli. Serving as its secretary, she organized a public meeting of rural women. A solemn oath to boycott all foreign goods and not to rest until freedom was won was taken by the gathered Hindu and Muslim women and after that a fund collection drive was launched. Women took off their jewellery and donated it to the Congress.

> My mother was so wonderful. She was my one ally in all these activities. Ignoring all the protestations of the family, in complete disregard of all the objections, she helped me collect funds [for the Congress]. When I took the jewellery that she had given me—what wealth did I have besides?—and put it into the collection, she did not protest, though I could see her pain.

When bonfires of British goods were to be lit one day in Barabanki in 1920, she briefly turned her Masauli household into a site of anti-colonial resistance. She declared that she would consign her wedding gharara (the only expensive clothes she had) to flames. Although her *dada* was horrified, Rafi laughed and asked her to take Shafi's marriage *achkan* too. To attend the meeting in Barabanki, village women from across the district had hitched purdahs over *ekka*s and tangas and travelled large distances:

> A huge pile of brightly coloured clothes shimmered in the middle of the massive field that was the venue. The glitter of gold trim, zardozi and sequins dazzled the eye. With my mother's moist eyes and my dada's flushed face in my mind's eye, I too reached the venue . . . A huge crowd had gathered in front of the stage, near which there was also an enclosure for women like us. In this tent stood ladies from some of the most venerable Thakur families of the zila as well as women like me, all desperate to see and hear Jawaharlalji.
>   Shortly, amidst wild applause and slogans of 'Victory to Gandhiji! Victory to Jawaharlal Nehru! Inquilab Zindabad!' a handsome, pristine, smiling Jawaharlalji appeared on stage. And though Chaudhary

Khaliquzzaman, Gokaran Nath Mishra and other local leaders were already present at the dais, the only one that all eyes in the crowd sought out was this emerging young leader, who was to go on and take in his hands the reigns of the nation.

The tent was abuzz with whispers.

'He's the son of a rich man, used to playing with gold coins!' one said. Another interjected, 'To think that his clothes used to be washed in Paris at one time, and today he stands before us in such a thick white khaddar sherwani!' Another tipped over the treasure of all the information she had, 'Do you know how many things in his house have already been burnt—the shirts alone numbered 700!' Overcome, a few old ladies broke out into a slogan, 'Blessed be the house that produced such a scion!'

Even though this meeting sparked off tumultuous times for the district, Anis apa was not to be privy to much more of this changing discourse in the women's world. Not only was the purdah an impediment, the responsibility of the household was also hers once Rafi and Shafi were arrested in 1921. Moreover, in 1921, she became a mother for the first time. But 'the poor frail little thing could manage only a few days of breathing in the air of this world before he departed'. Anis apa was inconsolable. Shafi had despatched a trained midwife from Lucknow (where he was spending the year working with Maulana Mohammed Ali and Seth Umar) but by the time she arrived, Anis apa had been already been subjected to the depredations of the old village midwife.

As expected, my mother took me to Lucknow for treatment. But when I returned to Masauli after having fully recovered a month later, I was again inexplicably caught in the grip of an inconsolable grief. This was so contrary to my usual temperament but the tears for that lost child continued to fall from my eyes. But in a few days, I was able to tell my friends cheerfully, 'It's just as well he went back; had he stayed, he would have just troubled me.'

What must Anis apa, herself ushered into the world just fifteen years ago by the experienced hands of Barabanki's first medically trained midwife, have felt in this world where even as the clock moved forward for so many, its hands wound backward for her? And even as she wrestled with the feelings that she was 'a bird whose wings had been clipped (*ek parkata parinda*)', she was to revisit this paradox again, when she gave birth to her eldest daughter just a year later, in 1922. And even choosing a name that held the promise of release for her child was denied to her:

> This little girl was just sixteen years younger than I was. The struggle for freedom was so inspiring that I named her Azadi. But my mother found it to be an awkward name, and so the child's *aqeeqa* was done with the name of Rafia Sultan.

Azadi was born in Masauli, but we don't know much about Kishwar's birth three years later in 1925. Shafi had returned to Masauli by then, but Apa's mother would certainly have not been there. In 1924 she fell ill and was taken to Lucknow. Rafi and Shafi rushed to Lucknow to look after her but her condition didn't improve. In her last moments, she called Rafi to her bedside and placed the hands of Bilqees and Anis apa in his, and then departed this world. Eighteen-year-old Anis apa, fourteen-year-old Wajahat, thirteen-year-old Midhat, eleven-year-old Bilqees and eight-year-old Jamal were orphans now.

The next three years were terrible for Anis apa and Shafi. Shafi had to abandon all his political aspirations, as the family's financial conditions were dire. He moved back to Masauli and tried to help his father turn around the beleaguered zamindari, with little success. As for Anis apa, all thoughts of political activism were driven from her mind by her mother's death; she had to care for her younger brothers and sister as well as her two children. Dogged by persistent ill-health and repeated miscarriages, she only had the support of her nani who came to live with her. And when Rafi and his wife suffered a terrible tragedy in 1926—Majidun Nisa accidentally caused the death of her own son; being illiterate, she gave him the wrong medicine—Anis apa had to care for her as well. In 1927 her sorrow was compounded when her chacha and chachi, in haste to leave for the Haj, married their two daughters to her brothers Wajahat and Midhat (seventeen and fifteen, respectively) almost overnight, without celebration or ceremony.

Things improved only in 1928, when Nehru became a member of the Allahabad Municipal Board and arranged a job for Shafi there. Meanwhile, Rafi had won a seat in the Central Assembly in 1926 and taken up a house in Daryaganj. In 1928 the ill-health of her friend Farida occasioned a visit to Delhi. Farida was dying of tuberculosis and the family wished to consult Rafi's friend and Congress colleague, the famous Dr Ansari, hoping that he could somehow save her. Anis apa with her two daughters and sister Bilqees accompanied Farida to Delhi. But instead of staying by her sickbed, Anis apa ruefully confesses that she and Bilqees were taken up with this new experience:

> A Muslim League meeting was going on so the palatial houses owned by various kingdoms and principalities were full of people. Delhi's beauty had been enhanced manifold by an exhibition—gold and silver artefacts and jewellery were being bought and sold, as the rajas and Nawabs who could buy chairs and cradles made of gold and silver were all at the exhibition. Bilqees and my delight knew no bounds. Allah! We hadn't truly known the world until now. What a beautiful, colourful, dazzling world it was! And to think that thus far our eyes had been blindfolded to its very existence![10]

Though the two young women were in strict purdah, they clattered around in tangas exclaiming over Delhi's majestic sights and elegant women:

> One evening, we were invited to an Iftar party at Safdarjung Tomb, where we were introduced to some noblewomen of Delhi. Among them were princesses, Begums and other famous ladies: Begum Nawab Ismail's simplicity and sincerity, Wajida Khairi's delightful

conversation, Mrs Abdul Rahim's blushing ways, Begum Hakim
Zulfiqar Ali Khan's grandeur commanded our adulation.[11]

Another world of women, far removed from the one Anis apa had
seen thus far, and one she yearned to belong to.

As indeed was the world of men in Rafi's house in Daryaganj. A
hostel for any Congressman who needed a place to stay, it saw
ceaseless traffic of eminent leaders like Pandit Motilal Nehru, Srinivas
Iyengar and Maulana Mohammed Ali. The residents were not limited
to family or clan, were not always invited guests—most just sailed
in and chose their rooms—and spoke in many more languages than
just Awadhi or Urdu. Cloistered in one of the three rooms that
housed the Kidwais (of the fourteen bedrooms in the house), Anis
apa overheard the 'Bengali, Bihari and Madrasi guests sitting out in
the verandas, discussing politics and arguing with each other in their
own languages'.

However brief her exposure to this variegated world with its classes,
culture, politics and babble of tongues, this experience marked the
beginning of Anis apa's march to freedom. Happily for her, once she
joined Shafi in Allahabad in 1929, she became better acquainted with
the public world. Although until 1935 financial difficulties beset her
peace, these were also the years when she occasionally felt like a
participant in the liberation struggle. Rafi had also moved to Allahabad
by 1930 and Shafi's house became one of the headquarters of the
Congress publicity machinery. Through a door that opened out in a
back lane, came activists to collect the leaflets and posters prepared
secretly in the house. Rafi, frequently underground during this period,
also used the same door to make surprise visits.

But the Allahabad house was not always a home for Anis apa.
Though she had brought along her daughters and siblings, she would
return to Masauli for long periods whenever Shafi struggled to make
ends meet. In 1929, it was in Allahabad that she gave birth to a
premature baby boy, my father Taufiq Naseem. By the time the Salt
Satyagraha started in 1930, however, she was back in Masauli. But
she was too weak to breastfeed so a wet nurse, Chhuttan, was engaged.

Just a few months of this robust woman's milk ensured that my father became a tough little boy.

Apa doesn't tell us how often she returned to Allahabad from Masauli, but we do know that living in Masauli between 1930 and 1935 was tough for her, both financially and in terms of health. When she learnt that her brothers had decided not to accept any assistance from the zamindari, she also resolved to accept nothing but a bare subsistence. Her health had been seriously compromised by years of childbearing.

The year 1936, when Shafi got a job as an administrator in Dehra Dun, marked a turning point in their fortunes. Anis apa, Chhuttan and the children moved there, and lived uninterrupted with Shafi till 1947. She engaged in social work—what she called 'national service'. With other Muslim middle-class women, she started a small primary school in Karanpur, with which she was intimately associated till 1946. She was also active in the Dehra Dun unit of the All India's Women's Conference (serving as its vice president for two years) and a school for teaching handicrafts (as a member of the board). But most of all, she spent her time reading and writing. To the first article she published in *Ismat* in 1928, she added many more, also experimenting with drama and short stories.

The period from 1936 to 1947 appears to be the only quiet interval in Anis apa's life; perhaps it seems so because her autobiographical writings end here. In this period, she managed at last to break free from the purdah—a combination of escape from Masauli and a long period of hospitalization for removal of liver stones. In all the family memories I've been able to gather, Anis apa was always happy in the summer visits they made to her and Shafi's house. Every afternoon, the cousins would consume gallons of *kheer* made by Chhuttan, while Anis apa read and wrote. Every evening after rounds of cards, carrom and ludo, they would gather round her and she would tell them stories from the world and from her imagination. Shafi was, for these young children, mostly a distant presence, and more than one recalls being terrified of his anger.

But there were definitely periods of intense grief and anxiety. In the early 1940s my aunt Kishwar was diagnosed with a hole in her heart (an inoperable condition then) and was given only a few years

Anis Kidwai (seated second from the right in the middle row) c. 1946. From right to left in the same row: Anis's younger brother Wajahat; Badr-ul Hussain, a close friend of Wilayat Ali Bambooque; Wajahat's wife and her childhood friend, Jamila; and Anis's daughter Azadi. Top and bottom rows comprise family retainers.

to live. In the same period, my own nani was dying of tuberculosis in a sanatorium nearby. My mother recalls that the one time she was well enough to be discharged, it was Anis apa and Shafi's home that she stayed in, putting their children at risk. After my nani died in 1943, it was Anis apa who gave my mother (not yet her daughter-in-law, but still her brother Midhat's daughter) a home for life.

Also around this time, Anis apa's heart must have broken for her youngest brother Anwar Jamal, her beloved Jammu, when his first marriage at a very young age did not last more than a couple of years. In 1945, when Jammu got marriedz a second time, to Shakuntala, a Sikh fellow student, how Anis apa must have feared for their safety in those communally charged times! Shakuntala became a close friend, but Jammu's first wife also remained part of her family.

The decade between 1936 and 1947 must be responsible for the 'social worker' and 'litterateur' Anis apa of *Azadi*, so far removed from the strong-headed, rebellious young woman we encounter in *Ghubar*, fretting at her restraints. It was perhaps this period of a quiet family life and sustained social work that led her to accept the role she must play in the freedom struggle, given her circumstances, background and affiliations.

Perhaps, the Anis apa of 1936–47 thought the same as the one of 1979. In the closing pages of *Ghubar*, when she speaks of the roles of various classes of women in the liberation struggle, she observes that in many parts of Awadh, particularly Lucknow, the first Muslim women in the Congress were elite Begums and ranis:

> The only connection these ladies had with politics lay in the condolence motions they solemnly passed on the passing of some reputable personage or in the resolutions they adopted to condemn social evils like child marriage or in passionate support of women's rights. Usually, the activities of such ladies were confined to a handful of tiny schools in large cities, or the organization of zenana clubs and dinner parties.

While it would be easy for us to dismiss these women as dilettantes, Anis apa demurs. This would be 'rank ingratitude', because:

> These ladies, so in love with English culture and learning, were all Hindustani on the inside, seized with a genuine concern to rouse Indian women from their inertia. And the voices they raised through their writings in magazines and journals reached the ears of women living in the rural areas.

By giving literary flesh to illiteracy and superstition, these women's efforts sensitized women of all classes to the need for social reform. No, elite women did not participate as fully in the struggle as was needed. Well may this section 'console' itself—'I too was one such woman,' says Anis apa—the truth was that it was mostly lower middle-class and poor women who populated mass movements like the satyagraha. But, she argues, the non-participation of elite zamindari and middle-class women was not because of their insensitivity or depoliticization:

In the initial stages of the liberation struggle, women strained every nerve to break the bonds of tradition that shackled them to home and family. It was usually opposition from family elders that made them backtrack. Thus, the public saw only a few women from the upper classes entering the fray, going to jail. (Even of these women, only a few managed to stay in the battle and hold firm in the time's wildly swinging politics.)

For women like Anis apa, whatever their dreams of a more vital participation, the home and the space around it had to be the arena of their struggle for freedom:

It was a change Hindustan was not ready for yet—to stake the virtue of its women in the struggle for sovereignty was inconceivable. Even the most progressive individuals still considered women to be tender as flowers and—'deficient in mind' (*naqis-ul-aql*). Also, there is no gainsaying the fact that even the women from political families lacked expertise and experience to secure their places in the political sphere.

Moreover, they had to take care of their children. When the men went to jail, the entire burden of home and family shifted to the women's shoulders. At such times, women displayed a masculine vigour in rearing their children and arranging for their education and marriages, as in boycotting British goods. They faced the colonial debt collectors and auctions of their properties, the invasions and assaults of the police, and the opposition and disapproval of elders. And by doing all this, they forced the men to admit that they had an equal role in the fight for national independence.

Whether we read this passage as biographical rationalization or historical subversion, Anis apa's words bring us to the point at which *Azadi* comes to be written, and to some understanding of the person she was at the time that fate propelled her into the horrific drama being staged in Delhi then.

In her preface to the 1974 edition of *Azadi* (written in 1949), she says that her gaze on the events she has witnessed is constrained by a world view that derives from her being a 'qasbati woman'. Not just an apology for the shortcomings of insight, the term is her shorthand for her discursive synthesis of the various affiliations and alliances she accumulated in the first forty-one years of her life.

First, her origin from a somewhat down-at-heel zamindar family of an Awadhi qasbah made her affiliations rural rather than urban, distancing her from Lucknow's upper-class ladies. Second, as a woman who had spent most of her life in purdah, Anis apa had a lived experience of a syncretic tradition where gender solidarity and human empathy far outweigh public identities like religion or family. Third, as a politicized nationalist woman who critiqued practices that imprisoned young girls in their homes, denied them education and forced marriage and motherhood upon them, she was a social reformer, thus allied with all movements hinging on the liberation, education and welfare of women and children. Fourth, as a learned Muslim woman, she was not only connected to her co-religionists by the theological tenets of Islam, but by language (Urdu, Arabic, Persian) and a contemporary socio-politico-cultural identity. Fifth, as a member of a prominent political family, she was defined by the gender roles and attitudes within the family, as well as its social status.

For Anis apa, to be a qasbati woman is to be one in whom each of these alliances mediates the other. While her education and learning, her literary career and her family's political prominence affiliated her to an elite socio-political class, the fact that she was not urban but rural, that she had been an interlocutor of women behind the purdah and that her membership of the family had not implied autonomy, denied her a powerful identity. While she was Muslim, her politicized experience of the woman's world of faith and her learning of theology and the spiritual strands of South Asian Islam empowered her to redefine public religion as private faith—constituted by the political values of humanity, rationality, equality and resistance. She could thus dissociate herself both from a political Islam that imbricates the hierarchical structures of the clergy as well as a romanticized notion of faith that forever associates it with superstition, ritual, repression. Finally, while she was a member of a political family deeply committed to Congress politics, her experiences as a woman gave her quite a different understanding of secularism and the true meaning of political emancipation.

In terms of language and style as well, to be a qasbati woman of Anis apa's definition enables access to a great variety of lexicons and registers. Apa's language is remarked upon by anyone who reads her in the Urdu original—the use of lexical resources ranging from Awadhi, Hindi, Urdu, Farsi, Arabic to English impart a delightfully polyphonic quality to her language; there is as much delight in anticipating the words she will use to describe an event as in learning how that event propels the narrative. Her style can jump sharply in terms of which lexicon is used to narrate even a short passage.

Whereas in most of Anis apa's writings, the primary effect that this multi-codal Urdu seeks is humour, in *Azadi* it is employed to construct at least two different registers. Anis apa's personal reflections on society, history, religion are written in a High register using primarily Perso-Arabic stock, whereas the narrative of events employs a Middle register using an 'everyday', 'public', 'neutral' vocabulary. This quotidian language is multi-codal at its very core and, in Anis apa's understanding, the only claimant to a near universal intelligibility across speakers of Hindi, Urdu and any local/regional variety. Perhaps this is why Anis apa frowns so much at the monolithic linguistic choices made by the newly independent India in Chapter 1 of *Azadi*. To solely employ any one of the lexical stocks available to Hindi\Urdu\local speakers is to speak in a tongue that alienates all women, because in a woman's world, there is always another language besides Hindi or Urdu.

Equally importantly, Anis apa constitutes this voice of a qasbati woman to negotiate the confessional demands that the genre of autobiography makes on the writer. Having heard stories of how the family lived through the months after Partition, it is striking to find that almost nothing from those experiences appears in the book. Instead, Anis apa is alone, almost without family or even a home. To even mention the scores of people who took refuge for months in her house (Rafi's ministerial residence), the many abducted women she brought home and looked after, or even the insecurity that plagued many family members would perhaps be to surrender the long-yearned-for autonomy these two years of activism had finally given her.

The major differences between the initial drafts (from the two notebooks I found in her papers) and the final manuscript pertain to personal and family references. For example, in the draft of the opening of *Azadi* she begins her narrative thus:

> From the beginning of 1947, reports of Hindu–Muslim riots started flooding in. The first of these was the news of the Muslim League's celebrations of Direct Action Day in Calcutta. I remember vividly the consternation with which the news was received in Lucknow.
>
> Bhai sahab had gone to Delhi. As soon as he returned, we all surrounded him, pressing him for information, as he would have met the leaders from Bengal in the conference he went for. He would have the correct information—here in Lucknow, there were only contradictory speculations about which community had lost more members.
>
> Bhai sahab was very deeply disturbed. He said, 'These people have ensured that Muslims will be massacred! I am told that Suhrawardy was surrounded by goons and could barely save his life. And whatever followed was all his doing. When the mammoth crowd dispersed at the end of his meeting, it turned on the Hindus on its way back. For that whole day, the most brutal killing and looting of the Hindus took place. Then the massacre of Muslims began. For two or three days, the situation was out of control. This was a direct consequence of Suhrawardy's incitement, and now he has the gall to go around with folded hands, begging for help! Anyhow, Congress workers have pressed their very lives into an attempt to ameliorate the tension. Prafulla Ghosh had also said that Muslims were by far the worst affected, even though it was they who threw the first stone.[12]

Even though this is a more truthful and coherent beginning for the record, it is all wrong for Anis apa, as it reveals the two alliances she is most at pains to elide—affiliations to public religion and to a politically prominent family. For it to be *her* record, it must only be what *she* saw and *she* heard.

Another passage—in her notebooks but not in the manuscript—shows that she was at risk purely because she was a Muslim, and that she could react with the patience and fortitude she usually exhibited in all encounters where her security was compromised:

> Caravans of sanctuary seekers kept streaming in, and it was a crime to even take the name of Muslims on the streets of Delhi. In October 1947, even I had to travel with a police guard. The situation was so dangerous that he kept his rifle on the ready, as bullets would whizz past us all the time.
>
> One day, as I was going to Okhla, we had to stop at a military checkpoint. A soldier barked at us, 'Hindu or Muslim?' The driver replied, 'Hindu,' to which the answer was, 'All right, proceed.' The driver started the car but I told him to wait, and asked, 'And if one is a Muslim?' The reply was, 'If it is a Muslim, the order is to shoot.' Incensed, I rolled down the window and shouted, 'Shoot then! I'm a Muslim!'[13]

Luckily for Anis apa, no shots were fired as one of the other soldiers, who knew who she was, intervened just in time. He apologized, said she had misunderstood what the first soldier said and let the car go.

While one can only admire Anis apa's fierce defence of her right to be an autonomous witness, the information I have gathered from her other writings about those times has helped me appreciate that this absence of the personal exacts quite a cost. For one, it affects the completeness of her narrative. From my mother, I learnt that the two children Rasheeda and Babu whom she speaks of in Chapter 5 met very different ends. Babu died soon after the car ride, haunted by the blood that had seeped into his mind, but Rasheeda, though her head had been split by a cleaver, lived for many years. I'd met her many times and remember her as a slightly odd person, her mind affected by the injury. After nursing her back to health, Anis apa married her to a good-hearted man but every few years, Rasheeda would fight

with him, pack up her belongings and gaggle of children and return
to Anis apa. She would stay for many days until Anis apa calmed her
enough to return to her husband.

Nor do we fully comprehend the full facts of Shafi's death. Although
Anis apa tells us that this was a premeditated murder, we are not
told why. The answer is not found in family accounts, which were
often quite contradictory and vague: 'Your Shafi dadajan was fighting
corruption.' Only when we were well into our teens were we told
that he was murdered in 1947, for fear that our young minds would
misinterpret the information. And when we were told, it was always
with the warning that we shouldn't mention him in front of Anis apa,
as it would cause her tremendous pain. My sister Sonia recalls that
she was present when a distant relative spoke of him in front of Anis
apa and Sonia was startled by the bleak anguish she saw on our
grandmother's face. Each October, when Anis apa took my brother
Rafiq to Mussoorie to pray at his grave, they would spend their time
there in complete silence. Anis apa's notebooks reveal a little more than
what she includes in *Azadi* about the events leading up to his murder:

By the time he had been in Mussoorie just four months, the Congress,
the Hindu Mahasabha and the Muslim League had all passed
resolutions demanding that he be removed from his post (as
administrator of Mussoorie) and recalled to Lucknow. The fact was
that the administration was riddled with corruption. From top to
bottom, every employee took bribes. Shafi sahab had become
infamous for his incorruptibility and the inflexibility of his principles.

From the moment news arrived that he was to be the administrator,
the administration had been agitated. In the months before his
transfer, there were sustained efforts to ensure that he did not arrive,
but in vain. The government posted him to Mussoorie. Once he
was there, and because he made no distinctions on the basis of
religion, he dispensed with the services of one Hindu and one
Muslim officer. In effecting these dismissals, Shafi sahab was acting
on the CID inquiry that the municipality board had instituted
months before he reached. Grave charges had been levelled against

these officers and he was bound to act. In fact, he had written to me saying that he felt unfortunate about starting his service with such unpleasant duties.

The morning Shafi sahab was killed on his way to his office, he was carrying a termination order. The day after his death, that order was withdrawn.[14]

This information goes a long way in explaining not only why Shafi's murder was a conspiracy by vested interests using the pretext of communal strife but also why Anis apa is so arraigned against officials in *Azadi*. Nevertheless, the central questions—why did he have to be *murdered?*—remained unanswered for close to sixty years, until my sister Sabina went to Mussoorie to research a film on the differences between her relationship to Islam and that of Anis apa or my mother. We have no way of knowing whether the answer she received gets us closer to the truth, but this is what she found. Much of the property that Muslims owned in Mussoorie was in areas where today prosperous hotels stand. If Shafi had been allowed to continue confiscating all evacuated property, the window of opportunity that communal violence afforded for grabbing land and buildings would have been sealed.

Anis apa's silence on the facts around Shafi's murder springs from her Gandhian beliefs. Her decision not to insist on an inquiry into his murder was an act of resistance, not capitulation—in doing so, she could end the cycle of grief–betrayal–revenge–reprisal in the one part of the world that she still controlled. The reason that she gives for her silence—why should she make the killer's mother suffer?—ascribes to an Islam that requires its believers to follow the dictates of the conscience. How difficult Anis apa would have found it to reconcile herself to the political Islam of today, in which the only mode of resistance and protest is death (of oneself or of others); equally, how dismayed she would have been with the countering discourses about 'moderate Islam'—for her, no 'moderation' was possible in her religion of the conscience.

Anis apa's Islam was that particular construction of faith as national service that, across the globe, formed the bedrock on which liberation

The house in Mussoorie that Shafi Ahmad Kidwai lived in at the time of his murder in October 1947. So brutal was the attack on him that the identification of the body had to be made by the pen he carried.

Shafi Ahmed Kidwai's grave.

struggles were mounted. For Anis apa (and my mother), inherent to this belief system was a commitment to freedom and democracy, an integral part of the moral compass that religion provided her. At the point of Partition therefore, Anis apa (and the rest of her family) could not have wavered, because Pakistan was not a state created by the Islam she practised. And even though her experiences through *Azadi* made her realize that not every Muslim in India could make the choices she could, her Islam told her that she must stop those Muslims from leaving. This is why, I think, throughout *Azadi*, Anis apa rues the fact that she didn't get enough opportunity to talk to the Muslims intent on leaving—were she able to, she would have convinced them that to stay on was their religious duty. Were she alive today, the same would have been her weapon against political Islam as well right-wing Hinduism. The problem that these two extremisms presented, she would have diagnosed, was their rejection of the 'Islamic' ideals of freedom and democracy and the dictates of the conscience.

Furthermore, because Anis apa's Islam is a religion of humanity, it also serves as an impetus to social reform. So, even while she empathizes with the many Muslim victims of communal violence she encounters and assists in *Azadi*, their vicissitudes do not automatically exempt them from a critique based on the goals of justice and equality. If Muslims resist the ideals of equality and fraternity, if their conduct is marked by communalism, injustice, violence and superstition, if they imprison women in the purdah or burqa, they have departed from the teachings of Islam. This perspective is instructive even today, when we are often content with a secularism that, at best, overlooks and, at worst, endorses the unequal, unjust practices of the victims of bigotry and discrimination.

In other parts of the book, Anis apa's silence deprives us of vital information. For example, it is only from her other writings that we discover the close and informal relationship she had with Jawaharlal Nehru for years. In her essay on him in *Ab Jinke Dekhne Ko*, she tells us that the case of the daughter of a noble family of Jind, which she mentions in passing in Chapter 6, was a protracted affair in which she herself played an important role:

Consider a brief example of the faith he [Jawaharlal Nehru] reposed in his colleagues and workers. A young girl, sole surviving heir of a Sharafat Ali's family that had owned large tracts of land in Jind. Her distant relatives in Pakistan had staked a claim to her whole inheritance; meanwhile, refugees had been settled on the property by the administration. Thus, both sides were conspiring to ensure that there would be no trace of this child's family left.

One day, when a meeting with Panditji (on some other matter) got over, and I was leaving, Panditji followed me out, saying, 'Wait a while. I have something to ask you.' We returned to his office and he asked his secretary to bring out the girl's file. He asked me whether I was familiar with the case. I replied that I was; in fact, not only me, Rameshwari Nehru too knew all the facts. He said, 'Well, then have a look at the notes she has written in the file.'

I showed him the diary in which I'd noted the girl's name, age, address and told him that I also knew that the person whom the girl was entrusted to was in the city these days. He asked me, 'Can I meet her? Can you bring her here tomorrow?' I agreed.

Panditji closed the file and asked his secretary to put it away. The man looked as if he wanted to say something but Panditji brushed him away. The next day, I took the girl to meet him. He sat her next to himself, ran a sympathetic hand over her head and immediately fixed a sum of Rs 200 per annum for her welfare.[15]

Similarly, why wasn't it possible for her to share what she knew from personal experience of the desolation of being married at thirteen and bearing a child at fifteen? Would mentioning personal biography turn our gaze to her from the victims? Or did she wish to be seen as acting on principle alone, not individually but as part of a collective? And why does she find it so difficult to reveal the full force of her dislike for the Ulema? In her notebooks she writes that when her sister Bilqees asks her to come meet the Tablighi Jamat preachers visiting the camp, she refuses, saying that she finds all clerics 'oppressive'. Must her criticism be veiled because she fears we will consider her a heretic? Whatever the reasons for her silence, these omissions indicate a conscious construction of the narrator of *Azadi*.

Anis apa's reticence about her home also sadly deprives us of many stories that she could have included in the narrative of *Azadi*. For me, the most unfortunate exclusion is the story of Savitri Devi and the months she spent in Apa's home:

> One evening, an old British woman, bag, baggage and all, sailed into the drawing room. Rafi sahab was not at home and she was desperate to meet him—she had come with the intention of living permanently in this house. Quite naturally, even as we made all the requisite noises of welcome and light conversation, we were curious to know who she was and why she had come. We didn't have to spend too much time in discreet enquiry; almost immediately, she showed us her sutured chest and told us her story. I cannot now recall the English name she gave for herself, but I do remember that she first came to India from London with her second husband Jafar Ali some years ago. When Jafar Ali departed from her life some time later (perhaps he died or the two separated), she became Savitri Devi. Soon, she was closely associated with Congress socialists and revolutionaries. And when Jawaharlalji and his other young colleagues started working in accord with revolutionaries like Bhagat Singh, she acted as a courier between the two groups, carrying secret messages and information.[16]

Anis apa realized that she had, in fact, heard of this woman, an important revolutionary. She had last heard of Savitri Devi in the context of Chandrashekhar Azad's escape and brutal execution. But though she tried to learn more from Savitri Devi about these events, she was unsuccessful:

> After every few sentences, Savitri Devi would keep on wandering back to the events in East Punjab and Patiala. In a strangely detached voice, her eyes fixed on the ceiling, she began to narrate the tale of East Punjab and the principalities: the horror that was wreaked on

trains, camps and homes, the way women were dishonoured, the cruelties committed upon them. On her as well.

'The goons held me down like this and molested me so, and then they raped me. Just look, they even cut off my breast!' She cursed the doctors and hospital staff, 'The evil people sent me away from the hospital, even though I have cancer. Don't you know? Rafi sahab had me admitted in hospital. That's why I have come back to him.'

All at once, she started to moan, 'Oh my God! They overturned the train. They set fire to all of us—me and the girls I had rescued and was bringing back. What happened to them I wonder? I pleaded with the men, "I'm an old woman!" But they didn't leave me alone. Then I wrote to Rafi sahab and he had me treated. Now I will just stay here. I cannot go anywhere else.'

After some days, I realized that the old woman had lost her mental balance. All the cruelty, sin and troubles that she had seen wrought on others, she had taken them upon herself. It was as if they happened to her. The truth was that she had tried to save many people but failed every time. She would cry and remind us that she too played a role in the liberation of the country, that she was an ally of its revolutionaries, that she had helped people, given sanctuary to victims and endured imprisonment and the excesses of the British government. Today, no one even knew who she was.

We will never know how much Savitri Devi and the scores of other women that Anis apa met in this time led her to write *Azadi*. What we know is that all the women she populates her book with—streaming into camps with bundles hoisted upon their shoulders, squatting under the open sky crazed with grief and rage, boldly thrashing through the fields to seek abducted women, fighting with government officials, or making unforgivable errors of judgement—ensure that while she appears before us without family or antecedent, Anis apa never stands alone. For it is in all these women and their stories that she found family and formulated an autonomous understanding of culture, religion and society.

It is thus no surprise that not once in *Azadi* is there a romanticized allusion to a composite culture ruptured at the moment of Partition. Rather, all her references to the pre-Partition era are located in the restraint that social norms imposed, rather than in some organic past to which we should return. That that past has discriminatory practices, she indicates most sharply through the exchange of the Gaur Brahmin hookah in Chapter 14. While there is definitely the sense of rupture, the question she asks (but cannot answer to her own satisfaction), is how long before Partition were the seeds for this moral decline sown.

Even though it was to be another twenty-five years before *Azadi* was published, Anis apa's life was radically transformed in writing it. Encouraged by Rafi, Anis apa took wing. She walked with more confidence in the public sphere, carrying with her all that she had learnt about herself, her nation, women and sisterhood between 1947 and 1949. Although she could not be the freedom fighter she so dearly wanted to be, she felt better equipped to fight with freedom so that no citizen, particularly no woman, would be excluded from that freedom and that fight ever again.

As yet, however, Anis apa was not the woman who wrote *Ghubar*, who could cast an amused but critical eye on the old social order and its moral and ethical values, with the quiet confidence that such a time is past. Where in *Azadi* she is hesitant to overtly question the social norms that constitute her standard of comparison for the decline that Partition violence signifies, in *Ghubar* her principles are reflections of the mirror that her activist experiences have trained on her own life.

This new Anis apa was forged over the next twenty years, mainly through close association with Mridula Sarabhai in the recovery of abducted women and with Subhadra Joshi in the Delhi State Congress Committee, of which Anis apa was a member (1952–54). She also continued her association with Jamia and Shafiq-ur-Rahman Kidwai and worked on the education of children and adults. Relentless in her pursuit to free Nizamuddin dargah from the clutches of the Custodian of Evacuee Property, she was successful in 1957.

Most importantly, Anis apa found a way to return to the Masauli and the women's world she had loved as a young girl, when she managed to establish a shelter for destitute women and children there. The Women's Service Home and Orphanage functioned for its first few months in Lucknow, but was moved to Masauli by 1952/53, registered under the Societies Registration Act in 1955. Though primarily intended to rehabilitate Muslim women and children victims of the 1947 disturbances, the Home's portals were (and are) 'open to all religions and communities without distinction of caste or creed'.[17] The aims and objectives of this institution underscore what Anis apa sought to achieve:

- To provide board, lodging and training to orphans, destitute children and deserving women on a purely charitable basis
- To help them achieve self-reliance
- To help them develop the responsibilities and duties of good citizens[18]

In the 1950s, I'm told by an old Najma apa (a Masauli resident closely associated with Anis apa), the first few 'batches of girls' were both Hindu and Muslim and 'generally excellent in temperament'. Within months, they became a part of Masauli life and, in a few years, had most of the skills that the Home could impart. One of them even studied nursing and worked in Lucknow for many years. Most of them married as well, some into families in Masauli itself. One such woman still comes to Masauli every year to tie rakhis to the women she knew from that time.

The Women's Service Home and Orphanage in Masauli, instituted by Anis Kidwai in 1952–53, is still in operation today.

Though Anis apa was intimately associated with the Home all her life, Kishwar actually administered it. Kishwar never married because of her heart condition; and though she suffered greatly because of it and the rheumatic pains, she stayed the same Kishwar of *Azadi*, who loved all children and aided any woman in trouble. It is through her and Anis apa's efforts that this unusual experiment in a UP village lives on to this day. When I last visited it in September 2009, I found it in a state of disrepair but functioning—now mainly as an orphanage and home for destitute children—with financial support from the Mridula Sarabhai Foundation and sporadically, the UP government. In the gaggle of children who greeted me was a young woman with an infant; she was home for the Id holidays.

Another major influence in making the writer of *Ghubar* was Anis apa's twelve years in the Rajya Sabha. Her tenure began on 3 April 1956, about eighteen months after Rafi's death on 24 October 1954. We don't have her own words to tell us what a great tragedy his passing was for her, but she must have been overwhelmed with the same grief and feeling of destitution that engulfed every other relative, friend, follower. Although Rafi died suddenly (leaving behind an astronomical debt of Rs 90,000), the respect for Anis apa's autonomy that he had fostered in the family became his legacy. Shortly after his death, Congress offered a Rajya Sabha seat 'to the family'; although Rafi and Shafi's younger brother Mahfuz could have assumed the seat, he asked that Anis apa be the nominee.

Anis apa served in the Rajya Sabha for two terms, retiring on 2 April 1968. She participated actively in the proceedings, in concert with women like Savitry Devi Nigam (also a member from UP, whom she had befriended in *Azadi*) and Dr Seeta Parmanand. Subhadra Joshi was also a Lok Sabha member for much of this duration, and on many occasions, the two women worked together in Parliament and outside.

The first ten years of the Indian parliament saw sustained attempts by women (and progressive men) to put in place laws that would guarantee the rights of women and children. While many of the bills were government-sponsored, such as the anti-dowry bills of 1953, many were introduced in the form of private members' bills. Such bills often sought, directly or indirectly, to enact laws that addressed the specific post-Partition difficulties that women faced.

Almost invariably, however, such bills lapsed, sometimes because a more comprehensive government legislation was later brought on the matter (like in the case of the bills first moved to regulate orphanages and widows' homes) but often because the issues raised were too discomfiting. Reading through some of these early debates, one is struck by not only how committed these women were but also how varied in the perspectives and experiences they brought to the business of making India better for its women citizens. All this can be seen in the debate on one such failed private member's bill, the Punishment for Molestation of Women Bill 1958, in favour of which Anis apa also spoke.

Anis apa would have approached her Rajya Sabha appointment with a deep sense of honour for her role in actualizing the socially transformative power of this newly independent nation. Given the active role other women were taking in proposing legislation, Anis apa must have thought that she too should bring her activist experiences to the Parliament. Although the actual bill was tabled by Savitry Devi Nigam, I'm told by Anis apa's former secretary Zubair Siddiqui that the two had thought it up together. Anis apa was to speak second, after Savitry Nigam's introduction, and before Dr Parmanand, the member from Madhya Pradesh.

Almost as soon Savitry Devi began her speech,[19] any misconception that Anis apa may have held that Parliament was a place where makers of modern India were equally seized by the concern to right the wrongs done to women in Indian society would have certainly been dispelled. Introducing the bill in a somewhat long-winded and muddled speech, Savitry Devi justified its provisions—a minimum of fifteen years of rigorous imprisonment and a minimum fine of Rs 20,000 for offences ranging from 'insult' to 'assault'—by alluding to the fact that most perpetrators walk free under existing provisions. There was a felt need for such a bill among not only social service workers, she said, but also the administration and the police: recorded complaints of sexual harassment of and assault on women students and working women had nearly doubled.

The prime targets of the bill, Savitry Devi emphasized, were 'hooligans' and 'inter-provincial gangs of traffickers and brothel-keepers' operating across India. Young men, misled by romantic films, were not its object, because she knew that 'as long as the human body persists, human weakness will too—love affairs will take place, romance will happen. Errors will be made, and forgiveness also given. But where such errors exceed the limits of romance and transgress into hooliganism, this bill is needed to put a stop to them'. She urged the members to understand that there was no room for anxiety and certainly no need for male members to bring on a legislation for men's protection that she'd heard being discussed.

The last comment drew the ire of at least one member, who cried out, 'This is a baseless charge!' Perhaps there was a hubbub and laughter too, so that when Savitry Devi continued, her nervousness took her away from the subject. The bill, she argued, would have a social impact that would go a long way in mitigating the effects of the protection that men have traditionally enjoyed in Indian society and religion. In a society where couplets that say 'women are impure' are uttered so casually in the Ramayana, where women are equated to animals, it was inevitable for young men to form the opinion that 'women are inferior, debased and weak and men are wonderful'.

These comments drew more interjections. One member even caustically asked her whether she would move to have the offending lines expunged. Clearly flustered, Savitry Devi moved into even riskier territory—the effects of patriarchal attitudes on the psychology of women. The prime example, she said, were the abducted women returned to India from Pakistan. Many were not accepted by their families. In many cases, even if the families were ready, the women themselves didn't want to return:

Let me tell you the pathetic story of one such sister. Although her husband was ready to take her back and treat her with dignity, other family members were adamant. When the woman was told that her husband was ready to accept her and asked whether she was ready to go to him, she said, 'But I am impure! I am a believer in Sanatan Dharm and I do not wish to go to him and pollute his home.'

The woman cried all the time, she was desperate, but still refused all her husband's requests to return, for fear that she would stain her husband and his family. So to all those people who think that legislations like these are of no consequence and take them lightly, I wish to say that the bill deals with a very serious matter that requires deep introspection. No one should think that they must oppose it or make fun of it just because it has been moved by a woman.

Although Savitry Devi managed to compose herself enough to wind up by making an appeal to all members—remember that the most exalted form of a woman is that of a mother and when women are discussed, this form should be uppermost in one's mind—the genie of the molested, abducted woman was out of the bottle. The debate was no longer just about the molestation of women but also about the men in the room.

It was Anis apa's turn to speak next. Did she feel as nervous about speaking in public as she did at the time of *Azadi*? Or did she now think herself a good enough speaker to take on these mocking men? In any case, she started cautiously, distancing herself from the muddle created by Savitry's long perorations:

Respected Chairman, Sir, in her introduction to the bill, Savitryji has confused two separate issues, so much so that the bill states one thing and her elaboration of the bill something else entirely. In her speech she has referred to a gang [of traffickers in women], a matter that we have already considered earlier and the government has already enacted a separate law for it. So this topic must be considered null and void in today's debate. Because to talk about a gang that indulges in immoral acts, causes trouble in different provinces, conveys women to brothels, buys and sells them three or four times, is quite a separate issue from speaking about those who disrespect and harass respectable women on the streets or in government offices. As far as I have understood, in this bill, my sister Mrs Nigam means to address the second type.

I will speak on the bill in this light. I think that she has brought forward a good proposal and tried to raise an issue that is better faced up to, rather than covered up. Because that is what people have been doing with it thus far—sweeping it under the carpet. I noticed that many of our brothers in the House were amused not so much by Savitryji's words but by the very idea that a bill on the subject should be brought before the House. They found it extremely odd.

Perhaps to boost her confidence, she used the language and the understanding of *Azadi*:

But perhaps my brothers have forgotten that years ago, there existed a social organization of community, caste, clan and panchayats that could keep the various constituents of society under control and, in 1947, the warp and weft of that old order came undone when so many people left and so many came. In lakhs and crores, people came from Pakistan, and in lakhs and crores, people left from here.

But she was still a little defensive and confused about how to continue with her arguments:

I've seen the ones who arrived here but those who left, I don't know what condition they are in. I've never set foot in Pakistan; even before Partition, I did not visit Lahore or Karachi. So I cannot say anything of them. But those who have come here, I do know something of their state. It is often said that man is a social animal and that if society were to disappear, there would be no difference between him and a beast. That was the very condition when the warp and the weft of our society came undone, and our society was no longer what it once was. We saw that among these people there was no decency, no shame, no consideration and no sympathy for each other . . .

Until she decided to abandon the high moral ground a minute or so later, and dirty her hands in the battle, by changing the topic and mounting an assault on the traditional values that enable men to smirk at a sexual molestation bill:

It is said that women abet men in their own harassment. I am of an age when I can say these things frankly. It is said that women's clothing, fashion, lipstick and powder is aimed at enticing men, saying to them, 'Look at us.' Let that be true. Let it also be the reason why earlier our Muslim sisters wore burqas and our Hindu sisters ventured out swathed in a huge chadar with a long *ghoongat* covering their heads. But those times are past. We are now in times of progress and when men have adopted so many new things, it is not too much to expect that in terms of their intentions and habits, they should change too . . .

The example of Sati and Savitri has always been proffered before the Hindustani woman. [In earlier times,] she was indeed a Sati or Savitri. Her voice, her body, all that was hers was kept safe and secure for the home, for the family. No one from outside the home could ever catch even a glimpse of her . . . But today, when both women and men can receive education in the same colleges, when they can study together, work together, even do social work together, when in both social life and domestic life, there are no longer any restrictions, then neither can tell the other what they can or cannot do. The only restriction we can legitimately impose is that they respect each other . . .

I don't know whether this regard for women ever existed. Certainly from my childhood to this day, I have never noticed any special sentiment of respect for women in either the Hindus or the Muslims. A woman might well be worshipped as a goddess, but the choicest of abuses for women and sisters are also to be found here. No other culture perhaps has as many abuses for women as we do.

The reality of, Anis apa went on to say, the denial of public space to women was the symptom of an old evil running riot, once it was afforded the opportunity in 1947. If everyone agreed that girls and women were more insecure than ever before, it was the government's responsibility to strengthen women's right to the public sphere. It was duty-bound to make laws for the protection of women, because 'it is on the basis of the assurances that the government gives us that we send young girls to school and college'.

In Anis apa's understanding, moreover, the government's credibility couldn't be established by the mere enactment of Savitry Devi's bill, because the government machinery was itself riddled with such offenders. The government's failure to punish its own officials for abduction was also a legacy of 1947:

> I did not want to say this here . . . But I, and many other colleagues, recovered abducted women from the houses of officials in different government departments. We requested the government that it should somehow punish these people who did such things and took advantage of people in distress. The minimum action that should be taken is to dismiss them from service, if the government thinks what they did is wrong. But that did not happen and the same conditions hold today as well.

Like Savitry Devi, by the end of her speech, Anis apa too lost her composure, perhaps because her comments invited expressions of outrage. But, unlike her friend, when she concluded, all she could muster up were a few sarcastic comments about how it would be far simpler for the government to pass a law that covered up women completely:

> Because otherwise women will believe that just because freedom is theirs, they too have the right to choose their clothing and will want to dress well. This is a great infirmity in women's temperament that they cannot remove: they will insist on wearing good clothes, looking pretty and being well turned out in public. You will not be able to make them appear dishevelled, so the only solution is a drab, thick uniform. I think that will have a good effect!

Although Anis apa's speech was more focused than Savitry Devi's, the debate had wandered far from the bill's subject. Both women, in fact, were at pains to indicate a lack of expertise about the specific provisions for punitive action included in it: all they knew was that the existing maximum imprisonment of two years and fine of a few hundred rupees was not an adequate deterrent. And while they weren't wrong in raising the spectres of molested women and patriarchal mindsets, they did so as indignant reaction rather than cogent argumentation.

It was then up to the most experienced woman member of Rajya Sabha to speak. Dr Seeta Parmanand—a DPhil from Oxford and a barrister, to this day responsible for the most number of private bills moved in Parliament (almost all on matters relating to women)— tried to restore the focus to the content of the legislation, without compromising with the patriarchal mindsets in the room:

> Sir, at the outset I would like to make it clear that though it is not possible to support the bill in the form in which it has come, it is very necessary that the House give its serious consideration to the situation to which the bill points. I would also like to appeal that when members speak on this bill, they will keep, with all due deference to the subject and the same standard which the mover of the bill and the speaker who followed her have maintained.

Dr Parmanand found the bill lacking in clarity: 'the term *insult* is beautifully vague,' she observed (quite correctly). It was wrongly framed—it should have been an amendment bill to the Indian Penal Code—and its proposed penalties were too 'harsh' and 'impracticable'. Nevertheless, she argued, such amendments to the IPC were needed because women government servants working in villages as social workers needed protection: 'It is necessary that some sort of deterrent is introduced in legislation by which the growing goondaism of insulting and unseemly attitude to *women in public work* can be checked [emphasis mine].' She suggested to the government to appoint a small committee of social workers to draft an amendment bill to the IPC.

The genie was stuffed back into the bottle, but at a price. Where Savitry Devi and Anis apa had asked for protection from molestation for all women by any class of offender in any circumstance, now it intended to benefit only women employees of the government's social work departments. And where the two proponents articulated the necessity of the legislation as part of an agenda of social reform, Dr Parmanand couched it in terms of creating favourable conditions for the implementation of government policy. But in the end, while Dr Parmanand's pitch for legislation may well have been more tactical, seasoned and mature than Anis apa's and Savitry Devi's, even the committee she recommended was never constituted. As was the norm, Savitry Devi's bill lapsed that year and was never taken up again. In fact, the Indian parliament has never been able to bring itself to enact specific laws on molestation and sexual harassment.

As this seems to have been Anis apa's only foray into the area of initiating legislation (though she spoke on the subject of a few), she appears to have concluded that she was not up to the task of a tactical redeployment of her own experiences that moving legislation required. In all her subsequent interventions in the Rajya Sabha—even as she grew as a speaker—she spoke on matters that she could emotionally relate to, and always within the parameters of her own experience and understanding of the nation as the arbiter of a new morality. This resulted in speeches about the state of agriculture and rural India and some purely political interventions on matters that confronted the nation (always ones with which she had a personal connect). In her papers I found notes for one such speech she may have given, where she argues for the reservation of seats for women in Parliament and the legislative assemblies. Although the ideal situation would be one where political parties earmark a percentage of seats for women, Anis apa notes, a government committed to the welfare of women cannot wait for male-dominated parties to fulfil its responsibilities.

Another such intervention was her speech in the Motion of Thanks to the President's Address in March 1965, when Parliament reconvened after a stormy late 1964 and early 1965. In the two years preceding this session, the government had framed two important laws that were now the subject of large-scale consternation and protests across India. The southern Indian states in particular were up in arms against the Official Languages Act of 1963, which declared that Hindi would become the sole official national language in 1965; the people of Assam were wrestling with the Prevention of Infiltration of Pakistanis scheme started by the Assam Police in 1960. In 1964 a special provision was included in the Foreigners Act for producing suspected foreigners before a tribunal, by which the onus of proof was placed on the person alleged to be a foreigner. Anis apa reacted to both issues, beginning on an assured note:

Madam Deputy Chairman, I'd like to begin by endorsing the Motion of Thanks for the inaugural address given by the President of our democracy. Every year, the Presidential Address becomes the subject of our discussion and we look to it as the basis of our analysis of the events of the past year and the plans we are to make for the next. We are extremely fortunate that the President of India is a learned man and a philosopher of the highest order. And though he is the head leader of such a large republic, he is also a human. Which is why even as we expect him to have the measure of the pulse of the nation, we also expect his speech, moving beyond mere statistics, to encapsulate for us the way the heart of this nation beats. So when I found no mention of the difficulties and losses [over the past year] alongside the enumeration of progress and achievements that he has given us in his speech, I was a trifle disappointed.

After demanding stern action on the matter of labour unrest in heavy industries and the imposition of strict discipline on striking workers, Anis apa moved to the Assam issue and her visit as part of a three-member Parliament delegation in 1964:

The issue is not of those deceitful people who are citizens of another country and infiltrate into India. They can be sent to Pakistan for all I care. The question is of those who are citizens of this country, have lived on its land for years, have voted not once, but thrice in its elections—1952, 1957, 1962—and have in their possession receipts for taxes paid to the government and the municipality. An ordinary constable [in Assam] was given the right to arrest them and bundle them across the border overnight! . . .

[Although the provision for the tribunals in 1964 gave some relief,] violations continue. And to this day, there is no answer to the question of those citizens that India is pushing out but Pakistan refuses to accept. [When we visited Assam,] a sixteen-year-old girl was brought before us, whose husband had been forcibly sent off to Pakistan. She must now live dependent on the goodwill of the other villagers. We met an old man whose two breadwinning sons had been despatched to Pakistan. He stays alive by begging. Scores of such cases were presented to us. We saw so many fields ready to be harvested but lying untended, as their owners had been sent off to Pakistan.

But to include even a couple of words in the President's Address about this sorry situation was considered inappropriate. I find this regretful. Every Indian citizen could at least have been given the assurance that, without investigation and proof, no one would be subjected to such excesses.

On the language issue, Anis apa's route to a progressive position was through both her experience of the marginalization of Urdu and her belief that the assurances that Gandhi and Nehru gave regional languages and Urdu must be fulfilled:

I cannot stay without expressing my disapproval of the means employed by the people of Madras and south India. Even taking into consideration all the social and cultural pain they have felt, I am forced to say that what they have done is wrong, very wrong, for their own communities as well as the nation. The use of protests, strikes and boycotts I can understand, but a mode of protest that involves setting oneself, libraries, or community and government properties on fire is simply unacceptable.

I say this with the awareness of one who has some idea of their predicament. As the rural proverb goes: *jake pair na phatee biwai, wo kya jane peed parai* [he who has never felt the pain of cracked feet, how can he sympathize with pain of another]? We Urduwalas are in a better position to understand their grief. Rendered homeless in our own province and slandered in the Hindi area, we too have suffered . . .

The time has come for the government to lay all doubts to rest once and for all. Every regional and local language must be given such firm assurances that . . . even the thought that Hindi imperialism or Aryan culture is sought to be foisted on them is banished from their minds for all time to come.

These assurances should be extended to Urdu as well. Anis apa demanded that it be made an official second language in the five states as well as assorted districts where it is spoken. Because the real issue, she said, was the unity of the nation, which must be maintained at any cost. It is impossible for us to know whether the Urdu that Anis apa was speaking of here was her own multilingual variety or the more rigidly Perso-Arabic language that many of her co-religionists spoke. Perhaps it is irrelevant as well, as both kinds of Urdu are Urdu for her.

In the 1960s Anis apa began to feel that the more inclusive nationalist Muslim identity that she had worn until now was beginning to tarnish—from within and without. For one, the pressure on her to think of herself as a Muslim woman first was mounting. In 1961 she was the sole woman member of a six-member parliamentary committee constituted by Nehru to look into possible reforms of Muslim Personal Law. The committee was disbanded almost immediately, as its very first meeting drew vociferous protests by Muslim MPs and ministers. Muslim Personal Law reforms must be left to the Muslims themselves, said this powerful group of men, led by a man she admired very much, Dr Hussain, then India's vice president. Though we cannot definitively know Anis apa's own position, the fact that she accepted to be part of the committee would suggest that she was not averse to the state's involvement in reform, particularly since all other members were Muslims as well. But on witnessing the uproar among people she respected and that too in a way that questioned the basis of her nationalism, Anis apa may have been somewhat confused. Although in the Anis apa I grew up with, there was a great commitment to reform, she also believed that the Shari'a was sacrosanct.

Secondly, the 1960s saw the return of communal violence to India, starting with the Aligarh riots in 1961. The next few years saw the

Note on problems of rehabilitation of riot victim
destitute women and children in Ahmedabad.

There is lot of confusion in tackling the problems facing the
rehabilitation of riot victim destitute women and children.   The
Government has encouraged one Begum Tanis Qureshi, a woman Corporation
member to house about 40 women of this category in an improvised hut
tenement in Shah Alam ka Roza.   Begum Anis Kidwai and I have visited
this camp.   Begum Kidwai has written a letter to Begum Tanis Qureshi
which gives one an idea of the problems that exist in this shelter
camp.   As far as we know no account has been taken of this letter
and the condition of the women in this camp is getting worse.   It is
said as to the number of riot victim destitute women and children,
there is a lot of dispute.   It is not know what figure the Government
has accepted, but it has been said that about 166 claim applications
from such women have reached the Government.   New applications are not
being entertained due to time bar or some other reason.   Non-official
popular figure of such category of women is between 250 to 300; with
an average of 4 children per woman, it comes to 1000 to 1200 children
who have to be attended to.   These women and children are scant
scattered in the city.   Some of them are staying in private homes
while a number of them are staying in private camps which have now
been dispersed.   We have requested those who have been running the
private camps to give these women and children temporary shelter till
we are able to make some arrangement for them.   Hence there is an urgent
need to start a transit camp.

Narayanbhai, Secretary, Shanti Sena has talked to Hitendrabhai
the Chief Minister and to the Governor Sriman Narayanji.   He has come
back with the impression that the Government would give rations etc.
to a camp conducted by the Shanti Sena.   They might also help in
expediting cases of claims and if Shanti Sena authorises, then perhaps
they may recognise and include women who are not included in the

*This note written by Mridula Sarabhai on the aftermath of the Ahmedabad riots of 1969
bears witness to the fact that the concerns she and Anis Kidwai shared from December
1947 onwards endured in the years to come.*

violence repeated in Jabalpur, Ranchi and Bhiwandi. Until Nehru was alive, Anis apa appears to have had faith in the state's intentions in combating this old contagion—mainly because she, Subhadra and Mridula still had access to his trust and support. In 1961 Anis apa and Subhadra could rush off to riot-affected Jabalpur leaving him a note that they expected his cooperation because, if need arose, they would have to say that he sent them. The need did arise and Nehru backed them to the hilt. Nevertheless, her faith must have wavered somewhat, as Nehru's government failed in stemming the growing communalization of Indian society and polity.

Perhaps these were the reasons that underlay her brief flirtation with the All-India Muslim Majlis-e-Mushawarat in the mid-1960s. This organization of Muslims, formed on 9 August 1964, set itself up as a pressure group to influence 'the political behaviour of Muslims in a bid to obtain a parliament and legislative assemblies more favourably disposed to what it considered to be the Muslim interests'.[20] All shades of Muslim opinion and ideology—from religiously conservative Ulema to politically influential nationalist Muslims—were represented in its meetings but Anis apa didn't last long enough, my aunt Tazeen tells me, to play an active role.

The Majlis had its sights set on the 1967 elections to the Lok Sabha, and in the debate on which candidates were truly 'Muslim-friendly' Anis apa made her break with the organization, perhaps in 1966. The candidate under discussion was Anis apa's old friend Subhadra Joshi. When Dr A.J. Faridi (a founder member of the Majlis) spoke against Subhadra's secular credentials and a Majlis endorsement of her candidature, Anis apa was incensed. Standing up tall to her five-foot height, Anis apa made a passionate, though somewhat intemperate, speech in defence of Subhadra, concluding with a public announcement of her resignation from the Majlis and a prediction that Dr Faridi would prove to be no less than a Nathuram Godse to the Muslims. Apparently her outburst did influence the Majlis's eventual official support for Subhadra, but Anis apa never participated in the Majlis again.

In the family narrative of this incident, Anis apa's anger was not limited to the slur on Subhadra but was also focused on Indira Gandhi, who reportedly kept tugging at Anis apa's sari to make her sit down and keep quiet. In the heat of the moment, Anis apa told several family members that she would resign from the Rajya Sabha, but that did not happen. When she was offered a third Rajya Sabha term, Anis apa politely declined and settled down to a life of writing. Ironically, Subhadra lost the 1967 election from the Chandni Chowk constituency she had represented thus far, perhaps because of the very endorsement that Anis apa had fought for.

The last fifteen years of Anis apa's life were relatively quiet in terms of political activity, but most successful in terms of appreciation for her literary work. In 1978 she began writing *Ghubar*, which at least when she began to write, she thought of as her final farewell. However, once *Azadi* was published in 1974, both literary acclaim and more publications followed: in 1976 and 1980 Jamia brought out two collections of her essays, *Nazre Khush Guzre* and *Ab Jinke Dekhne Ko*, and Anis apa finally had a career as a writer. For her, this recognition was a source of great pride and joy and she had no hesitation in showing it. And what a source of satisfaction it must have been for Subhadra that she was instrumental in bringing this happiness to her friend of twenty-seven years, because had Subhadra and QET not taken on the manuscript, it would still be searching for a publisher.

But mixed in with this happiness was great sorrow as, in 1973, her daughter Azadi passed away after many years of battling rheumatic heart disease, leaving behind my eighteen-year-old cousin Seema and her two elder brothers Parvez and Kamal. And just when Anis apa was climbing the first rung of the ladder of success, Mridula left her on 27 October 1974. And if Anis apa had thought even for a moment that the commendations that *Azadi* received were in any way a sweeping societal endorsement of the politics of conscience that she shared with her two friends Mridula and Subhadra, these thoughts would have been quelled by the mere recollection of Mridula's name.

In a moving tribute to Mridula in *Ab Jinke Dekhne Ko*, Anis apa's memories of a dear comrade and friend, the inspiration behind Women's

Service Home, a skilful organizer of an army of women and a selfless indomitable fighter are tinged with anger at the way she was treated in independent India. Thrown out of the Congress and incarcerated twice (in Tihar Jail in 1958–59 and in house detention in 1965–67) for her 'anti-national' critique of the Indian government's violation of civil liberties in Jammu and Kashmir and its repeated detentions of Sheikh Abdullah, Mridula was isolated. Even those who acted against her admitted that she was an 'institution', a 'patriot', a 'freedom fighter' and a 'brave warrior for principles, truth and justice'; but no one ever said, 'If only I could have been a traitor like her, I could have tried to save the nation from the nationalism of its self-styled patriots.'[21]

This political isolation within her own party was also Subhadra's ultimate fate. Though she won the 1971 elections from the Chandni Chowk constituency she had represented in the first three Lok Sabhas, her strained relationship with Indira Gandhi saw her in constant conflict with the leadership. Subhadra had spent the last decade dashing from the scene of one riot to another, trying in vain to rouse the Congress to act against the RSS. Like Mridula, she was valiant in her determination to combat any group or institution that threatened civil liberties; in doing so, she always remained the Subhadra of January 1948 who had spilled 100 children onto the streets during Gandhiji's fast. Through the Sampradayikta Virodhi Andolan that she and D.R. Goyal instituted in the 1960s, she mobilized thousands of ordinary people against communalism. During the Emergency, she was always the first Congress leader out on the streets against forced sterilizations and attacks on the press and lawyers, but to no avail. As she wrote in her letter to Indira Gandhi on 24 April 1976, protesting the brutality of Jama Masjid and Turkman Gate: 'people at the top are a little hard of hearing'.[22] In 1977, Subhadra—the woman who defeated Vajpayee in 1962—lost the general elections and was never elected again. But she fought on regardless, until the end on 30 October 2003.

Mridula didn't live to see the Emergency but Anis apa did. For the first time in her life, she appears to have felt fear of the Indian state. My mother recalls that when she and Anis apa were having a political discussion, Anis apa signalled to her to be quiet until she could peep out of the window to ensure that no one was eavesdropping. In my own child's memory, another scene is engraved: the doorbell rings in our Munirka flat, a middle-aged neighbour asks to see Anis apa. A schoolteacher in a government school, she has come to ask Anis apa whether she could supply her some women from the Home for sterilization. I'm shooed away but I remember hoping that Anis apa wouldn't agree. She did not, of course.

That Anis apa disapproved of the Emergency is undoubted—in her preface to the 1978 edition of *Azadi*, she says so frankly—however, she didn't write anything about it. Perhaps her silence was because Mridula was no longer there and that more bereavement after Azadi had followed; in 1976, her brother Wajahat had died. Or perhaps she didn't know how to fight this battle. Unlike Subhadra and Mridula, whose politics were evolved and honed in the freedom struggle to the point that they knew that the cause was not won just by political freedom, Anis apa's articles of faith were formed at a time when she felt that the newly liberated state and government were in danger. Where Subhadra and Mridula saw opposition to the government for its injustices as their affirmation of an ideally democratic Indian state, Anis apa could not separate state from government with the same ease.

The Emergency was the point when this conceptual separation had to be made. Anis apa may initially have refused to condemn the Emergency—to acknowledge the government's totalitarianism was to cast the democratic state as immoral—but the excesses of the Emergency did not let her avert her gaze for too long. Forced sterilizations, demolitions and firings at Turkman Gate in April 1976 forced her to acknowledge that her leaders had abandoned democracy. Seema tells me that Subhadra and Anis apa went to meet Indira to protest. When Anis apa returned home, she was white as a sheet. Indira—the daughter of her Jawaharlalji, the woman she had turned to so often in 1947–48—had refused to hear them and asked them to speak to her son Sanjay instead. After that day, Anis apa never again asked Seema for restraint in her exertions against the Emergency.

By 1979 Anis apa had become quite frail. She had lost her sister Bilqees that year and now took to spending most of her time in

Delhi, shuttling between her son Taufiq's home in Tara Apartments and Jamal's in Jamia. Every house that she ever lived in was first and foremost Anis apa's home and holidays would be marked by a ceaseless stream of visitors to meet her and Kishwar. Among the regulars, mostly single women friends of Kishwar, my particular favourite was (and is) Prema Mandi, whose long association with the family since she came to Anis apa's home in the 1950s, nursing a broken heart, has led many outsiders to address her as Prema Kidwai. My brother Rafiq's favourites were Begum Pataudi and Mridula from the years of his childhood. But the most intriguing was Sanath, whose visits we eagerly anticipated, not only for her very public declamation of her affairs of the heart and domestic troubles, but also for the frequency with which she changed her religion. The last time I met her (it was in Anis apa's lifetime, I think), she had shaved her head and donned orange robes. Once or twice a year, a bearded gentleman from her past would arrive, and

Seated from right to left: Anis Kidwai, her daughter Kishwar and Hamida Habibullah, a prominent Congress leader from UP, in Masauli in the 1970s. Standing at the far left is Farid Kidwai—the only Masauli Kidwai in politics—a member of the Bahujan Samaj Party.

Anis apa would race across the lawn to welcome him and later cackle with delight when I teased her about her 'boyfriends'.

I think of Anis apa's diminutive frame on the bed, a sheaf of papers on her lap, writing for hours on end. As her eyesight dimmed, and she couldn't write or read as much as she wanted to, she tried something she had never attempted—cooking. Being a woman of boundless ambition, all her culinary experiments naturally required skills on the expert end of the spectrum (much to the dismay of us grandchildren). As soon as she entered the kitchen, we would scatter to the furthest reaches of Tara. We knew that our desertion would make Anis apa take to the streets almost immediately and, taking shameful advantage of her age and service to the nation, forcefeed her latest failure to the first unfortunate passer-by.

Every evening, Anis apa would go for a walk with our two dogs, stopping at Arpita and Paramjeet Singh's garden for a visit. By 6 p.m. she would be home and the television would be switched on for her regular show, *Krishi Darshan*. Occasionally, a film would be aired, and it didn't really matter which language it was in. I remember watching Satyajit Ray's *Apur Sansar* with her one such evening. My eleven-year-old self puzzled through the film over the fact that even though it was I who could read the English subtitles, it was Anis apa who seemed to know what the film was about. We watched in complete silence. Even when it ended, nothing was said, but I knew that something important had happened to me at that moment. I had just been introduced, with Anis apa seated silently by my side, to learning how to feel the pain and relief of others.

Anis apa died on 16 July 1982. Of her siblings and children, she was the only one who did not suffer the indignities of protracted ill-health. All she left behind were Shafi's bloodstained pen and his last letters, her own two pens, a kafan of the prescribed length, a pile of handwritten pages, a few letters from her brothers, sister and Kishwar, the letter from the Custodian releasing the property of the Nizamuddin dargah, a copy of a report by Mridula on the relief efforts needed for riot victims in Gujarat in 1969, two sequinned cloth pouches made by women from the Home stuffed with cloves and cardamoms, a pair of spanking new scissors and a luridly golden metal box. All this was packed neatly into the small shiny aluminium suitcase that her Jammu had given her as a present.

At this point of ending her story, Anis apa would have liked me to pluck this couplet from Ghalib to weave in the rich intertextuality of life and literature she was so fond of:

> *chand tasweer-e-butaan, chand haseeno-ke khutoot*
> *baad marne ke mere ghar se ye samaan nikle*
> Some tattered images, a few epistles from beautiful women
> After my death, these were the things found in my house

Or perhaps to quote the concluding lines of her sketch of a defeated Dr Kitchlew in *Ab Jinke Dekhne Ko*:

> Most nationalist Muslims came to the same end as he did. Some were driven mad by grief and anger, some silenced by a regard for cordiality and civility, some began to aspire to the heights of power and some put on display forever their mortally wounded breasts. Only a few could stay the course they had set out on.

I cannot let her have the last word. Even as we are moved by Anis apa's summing up of her own life in her preface to *Ghubar*:

> Life in all events is simply life. To spend it in happiness, to always look to separate flowers from thorns and search out a reason for cheer amidst grief is something only humans can do. It is only our courage and strength that despite being fettered by the most unfavourable of circumstances and plagued by grief and a host of difficulties, we are still able to add lustre to this world. Angels would have fled the ground long ago . . .
>
> In this long and laborious journey of life, there has been a succession of a crowd of fellow travellers, an immeasurable multitude of people, an incessant stream of actions and events. Each link of this chain is discrete, but also integrated. Or to say, it is a tale within a tale.

Those eyes that have the ability to bear witness to the whole world and gain their insight in universities and colleges in the radiance of science and philosophy are quite something else. The vision of my own tiny eyes was fed only by the gleam of surma and kajal, within the confines of four walls, and could not therefore extend beyond the immediate.

This will not be the only appraisal that we—our eyes lit by science, literature, history, philosophy—*and* streaked with kajal—can give of her. For, in Anis apa's story, as she would herself agree, lie the gardens of our mothers and a room of one's own. And with each such story, another integrates and inheres. I am grateful for the opportunity of being a part of telling Anis Kidwai's.

Endnotes

～

1. *From Pluralism to Separatism: Qasbas in Colonial Awadh* by Mushirul Hasan, Oxford University Press, Delhi 2004.
2. Hasan, ibid. pp. 56–58.
3. Hasan, ibid. p. 57.
4. *Ghubar-e-Karwaan* by Begum Anis Kidwai, Maktab-e-Jamia, Delhi 1983.
5. *Ab Jinke Dekhne Ko* by Begum Anis Kidwai, Maktab-e-Jamia, Delhi 1978.
6. Hasan, ibid. p. 87.
7. Unless otherwise specified, all quotations in this section are from *Ghubar-e-Karwaan*, ibid.
8. Unpublished notes for *Ghubar.*
9. Unpublished notes for *Ghubar.*
10. Unpublished notes for *Ghubar.*
11. Unpublished notes for *Ghubar.*
12. Notebook I, Draft Notes for *Azadi Ki Chhaon Mein* by Begum Anis Kidwai, Qaumi Ekta Trust, Delhi 1974.
13. Notebook I, Draft Notes for *Azadi.*
14. Notebook II, Draft Notes for *Azadi.*
15. From 'Jawaharlal Nehru' in *Ab Jinke Dekhne Ko*, ibid.
16. From 'Ajtamae Ziddain' in *Nazre Khush Guzre*, ibid.
17. Annual Report of the Women's Service Home, Masauli 1989–93.
18. Rules and Regulations of the Women's Service Home, Masauli.
19. All quotations in this section are from the published debates on the

bill. Savitry Devi and Anis Kidwai spoke in Hindi\Urdu (reproduced here in my translation), while Seeta Parmanand spoke in English.

20. Zaheer Masood Quraishi (1971), 'Emergence and Eclipse of Muslim Majlis-e-Mushawarat', *Economic and Political Weekly* 6 (25): 1229–34.
21. From 'Mridula Sarabhai' in *Ab Jinke Dekhne Ko*, ibid.
22. As reproduced in translation in Janak Raj Jai's *Emergency excesses, a daylight robbery of human rights and JP, the saviour*. Regency Publications, New Delhi 1996.